DEBT AND CRISIS IN LATIN AMERICA

POWER AND CRISIS IN LATIN AMERICA

ROBERT DEVLIN

DEBT AND CRISIS IN LATIN AMERICA

The Supply Side of the Story

PRINCETON UNIVERSITY PRESS

PRINCETON, NEW JERSEY

Published by Princeton University Press, 41 William Street,
Princeton, New Jersey 08540
In the United Kingdom: Princeton University Press,
Chichester, West Sussex

Devlin, Robert.
Debt and crisis in Latin America : the supply side of the story /
Robert Devlin.
p. cm.   Bibliography: p.   Includes index.
ISBN 0-691-07797-5
ISBN 0-691-00079-4 (pbk.)
1. Loans, Foreign—Latin America.   2. Debts, External—Latin
America.   3. Latin America—Foreign economic relations.   I. Title.
HG3891.5.D48   1989
336.3'435'098—dc19   89-3724

This book has been composed in Linotron Sabon

Princeton University Press books are printed on acid-free paper
and meet the guidelines for permanence and durability of the Committee on Production
Guidelines for Book Longevity of the Council on Library Resources

First Princeton Paperback printing, 1993

Printed in the United States of America

3 5 7 9 10 8 6 4 2

For Martine

CONTENTS

LIST OF FIGURES

LIST OF TABLES

IN 1985 the Chilean economist Aníbal Pinto remarked to me that the Latin American debt crisis would be an epic tale of twenty chapters, of which we have seen only four. Three years later the debt saga is indeed very much alive and full of unexpected twists and turns. Thus writing an ending to this book was a somewhat uncomfortable task. I decided to use early 1988 as the cutoff point of my analysis, knowing very well that by the time the study reached print new developments could overtake some aspects of the text. I trust the reader will understand this occupational hazard facing students of the Latin American debt issue.

Much of the book has been inspired by my work in the Economic Development Division of the United Nations Economic Commission for Latin America and the Caribbean (ECLAC), where I have been entrusted for a number of years with the study of the dynamics of foreign debt in the region. I am very grateful to the Commission for a stimulating professional environment that effectively acted as a catalyst for many of the ideas developed in this volume.

Institutions are, of course, made up of people, and some of my colleagues have been especially instrumental in creating that environment. The late Raúl Prebisch and Aníbal Pinto actively encouraged my study of bank lending to Latin America, beginning when I first arrived at ECLAC as a young "gringo" economist in 1975. Andrés Bianchi, the director of the Economic Development Division, as well as Enrique Iglesias, the former executive secretary of the Commission, provided me with the intellectual and administrative support I needed to enmesh myself in the subject matter. Meanwhile, my friendly ongoing intellectual sparring with Andrés and divisional colleagues Joseph Ramos, Enrique de la Piedra, and Richard Ground has contributed more to my thinking on the issue of debt and development than they are probably aware of.

Over the years I also have benefited from exchanges with a number of individuals outside the organization. I would not want this book to appear without acknowledging the importance of my discussions with Ricardo Ffrench-Davis, Manuel Marfán, Carlos Santistevan, James Weaver, and John Willoughby.

I also want to express appreciation to several institutions for the financial support that made the preparation of the book possible. Most of the drafting was done while I was a Visiting Researcher at the Corporación de Investigaciones Económicas para América Latina (CIEPLAN) in Santiago, Chile, and a Faculty Fellow at the Helen Kellogg Institute for International Studies of the University of Notre Dame. I also am grateful to the United Nations External Studies Program, which financed part of my extended leave of absence from ECLAC to work on the manuscript.

Helpful comments on one or more chapters of the manuscript were received from most of the individuals cited above. I am also grateful for the criticisms and suggestions of Jorge Daly, Martine Guerguil, Kenneth Jameson, Mimi Keck, John McDermott, Al Watkins, Roberto Zahler, and two anonymous referees.

Efficient statistical assistance came from Guillermo Mundt and Raúl Labán. Ximena Sepúlveda cheerfully typed the manuscript, and Hilary Berg gave me some valuable editorial help. I owe a special measure of thanks to Cathy Thatcher of Princeton University Press for her patience and excellent copyediting.

Finally, none of the previously mentioned individuals or institutions would agree with all that I say in this volume; its contents and any remaining errors are my exclusive responsibility.

DEBT AND CRISIS IN LATIN AMERICA

CHAPTER ONE

Introduction: The Crisis in Latin America

SINCE mid-1982 Latin America has been suffering through one of the most serious economic crises in its history. A good summary statistic of the region's plight is per capita income: at the end of 1987 it was nearly 6 percent lower than the figure registered in 1980.[1] At the outset of the crisis even the most optimistic observers expected the 1980s to be a "lost decade" for Latin America, estimating that by 1990 per capita income would barely exceed its 1980 level.[2] Now, with six years of crisis behind us, that bleak prognosis indeed appears to have been too bright, just as some analysts feared.[3] Barring a favorable turn of events regarding the level of debt service or the performance of the world economy, it now appears that it will be difficult for the region to recover 1980 per capita income before 1992.[4]

While the region's crisis is a development crisis, it is most frequently referred to as "the debt crisis." Attention has tended to center on the whole issue of debt because it constitutes one of the crisis's most immediate links between North and South. On the one hand, the debtors' difficulties in servicing their obligations have represented a potential threat to the viability of the creditor nations' financial systems. On the other hand, debt servicing drains an extraordinary amount of resources

---

[1] For complete data on the recent evolution of the economies of Latin America see United Nations Economic Commission for Latin America and the Caribbean, "Preliminary Overview of the Latin American Economy 1987" (Santiago, Chile, December 1987).

[2] This is the conclusion that can be drawn from the statistical projections in William Cline, *International Debt: Systematic Risk and Policy Response* (Washington, D.C.: Institute for International Economics, 1984), p. 195.

[3] For a technical critique of Cline's optimism see Albert Fishlow, "Coping with the Creeping Crisis of Debt," in *Politics and Economics of External Debt Crisis*, ed. Miguel Wionczek in collaboration with Luciano Tomassini (Boulder, Colo.: Westview Press, 1985), pp. 111–122; Rudiger Dornbusch and Stanley Fischer, "The World Debt Problem: Origins and Prospects," *Journal of Economic Planning*, no. 16 (1985), pp. 75–78; and Jonathan Eaton and Lance Taylor, "Developing Country Finance and Debt," paper prepared for a conference on New Directions in Development Theory, Cambridge, Mass., Massachusetts Institute of Technology, 17–19 January 1985, pp. 77–78.

[4] See, for instance, United Nations Economic Commission for Latin America and the Caribbean, "Restrictions on Sustained Development in Latin America and the Caribbean and the Requisites for Overcoming Them" (Santiago, Chile, February 1988), pp. 10–26.

from Latin America and has had strong depressionary effects on economic activity. Indeed, in the face of the high burden of payments, development policy in the 1980s has taken a back seat to the exigencies of crisis management and the politics of international debt.

Latin America found its debt burden unsustainable in 1982, a fact that was dramatically brought to the world's attention by Mexico's announcement of a temporary moratorium in August of that year. This date initiated a process in which most countries have fallen into a state of de facto default, repeatedly breaking scheduled repayment calendars. De jure default has been avoided only because the banks and their OECD governments effected widespread rescue operations, which facilitated the multiple rescheduling of debt payments. The reschedulings—undertaken in no less than seventeen countries of the region—helped to avoid the feared collapse of the international financial system. Yet we will see that the same exercises that so successfully saved the world financial system have also decisively undermined the growth and development process in the debtor countries.

The advent of crisis, and the dramatic and controversial nature of the rescue operations, has brought debt to the forefront of research agendas. Indeed, there has been a virtual explosion of writings on the debt crisis, both as to its origins as well as to potential solutions.

Analysts have tended to stress different underlying factors behind the emergence of the crisis. Perhaps the most popular argument to appear in the North referred to what some simply called bad economic management in the debtor countries. In this school of thought, primary attention is placed on expansionary macroeconomic policy, and above all on fiscal deficits.[5] In other words, lack of fiscal and monetary discipline in the 1970s induced public-sector deficits and an unsustainable accumulation of debts. The prescription following from the diagnosis involved austerity in the debtor countries, a rolling back of the public sector, the elimination of price distortions, seen as inhibiting the functioning of the market mechanism, and export-led growth. Some of these analysts expressed support for the conventional crisis management involving commercial bank reschedulings, which leave creditor portfolios largely undamaged, while others argued that the bad economic policies have made many debtors incapable of servicing the nominal value of the debt and therefore the banks must assume write-downs and losses on their

[5] Two representative statements are Larry Sjaastad, "International Debt Quagmire: To Whom Do We Owe It?" *The World Economy* 6 (September 1983): 305–324; and Eduardo Wiesner, "Latin American Debt and Pending Issues," *American Economic Review* 75 (May 1985): 191–195.

loans. Sometimes these latter analysts proposed a type of internationally supported financial plan that would help the banks write off part of their asset values in the developing countries.

A second popular interpretation supported the notion that the debtors mismanaged their economies but placed relatively greater emphasis on the role of unforeseen exogenous shocks brought on by OPEC pricing policies, high world interest rates, and prolonged world economic recession.[6] This diagnosis leaned toward a conjunctural explanation of the problem and consequently placed greater weight on a conjunctural solution: lower interest rates, recovery of the OECD economies, and improved commodity prices. There also was recognition of the need to introduce austerity and better economic management in the borrowing countries. But given the stress on conjunctural developments, it viewed the problem in the countries as one of illiquidity and strongly supported the conventional strategy of commercial bank reschedulings and austerity in the debtor countries.

A third interpretation of the problem pointed to an overall systemic crisis of capitalism, of which debt was a major manifestation.[7] Much of this analysis has its roots in the Marxian tradition. Solutions are not well articulated, but integral to the classic Marxian approach is the notion that a capitalist system in crisis regenerates itself through defaults, financial collapse, and the devaluation of financial assets.[8]

In a fourth interpretation some analysts focused primarily on the tendency of banks—Latin America's principal creditor—to overlend in the 1970s.[9] The prescription emerging here was more effective control of bank-lending practices.

While the diverse arguments have been in practice often treated as competing explanations, they all capture important dimensions of the crisis. For instance, it is difficult to quarrel with the argument that many debtor countries mismanaged their economies. There is much evidence to support the hypothesis that many of the countries in Latin America had excessively debt-leveraged development strategies in the 1970s. It

[6] See Cline, *International Debt*, chap. 1, for a representative statement.

[7] Arthur MacEwan, "The Current Crisis in Latin America and the International Economy," *Monthly Review* 36 (February 1985): 2–3. The crisis itself is analyzed in depth in Ernest Mandel, *The Second Slump*, trans. John Rothschild (London: New Left Books, Verso edition, 1980).

[8] See John Weeks, *Capital and Exploitation* (Princeton, N.J.: Princeton University Press, 1981), pp. 123–217.

[9] For example, see Jack Guttentag and Richard Herring, "Commercial Bank Lending to Developing Countries: From Overlending to Underlending to Structural Reform," in *International Debt and the Developing Countries*, ed. Gordon Smith and John Cuddington (Washington, D.C.: World Bank, 1985), pp. 129–150.

also is evident that the OPEC shocks, as well as the prolonged world recession and high interest rates of the 1980s, contributed to the massive accumulation of debt and simultaneously undermined the capacity to repay it.

As for capitalist crisis, the slowdown in the world economy since the late 1960s is a matter of record. There are a number of studies that point to structural crisis in capitalism, and some are from very orthodox circles.[10] Moreover, the external shocks that have been stressed by certain authors could easily be incorporated into a comprehensive theory of capitalist crisis. This would, however, admittedly change the underlying assumption of the shock literature, which was that the crisis is short-term and conjunctural and not a protracted structural problem.

Concern about market supply and bank lending also seems eminently reasonable since the other side of overborrowing is overlending. Nearly one hundred years ago Marshall eased the debate between the classical and neoclassical schools on whether supply or demand was the more important determinant by pointing to the two blades of his now famous scissors.[11] Yet, unfortunately, the supply side of the debt crisis remains relatively untold, as most analytical studies in the North have largely ignored creditor behavior when evaluating the causes of the crisis; even when banks were brought into the picture they were treated, at best, parenthetically.[12] Curiously, Latin American observers have been more respectful of Marshall; while from the outset not denying serious mistakes in the management of their economies, they also pointed to the dynamics of supply in the crisis in order to establish the principle of co-responsibility.[13] Yet their position generally has lacked a technical base

[10] See Mandel, *Second Slump*; W. Arthur Lewis, "The Slowing Down of the Engine of Growth," *American Economic Review* 70 (September 1980): 555–564; and Bank for International Settlements, *Forty-Eighth Annual Report* (Basel, 1978), p. 8.

[11] Alfred Marshall, *Principles of Economics* (London: Macmillan, 1961), app. 1, p. 820.

[12] Examine, for example, Cline, *International Debt*; Sjaastad, "International Debt Quagmire"; Beryl Sprinkel, "Grounds for Increasing Optimism," *Economic Impact*, no. 2 (1984), pp. 35–39; Thomas Enders and Richard Mattione, *Latin America: The Crisis of Debt and Growth* (Washington, D.C.: Brookings Institution, 1983); and Rudiger Dornbusch, "The International Debt Problem," Cambridge, Mass., Massachusetts Institute of Technology, Department of Economics, 1984. Since the outbreak of the crisis interesting anecdotal-type studies on bank-lending behavior have appeared, and I draw on some of them in later chapters. But analytical work on this subject still remains a relatively scarce commodity. Jack Guttentag and Richard Herring have been a major exception, although their excellent analysis of the supply of credit is in the business school tradition and does not really address very well the issue of development.

[13] See, for instance, United Nations Economic Commission for Latin America and the

and has rested on the assertion that loans were pushed on the Latin American economies.

THE PURPOSE of this study is to explore more thoroughly the dynamics of supply in the current crisis and thereby help to round out the analytical story of Latin America's debt problems. The general argument to be presented is that banks were an endogenous source of instability in the credit cycle of Latin America, tending to overexpand on the upside and overcontract on the downside. Taken broadly, my argument about the procyclical behavior of capital is not wholly original. Such diverse economists as Karl Marx, Thorstein Veblen, and, in modern times, Hyman Minsky, have posited in their different ways that unregulated private financial markets are prone to overexpansion and crisis.[14] Their theories, however, are developed at the very macrolevel for the capitalist economy as a whole. My analysis of the phenomenon will be more focused on the modern international bank during the 1970s, with special reference to lending to developing areas, and Latin America in particular. This approach will allow me to give an institutional dimension to the role of supply in a credit crisis as well as derive insights on bank behavior that often run counter to conventional wisdom. It also will provide some technical support to the Latin American argument of coresponsibility in the crisis.

Banks have been conventionally viewed as the most conservative of lenders, which in the context of a credit market impose discipline on the borrower. They also have been traditionally perceived as efficient intermediaries, in contrast to the public sector, which distorts credit allocation. This partly explains why many analysts were so optimistic about the expansion of the unregulated eurocurrency market and its lending to LDCs in the 1970s. It also perhaps explains why the most popular evaluations in the North of the causes of the crisis were so quick to implicate the economic management of the debtors and/or exogenous

---

Caribbean, "Preliminary Balance of the Latin American Economy in 1982," *Notas sobre la Economía y el Desarrollo de América Latina* 373 (January 1983): 7–8; and "Latin American Economic Conference," *CEPAL Review*, no. 22 (April 1984), pp. 39–52.

[14] Karl Marx, *Capital*, 9th ed. (New York: International Publishers, 1967), vol. 3, pt. 5; Thorstein Veblen, *The Theories of Business Enterprise* (New York: Charles Scribner's Sons, 1904), chap. 7; and Hyman Minsky, *Can "It" Happen Again?* (Armonk, N.Y.: M. E. Sharp, Inc., 1982). An excellent modern interpretation of Marx's theories of credit and crisis is found in Weeks, *Capital and Exploitation*, pp. 95–219. A helpful summary of seven early and modern theories of financial crisis can be found in Martin Wolfson, "Financial Crisis: Theory and Evidence in the Post-War U.S. Economy" (Ph.D. diss., The American University, 1984), pp. 16–72.

shocks but not really the banks. By examining how banks lend in practice, I will show that there was an inherent tendency of unregulated banking to overlend in the 1970s. Moreover, I will illustrate how credit markets could aid and abet any domestic forces in the debtor country directed toward overborrowing. In other words, there were important dynamics on the supply as well as the demand sides of the debt equation that pushed the system in the direction of excessive debt accumulation.

On the downside of the credit cycle the rescheduling of debts often has been touted as exemplary of the modern management of crisis at the global level, where the banks, OECD governments, and debtor countries have all assumed a fair share of the burden to protect the viability of the world financial and trading systems and to restore the debtors' creditworthiness. The rescheduling policies have conventionally been seen as market-based, efficient, and designed in the interests of the debtors and creditors alike. In contrast, I will demonstrate that with the advent of problems, banks shifted from overlending to underlending and that the management of the ensuing crisis has been primarily designed to protect the loan portfolios of the banks at a disproportionate cost for the debtors. I will also show that the technical arguments employed by the creditors to justify their policies were theoretically inconsistent, arbitrarily formulated, and could be construed as an attempt to mask the fact that debtors have been shouldering an unnecessarily large share of the costs of the crisis.

THE SUBSTANTIVE PART of the study begins with Chapter Two, which provides a historical overview of the role of private banks and capital in external finance from the nineteenth century up through the 1980s. Special attention is given to the postwar expansion of banking: its origins, the magnitude of lending, and eventual articulation with the periphery.

Chapter Three retraces the postwar expansion of banking found in Chapter Two, but at a higher level of abstraction. The analysis proposes to establish generally why banks were such profusive lenders in the upside of the credit cycle and how they could contribute endogenously to an overexpansion of debt. It first presents the conventional analysis of bank behavior, which relies on ahistorical portfolio theory and concludes that banks are cautious and efficient lenders that enforce discipline on borrowers. This is later contrasted with an alternative analysis that examines the modern bank as a historical institution operating in the dynamics of a specific market structure. The approach allows me to demonstrate "why" and "how" private banks during the 1970s were inclined to lend very aggressively in the expansive phase and become an active agent in overindebtedness and crisis.

The general proposition of Chapter Three is given greater focus in Chapter Four by analyzing more specifically the transmission of overlending into overborrowing. This is done by developing an analytical framework of the bank-borrower relationship patterned on the experiences of Peru and Bolivia, two countries that went through important credit cycles with the banks during the 1970s and for which I was able to secure unusually detailed primary data concerning credit transactions.

The fifth chapter turns its attention to the downside of the credit cycle and the political economy of rescheduling. It examines how banks dealt with the debtor country once it accumulated more debt than it could pay and entered into crisis. It will demonstrate that both the theory and practice of rescheduling has been arbitrarily formulated and rooted in the monopoly power of the creditors, which has been used in turn to pass the bulk of the costs of the crisis on to the debtors. In effect, just as the banks' behavior helped to exaggerate the expansive phase of the cycle, in the contractionary phase bank management of the crisis tended to aggravate the debtors' problems and helped to induce a socially inefficient, forced adjustment process that will have long-term negative consequences for Latin America's development.

The sixth and final chapter will explore the various options for resolving Latin America's debt crisis. It will show that the debtor countries should not passively await the arrangement of international public solutions that would manage the debt crisis in a more socially efficient way. This is because disproportionalities in creditor-debtor bargaining power and other objective conditions create an inertia in the North that could make the emergence of such international public initiatives painfully slow. To relieve the excessive burden of the debt now the countries must imaginatively defend their own economic interests by developing new payments options, which can include, among other things, a unilateral limitation of debt service. To this end the chapter reviews possible nonconventional alternatives for reducing the transfer of resources from debtor to creditor country.

CHAPTER TWO

Growth and Transformation of International Banking: An Overview

RATHER than any claim to originality the purpose of this chapter is to present background material on international bank lending that will be supportive of hypotheses and analysis developed in subsequent chapters. My main focus will be on institutional and structural aspects of private banking that I feel are important for understanding the nature of the banks' interface with Latin America during the expansionary credit cycle of the 1970s and its collapse in the 1980s.

PRIVATE BANK LENDING IN HISTORICAL PERSPECTIVE

There is a growing analytical literature on private international capital markets. A number of good works are available on the evolution of international lending prior to the great financial collapse of 1929.[1] The

---

[1] Barbara Stallings, *Banker to the Third World* (Berkeley: University of California Press, 1987); Douglass North, "International Capital Movements in Historical Perspective," in *U.S. Private and Government Investment Abroad*, ed. Raymond Mikesell (Eugene, Ore.: University of Oregon Books, 1962), pp. 10–43; Arthur Bloomfield, *Patterns of Fluctuation in International Investment before 1914*, Princeton Studies in International Finance, No. 21 (Princeton, N.J.: Princeton University, Department of Economics, 1968); United Nations Economic Commission for Latin America and the Caribbean (ECLAC), *External Financing in Latin America* (New York, 1965), pp. 5–34; Albert Fishlow, "Lessons from the Past: Capital Markets during the 19th Century and the Interwar Period," *International Organization* 39 (Summer 1985): 383–440; Steven Davis, *The Eurobank: Its Origins, Management, and Outlook* (London: Macmillan, 1976), pp. 6–21; Charles Kindleberger, *Manias, Panics, and Crashes* (New York: Basic Books, 1978); Herbert Feis, *Europe the World's Banker, 1870–1914* (New York: W. W. Norton, 1965); Karl Born, *International Banking in the 19th and 20th Centuries*, trans. Volker Berghahn (New York: St. Martin's Press, 1983); Marilyn Seiber, *International Borrowing by Developing Countries* (London: Pergamon Press, 1982), pp. 19–32; David Gisselquist, *The Politics and Economics of International Bank Lending* (New York: Praeger, 1981), pp. 1–57; Henry Bishoff, "British Investment in Costa Rica," *Inter-American Economic Affairs* 7 (Summer 1973): 34–47; and Carlos Díaz-Alejandro, "The Early 1980s in Latin America: 1930s One More Time?" paper presented at the Expert Meeting on Crisis and Development in Latin America and the Caribbean, United Nations Economic Commission for Latin America and the Caribbean, Santiago, Chile, 29 April–3 May 1985.

reemergence of dynamic private international capital flows in the post-war period is covered in a large literature on the eurocurrency market,[2] and the massive expansion of private lending to less-developed countries during the 1970s has come under increasing scrutiny.[3] Here I will draw on this and other literature to interpret some of the more relevant aspects of international banking as it pertains to the contemporary financial situation of Latin America and developing countries more generally.

Private Capital and Latin America Prior to 1929

Incompleteness of data on capital flows makes precise estimates of private transactions impossible. Nevertheless, it is well known that private foreign capital actively flowed to Latin America on a significant scale in the nineteenth and early part of the twentieth centuries.[4] While avoiding a detailed description of these transactions, I would like to highlight some of their more interesting characteristics, because as will be seen later in the study, there are some important parallels as well as differences with modern international finance.

Chronic Cyclical Booms and Crashes   One notable feature of private capital flows was that they were highly cyclical, characterized by boom periods that were followed by systemic payment problems and financial

---

[2] Some works worth mentioning are Stuart Robinson, *Multinational Banking* (Leyden, Netherlands: A. W. Sythoff Leiden, 1974); Anthony Angelini, Maximo Eng, and Francis Lees, *International Lending, Risk, and the Euromarkets* (New York: John Wiley & Sons, 1979); Jonathan David Aronson, *Money and Power* (Beverly Hills, Calif.: Sage Publications, Inc., 1977); Gunter Dufey and Ian Giddy, *The International Money Market* (Englewood Cliffs, N.J.: Prentice-Hall, 1978); Ronald McKinnon, *The Eurocurrency Market*, Princeton Essays in International Finance, No. 125 (Princeton, N.J.: Princeton University, Department of Economics, 1977); T. H. Donaldson, *Lending in International Commercial Banking* (London: MacMillan Publishers Ltd., 1983); and Davis, *The Eurobank*, pp. 22–188.

[3] P. A. Wellons, *Borrowing by Developing Countries on the Euro-Currency Market* (Paris: Organization for Economic Cooperation and Development, 1976), pp. 7–31; Robert Devlin, "External Finance and Commercial Banks: Their Role in Latin America's Capacity to Import between 1951 and 1975," *CEPAL Review*, no. 5 (first half of 1978), pp. 63–98; David Beek, "Commercial Bank Lending to Developing Countries," *Federal Reserve Bank of New York Quarterly Review* 2 (Summer 1977): 1–8; Howard Wachtel, *The New Gnomes: Multinational Banks in the Third World*, TNI Pamphlet No. 4 (Washington, D.C.: Transnational Institute, 1977); Seiber, *International Borrowing*, pp. 79–122; Gisselquist, *Politics and Economics of Bank Lending*, pp. 148–195; and Stallings, *Banker to the Third World*.

[4] Data on capital flows up to 1930 are found in ECLAC, *External Financing in Latin America*, pp. 5–36. These data, however, are reported in nominal terms and are incomplete due to unpublicized transactions.

collapse.[5] In Latin America there were several well-defined cycles. The first significant financial wave came in 1822 as newly independent Latin American countries attracted European capital. The financing boom was short-lived, however, as debtors and investors overestimated the region's export earnings; servicing problems and financial panic broke out shortly thereafter in 1827. The severe losses experienced by creditors helped keep foreign investors away from the region for more than two decades. Nevertheless, foreign capital returned with some enthusiasm in the 1850s due to expansive forces in some European capital markets and the fading memories of the past losses. The second wave of credit was also followed by severe payment problems: 58 percent of the Latin American public debt to Great Britain was in default by the end of 1880.[6]

Notwithstanding the aforementioned collapse, capital once again renewed its flow to Latin America during the rest of the nineteenth century and the early part of the twentieth century (although there was another payments crisis in the 1890s). This era was a classic one of very intensive private international investment, glowingly coined the "Golden Age of Foreign Capital" by mainstream analysts impressed by the free flow of capital, but more disparagingly termed the "Age of Imperialism" by Marxists, who focused on the hegemonic rivalry of creditor nations and the forceful economic and political penetration of the periphery.[7] During this period Latin America's attraction of foreign investors grew steadily, and "by the eve of the First World War the region had become the target of keen competition among the great international financial centers."[8]

During the First World War capital flows to Latin America slumped, but serious payment problems did not develop, in part because exports and payment capacity were boosted by wartime purchases. Then, in the 1920s another investment boom ensued, followed by the famous crash in the 1930s, which was brought on by the Great Depression and the dramatic fall in the region's export prices. (Export earnings dropped by 48 percent between the periods 1925 to 1929 and 1930 to 1934.)[9] Private capital flows dried up almost completely for the fifteen years fol-

---

[5] Gisselquist, *Politics and Economics of Bank Lending*, p. 56.

[6] ECLAC, *External Financing in Latin America*, pp. 6–7.

[7] The Marxist concept of imperialism has changed over the years from the classic interpretation of Hilferding, Lenin, and Bukharin that is used in the text. For a detailed survey of Marxist interpretations of imperialism refer to Anthony Brewer, *Marxist Theories of Imperialism* (London: Routledge & Kegan Paul, 1980).

[8] ECLAC, *External Financing in Latin America*, p. 7.

[9] Ibid., p. 23.

lowing the 1929 depression, and it was only after the Second World War that Latin America's access to private international capital began to be gradually restored.

Sources and Uses of Funds   The biggest source of foreign investment flows prior to World War I was England, with more than 50 percent of the foreign capital in the region. Far behind were the United States (15 percent) and France (8 percent).[10] About a third of the investment was of a portfolio type, namely bonds, the remainder being direct investment by private firms.[11]

The bonds emitted by Latin American countries were purchased by small and large investors in the great financial centers. As for commercial banks, it is important to note that in this period they acted mostly as an intermediary between investors and borrowers, undertaking the relatively risk-free business of underwriting issues. Their own liability in the debtor countries was limited to a short-term floating debt, much of which was accumulated as bridge financing between the bond issues.[12]

The users of foreign capital were governments and private firms. Most of the portfolio investment was with the public sector directly, or indirectly via government guarantees of private issues. The most important users of foreign capital were, as one might expect, Argentina (41 percent of the total), Brazil (20 percent), and Mexico (14 percent).[13]

After the First World War the major change in the picture was the emergence of the United States as the principal investor in Latin America and the world more generally, a role it has maintained until today.

Finally, it also must be mentioned that during the 1920s, portfolio investment took a growing share of capital transactions; in the United States its participation in total investment rose from 17 percent in 1919 to 32 percent in 1929.[14]

The Long-Term Nature of Capital Flows   Capital flows to Latin America were of a long-term character. Direct investments are, of course, an equity participation in firms, and thus the major financial burden was profit remittances, which are flexible and can fluctuate in an anticyclical way; that is, when the economic cycle declines, so do profits and remittances and vice versa. Bond issues also were of a very long

---

[10] Ibid., tables 16 and 17.
[11] Ibid., p. 21.
[12] Gisselquist, *Politics and Economics of Bank Lending*, p. 32.
[13] ECLAC, *External Financing in Latin America*, tables 16 and 17.
[14] Ibid., p. 20.

tenor, with maturities sometimes extending up to ninety-nine years.[15] Unlike profit remittances, however, debt service payments were contractually fixed and not formally adjustable to the economic cycle.

Market-Induced Debt Relief   Even though it was fixed, de jure debt service encountered a de facto mechanism that adjusted payments to severe swings in the economic cycle: default. In effect, the frequent defaults of the period acted as a risk-sharing device that passed a significant part of the costs of the adjustment to an excessive buildup of credit onto the lenders.

During the years of the Great Depression, the massive slump in export earnings caused all Latin American countries except Argentina (on federal obligations), the Dominican Republic, and Haiti to suspend service of their debts. By 1937, 85 percent of the region's public dollar bond debt was in arrears. These payment difficulties in turn caused the prices of Latin American paper to fall sharply in foreign capital markets. Bonds issued by the region at a nominal value of $2 billion in 1920 to 1931 lost a staggering 75 percent of their value by 1935. Countries could take advantage of this situation to relieve their debt burden. Indeed, many countries ceased paying interest so that they could earmark funds for redeeming bonds at market prices that were falling precisely because of the arrears on interest payments. For example, in 1935 Chile reduced its public debt by $88 million, paying fifteen cents on every dollar withdrawn from the market.[16]

When countries entered into default, there was very little creditors could do about it. Bondholders were dispersed, anonymous, and not easily able to organize themselves to enforce collection. Moreover, while there are examples of gunboat diplomacy to protect creditor interests in the nineteenth and early twentieth centuries, creditor governments largely did not interfere in the frequent defaults of the period.[17]

The basic cost for the debtor of default was loss of access to new pri-

---

[15] Helen Hughes, "Debt and Development: The Role of Foreign Capital in Economic Growth," *World Development* 7 (February 1979): 96.

[16] ECLAC, *External Financing in Latin America*, pp. 29–30. Losses should not be exaggerated, however. Prior to the suspension of payments, bondholder returns were high and interest rates perhaps compensated for much of the risk of default. Some researchers have found that bonds in default during the period nevertheless produced a 3 percent rate of return, which was comparable to the return on Aaa bonds in the United States. David Folkerts-Landau, "The Changing Role of International Bank Lending in Development Finance" (Washington, D.C.: International Monetary Fund, December 1984), p. 6.

[17] Richard Dale and Richard Mattione, *Managing Global Debt* (Washington, D.C.: Brookings Institution, 1983), p. 3; and ECLAC, *External Financing in Latin America*, pp. 29–30.

vate credit. As has been mentioned, there was a virtual cutoff of private credit to Latin America for twenty years following the massive suspension of payments in the 1930s. But on the other hand, debtor countries avoided sharp falls in output as market-induced debt relief helped them sustain domestic economic activity;[18] moreover, after the defaults, private expectations and markets were often in such disarray that new autonomous financing was problematical in any event.[19]

Importantly, countries did not repudiate their debts. Thus, when export earnings recovered, debtor governments usually attempted to renegotiate payments and reestablish their creditworthiness. For instance, after World War II there were negotiations with creditors to renew the servicing of obligations. Arrangements usually had a strong concessionary element that at least partially acknowledged the market discounts at which the loans were traded, for example, the payment of interest arrears with new bonds at a rate of interest inferior to the original rate and stretchouts of overdue principal repayments, the value of which was often reduced in negotiations to below original amounts outstanding.[20]

Creditor Myopia   Private financial markets are traditionally viewed as efficient, with capital migrating to the highest rate of return. Retrospective macroeconomic analysis of the long period in question suggests that this might have been the case.[21] Yet the socially costly cyclical credit pattern of booms and crashes has caught the critical attention of other observers with an institutional focus on the borrowing and lending process. In effect, during periods of economic prosperity generalized euphoria often generated a pyramiding of credit as more and more investors with less and less understanding of the situation entered the market for profit making. As John Kenneth Galbraith has observed in his uniquely sardonic way:

> As banking developed from the seventeenth century on, so, with the support of other circumstance, did the cycles of euphoria and panic. Their length came to accord roughly with the time it took people to forget the last disaster—for the financial geniuses of one generation to die in disrepute and be replaced by new craftsmen who the gullible

[18] Díaz-Alejandro, "The Early 1980s in Latin America," p. 13; and Charles Kindleberger, "The 1929 World Depression in Latin America—From the Outside," in *Latin America in the 1930s*, ed. Rosemary Thorp (New York: St. Martin's Press, 1984), p. 323.

[19] ECLAC, *External Financing in Latin America*, p. 30.

[20] See ibid., pp. 30–31; and Stallings, *Banker to the Third World*, pp. 79–80.

[21] Bloomfield, *Patterns in International Investment*, pp. 35–40.

and the gulled could believe had, this time but truly, the Midas touch.[22]

Galbraith's view of financial developments, though witty, finds ample support in the numerous government inquiries that followed major financial collapses. For instance, in 1875 the Select Committee on Loans to Foreign States of the English Parliament published a report on recent defaults in Latin America with findings of "reckless disregard for the borrower, misuse of the loan proceeds, commissions so usurious that no honest borrower would submit to them, collusion between government representatives and issuers, and falsification of the market to dispose of the bonds."[23] Meanwhile, a U.S. government report summarized international lending practices in the 1920s this way:

> Under the high-pressure salesmanship methods by which foreign issues were solicited and sold, our loans proved to be their undoing. The flotation of one loan frequently came to be regarded as adequate justification for further issues to the same borrower or the same country without regard to the growing burden of indebtedness.[24]

Problems in the financial system and scrutiny by government officials often led to pressures for regulation and reform. In the United States, controls of national banking systems began to take shape in 1863 and 1864, but it was the great financial collapse of the 1930s that gave rise to the comprehensive regulatory system that oversees banking in that country today. Other national banking systems in the OECD also promoted increased supervision of their lending institutions.[25]

After the Second World War

Immediately following the war, the region's foreign finance was heavily dependent on direct foreign investment flows and government-to-government lending. This was complemented by World Bank funding at the end of the 1950s, as that institution turned its attention from the

[22] John Kenneth Galbraith, *Money* (Boston: Houghton Mifflin, 1975), p. 21.

[23] Feis, *Europe the World's Banker*, pp. 105–106.

[24] Hal B. Lary, *The United States in the World Economy* (Washington, D.C.: U.S. Department of Commerce, 1943), quoted in Davis, *The Eurobank*, p. 21.

[25] For a description of the regulation of the U.S. depository system in this period see Lewis Spellman, *The Depository Firm and Industry* (New York: Academic Press, 1982), pp. 16–28; and Milton Friedman and Anna Schwartz, *A Monetary History of the United States, 1867–1960* (Princeton, N.J.: Princeton University Press, 1963), pp. 420–462. For information on European systems see Ulrich Immenga, *Participation by Banks in Other Branches of the Economy* (Brussels: Commission of European Communities, 1975).

reconstruction of Europe to development finance. Additional multilateral finance became available in the early 1960s with the establishment of the Inter-American Development Bank. Private commercial banks for their part had a very low profile in the region's external finance, generally limiting themselves to home government guaranteed export credits and relatively risk-free short-term trade credit. Meanwhile, bond issues were for only modest amounts, both due to the lingering memories of investors of the 1929 crash as well as the creditor governments' official red tape and other institutional restrictions that limited LDC access to these markets.[26] With regard to the actual volume of finance, it was of limited proportions.

The picture was of course altered radically in the 1970s as finance became abundant and was largely provided by private commercial banks. These dramatic changes can be examined from various angles.

The Flow of Foreign Resources   Tables 2.1 and 2.2 present the flow of external financial resources to Latin America and a subgroup of nonoil exporters for the postwar period up until the crisis. The first table presents the data in nominal dollars, while the second uses constant 1970 dollars to abstract from the effects of inflation.

Examining first Table 2.1, it can be observed that up through 1970 Latin America encountered a restrictive environment with regard to external finance. Through 1965 loans and direct investments were roughly equal in their contribution to external finance, but on a net basis, after accounting for factor payments, the transfer of these resources (column 8) was slightly negative for the region as a whole (the outflow being equivalent to somewhat more than 1 percent of export earnings) and modestly positive for the nonoil exporters (the inflow being equivalent to 5 percent of export earnings).[27] The external environment for finance remained relatively restricted in the latter half of the 1960s as well.

The changed environment after 1970 is rather striking. Here we ob-

[26] Many governments of the industrialized countries prohibit pension funds from buying the securities of developing countries, limit the percentage of the portfolio that can be placed in such assets, and place open restrictions on the floating of LDC bonds in their capital markets. See Donald Lessard and John Williamson, *Financial Intermediation beyond the Debt Crisis* (Washington, D.C.: Institute for International Economics, 1985), pp. 100–101; and Francis Lees and Maximo Eng, "Developing Country Access to the International Capital Markets," *Columbia Journal of World Business*, Fall 1979, pp. 80–81.

[27] The negative effect of the oil producers on the transfer of resources to the region was largely due to profit remittances out of Venezuela.

TABLE 2.1. Latin America: External Financial Flows and Resource Transfers, 1951–1983 (billions of dollars)

Annual Averages (1)	Foreign Direct Investment (2)	Net Noncompensatory Loans			Total Flows (2 + 5) (6)	Factor Payments[b] (7)	Net Transfer (6 − 7) (8)	Net Transfer Plus Unregistered Transactions[c] (9)	Memorandum Items	
		Medium-/Long-term[a] (3)	Short-term (4)	Total (3 + 4) (5)					(8) ÷ Exports[d] (10)	(9) ÷ Exports[d] (11)
					Latin America[e]					
1951–65	0.5	0.4	0.1	0.5	1.0	1.1	− 0.1	− 0.3	− 1.1	− 3.3
1966–70	0.7	1.3	0.5	1.8	2.5	2.3	0.2	0.1	1.4	0.7
1971–75	1.7	6.6	1.1	7.7	9.4	4.2	5.2	4.6	17.1	15.1
1976–80	3.7	18.2	1.9	20.1	23.8	11.5	12.3	12.1	17.4	17.4
1981	7.2	38.6	2.0	40.6	47.8	28.1	19.3	8.1	16.6	7.0
1982	5.7	28.0	− 5.4	22.6	28.3	39.7	−11.4	−20.7	−11.0	−20.0
1983	3.1	15.0	−13.0	2.0	5.1	35.0	−29.9	−33.1	−29.2	−32.3

Latin America: Nonoil Exporters[f]

1951–65	0.3	0.3	0.1	0.4	0.7	0.4	0.3	0.2	5.4	3.6
1966–70	0.4	0.9	0.3	1.2	1.6	1.2	0.4	0.3	4.4	3.3
1971–75	1.2	4.8	0.8	5.6	6.8	2.5	4.3	4.1	23.4	22.3
1976–80	2.7	10.9	1.9	12.8	15.5	7.8	7.7	7.7	18.0	18.0
1981	4.4	26.4	– 5.1	21.3	25.7	18.3	7.4	6.6	11.7	10.4
1982	3.7	16.3	1.0	17.3	21.0	24.3	– 3.3	– 4.9	– 5.8	– 8.6
1983	2.5	9.2	– 0.5	8.7	11.2	22.6	–11.4	–13.5	–20.1	–23.8

SOURCE: Calculated from balance of payments data of the United Nations Economic Commission for Latin America and the Caribbean (ECLAC), Division of Statistics and Quantitative Analysis, which are in turn prepared from the magnetic tapes of the International Monetary Fund's *Balance of Payments Yearbook*.

NOTES:

a Includes portfolio investment.
b Interest payments and profit remittances (net).
c Unregistered transactions are those that appear in the "errors and omissions" line of the capital account of the balance of payments.
d Goods and services. By dividing the net transfer by exports one gains an idea of the degree of positive or negative contribution that external financial transactions have on the total availability of foreign exchange.
e All Spanish-speaking countries (less Cuba) plus Brazil and Haiti.
f All countries in (e) less Mexico, Venezuela, and Ecuador.

TABLE 2.2. Latin America: External Financial Flows and Resource Transfers, 1951–1982 (billions of 1970 dollars)

| Annual Averages (1) | Foreign Direct Investment[a] (2) | Net Noncompensatory Loans | | | Total Flows (2 + 5) (6) | Factor Payments[b] (7) | Net Transfer (6 − 7) (8) | Memorandum Items | | |
		Medium-Long-term[a] (3)	Short-term (4)	Total (3 + 4) (5)				Effect of Change in Terms of Trade[c] (9)	Export Volume[d] (10)	Imports[e]/Exports (11)
					Latin America[f]					
1951–65	0.6	0.5	0.1	0.6	1.2	1.5	−0.3	1.3	60.6	107
1966–70	0.8	1.3	0.5	1.8	2.6	2.5	0.1	−0.4	91.6	96
1971–75	1.2	4.4	0.7	5.1	6.3	3.0	3.3	2.2	114.2	118
1976–80	1.6	8.0	0.7	8.7	10.3	4.7	5.6	4.1	155.2	126
1981	2.4	12.5	0.8	13.3	15.7	8.9	6.8	4.4	197.3	124
1982	1.9	9.4	−1.6	7.8	9.7	11.7	−2.0	0.2	192.4	104

Latin America: Nonoil Exporters[g]

1951–65	0.3	0.4	0.1	0.5	0.8	0.5	0.3	−0.1	58.3	104
1966–70	0.4	0.9	0.4	1.3	1.7	1.3	0.4	−0.4	89.7	96
1971–75	0.8	3.2	0.5	3.7	4.5	1.7	2.8	−0.3	116.2	114
1976–80	1.1	4.3	0.8	5.1	6.2	3.0	3.2	−1.6	166.9	102
1981	1.3	7.6	−1.4	6.2	7.5	5.3	2.2	−6.0	215.3	89
1982	1.2	4.8	0.3	5.1	6.3	6.9	−0.6	−6.8	207.5	76

SOURCE: Same as Table 2.1.

NOTES: Data were deflated by price indexes of imports of goods and services. The indexes are prepared by ECLAC's Division of Statistics and Quantitative Analysis and are based on the prices of a sample of imported goods by country. The data presented here are weighted averages for the region. A comparable observation for 1983 was unavailable due to a change in ECLAC's data base for balance of payments accounting.

[a] Includes portfolio investment.

[b] Interest payments and profit remittances (net).

[c] $\bar{X}_t[(PX_t/PM_t) - 1]$ = the terms of trade effect, where $\bar{X}$ is the annual value of goods and service exports in constant 1970 dollars, PX is the deflator for exports, PM the deflator for imports, and t is the year of observation. For more information on the methodology see ECLAC, *América Latina y el Caribe: Balance de Pagos, 1950–1984* [Latin America and the Caribbean: Balance of Payments, 1950–1984] (Santiago, Chile, 1986), p. 18.

[d] Index with 1970 = 100.

[e] Constant dollar imports of goods and services divided by constant dollar exports of goods and services. A figure greater than 100 indicates a trade deficit, while one less than 100 indicates a trade surplus.

[f] All Spanish-speaking countries plus Brazil and Haiti.

[g] All countries in (f) less Mexico, Venezuela, and Ecuador.

serve a dramatic turnaround in the behavior of financial flows. The relatively arid years of the 1950s and 1960s turned into a virtual torrent of finance in the decade of the 1970s: the net transfer was gigantic, equivalent to 17 percent of the value of exports of the region as a whole, while for the nonoil exporters the net transfer was equivalent to 23 percent and 18 percent of its exports in the first and second half of the decade, respectively. It is also evident from the table that practically all the growth in financial flows was attributable to loan transactions, which by the end of the 1970s dwarfed direct foreign investment flows (DFI) in terms of their direct contribution to the balance of payments.[28]

Finance continued to be abundant in 1981, but in 1982 and 1983 the situation was dramatically reversed as net lending fell sharply, while factor payments skyrocketed. For the region as a whole and the subgroup of nonoil exporters the net transfer turned negative; by 1983 (the first full year of crisis) it was equivalent to 29 percent and 20 percent of export earnings, respectively. This meant that the corresponding turnarounds of flows between 1981 and 1983 was a staggering 46 percent and 32 percent of exports ($[16.6 - (-29.2)]$ and $[11.7 - (-20.1)]$). The situation was, moreover, aggravated by considerable capital flight, which increased the migration of resources to creditor countries. As seen in column 9 of Table 2.1, when unregistered balance of payments transactions (a rough and ready proxy for capital flight) are added to registered financial transactions, the export of resources to the North in 1982 nearly doubled for the region as a whole and increased by nearly 50 percent for the nonoil exporters. These unregistered outflows put heavy pressure on some countries and were both a cause and a consequence of the outbreak of financial crisis in Latin America in mid-1982.

Further insight into the dynamics of financial flows can be found in the constant dollar data of Table 2.2. The message is similar in terms of the magnitude of flows: a relatively restricted financial environment until 1970, abundant finance in the 1970s, and a collapse of net financial transfers beginning in 1982. The dynamics of finance were almost entirely determined by loan transactions, the volume of which rose roughly fourfold between the periods 1966 to 1970 and 1976 to 1980 for the region as a whole. The net transfer of financial resources increased only somewhat less dramatically over the same period. The large transfer (coupled with a favorable terms of trade for the oil exporters) permitted a big and growing trade deficit even after discounting the effects of infla-

---

[28] Here, of course, one is only considering financial flows and not the spinoff effects of DFI on the volume of imports or exports.

tion. This in turn meant that real domestic expenditures could exceed real domestic output, which in turn can provide a strong stimulus to growth.[29] Indeed, while the Latin American economies are quite diverse, abundant foreign credit was a common factor that contributed to strong economic growth in the region even in the face of the sluggish expansion of the OECD area; moreover, the traditional growth premium enjoyed by the Latin American economies with respect to the OECD was accentuated in that decade (Table 2.3).

By 1982, however, the region experienced unfavorable trends on all fronts: a negative net transfer of external finance and a further loss of resources due to an adverse movement of the terms of trade and lower export volume on account of a prolonged recession in the industrialized countries. In light of this situation the trade deficit and economic growth contracted severely (see tables 2.2 and 2.3). But the inversion of trends is even more dramatic when one excludes from the analysis the oil exporters, which in 1982 still had terms of trade that were superior to pre-1974 levels.

Table 2.2 indicates that the nonoil exporters had, on average, a generally unattractive terms of trade throughout the postwar period. Thus, the large net financial transfers were decisive in permitting the trade account in real terms to evolve from rough balance during the 1950s and 1960s to a significant deficit in the first half of the 1970s. As mentioned, this provided an impulse for growth during a period in which the OECD economies were sluggish. Although the real net transfer of financial resources was larger in 1976 to 1980 than during the previous five years, the trade deficit contracted considerably in real terms and approached a rough balance. This is explained in part by the fact that inflows of finance were offset by a marked deterioration of the terms of trade and the fact that during this period many countries borrowed to accumulate foreign exchange reserves.

In 1981, and above all in 1982, the nonoil exporters displayed clear signs of severe financial stress. On the one hand, the real net transfer of financial resources underwent marked contraction, turning negative in the latter year. This was coupled with a much graver loss of resources due to a further unfavorable shift in the terms of trade. In these circumstances the countries could no longer run trade deficits in real (or for that matter in nominal) terms; indeed, by 1982 a very large surplus was

---

[29] While this situation can stimulate growth, sustainability depends partly on how efficiently the additional resources are absorbed. This point receives more attention in Chapter Four.

TABLE 2.3. OECD and Latin America: Gross Domestic Product
(rates of growth)

Countries	1962–72	1973	1974–75	1976–79	1980	1981	1982	1983	1984	1985	1986	1987[a]
OECD countries	4.8	5.8	0.1	4.0	1.1	1.6	−0.5	2.7	4.9	3.2	2.8	2.8
Latin America[b]	5.7	8.4	4.1	5.4	6.2	0.7	−1.2	−2.5	3.8	3.6	3.8	2.5
(Nonoil exporters)[b]	(5.4)	(8.3)	(4.8)	(5.3)	(6.6)	(−2.4)	(−1.6)	(−1.5)	(−4.3)	(4.4)	(6.9)	(3.2)

SOURCES: Organization for Economic Cooperation and Development (OECD), *Economic Outlook* (Paris), various numbers; and ECLAC, Division of Statistics and Quantitative Analysis.

NOTES:

[a]Preliminary estimates.

[b]Same as Table 2.1, note f.

generated. Thus for the first time since the late 1960s real expenditures were sharply less than real output. This—in the absence of a very strong expansion of exports—tends to have depressive effects on the economies, as demonstrated in Table 2.3.

In sum, the boom in Latin America that was stimulated by external finance during the 1970s turned into the bust of the 1980s; as has been mentioned, per capita income in 1987 was almost 6 percent lower than in 1980 and was similar to that already obtained by the region in 1978.[30]

The Sources of Finance   Tables 2.1 and 2.2 demonstrated that the buoyant external finance during the 1970s had its origins in a massive expansion of foreign lending. I will now document that this new lending was accounted for by the credit decisions of private international commercial banks.

Table 2.4 breaks down net financial flows by source over the period 1961 to 1981. The data are not wholly compatible with those of Table 2.1 because they exclude short-term finance, flows to the private sector, and also incorporate a number of English-speaking Caribbean countries that were not considered in the earlier data base. Nevertheless, the table does sufficiently illustrate the radical change in the role of commercial banks in Latin America's external finance.

It can be seen that in the early 1960s the split between official and private financial flows was 60/40. Within this framework private banks had a meager participation, with only 2 percent of the total resource flows. Their participation rose to a modest 8 percent in the latter half of the 1960s as part of a general rise in the profile of private finance. By the late 1970s, however, the picture had substantially altered. The split between official and private finance by then had become 13/87, with the share of commercial banks a towering 58 percent, a figure that dwarfed all the other sources of finance. Moreover, if one assumes that short-term balance of payments finance during the period 1976 to 1980 was basically from private banks and adds these sums to the medium- and long-term finance that forms the basis of Table 2.4, the participation of commercial banks is even greater, accounting for 62 percent of total flows. It is thus safe to say that the 1970s represented a decade when financial flows to the region were "privatized" and even more specifically "bankerized."

---

[30] United Nations Economic Commission for Latin America and the Caribbean, "Preliminary Overview of the Latin American Economy 1987" (Santiago, Chile, December 1987), table 2.

TABLE 2.4. Latin America: Net Financial Flows by Source (percentages)

Year	Official			Private						Grand Total
	Multilateral	Bilateral	Total	Suppliers	Banks	Bonds	Direct Investment	Other	Total	
1961–65	19.4	40.7	60.1	7.9	1.6	5.1	25.3	. . .[a]	39.9	100
1966–70	16.6	26.9	43.5	11.7	8.1	2.6	33.2	0.9	56.5	100
1971–75	13.5	11.2	24.7	4.0	42.4	2.2	25.8	0.9	75.3	100
1976–80	8.5	4.5	13.0	1.3	58.3	9.0	18.6	−0.2	87.0	100
1981	10.4	5.4	15.8	. . .	53.5	6.4	24.6	−0.3	84.2	100

SOURCE: Inter-American Development Bank, *External Financing of the Latin American Countries* (Washington, D.C., December 1978, 1981, and 1982), table 4 in each source.

NOTES: Information is for developing country members of the Inter-American Development Bank. Includes only medium- and long-term capital flows to the public sector.

[a](. . .) = zero or not large enough to quantify.

SOME FACTORS UNDERLYING THE ASCENDANCE OF PRIVATE BANKS IN THE POSTWAR ERA

There have been a number of general approaches to explaining the rather remarkable rise of bank lending to Latin America and other developing areas. The most widely accepted view has primarily stressed conjunctural factors. These were primarily exogenous shocks such as the oil price hikes that generated a demand for external finance in developing countries that for diverse reasons could only be met by private commercial banks.[31] Meanwhile, analysts linked to private banks typically stressed the growing awareness of developing countries of the attractiveness of banks as a source of funds: flexible and efficient intermediaries capable of raising finance on reasonable and nonpolitical terms.[32] Others, steeped in the Marxist tradition, have focused on the progressive socialization of capital in mature capitalism and the ascendance of finance capital over industrial capital. This, coupled with structural crisis in the center (due to overaccumulation or underconsumption) was responsible for a massive export of capital to the periphery by private banks.[33] Finally, some observers have placed emphasis on an endogenous process of institutional change within the world banking industry in the 1950s and 1960s, which induced a massive expansion of overseas lending that eventually incorporated developing countries.[34]

Monocausal explanation, while often popular, usually hides more than it reveals in the evaluation of social phenomena. The diverse focuses on why commercial banks expanded their lending to LDCs are, in fact, not incompatible and merely reflect various dimensions of the basic supply-demand relation. As I mentioned in Chapter One, the central thrust of the present study is to develop an analysis of the role of the supply side in the current financial crisis, since that aspect of the problem has undergone relatively less scrutiny. Because of this, and my

[31] As an example see Marina Whitman, "Bridging the Gap," *Foreign Policy* 30 (Spring 1978): 148–149.

[32] See, for instance, Irving Friedman, *The Emerging Role of Private Banks in the Developing World* (New York: Citicorp, 1977), p. 61.

[33] See, for example, María de Conceicão Tavares and Luiz G. de Mello Belluzzo, "Capital Financiero y Empresa Multinacional" [Finance Capital and the Multinational Enterprise], in *Nueva Fase del Capital Financiero* [New Phase of Finance Capital], ed. Jaime Estévez and Samuel Lichtensztejn (Mexico City: Editorial Nueva Imagen, 1981), pp. 35–48.

[34] To my knowledge, the argument was first developed in a seminal article by Richard Weinert, "Eurodollar Lending to Developing Countries," *Columbia Journal of World Business*, Winter 1973, pp. 34–38.

special institutional concern about banking, I want to highlight the structural transformations in the banking industry that induced the expansion of lending in the periphery. My special focus, however, is not meant to diminish the importance of the other contributory factors that have come forth in the literature.

The Seeds of Change: New Developments in the U.S. Market

We begin in the United States, the only major industrial country that escaped the ravages of World War II. The conservative lending policies of domestic banks that evolved out of the 1929 financial collapse, coupled with wartime financing of government, gave these institutions a very conservative portfolio: only about 23 percent of the banking system's investments were in loans, the relatively most risky asset, but one that traditionally generates the highest rate of return. Immediately following the war banks liquidated many of their bonds, but even then government securities still exceeded the loan account. In fact, the banking industry was sluggish and of declining importance as a financial intermediary in relative terms. During the 1950s and 1960s, however, U.S. domestic banking underwent some fundamental changes in portfolio strategy; it became more aggressive as the marketing of loans and services developed into a central business concept.[35] This would later have important repercussions for international lending.

At the outset of the 1950s U.S. banks were highly liquid. As noted previously, their portfolio was skewed in the direction of low-risk, low-yield securities. Corporations were also very liquid and could finance investment internally, thus reducing the demand for bank loans. Consumer and real estate finance—traditionally viewed by the banks as more risky and of low priority—were the only major source of loan demand.[36]

Parallel to this situation was the retiring from service of bankers whose conservative view had been conditioned by the depression years and their replacement in top management by a young, new breed of upwardly mobile career-minded bankers who were to become the "go-go guys" of international banking in the 1960s.[37]

[35] Douglas Hayes, *Bank Lending Policies* (Ann Arbor, Mich.: University of Michigan, School of Business Administration, 1977), p. 32; and Howard Crosse and George Hempel, *Management Policies for Commercial Banks*, 2d ed. (Englewood Cliffs, N.J.: Prentice-Hall, 1973), p. 273.

[36] Hayes, *Bank Lending Policies*, p. 32.

[37] Jonathan David Aronson, "The Changing Nature of the International Monetary Crisis, 1971–1974: The Role of the Banks," paper presented at the Seventeenth Annual Meeting of the International Studies Association, Washington, D.C., February 1975, p. 16.

As Douglas Hayes points out, the above circumstances were conducive to the introduction of innovative asset management, that is, the boosting of earnings and career mobility by shifting the portfolio from low-yielding bonds to high-return loan accounts. With the banks very liquid and corporate borrowers scarce, the portfolio adjustment induced intense competition among the lenders for customers. In this environment the image of a successful loan officer changed; he now became a salesman at heart, aggressively soliciting clients. According to Hayes, circumstances were such that lending criteria were greatly liberalized in the 1950s; indeed, procedures were instituted internally within a bank that often "made it more difficult for a loan officer to reject than to grant a loan request."[38] The drive for loan expansion was intensified by the establishment of a large infrastructure of services to promote lending; with substantial fixed costs, there was a further inducement to lend. In effect, developments in the 1950s had created a strong growth bias in the loan program of the banks.

The aggressive expansion of U.S. private banks described above was largely a domestic phenomenon; indeed, prior to 1960 the U.S. banking system's profile abroad had changed little since the 1920s, with just seven banks having branches abroad.[39] But as the reader might now suspect, the change in attitude within the U.S. banking industry eventually made an imprint on the nature of international lending in the decades to follow. In effect, for reasons I will set out below, the aggressive posture of U.S. banks spilled over into international markets and helped to set off a frenzied expansion of world banking.

International Expansion: The Regulatory Factor

The revival of international lending in the 1960s has strong roots in an asymmetry between domestic and international banking regulation. As noted in the earlier historical overview there had evolved in the United States a growing regulation of national banking, especially after the 1929 collapse. Regulations tend to restrict the ability of banks to minimize their opportunity costs in the management of deposits and loans, and hence can limit short-term profit making.[40] Thus, the banks' increasing interest in earnings growth was frustrated by the maze of controls over their operations.

First, depository controls restricted commercial bank activity to state

[38] Hayes, *Bank Lending Policies*, p. 34.

[39] Robinson, *Multinational Banking*, p. 198; and United Nations Centre on Transnational Corporations, *Transnational Corporations in World Development* (New York, 1988), p. 23.

[40] However, well-designed regulation can increase overall social welfare if it enhances the banks' longer-term performance and avoids systemic collapses of financial systems.

frontiers; for the big New York money-center banks the regulatory fences were more severely placed around the city of New York. Needless to say, these controls frustrated the growth ambitions of many institutions.

Commercial banks also faced a law called Regulation Q, which put limits on the rates banks could pay for deposits. When these institutions were highly liquid, the law was of little consequence. But with a tightening of the money supply in the second half of the 1960s, banks found depository rate controls to be an obstacle to expanding their loan portfolio. This introduced a new need for aggressive liability management to support the ambitious growth goals of the industry.

Further obstacles were confronted with the capital controls that the U.S. government introduced in the 1960s to stem a growing balance of payments deficit. During this period, U.S. nonfinancial multinationals (MNCs) had been expanding abroad. But official restrictions on capital outflows made it difficult for U.S. banks to service the overseas needs of these traditional corporate customers.[41] Moreover, under the circumstances MNCs had an incentive to deposit their foreign earnings abroad in order to avoid domestic controls. Thus, banks had to face the dilemma of establishing overseas financial services for their big corporate customers or risk losing their deposit and loan business to foreign banks. The domestic restraints on asset and liability management provided a natural incentive to open branches and subsidiaries abroad; indeed, the number of U.S. banks with foreign branches rose from just seven prior to 1960 to seventy-nine by 1970.[42]

The incentive to go abroad was greatly enhanced by the development of an offshore money market that fell into a "no-man's land" with regard to national regulation: the so-called eurodollar or eurocurrency market. This funding center was devoid of government controls and indeed did not even have conventional regulations such as reserve requirements. As Lees and Eng point out:

> The origin of the Eurodollar market can be traced back to the 1920s when U.S. dollars were deposited in Berlin and Vienna and converted into local currencies for lending purposes. These practices did influ-

[41] The restrictions were the Interest Equalization Tax and the Voluntary Credit Restraint Program. These are described in Aronson, *Money and Power*, pp. 69–91; and John Haley and Barnard Seligman, "The Development of International Banking by the United States," in *The International Banking Handbook*, ed. William Baughn and Donald Mandich (Homewood, Ill.: Dow Jones-Irwin, 1983), pp. 38–40.

[42] U.S. Congress, House, Committee on Banking, Currency, and Housing, *International Banking: A Supplement to a Compendium of Papers Prepared for the FINE Study*, 94th Cong., 2d sess. (Washington, D.C.: U.S. Government Printing Office, 1976), p. 79.

ence the local money markets. After World War II, the U.S. dollar was designated by the IMF as an intervention currency in the foreign exchange market. This established the common acceptability of the U.S. dollar as a key currency for international trade, investment, exchange arbitrage, and balance-of-payments settlements. The continuous balance-of-payments deficits of the United States resulted in a growth of official reserve assets in West European countries, and their central banks looked for investment opportunities for short-term gains. In the 1950s, Russian banks in Western Europe preferred to place their holdings in U.S. dollars with British and French banks against the risk of possible seizure by the U.S. authorities in case of crisis. Under these circumstances, Eurobanks simply practiced the principles of free economy by establishing competitive spreads between creditor and debtor rates of interest. Some French banks extended U.S. dollar loans to Italian banks during the 1950s as typical operations in small amounts.[43]

Thus the freewheeling unregulated market was undoubtedly attractive to banks interested in growth and profits. Furthermore, for U.S. banks it became a vital source of funding to overcome the aforementioned capital export controls and tight money policies in their domestic market during the 1960s.

It is a historical curiosity that the eurocurrency market was actively promoted by the very governments that thought it appropriate to tightly regulate their domestic banking systems. England promoted London as the major offshore dollar center, even while preventing its banks from carrying on dollar transactions in its domestic market. In the late 1960s the U.S. government gave impulse to the expansion of the eurocurrency market in the Caribbean—Panama, Nassau, and Grand Cayman—by authorizing U.S. banks to establish "one-man shell" branches there to carry out accounting of international transactions that were actually undertaken in the United States. In this way U.S. banks could lend internationally from New York without violating official capital controls.[44] Moreover, smaller U.S. banks found the Caribbean shells exceptionally useful because they could "go international" without incurring the high expenses of opening up a full-fledged branch in London, the center of the eurocurrency market. An additional attraction was the fact that U.S. tax laws made it profitable for U.S. banks to transfer funds to tax havens, which these Caribbean money centers

---

[43] Frances Lees and Maximo Eng, *International Financial Markets* (New York: Praeger, 1975), p. 435.

[44] U.S. Congress, House, *International Banking*, p. 72.

were in every sense of the word.[45] What the Caribbean became for the U.S. banks was eventually duplicated by Luxembourg for the German banks and Hong Kong and Singapore for Asian financial institutions.

Once U.S. banks had invested in a costly international branch network to improve asset and liability management, fixed costs could be reduced by increasing the volume of their operations. Thus there was a further incentive to expand services and raid the traditional clients of foreign banks. The aggressive posture of U.S. banks soon brought with it a defensive reaction from European, Canadian, and Japanese institutions, which also went international to avoid losing their market share to the invading Americans. As in the case of U.S. banks the first to venture overseas were the largest institutions, but they were soon followed by smaller banks interested in avoiding the loss of clients to their bigger brethren.

The successive waves of new banks entering the eurocurrency market, coupled with the absence of reserve requirements, obviously fueled its expansion. As Weinert has pointed out:

> The size of the Eurodollar pool grew steadily, fed partly by continued U.S. deficits but also by deposit creation on the part of proliferating financial institutions. Each U.S. bank branch and consortium bank established in London enlarged the Eurodollar pool by redepositing their deposits with each other, thereby creating new deposits. Moreover, the increased number of financial institutions created an ever greater will to lend as each institution sought to build a portfolio.[46]

International Expansion:
The Technological and Organizational Factor

Another very important factor in the growth of international banking was technological and organizational innovation in the industry. In effect, new techniques in banking lowered perceived risks and raised the expected profits, and hence attractiveness, of international lending.

The first innovation involved a technique to break out of the traditional reliance on short-term trade credits and move into significant term lending, which in turn opened up new market opportunities. In the 1950s and 1960s, loans out of the eurocurrency market were basically

---

[45] Tax officials permitted U.S. banks to credit taxes paid on foreign income in excess of the U.S. rate of 48 percent to other foreign income taxed at lower rates than the U.S. rate. The U.S. institutions thus had an incentive to generate income in low-tax areas. This is analyzed in more detail in Karin Lissakers, *International Debt, the Banks, and U.S. Foreign Policy* (Washington, D.C.: U.S. Government Printing Office, 1977), pp. 18–21.

[46] Weinert, "Eurodollar Lending to Developing Countries," p. 35.

short-term (less than one year), reflecting the short-term deposit base of the market and the need to roughly match the tenor (i.e., maturity) of assets and liabilities. However, banks soon discovered that aggressive liability management in the eurocurrency market could liberate them from the straightjacket of short-term deposits. In practice, banks could "buy" short-term deposits in the interbank market and, through the continuous roll over of bank-to-bank loans, thereby finance lending to third parties over a medium- to long-term period. Moreover, banks learned how to pass the interest rate risk on to the borrower: they abandoned fixed-rate loans and inserted a variable-rate clause into the loan contract. Typically the base lending rate was adjusted every three or six months according to movement of the London Interbank Offer Rate (LIBOR), which was the rate charged by banks to each other in the interbank market. In this way lenders could ensure an approximate correspondence between their cost of funds (the LIBOR) and the price of credit to the borrower (which included a margin, or spread, over the LIBOR to provide for risk coverage and profit). Thus not only did longer-term lending become technically possible, it was financially lucrative as well.

By the end of the 1960s international credits could carry a maturity period of up to five years,[47] and as we will see later, even much longer periods were available in the 1970s. Naturally this mismatching of liabilities and assets incurred risks. These were at least three:

—The possibility that the interest rate of the interbank funds would rise substantially before the date of adjustment of the variable-rate loan;
—The possibility of a crisis of confidence in the interbank market that would cause banks to charge a premium mover LIBOR to their cohorts in the market; and
—The possibility that a crisis of confidence—either due to the state of the bank or the market more generally—would make it impossible to purchase deposits at any price.[48]

Any of the mentioned risks would raise the cost of funds above the price of loans, inducing losses. The first risk was minimal, however, given that variable-rate loans were adjusted frequently, every three or six months. As for the latter two risks, they were generally not considered to be serious because of a buoyant attitude about the interbank market and the ability to roll over funds. Indeed, banks of all sizes con-

---

[47] Robinson, *Multinational Banking*, p. 254.
[48] Rae Weston, *Domestic and Multinational Banking* (New York: Columbia University Press, 1980), pp. 312–320.

sidered access to the market to be immediate, automatic, and nondis-criminatory.[49]

A second important technical innovation was the loan syndicate. In the 1960s credits from the eurocurrency market were extended by individual banks, and the amount of each transaction rarely exceeded 15 million dollars.[50] The creditors, however, discovered that individual institutional risk could be minimized by joining together in a group to extend a loan. On the one hand, banks acting as a group in a syndicated loan could lend a large amount of total credit, yet the exposure, or share, of each bank participating in the loan could be kept within prudent limits. The syndicated loan was especially important to the entrance of smaller banks into the market inasmuch as they could tailor the size of their loan to their individual situation, sometimes participating with as little as $250,000. On the other hand, the syndicate provided for one loan contract for all the lenders, which ostensibly raised the bargaining power of each institution, since the failure of a borrower to pay meant confronting a large number of lenders simultaneously. With the rising popularity of the syndicated loan, individual transactions eventually grew to as much as a billion dollars or more, with a hundred or more participating lenders.[51]

A third innovation that in practice reduced perceptions of risk and raised expected profits in international lending was the standard introduction of cross-default clauses into loan contracts. This clause essentially stated that nonpayment to one lender was equivalent to nonpayment to all lenders. Thus, unlike the 1930s, selective default became legally impossible, and should a country decide not to pay, it risked the wrath of not only the bank on which the default occurred but all the other banks that the clause forcibly drew into the argument as well. Clearly, a simultaneous conflict with hundreds of banks might make a borrower extremely reluctant to default on a loan.

A fourth innovation had less to do with the banks than their regulatory authorities. As mentioned, as a consequence of systemic bank failures in the 1930s, the United States and some other industrialized countries had introduced insurance programs on bank deposits designed to discourage panic withdrawals. Effectively, either via direct or indirect mechanisms, domestic banking systems had the official protection of a lender-of-last-resort. Some analysts have argued that many banks went

[49] Richard Cummings, "International Credits: Milestones or Millstones?" *Journal of Commercial Bank Lending*, January 1975, pp. 40–52.

[50] "Syndicated Loans" (Special Supplement: World Banking Survey), *Financial Times*, 21 May 1979.

[51] More will be said on the syndicated credit in the next chapter.

abroad with the implicit assumption that should problems develop the domestic lender-of-last-resort would, even if only in an ad hoc manner, be extended internationally.[52]

A fifth and final innovation supporting international lending that might be mentioned is improvements in international communications and computation, which facilitated the around-the-world profit making that today so characterizes the transnational bank.

International Expansion: The Macroeconomic Factor

Economists as diverse as Smith, Marx, and Schumpeter all recognized that accumulation and growth were intimately linked to an expanding and ever-sophisticated credit system. For Smith credit permitted the conversion of "dead stock into active and productive stock." For Marx credit was essential to the "concentration" and "centralization" of capital (somewhat akin to the concepts of capital deepening and the re-allocation of capital between sectors, respectively) during the process of capitalist accumulation and the development of the forces of production. Meanwhile, Schumpeter viewed credit as a fundamental condition for the entrepreneurial innovation that broke his static circular flow economy and provided for a dynamic burst of economic development.[53] There was an unprecedented expansion of the world economy after the Second World War. Moreover, the introduction of convertibility of European currencies and the formation of the European Economic Community in 1958, coupled with liberalization of domestic markets, brought a boom in trade that significantly overshadowed growth of world product.[54] Employing the theoretical insights of the aforementioned economists, it is no surprise that the internationalization of finance accompanied the postwar internationalization of production.

Mandel has suggested another macroeconomic factor that perhaps accentuated the role of the banking system in the postwar boom. According to his analysis of "late capitalism," in the first three decades

[52] Folkerts-Landau, "The Changing Role of International Bank Lending," pp. 7–8. For a recent discussion of contemporary lender-of-last-resort facilities see P. A. Wellons, *Passing the Buck* (Boston: Harvard Business School Press, 1987), pp. 241–272.

[53] Adam Smith, *The Wealth of Nations* (1937; reprint ed., New York: The Modern Library, 1965), pp. 304–305; Karl Marx, *Capital*, vol. 3, *The Process of Capitalist Production as a Whole*, 9th ed. (New York: International Publishers, 1967), pp. 435–441; Joseph Schumpeter, *The Theory of Economic Development*, trans. Redvers Opie (1961; reprint ed., New York: Oxford University Press, 1980), pp. 95–127.

[54] "Between 1953 and 1963 the volume of industrial production in the capitalist countries rose 62%, while exports rose 82%. Between 1963 and 1972 industrial production rose 65%, exports 111%." See Ernest Mandel, *The Second Slump*, trans. Jon Rothschild (London: New Left Books, Verso edition, 1980), p. 19.

after the war governments became unwilling to subject their economies to the free forces of the market and the economic cycle. The main instrument to curb depression and sustain the economic expansion was easy money and credit policies, which naturally gave greater stimulus to the expansion of banking, both domestically and internationally.

> The combination of inflationary creation of money to mitigate crises and growing competition on the world market give the industrial cycle in the first "expansionary" phase of late capitalism the particular form of a movement interlocked with the credit cycle. In the epoch of freely competitive capitalism, when there was a gold standard and the central banks only intervened marginally in the development of credit, the credit cycle was completely dependent on the industrial cycle. In late capitalism, when institutionalised inflation makes the monetary sphere much more autonomous and capable of independent action—running counter to the industrial cycle—to moderate conjunctural fluctuations, a credit cycle temporarily distinct from the industrial cycle comes into being.[55]

As pointed out earlier, the aggressive expansion of U.S. banking, first domestically, then overseas, was fueled in part by the relatively high liquidity of the banking system in the 1950s and the first half of the 1960s. A further impetus to the ascendancy of banking could have come from what some analysts have seen as a structural downturn in the postwar boom in the late 1960s and early 1970s that eventually put greater pressures on governments to pursue expansionary fiscal and monetary policies.[56] The rapidly expanding eurocurrency market also gave a further degree of independence to banks as they could use these unregulated deposits to counter the periodic restrictive policy of their own monetary authorities—as was done by U.S. banks in the late 1960s.[57] And, of course, the banks' expansion was given a special impetus by the oil price shock in 1973 and 1974 and the OECD governments' ready encouragement of petrodollar recycling via private economic agents.[58] It thus seems at least plausible that the nature of world monetary policy in the postwar period added its own special dimension to the expansion of world banking. Moreover, the sharp slowdown in international

---

[55] Ernest Mandel, *Late Capitalism*, trans. Joris de Bres (London: New Left Books, Verso edition, 1980), p. 454.

[56] Mandel, *Second Slump*, pp. 22–39, and Ricardo Parboni, *The Dollar and Its Rivals*, trans. Jon Rothschild (London: New Left Books, Verso edition, 1981), pp. 79–82.

[57] Martin Wolfson, "Financial Crisis: Theory and Evidence in the Post-War U.S. Economy" (Ph.D. diss., The American University, 1984), p. 164.

[58] See Wellons, *Passing the Buck*, pp. 58–63.

TABLE 2.5. The Size of the Eurocurrency Market
(billions of dollars)

Year[a]	1965	1970	1975	1980[b]
Gross	24	110	420	1,200
Net[c]	17	65	245	650

SOURCE: Rosario Green, *Estado y Banca Transnacional en México* [The State and Transnational Banks in Mexico] (Mexico City: Editorial Nueva Imagen, 1981), p. 188 (based on data from Morgan Guaranty Trust Company).
NOTES:
[a]End of period.
[b]June.
[c]Data adjusted for redepositing within the interbank market.

banking coincident with the advent of generalized tight monetary policy in the 1980s is consistent with the notion of a distinguishable role for this macroeconomic variable in overall trends.

MODERN INTERNATIONAL BANKING: A BRIEF LOOK AT THE DATA

Before proceeding to the banks' penetration of the periphery, it is useful to pause briefly to examine some data on the general phenomenon of the internationalization of banking. The focus will unfortunately be oriented almost exclusively toward U.S. banking since it is one of the few national systems with comprehensive published data.

Table 2.5 documents the massive expansion of the eurocurrency market, which was the basic platform for the international operations of private banks. The market grew quite slowly in the 1950s and did not really begin its now famous hyperexpansion until the mid-1960s.[59] But from 1965 to 1970 its net size (which excludes interbank operations) rose by fourfold (an average rate of more than 30 percent per annum). Between 1970 and 1975 it grew another fourfold, slowing down to a roughly threefold increase in the last half of the 1970s. This phenome-

[59] Dufey and Giddy, *The International Money Market*, p. 111. There is a great and conflictive debate surrounding the causes of the growth of the market—U.S. balance of payment deficit, infinite multiple deposit creation due to zero official reserve requirements, the attraction of deposits from domestic markets, et cetera—but to enter into this here would be an excessively long and a not too relevant digression from the thrust of my analysis.

TABLE 2.6. Foreign Branches and Assets of U.S. Commercial Banks

Variable	1950	1960	1970	1979
Number of banks with over-seas branches	7	8	79	139
Number of overseas branches	95	124	536	796
Assets of overseas branches			47[a]	364[a]

SOURCE: Christopher M. Korth, "The Evolving Rate of U.S. Banks in International Finance," *The Bankers Magazine* (July-August 1980), p. 69. Copyright © 1980, Warren, Gorham, & Lamont Inc., 210 South St., Boston, MA, 02111. Reprinted with permission from *Bankers Magazine,* as reproduced in John Haley and Barnard Seligman, "The Development of International Banking in the United States," in *The International Banking Handbook,* ed. William Baughn and Donald Mandich (Homewood, Ill.: Dow Jones-Irwin, 1983), p. 38.
NOTE:
[a]In billions of U.S. dollars.

nal growth made the market the largest single financial pool outside the United States.[60]

Table 2.6 provides information on investments by U.S. banks in foreign branches. Growth was robust in the 1960s and 1970s. From only 8 banks with foreign branches in 1960, the number rose to 139 by 1979. Moreover, these branches became very important in funding the overall operations of U.S. banks; data by Salomon Brothers indicate that by the late 1970s the top ten banks gathered over 50 percent of their deposits from overseas.[61]

Table 2.7 confirms that the action was in the global banking market and not at home. While the ten largest U.S. banks had a phenomenal expansion of international earnings in 1970 to 1976, profitability in the domestic market was generally flat. By the mid-1970s most of the large banks had 50 percent or more of their earnings from abroad. In the case of Citicorp and Bankers Trust the internationalization was extreme: by 1977 over 80 percent of all earnings came from their international operations (see Table 2.8).

Data in tables 2.7 and 2.8 for the late 1970s and early 1980s display a

[60] Christopher Korth, "The Eurocurrency Markets," in *The International Banking Handbook*, ed. William Baughn and Donald Mandich (Homewood, Ill.: Dow Jones-Irwin, 1983), p. 23.
[61] Salomon Brothers, *A Review of Bank Performance: 1984 Edition* (New York, 1984), p. 66.

TABLE 2.7. Ten Largest U.S. Banks: Growth in Domestic
and International Earnings, 1970–1976 and 1978–1981
(compound annual rates)

Bank	1970–76		1978–81	
	Domestic	International	Domestic	International
Citicorp	4.3	31.0	25.7	−6.0
Bank of America Corp.	6.1	32.4	−21.4	16.8
J. P. Morgan & Co.	3.6	27.1	− 2.3	24.1
Chase Manhattan Corp.	−22.8	17.8	28.9	33.0
Manufacturers Hanover Corp.	− 3.1	38.4	− 1.5	11.4
Chemical New York Corp.	− 5.0	32.1	25.7	12.5
Bankers Trust New York Corp.	−12.6	29.6	38.7	28.9
Continental Illinois	7.8		10.1	35.1
First Chicago Corp.	4.0	53.7		
Security Pacific Corp.	3.6	72.7	12.4	34.1

SOURCES: 1970–1976, Salomon Brothers as cited in Michael Moffit, *The World's
Money* (New York: Simon & Schuster, Touchstone Paperback, 1984), p. 52; 1978–
1981, Salomon Brothers, *A Review of Bank Performance: 1983 Edition* (New York,
1983), p. 66.

greater degree of ambiguity about the international earnings of U.S. banks,
as a number of institutions experienced a slowdown of profits in their
overseas operations, while for some banks domestic earnings picked up.
This situation reflects new trends in banking, in which domestic deregulation and problem international loans have encouraged the banks to
shift their portfolio strategy and explore profit opportunities at home.

Finally, while data have unavoidably been concentrated on U.S.
banking, it is safe to assert that trends similar to these—though perhaps
less pronounced—have occurred for the national banking systems
of other OECD economies. An indicator of the aggressive expansion of
European and Japanese banks is in a U.S. House committee report of
1976 that studied foreign banking in the U.S. economy and concluded
that the international expansion of European and Japanese banks was
"almost as dramatic as that of the American banks."[62]

[62] U.S. Congress, House, *International Banking*, p. 11.

Table 2.8. Ten Largest U.S. Banks: Foreign Earnings as a Percentage of Total Earnings, 1970–1982

Bank	1970	1971	1972	1973	1974	1975	1976	1977	1978	1979	1980	1981	1982
Citicorp	58.0	43.0	54.0	60.0	62.0	70.6	72.4	82.2	71.8	64.7	62.1	51.7	60.0
Chase Manhattan Corp.	22.0	29.0	34.0	39.0	47.0	64.5	78.0	64.9	53.3	46.9	49.1	55.6	64.7
Bank of America Corp.	15.0	19.0	21.0	24.0	29.0	54.7	46.7	43.0	34.4	37.5	44.5	63.3	65.1
Manufacturers Hanover Corp.	13.0	24.0	29.0	36.0	47.2	49.1	59.3	60.2	51.2	48.8	49.1	60.2	49.6
J. P. Morgan & Co.	25.0	28.9	35.0	45.9	45.0	60.2	46.1	47.9	50.8	52.2	59.3	68.1	63.9
Chemical New York Corp.	10.0	17.0	14.2	18.5	34.0	41.6	41.1	38.8	42.0	31.7	38.4	34.2	38.7
Bankers Trust New York Corp.	14.5	19.1	31.0	40.0	52.0	58.6	60.4	82.8	67.9	51.5	57.5	62.4	49.5
First Chicago Corp.	2.0	7.0	11.0	12.0	3.0	34.0	17.0	20.7	16.0	3.5		19.7	30.3
Continental Illinois	0.2	3.0	17.0	20.0	4.0	13.4	23.0	16.7	17.8	16.5	28.1	28.4	62.8
Security Pacific Corp.	0.4	2.0	5.0	12.0	16.0	12.6	6.9	11.2	16.6	10.9	12.9	25.4	31.6
Total	17.5	23.8	29.3	35.6	39.6	52.5	50.8	50.8	45.5	42.3	46.3	51.0	54.7

SOURCES: 1970–1979, Salomon Brothers as cited in Moffit, *The World's Money* p. 53; 1980–1982; Salomon Brothers, *A Review of Bank Performance: 1983 Edition*, p. 66.

THE PENETRATION OF THE PERIPHERY

Prior to 1970 the internationalization of banking was almost entirely concentrated in the OECD area; lending to the periphery was relatively marginal. In Latin America only Brazil and Mexico, and to a lesser extent Peru, had begun to establish significant commercial ties with private banks, and this was in the latter half of the 1960s. Moreover, much of the activity of banks in these countries had been initiated by the servicing of the needs of locally based subsidiaries of home-country nonfinancial MNCs; foreign governments were generally not significant borrowers.[63]

Around 1970, however, loans from private banks began to grow significantly and LDC governments—as opposed to foreign firms—had become clients of increasing importance. It was evident that the banks' commercial contacts with LDCs were expanding beyond the need to service MNCs. From here on in, developing countries would become important clients in their own right.

Until 1973 there was no systematic collection of data on eurocurrency transactions. Table 2.9 presents information on publicized eurocurrency term credits as collected by the World Bank and published by the United Nations Conference on Trade and Development (UNCTAD). It can be seen that by 1973, prior to the famous petrodollar recycling process, developing countries were already absorbing around 50 percent of the international market lending of the banks. Moreover, within the developing country group, Latin America accounted for about half of the borrowing. In this latter region Brazil, Mexico, Peru, Colombia, Nicaragua, Panama, and Jamaica had by then what might be termed regular access to the banks.

With the beginning of the petrodollar recycling process in 1974, eurocurrency lending to developing countries of course underwent a marked and accelerated expansion. A growing number of developing countries were incorporated into the market, and these curiously even included many oil producers who had experienced a foreign exchange bonanza due to the higher price of petroleum.[64]

While the next chapter will have more to say on the nature of the borrowers, it is worthwhile to emphasize here that the boom in eurocurrency lending was to a large degree a Latin American phenomenon.

---

[63] Hayes, *Bank Lending Policies*, p. 46; Gisselquist, *Politics and Economics of Bank Lending*, pp. 148–149; and Wellons, *Borrowing by Developing Countries*, p. 24.

[64] This is evident from reviewing the detailed breakdown of credits by country in United Nations Conference on Trade and Development (UNCTAD), *Handbook of International Trade and Development Statistics 1981 Supplement* (Geneva, 1982), pp. 336–338.

TABLE 2.9. Gross Eurocurrency Credits to Developing Countries
(billions of dollars)

Countries	1973	1974	1975	1976	1977	1978	1979	1980
Developed[a]	13.0	19.5	6.5	10.2	12.7	32.0	25.7	38.2
Less developed	7.1	7.6	11.3	15.5	18.3	35.2	35.3	28.8
(Latin America)	(3.4)	(4.6)	(6.0)	(9.2)	(9.4)	(18.5)	(22.0)	(18.1)

SOURCES: United Nations Conference on Trade and Development (UNCTAD), *Handbook of International Trade and Development Statistics 1980 Supplement* (Geneva, 1981), pp. 322–324; and UNCTAD, *Handbook of Interational Trade and Development Statistics 1981 Supplement* (Geneva, 1982), pp. 336–338.
NOTES: Gross eurocurrency credits = publicized credits, excluding short-term.
[a]The OECD countries plus Yugoslavia.

Starting in 1975, the Bank for International Settlements (BIS) began to publish data on total private bank exposure, including short-term credits, around the world. Although some lending escapes the BIS survey, its data are at least a close approximation of trends. I have calculated regional distributions of lending to developing countries for the years 1975 and 1981 (Table 2.10). It can be observed that close to two-thirds of all gross exposure of the banks in the developing world was in Latin America, and on a net basis (gross debt less deposits in the banks), Latin America carried the overwhelming share of overall obligations.

Why the bankers' interest in developing countries during the 1970s? I will suggest some factors below.

The Developing World: A Last Frontier

It has already been shown in the earlier section analyzing the ascendance of the private banks that as far back as 1950 there is evidence that the banking industry was undergoing an aggressive portfolio adjustment following many years of a conservative low-yield, low-risk investment strategy. The process first began in the U.S. domestic market, as banks sought to expand their loan account. We also saw that the U.S. banks' growth drive progressively shifted to the international area, where it induced a defensive reaction on the part of European, Canadian, and Japanese banks, which also decided to expand their international operations. The battleground was the OECD area.

With the increasing competition among the banks "going international," the OECD market became very crowded. The situation was perhaps aggravated by the slowdown in the postwar economic boom,

TABLE 2.10. Distribution of Total Bank Debt among Developing Regions, 1975 and 1981 (billions of dollars)

Year	Latin America[a] Amount	%	Middle East[b] Amount	%	Africa[c] Amount	%	Asia[d] Amount	%	Total LDC Amount	%	Total World Amount
1975[e]											
Gross debt	50.9	65.6	6.7	8.6	5.5	7.0	14.7	18.8	77.8	100	442.6
Net debt[f]	24.0		-36.1		-0.7		3.2		-9.6		
1981[e]											
Gross debt	185.3	63.3	30.7	10.5	29.2	10.0	47.5	16.2	292.7	100	1,541.4
Net debt[f]	124.7	238.7	-96.4	-184.5	13.3	25.5	10.6	20.4	52.2	100	

SOURCES: Calculated from data of the Bank for International Settlements (BIS), *International Banking Statistics, 1973–1983* (Basel, April 1984), p. 41; and BIS, *International Banking Developments: Fourth Quarter 1983* (Basel, April 1984), Statistical Appendix, p. 10.
NOTES:
[a]Includes the Caribbean. Countries excluded are Bahamas, Barbados, Bermuda, Cayman Islands, Netherland Antilles, Panama, and West Indies.
[b]Excludes Lebanon and Israel.
[c]Excludes Liberia.
[d]Excludes Hong Kong and Singapore.
[e]End of period.
[f]Gross debt less deposits in the banks.

marked by the significant 1970 recession in the U.S. economy. Loan demand and interest rates fell in the United States. American banks tried to absorb their liquidity by intensifying their lending to Europe, but demand was not adequate. Further obstacles to lending in Europe came because some countries—in the face of capital inflows and inflationary pressures—introduced exchange controls that limited the activities of U.S. foreign branches in Europe. Hence, growth ambitions were stymied.

To sustain growth and expansion of earnings, new frontiers were opened up. First, U.S. banks sought new markets at home; in the early 1970s a major effort was made to raise real estate lending, manifested in a massive expansion of loans to the so-called Real Estate Investment Trusts.[65] Another frontier was developing countries.

The drive to enter developing countries could have appeared as a logical extension of the aforementioned portfolio adjustment that began to first take place in the 1950s. The commercial banks' articulation with developing countries had been weak for nearly forty years; thus portfolios could be built up without much concern for excessive exposure. Moreover, many of the developing countries had participated in the postwar boom and looked relatively prosperous; for instance, Latin America's gross domestic product rose by an average of 6 percent per annum between 1965 and 1970, compared to 5 percent in the previous fifteen years. Some countries experienced extremely strong growth between 1965 and 1970: Brazil, Mexico, Panama, and the Dominican Republic all achieved annual rates of growth of 7 percent or more. Export expansion was also generally good in Latin America, and quite exceptional in Brazil, where earnings nearly doubled over the last half of the 1960s.[66]

Profit motives were also an important consideration. Competition and excess liquidity had driven down interest spreads in the OECD area, but developing countries, representing a new frontier unscarred by competition, offered higher rates of return. Indeed, in the early 1970s developing country borrowers were willing to pay high premiums of 2 percent or more over LIBOR. Moreover, the new lending was to governments and therefore the risk was perceived as low since conventional wisdom within the industry argued that governments—

---

[65] Hayes, *Bank Lending Policies*, p. 46; U.S. Congress, House, *International Banking*, pp. 72–73.

[66] United Nations Economic Commission for Latin America and the Caribbean, *1983 Statistical Yearbook for Latin America* (Santiago, Chile, 1984), p. 120 and pp. 518–519.

unlike private firms—could not go bankrupt and therefore would always be around to service their debts.[67]

The expansion into the periphery was begun by the big U.S. banks and focused initially on the most prosperous countries where these institutions already had considerable experience in lending to multinational corporations, namely Brazil and Mexico. They were followed by other U.S. banks, the Japanese and Europeans, with many institutions reacting defensively to the expansion of the bigger banks into the periphery. As competition became keener, lending spilled over into less prestigious countries such as the aforementioned Latin American countries, and Zaire, the Ivory Coast, Senegal, Algeria, Indonesia, and the Philippines.

Thus the lending drive was well underway prior to the first oil shock in 1973/1974. With the historical rise in oil prices, however, banks became much more active lenders, and the scope of their operations expanded enormously. In effect, in 1974 the euromarkets were the largest single depository of OPEC funds; Kane estimates that fully 41 percent of that year's total surplus of 56 billion U.S. dollars entered the international private banking system.[68] These new deposits essentially fueled the fires of an expansion that had been well underway. Private banks, highly liquid with funds, now had even more raw material with which to pursue the drive for portfolio diversification and growth of earnings. However, at the end of 1974 and through 1975 the recession in the industrialized countries greatly reduced the demand for loans (see Table 2.9), making the periphery—where there was less willingness to accept recession—the only dynamic outlet for lending.

Individual developing countries dropped in and out of favor with the banks throughout the 1970s, but as already shown in Table 2.9 the gross amount of term credits to this group rose dramatically throughout the decade. Expansion of bank exposure in developing areas was exceptionally rapid, reaching an average annual rate of 30 percent per annum in the latter half of the decade.[69] Of course, the second oil shock of 1979/1980 gave more impetus to the process as once again banks be-

[67] This factor is highlighted in Pedro-Pablo Kuczynski, "Latin American Debt," *Foreign Affairs* 61 (Winter 1982/1983): 352.

[68] Daniel Kane, *The Eurodollar Market and the Years of Crisis* (New York: St. Martin's Press, 1983), pp. 110–111.

[69] The data on rates of growth of bank exposure are from Morgan Guaranty Trust Company, *World Financial Markets* (New York, February 1983), p. 3. The data are for twenty-one major LDC borrowers that accounted for 85 percent of all bank loans in the Third World. Nearly 70 percent of the value of this debt was in Latin American countries.

TABLE 2.11. Latin America and All Developing Countries: Participation of Private Banks in Total Debt Prior to the Crisis (percentages)

Countries	1973	1975	1977	1980
Latin America	60	69	70	78
All developing countries	40	46	49	59

SOURCE: Ricardo Ffrench-Davis, "Deuda Externa y Balanza de Pagos de América Latina" [External Debt and the Balance of Payments of Latin America], in Inter-American Development Bank, *Progreso Económico y Social en América Latina, Informe 1982* [Economic and Social Progress in Latin America, 1982 Report] (Washington, D.C., 1982), table 3.

came major depositories of OPEC funds. Although data on the foreign debt of developing countries are notoriously poor, estimates are available. An early study by Ffrench-Davis estimated that by the end of 1980 total LDC debt exceeded $441 billion, of which 59 percent belonged to private banks (Table 2.11). His figure for Latin America is US $205 million, 78 percent of which originated in the banks.

The expansive phase of international banking in the periphery came to an end in mid-1982, when in August Mexico unilaterally declared its inability to service debts. This was followed by a wave of rescheduling requests, above all in Latin America, but also in Africa, Asia, and the socialist countries. Already by early 1983 more than twenty-five countries of the periphery had initiated rescheduling proceedings with their bankers, representing about half of the portfolio invested in these areas.[70] While banks continued to lend voluntarily to a few selected developing countries (especially the Asian NICs), the aforementioned portfolio adjustments of the banks in the direction of expanded international lending to the pheriphery has been virtually halted. Table 2.12 documents the marked falloff since 1982 of lending to developing countries and Latin America in particular. Moreover, and as will be shown in greater detail later in the study, much of the lending that has appeared since 1982 (and practically all of it to Latin America) has been "involuntary," that is, new loans materialized as part of bailout agreements between the banks and the borrowers during rescheduling exercises.

The sharp slowdown in new credit for Latin America is reflected in its debt statistics. Table 2.13 presents data on total debt for the region. The

[70] Ibid., pp. 1–2.

TABLE 2.12. Financial Flows between International Banks
and Developing Countries
(billions of dollars)

Countries	1980	1981	1982	1983	1984	1985	1986
Developing countries	45.9	44.1	28.0	22.4	7.9	11.3	−0.1
OPEC[a]	7.0	4.2	8.2	9.8	−1.9	0.2	−0.2
Non-OPEC countries	38.9	39.9	19.8	12.6	9.8	11.1	0.1
Latin America	27.4	30.5	12.1	8.3	5.3	1.7	−1.6
Middle East	2.1	2.3	1.7	0.3	−0.4	0.2	−0.6
Africa	2.0	2.0	1.7	0.6	0.1	0.9	−0.4
Asia	7.4	5.1	4.3	3.4	4.8	8.3	2.7

SOURCE: Bank for International Settlements, *Fifty-Seventh Annual Report* (Basel, 15
June 1987), pp. 100–101.
NOTES: Information includes short-term transactions.
[a]Includes Venezuela and Ecuador.

estimates are those of the United Nations Economic Commission for
Latin America and the Caribbean (ECLAC) and are uniformly higher
than the aforementioned data prepared by Ffrench-Davis, in part because subsequent to this latter author's pioneering work the Bank for
International Settlements and the countries have been continuously re-

TABLE 2.13. Latin America: Total Disbursed External Debt
(billions of dollars, end of year)

Countries	1978	1981	1982	1983	1984	1985	1986	1987[a]
Latin America	152.6	287.8	330.1	353.3	366.5	376.6	392.9	409.8
Brazil	53.4	80.0	91.3	97.9	102.0	105.1	111.0	116.9
Mexico	34.0	74.9	87.6	93.8	96.7	97.8	101.5	105.6
Argentina	12.5	35.7	43.6	45.1	46.9	48.3	51.5	54.5
Venezuela	16.4	33.4	35.1	36.0	34.7	33.9	32.3	32.2
Chile	7.0	16.0	17.2	18.0	19.7	20.4	20.7	20.5
Peru	9.3	9.7	11.5	12.5	13.3	13.7	14.5	15.3
Colombia	4.1	7.9	10.3	11.4	12.3	13.8	15.0	15.7

SOURCE: ECLAC, Division of Statistics and Quantitative Analysis.
NOTES: Total disbursed external debt = total debt, including IMF.
[a]Preliminary.

vising their country debt estimates to account for newly discovered obligations. In any event, from the ECLAC figures it can be observed that the rate of growth of the region's debt slowed from the buoyant average pace of roughly 25 percent per annum in 1978 to 1981 to 15 percent in 1982, and 7 percent in 1983. In more recent years the region's debt has expanded by only 3 to 4 percent per annum; that is, barely ahead of the international rate of inflation. Moreover, while debtors could have been expected to have responded to a difficult credit environment with a more cautious stance on borrowing, most of the slowdown in the growth of debt was involuntarily induced by the retreat of the region's main creditors, the international private banks.

The Demand for Finance

Not only were private banks willing to lend to the periphery but the developing nations were eager borrowers. Some of the attractions of bank loans are itemized below.

The Stagnation of Official Lending   The traditional literature on economic development that arose in the 1960s stressed savings, or capital, as a major constraint on growth. While schemes were devised to mobilize "latent" domestic savings in so-called labor surplus economies, it also became fashionable to advocate foreign loans (savings) as a way to raise capital formation and growth in LDCs.[71] Indeed, the developing country savings constraint was officially the raison d'être of official multilateral and bilateral lending agencies such as the World Bank and USAID. Unfortunately, in the late 1960s and early 1970s political support for concessionary development lending waned in the North. Official finance thus became increasingly inadequate for developing countries; indeed, the Development Assistance Committee of the OECD estimated that in this period official development assistance virtually stagnated in real terms.[72] Thus, to some extent there was a vacuum created with respect to the meeting of the demand for development finance, and this was eagerly filled by private commercial banks.

[71] Two classic works that stress the role of savings are Ragnar Nurske, *Problems of Capital Formation in Underdeveloped Countries* (New York: Oxford University Press, Galaxy Books, 1967); and J.C.H. Fei and Gustav Ranis, *Development of the Labor Surplus Economy: Theory and Policy* (Homewood, Ill.: Richard D. Irwin, 1964). Classic works on the role of foreign savings in boosting domestic capital formation are Hollis Chenery and Alan Strout, "Foreign Assistance and Economic Development," *American Economic Review* 56 (September 1966): 679–733; and Dragoslav Avramovic et al., *Economic Growth and External Debt* (Baltimore: The Johns Hopkins University Press, 1965).

[72] Organization for Economic Cooperation and Development, *1976 Review of Development Cooperation* (Paris, 1977), p. 153.

Of course, the demand for finance rose dramatically with the decision of OPEC to raise petroleum prices fourfold. Unfortunately, as Cohen observes, "the expansion of official financing sources did not manage to keep pace with increased need."[73] It was private financial markets that responded most nimbly, accounting for more than one-third of the finance of the cumulative current account deficit of the nonoil-exporting developing countries in the crisis years of 1974 to 1976.[74] For Latin America, banks were even more important for balance of payments support, financing almost 60 percent of the cumulative deficit over the stated period.[75] It was the quick response of the private banks that led many to believe that they had saved the Western World from severe upheaval; as Marina Whitman once put it, "the main factor in avoiding collapse was that the international financial markets proved remarkably resilient in rising to the challenge."[76]

Unconditional Lending of Banks   Another important consideration is the terms of financing. Official lenders usually tied their loans to projects—with rigorous requirements related to project formulation—and macroeconomic programs involving tough conditionality. This type of lending also was perceived in some circles to introduce severe political conditions as well.[77] In contrast, during the 1970s banks processed loans rapidly with few conditions, technical or political. Thus there is some merit in the observation by some bank analysts that the attractiveness of these creditors for developing countries was a factor in the penetration of the periphery: borrowing was indeed quick and easy.

The Convenient Financial Terms of Bank Credit   The financial terms of lending by private banks in the 1970s also could be convenient. As mentioned, at the turn of the decade private banks looked to the periphery to expand their loan portfolio and earnings. For a country that became a focal point of competition among the banks the terms of lending became extremely attractive:

> Competitive pressures became so hectic that banks—many of them new entrants to the international scene—saw their lending spill over

[73] Benjamin Cohen in collaboration with Fabio Basagni, *Banks and the Balance of Payments* (Montclair, N.J.: Allanheld, Osmun, 1981), p. 19.

[74] Ibid.

[75] United Nations Economic Commission for Latin America and the Caribbean, *América Latina en el Umbral de los Años 80* [Latin America on the Threshold of the 1980s] (Santiago, Chile, 1979), p. 144.

[76] Whitman, "Bridging the Gap," p. 148.

[77] Teresa Hayter, *Aid as Imperialism* (Baltimore: Penguin Books, 1971); and Cheryl Payer, *The Debt Trap* (New York: Monthly Review Press, 1974).

into the smaller, less developed countries of the region; countries traditionally accustomed to obtaining capital from official sources found the Eurocurrency market to be more than a willing supplier of funds. Indeed, by 1972 countries had discovered it to be a borrower's paradise; not only was there easy access to credit, but competition caused margins to be drastically reduced and maturities to reach unprecedented lengths. By way of example, Brazil, which was a leading borrower within the developing world, found that it could regularly secure credits with a 10–15 year maturity. As for spreads, they declined from 2¼% in 1971 to 1½% in mid-1972 and ¾–1% in 1973. At the same time lending was so voluminous that the country even found it necessary to introduce policies to discourage foreign bank loans.[78]

Brazil was not the only country to find itself facing increasingly favorable terms. Countries such as Singapore, Panama, Indonesia, Colombia, and Peru confronted similarly buoyant conditions for borrowing.[79]

The market conditions turned less favorable for borrowers in mid-1974 and 1975. In the latter half of 1974 a crisis of confidence exploded in the interbank market as a result of large losses on foreign exchange speculation at some banks. The two most publicized cases were Bank Herstatt of West Germany and Franklin National Bank of the United States.[80] The formerly democratic interbank market now came face to face with the risk of tiering, mentioned earlier, in the analysis of the roll over of bank-to-bank credits in order to finance medium-term loans to third parties. In effect, during the crisis many small and medium-sized banks had to pay high premiums over base offer rates for interbank funds or were denied access to these funds altogether. Losses ensued, and as Aronson has observed, "Overnight, banks active in the Euromarkets fell from over 200 to less than 40."[81]

With the withdrawal of many banks, the lending market tightened severely. Publicized eurocurrency credits for nonoil-exporting developing countries declined markedly; in the first quarter of 1975 the $1.2 billion of newly authorized loans was less than half that recorded for the same quarter of the previous year. Spreads over the LIBOR rose dra-

---

[78] Devlin, "External Finance and Commercial Banks," pp. 77–78. In 1973—in order to stem the flow of loans—Brazil established minimum maturities of eight years on new credits. See Wellons, *Borrowing by Developing Countries*, p. 35.

[79] Wellons, *Borrowing by Developing Countries*.

[80] For a comprehensive analysis of the Franklin experience see Joan Spero, *The Failure of the Franklin National Bank* (New York: Columbia University Press, 1980).

[81] Aronson, *Money and Power*, p. 119.

matically from 1 percent or less to 1.5 to 2.25 percent. Meanwhile, maturities on loans contracted violently: in the second quarter of 1974, 83 percent of the loans to developing countries had maturities of seven years or more, but by the second quarter of 1975 these longer maturities had fallen to just 20 percent of all lending.[82] The restrictive market put severe cash flow pressures on borrowing countries, and some of the borrowers with more precarious economic situations—for example, Peru, Jamaica, Zaire, and Turkey—suffered open payments crises.

By the third quarter of 1975 the market began to open up again. On the one hand, banks had recruited the OPEC deposits and could not keep them lying idle; on the other, as mentioned earlier, the depressed OECD economies had little demand for credit. While loans to LDCs began to flow once again, the banks were initially cautious and spreads remained high. Nevertheless, credit was still attractive to developing countries because it assuaged the adjustment process; moreover, throughout the recycling period unexpected inflation turned interest rates negative in real terms, perhaps making debt appear as "good business" (see Table 2.14).

By 1977 not only did loan volume continue to rise but the terms of lending softened as the situation moved back into a so-called borrowers' market. It can be observed in tables 2.15 and 2.16 that beginning in 1977 spreads came down sharply and maturities were commonly awarded in excess of five years. The trend toward lower spreads and longer maturities became sharply accentuated in 1978 to 1980. About the only unfavorable note during this period was a drift upward of the interest rate in real terms (Table 2.14), but even so it remained in the range of 2 to 3 percent, which is generally considered to be a normal historical rate. Thus borrowing conditions were relatively favorable even during the second petrodollar recycling.

The return to a borrowers' market had its roots in several factors. On the one hand, memories of the 1974/1975 interbank market crisis had waned. Second, banks remained quite liquid. Third, many banks that had left the market returned to active lending (for example, the Japanese and German banks), while other institutions, not previously active in international lending, jumped into the pool in pursuit of profits. Fourth, prior to the second oil shock in 1979/1980 most countries had

[82] All these data have been calculated from the World Bank, *Borrowing in International Capital Markets* (Washington, D.C., August 1975 and August 1976), pp. 46–52 and pp. 55–149, respectively. This was a periodic publication on eurocredits that the bank discontinued in 1981. It should be noted that the World Bank included in its definition of developing countries the lower-income OECD nations such as Spain, Greece, Portugal, and Turkey.

TABLE 2.14. International Interest Rates, Nominal and Real, 1972–1987

Year	Nominal LIBOR	Nominal U.S. Prime Rate	Consumer Prices OECD (% Change)	LIBOR Real Terms	Prime Rate Real Terms
1972	5.41	5.25	4.7	0.7	0.5
1973	9.31	8.03	7.7	1.5	0.3
1974	11.20	10.81	13.3	−1.9	−2.2
1975	7.61	7.86	11.1	−3.1	−2.9
1976	6.12	6.84	8.3	−2.0	−1.3
1977	6.42	6.83	8.4	−1.8	−1.4
1978	8.33	9.06	7.2	1.1	1.7
1979	11.99	12.67	9.2	2.6	3.2
1980	14.15	15.27	11.9	2.0	3.0
1981	16.52	18.85	9.9	6.0	8.1
1982	13.25	14.77	7.5	5.3	6.8
1983	9.79	10.81	5.0	4.6	5.5
1984	11.20	12.04	4.8	6.1	6.9
1985	8.64	9.93	4.2	4.3	5.5
1986	6.82	7.99	2.3	4.4	5.9
1987	7.29	8.14	3.1	4.2	5.0

SOURCES: ECLAC, *Estudio Económico de América Latina y el Caribe 1983* [Economic Survey of Latin America and the Caribbean 1983] (Santiago, Chile, (1985), 1: 59); Morgan Guaranty Trust Company, *World Financial Markets* (New York, January 1985), pp. 13 and 19; International Monetary Fund, *International Financial Statistics* (Washington, D.C.), various numbers.

managed to improve their balance of payments and raise their image of creditworthiness. Thus about the only sign of restraint in the market was exhibited by the U.S. banks, which had been at the vanguard of the expansion in the early 1970s. These institutions had apparently built up portfolios that approached prudential limits and they thus attempted to slow down their lending. But the restraint of American banks was more than offset by the reappearance of Japanese and German institutions after 1976, as well as the entrance of many latecomers to the market. While outstanding claims by U.S. banks on major developing country borrowers grew by only 17 percent per annum between 1976 and 1979, those of non-U.S. banks to the same countries rose by over 42 percent.[83]

[83] Morgan Guaranty Trust Company, *World Financial Markets* (New York, September 1980), pp. 8–9.

TABLE 2.15. Weighted Average Spread on Publicized Variable-Rate Eurocurrency Loans to Developing Countries (percentage distribution)

Spread	1975	1976	1977	1978	1979	1980
Up to 0.500	. . .[a]	. . .	0.2	1.3	16.2	16.9
0.501–0.750	. . .	. . .	0.2	15.4	39.2	38.9
0.751–1.000	. . .	. . .	18.9	30.5	25.4	21.4
1.001–1.250	1.9	7.8	13.1	21.2	12.5	9.9
1.251–1.500	35.8	25.0	15.5	16.6	3.7	7.3
1.501–1.750	36.1	31.9	32.3	6.5	1.7	1.6
1.751–2.000	23.0	27.0	14.1	5.2	0.7	1.5
2.001–2.250	2.6	7.0	3.0	1.6	0.1	0.1
2.251 or more	0.2	1.2	2.6	0.3	0.1	2.1
Unknown	0.3	0.1	0.2	1.3	0.3	0.2
Total	100.0	100.0	100.0	100.0	100.0	100.0

SOURCE: World Bank, *Borrowing in International Capital Markets* (Washington, D.C.), December 1978 [for 1975], p. 143; January 1980 [for 1976], p. 146; November 1980 [for 1977], p. 109; November 1981 [for 1978–1980], p. 107.

NOTES: The World Bank includes in the category of developing countries the lower-income OECD nations such as Spain, Greece, Portugal, and Turkey.

[a](. . .) = zero or not large enough to quantify.

The Needs for Refinance   A final reason for LDCs' demand for bank loans relates to the peculiar aspect of those credits. While bank loan maturities lengthened in the 1970s, they continued to fall far short of the twenty- to thirty-year maturities commonly associated with official development finance. Thus there was often an asymmetry between the repayment dates on the loans and the financial return generated by the deployment of that loan capital in the countries. To bridge this gap, and also to avoid a net outflow of resources, countries felt obliged to return to the market to refinance upcoming debt service, in effect paying old loans with new ones. While refinance is an awkward way to support development, it was in practice quite easy to do in the euphoric years of eurocurrency lending.

One consequence of this is that due to the law of compound interest, greater and greater proportions of a given level of borrowing were committed to repaying old debt. Thus, to maintain a given net transfer (*new loans > debt service*) a country had to borrow ever greater amounts. In essence, there was a treadmill effect in the market, where borrowing today in the market introduced a greater demand for credit tomorrow.

TABLE 2.16. Average Maturity Period on Publicized Eurocurrency Loans to
Developing Countries
(percentage distribution)

Maturity (years)	1975	1976	1977	1978	1979	1980
1–3	5.7	2.3	3.9	2.8	4.9	6.3
3–5	62.9	54.8	19.4	5.2	10.1	4.6
5–7	24.1	30.0	63.9	26.7	7.4	19.2
7–10	3.3	4.5	8.8	56.4	56.1	63.2
10–15	1.7	. . .a	. . .	6.3	16.1	4.5
15–20	. . .	. . .	. . .	. . .	0.3	0.2
Unknown	2.2	8.5	4.0	2.5	5.1	2.0
Total	100.0	100.0	100.0	100.0	100.0	100.0

SOURCE: World Bank, *Borrowing in International Capital Markets* (Washington, D.C.),
December 1978 [for 1975], p. 136; January 1980 [for 1976], p. 139; November 1980
[for 1977], p. 102; November 1981 [for 1978–1980], p. 100.
NOTES: The World Bank includes in the category of developing countries the lower-
income OECD nations such as Spain, Greece, Portugal, and Turkey.
a(. . .) = zero or not large enough to quantify.

Moreover, since countries generally wanted to avoid outward net transfers of resources to their creditors, this demand for credit, endogenous
to the process of indebtedness with the banks, was relatively inelastic to
the price of credit.

The refinancing of medium- and short-term debt to accommodate the
long-run returns of a development strategy is a process that of course
has its limits because it always risks pushing up gross borrowing to
points where creditors become alarmed. This in fact is one element in
the recent financial crisis, a subject I will return to in the next section.

THE CRISIS OF THE 1980s

As already noted, the financial crisis of the 1980s exploded in mid-1982
with the declaration of moratorium in Mexico. Most Latin American
countries have requested reschedulings from their creditors and the exercises have been multiple; indeed, by 1987 negotiations for a fourth
round of reschedulings in the region were well underway. The only major borrower of the banks to avoid a rescheduling has been Colombia,

whose traditionally cautious demand management policies induced an unusually careful articulation with private credit markets during the 1970s.[84]

Table 2.17 shows how the main indicators of debt service evolved during the years leading into the crisis. It can be observed in the table that the refinance of debt service was absorbing an ever greater amount of new lending in the late 1970s. By 1982 debt service far exceeded new medium- and long-term lending, meaning that the refinance mechanism had been broken and countries were required by the creditors to actually pay their debts. This of course had its counterpart in the beginning of an outward net transfer of resources, broached earlier in the chapter. For all but the most resilient economies the cutoff of the refinance mechanism in the middle of a world recession was sufficient to throw the debtors into crisis and disrupt normal servicing of obligations.

The table also demonstrates that practically all the rising burden of debt service was from interest payments. Referring to Table 2.14, one can see that a major cause of rising interest payments was the skyrocketing of nominal rates. However, in the early 1980s, unlike the 1974/1975 crisis, there were tight monetary and fiscal policies in the center that also raised rates in real terms. Indeed, in the years of crisis the LIBOR in real terms tripled what many consider to be the historically normal real rate of 2 percent. The situation was further aggravated by an escalation of spreads on the loans to LDCs in 1982 and 1983 (see Table 2.18). In any event, by 1982/1983 more than 40 percent of the region's exports were absorbed by interest payments on the debt. This situation was highly conducive to crisis, since bankers normally consider a coefficient of interest payments/exports in excess of 20 percent to already be a sign of great burden.[85]

Finally, examining the relation of debt to GDP and to exports provides some insight into the nature of the crisis in the region. The Latin American debt-to-product ratio of roughly 38 percent just prior to the crisis year of 1982 was not unduly high; according to the World Bank, some Asian countries that have not experienced debt problems, such as South Korea, also had coefficients in excess of 30 percent. But on the same criterion, the debt-to-exports ratio was indeed high, 2½ to 1,

---

[84] In his evaluation of Colombia's borrowing strategy in the eurocurrency market Wellons classified this country as an "ambivalent borrower" (*Borrowing by Developing Countries*, pp. 313–347). Of the larger Latin American economies, Colombia is the least indebted with the banks.

[85] American Express Bank, *Amex Bank Review* 10 (28 March 1983): 5.

TABLE 2.17. Latin America: External Debt Indicators, 1978–1983

Variable	1978	1979	1980	1981	1982	1983
			Billions of Dollars			
Medium- and long-term loan disbursements	38.7	46.0	43.8	60.2	47.7	28.7
Oil exporters	13.4	17.2	14.9	19.4	16.2	11.0
Nonoil exporters	25.3	28.8	28.9	40.8	31.5	17.7
Debt service	26.7	37.0	42.3	54.0	62.1	50.1
Oil exporters	9.7	15.2	15.9	20.3	24.7	21.1
Nonoil exporters	17.0	21.8	26.4	33.7	37.4	29.0
Total interest	9.5	14.2	21.0	31.5	40.8	36.0
Oil exporters	4.1	5.8	8.6	13.1	18.3	15.9
Nonoil exporters	5.4	8.4	12.4	18.4	22.5	20.1
Amortization (medium- and long-term loans)	17.2	22.8	21.3	22.5	21.3	14.1
Oil exporters	5.6	9.4	7.3	7.2	6.4	5.2
Nonoil exporters	11.6	13.4	14.0	15.3	14.9	8.9
			Percentages			
Memorandum items						
DS/DIS	69	80	97	90	130	175
Oil exporters	72	88	107	105	152	192
Nonoil exporters	67	76	91	82	119	164
DS/X	45	47	42	49	60	49
Oil exporters	38	41	31	35	45	41
Nonoil exporters	50	52	54	64	76	56
I/X	16	18	20	28	41	36
Oil exporters	16	16	17	23	36	31
Nonoil exporters	15	19	24	34	47	41
DBT/X	247	222	210	243	316	344
Oil exporters	254	207	180	210	268	300
Nonoil exporters	240	234	240	278	361	386
DBT/GDP	32	32	34	38	42	45
Oil exporters	36	34	36	40	43	47
Nonoil exporters	29	31	33	37	41	43

SOURCES: ECLAC, Division of Economic Development and Division of Statistics and Quantitative Analysis.
NOTE: Symbols are as follows: DS = debt service; DIS = disbursement of new medium- and long-term loans; X = exports of goods and services; I = gross interest payments on short-, medium-, and long-term debt; DBT = total disbursed external debt; GDP = gross domestic product.

TABLE 2.18. Average Spreads and Maturities on Eurocredits, 1981–1983

Countries	1981	1982	1983
Average Spreads[a]			
OECD	.58	.56	.64
Eastern Europe	.62	1.03	1.12
OPEC	.79	.94	.85
Other LDCs	1.04	1.14	1.70
Average Maturity[b]			
OECD	7.7	8.3	7.7
Eastern Europe	5.6	4.8	4.4
OPEC	7.8	6.0	7.2
Other LDCs	7.8	7.0	7.0

SOURCE: Organization for Economic Cooperation and Development (OECD), *Financial Market Trends* (Paris, October 1984), p. 44.
NOTES: Information is for publicized credits with a maturity of more than three years and greater than $30 million.
[a]Points over base interest rate.
[b]Years.

compared to somewhat less than 1 to 1 for South Korea. Although regional averages hide individual situations, this rough and ready comparison suggests that at the outset of the crisis Latin America as a whole was not necessarily overindebted with respect to its income but had contracted too much debt in comparison with its ability to transform income into foreign exchange for the service of obligations. In other words, the accumulation of debt was not wholly compatible with the degree of openness of the economies and export performance; servicing debt in foreign exchange depended to a large degree on refinance, and when this was cut off, the region got into trouble.[86]

[86] The data on Asian countries comes from the country pages of the World Bank's *World Debt Tables* (Washington, D.C., 1983). For an excellent detailed comparative analysis of the situation of debt and adjustment in Latin America and Asia see Jeffrey Sachs, "External Debt and Macroeconomic Performance in Latin America and East Asia," *Brookings Papers on Economic Activity*, no. 2 (1985), pp. 523–564.

CHAPTER THREE

International Banking: Its Structure and Performance during the 1970s

IT IS EVIDENT from the previous chapter that private banks have become important, high profile actors in the world economy. Yet research on the "global bank" has lagged well behind developments in the industry. As these institutions turned to a transnational growth strategy in the 1960s and 1970s most analysts focused their attention on the activities of the nonfinancial transnational corporation (TNC). For instance, the ground-breaking and controversial 1974 study by Barnet and Müller, which alerted public opinion to the possible socioeconomic repercussions of global profit-making corporate strategies, treated banks only parenthetically.[1] In the second half of the 1970s, and above all with the outbreak of the debt crisis in 1982, private banks received more scrutiny. Nevertheless, the overseas operations of these institutions remain relatively unexplored terrain, and there are serious gaps in our knowledge.

There is still no developed theory of transnational banking; when compared to the abundance of research and theory on transnational nonfinancial firms, banks are definitely the poorer cousins.[2] Second, much yet has to be done both on the empirical and theoretical level concerning the specific nature of the interface between private banks and developing countries, both in good times and bad, and the impact of their lending on macroeconomic policy and economic development.[3]

---

[1] Richard Barnet and Ronald Müller, *Global Reach* (New York: Simon & Schuster, 1974).

[2] Some early attempts at theory building include Herbert Grubel, "A Theory of Multinational Banking," *Banca Nazionale del Lavoro Quarterly Review*, December 1977, pp. 349–363; Robert Aliber, "Towards a Theory of International Banking," *Federal Reserve Bank of San Francisco Economic Review*, Spring 1976, pp. 5–8; Rae Weston, *Domestic and Multinational Banking* (New York: Columbia University Press, 1980); and Herbert Grubel, "The New International Banking," *Banca Nazionale del Lavoro Quarterly Review*, September 1983, pp. 263–284.

[3] There are relatively few detailed case studies designed to specially assess the bank-borrower relationship in an LDC. This remains, for all practical purposes, virgin territory. I have, however, prepared detailed case studies on Peru and Bolivia for ECLAC and will selectively draw on their findings in this chapter and the next. Following the methodology of these two studies (described in the Appendix), ECLAC is currently preparing

One possible reason for this situation is that private banks lagged about a decade behind nonfinancial firms in their global expansion. While banks had just begun their international expansion in the mid- and late 1960s, TNCs were already heavily embroiled in controversy in Europe and the periphery.[4] A second possible reason for the heavy attention given TNCs is that their expansion was built on highly visible direct investment, while most of the international banks' expansion was indirect investment via lower-profile cross-border lending, often shrouded in secrecy. Finally, a third, and perhaps the most important, factor may have been that until the eruption of the debt crisis in 1982 bank lending abroad was generally very robust and—with the exception of the already described brief minicrisis in 1974/1975—relatively free of controversy, thereby keeping it sidelined on research agendas.

Since international banking is still a relatively immature area of study, there is room for a wide range of interpretations about the nature of the market, its functioning and welfare effects. What I will do in this chapter is present a stylized picture of an interpretation of the functioning of private international banking markets, based on the notion of market efficiency that was very popular and influential in the 1970s. I will conclude that the popular version seriously underestimates the role of the banks' behavior as an endogenous source of financial problems and thus provides an incomplete explanation of how international financial markets really worked. This shortcoming, as mentioned in Chapter One, is a central concern of the study.

In developing the material I will retrace some of the terrain covered in Chapter Two but at a higher level of abstraction. The first section of this chapter will present the popular interpretation of international banking during the 1970s. We will see that it has much of its roots in traditional portfolio theory and the classic textbook model of efficiency through private atomistic markets. The popular view will be contrasted in the second section with another interpretation that draws on marketing theory, the behavior of the modern transnational firm, and oligopolistic market structure. Bringing these components together, one can more clearly understand the nature of debt accumulation in the 1970s. Moreover, we will find that by intensifying the institutional focus of the anal-

---

three more country cases. Since the studies are designed to generate primary data on bank loans they should contribute to filling out our understanding of the nature of bank lending to developing countries.

[4] The controversy itself is captured both in the analysis as well as the title of Raymond Vernon's *Sovereignty at Bay* (New York: Basic Books, 1971). The European side of the controversy is found in the classic work by Jean-Jacques Servan-Schreiber, *El Desafío Americano* [The American Challenge] (Barcelona: Plaza y Janes, S.A., 1968).

ysis one arrives at conclusions about the nature of supply that often run counter to conventional wisdom concerning the efficiency of private international credit markets. Although I do not pretend to present a complete alternative theory, the following analysis will hopefully offer direction for this type of work.

A POPULAR VIEW OF INTERNATIONAL BANKING: EFFICIENT INTERMEDIATION

Ever since Adam Smith made famous the Invisible Hand,[5] practitioners of economics and policy have been fascinated by the possibilities of self-regulating, free private markets. History, however, has not always been kind to Smith's paradigm; as pointed out so well by Polanyi, since the Industrial Revolution society has "protected itself against the perils inherent in a self-regulating market system" by establishing a network of measures and policies integrated into powerful public institutions designed to check the action of the market relative to labor, land, and capital.[6]

The Great Depression and the advent of Keynesianism of course greatly accelerated social intervention in markets, although not without controversy, as economic liberals consistently opposed policies that countered the ideal of freedom of markets. Indeed, I think it is fair to assert that even with the prosperity of the welfare state in the postwar era, along with oligopoly and monopoly in markets, the ideal of the free, self-regulating economy still captures the imagination of a vast number of economists. This is perhaps even more so today with the surge in popularity of Reaganomics and neoliberal principles.[7]

With domestic banking markets strictly controlled to avoid a repeat of the 1929 Crash as well as to facilitate deliberate public fiscal and monetary policy, the rise of the free-wheeling eurocurrency market and unrestricted private banking was viewed enthusiastically by those inclined toward the liberal tradition. It even received support from analysts traditionally sympathetic to public regulation of markets.

---

[5] Adam Smith, *The Wealth of Nations* (1937; reprint ed., New York: The Modern Library, 1965), p. 423.

[6] Karl Polanyi, *The Great Transformation* (Boston: Beacon Press, 1957), p. 76.

[7] A statement of the contemporary neoliberal ideal is in George Gilder, *Wealth and Poverty* (New York: Basic Books, Bantam paperback edition, 1981).

The Eurocurrency Market

The theoretical role of international capital markets has been well summarized by Charles Kindleberger:

> The main justification for international capital movement is that it shifts savings from locations where they are abundant and cheap relative to investment opportunities to places where they are scarce and expensive. The argument holds for all theories of interest, whether the movement equalizes the marginal efficiency of capital, differences in time preference (for consumption), or differences in preference for liquidity. Where capital is more productive in one country than another, it should be moved from the country where it is less to the country where it is more productive. Total output is increased by such movement. Where savers in one country have lesser preference for current consumption than those in another, total welfare is increased by shifting the consumption of one into the future and the other into the present. And even if there be no difference in the efficiency of capital or in time preference, gross capital movements, though not net, will increase overall world welfare under circumstances of different preferences for liquidity, if long-term capital moves from the country with low liquidity preference to that with high, and short-term capital moves in the other direction.[8]

Capital movements, of course, come in various forms and are the domain of various economic agents. As we saw in the earlier chapter, until the rise of euromarkets, contemporary international capital movements were effected mostly by nonfinancial firms (direct investments) and by governments, either directly by loans from official bilateral and multilateral institutions or indirectly by guarantees on private direct investment or bank lending. But with the emergence of the eurocurrency market in the 1960s and 1970s international capital flows became decisively privatized. Moreover, loans—the domain of private banks—were the primary financial instrument in the market: on a gross basis they accounted for 60 and 65 percent, respectively, of all publicized medium-to long-term transactions (loans and bond issues) in 1973

---

[8] Charles Kindleberger, "The Pros and Cons of an International Capital Market," *Zeitschrift fur die gesamte Staatswissenschaft*, October 1977, pp. 600–617, quoted in Gunter Dufey and Ian Giddy, *The International Money Market* (Englewood Cliffs, N.J.: Prentice-Hall, 1978), p. 193.

to 1975 and 1978 to 1980.[9] Moreover, the participation of loans would be even higher if short-term credits—which are not easily quantifiable—were incorporated into the calculation.

Thus, with the resurgence of private international capital markets banks became the dominant cross-border intermediary between savers and borrowers. Since eurocurrency markets were essentially unregulated and involved hundreds of lending institutions in competition, there was a presumption on the part of many that capital markets could approach the ideal functions outlined so well above by Kindleberger. In effect, the rise of euromarkets and unregulated banking raised expectations for the restoration of the classic laws of allocation in which credit flows are left to a market governed by the expected profit and risk perceptions of individuals. Implicit (and sometimes explicit) in the enthusiasm for euromarkets was the counterpart argument that international intermediation via domestic capital markets was biased in the direction of inferior return/risk ratios due to the considerable direct and indirect government interference in credit allocation. This general view is well summarized in an observation made by Dufey and Giddy: "In the international context the Euromarkets facilitate market-induced credit allocation at the expense of government-induced allocation. . . . Indeed, probably no other single force has made such a great contribution to the efficient international allocation of credit as have the eurocurrency markets."[10]

An even bolder statement on the efficiency of the eurocurrency market was made by McKinnon. According to him, there are three important functions of the market: (a) it facilitates foreign exchange trading among banks that permit forward exchange cover on loans and interest rate arbitrage; (b) it supplants financial intermediation between savers and investors that would otherwise be difficult to achieve in domestic markets; and (c) it acts as a great international conduit for the transfer of short- and medium-term capital from net savers to net borrowers. He goes on to characterize the market as extremely efficient in no uncertain terms:

> The competitive strength of the eurocurrency market in all three roles accounts for its astonishing growth and resiliency, on the one hand, and the great difficulty academic economists have had in developing a single theoretical model to describe it, on the other. Freedom from

[9] The calculations were made from data in the World Bank's quarterly report *Borrowing in International Capital Markets* (Washington, D.C.), August 1976, p. 17; November 1980, pp. 1 and 6; and November 1981, pp. 1 and 5.

[10] Dufey and Giddy, *The International Money Market* p. 193.

restraint has created a *paragon of international banking efficiency* [emphasis added].[11]

In effect, in his remarks McKinnon attributes to international banking activity both informational arbitrage efficiency and allocative efficiency. Here we are not far removed from the auction markets that underpin the neoclassical textbook parable of competitive efficiency. While not everyone went so far as McKinnon, the general sentiment of broad-based efficiency was clearly shared by most economists, policy makers, and bankers during the 1960s and 1970s, for otherwise serious attempts would have been made by governments to control the market and its banking functions. Evidently in the eyes of many the fast-growing eurocurrency market was not a "renegade" that threatened financial stability but rather a "freedom fighter" that had established a beachhead of rationality and efficiency in a financial world hamstrung by government intervention.

Private Banks and Lending to LDCs

The increased interest of banks in lending to developing countries during the 1970s was generally well received by policy makers and academics alike. Developing countries were seen to be facing external financial constraints and in need of more external savings. This need became magnified with the OPEC price shocks of 1973/1974 and 1979/1980. The first to embrace the new role of banks in development finance were the bankers themselves. While bankers are a heterogeneous group, they do have their spokespeople who maintain a high public profile. One of the most prominent of these is Dr. Irving Friedman, a former World Bank-IMF economist turned adviser to private banks. During the 1970s, Mr. Friedman made an important and well-publicized statement about banks and developing countries:

> The developing countries want private banks to play a significant role in their economic development process for several reasons. There has been evolving for some years—well before the OPEC crisis years—a new awareness of what private banks are capable of, an awareness that goes beyond the identification of a source of quick emergency help in time of need as well as normal trade-related financing. Private banks are seen as part of an extensive, expanding, *efficient nonpolitical international system* providing a great variety of services and tech-

[11] Ronald McKinnon, *The Eurocurrency Market*, Princeton Essays in International Finance, No. 125 (Princeton, N.J.: Princeton University, Department of Economics, 1977), p. 5.

nical assistance as part of their banking activities. They are seen as providing a major additional source of external finance to *countries whose chronic problem over time is how to find adequate external finance* [emphasis added].[12]

He went on to state:

Furthermore, private institutions are perceived as not being motivated or constrained by political considerations. At the same time, they offer advantages because of their diversities, competitiveness, international connections, magnitudes of lending capability (not limited by official budgetary restraints or the need for intergovernmental agreements), flexibility, reasonable terms and speed of response. At times the availability of finance on a nonpolitical basis is seen as a way to *reinforce the adoption or implementation of adjustment measures* without the appearance of outside political interference or involvement [emphasis added].[13]

Summarizing his views, Friedman additionally asserted:

The benefits of becoming—and remaining—creditworthy in the private bank markets are now seen in most developing countries to be of major proportions. In these countries, it is seen that *policies needed to maintain external creditworthiness with private banks are also needed to meet national development objectives* [emphasis added].[14]

In short, there is a perceived harmony of interests between efficient private banking practices and efficient development policies.

Seals of approval came from other diverse quarters as well. As early as 1970 Charles Kindleberger—a very insightful middle-of-the-road mainstream economist—pointed to the inefficiency of governmental development loans and the controversy surrounding the issue of control in direct foreign investment. He advocated a return to the "invisible hand" in credit allocation, as "in the long run, it is desirable that such private lending should, and conceivable that it could, replace some or most of such aid and lending."[15] Moreover, he anticipated Friedman's characterization of private markets as a source of discipline for development policy.

---

[12] Irving Friedman, *The Emerging Role of Private Banks in the Developing World* (New York: Citicorp, 1977), p. 61.

[13] Ibid.

[14] Ibid., p. 66.

[15] Charles Kindleberger, "Less-Developed Countries and the International Capital Market," in *Industrial Organization and Economic Development*, ed. Jesse Markham and Gustav Papanek (Boston: Houghton Mifflin, 1970), pp. 338 and 344.

More significant, perhaps, *the sensible fiscal management needed to restore credit worthiness in the international capital market is the same management needed for effective economic growth.* Applied impersonally, rather than by paternalistic officials of international institutions, such management and governmental borrowing from the private international capital market raise a prospect of enlisting local capital in national growth efforts, initially in roundabout, and ultimately in direct, fashion [emphasis added].[16]

Private banks, of course, also received high marks for the recycling of petrodollars to LDCs. Observers recognized that there were difficulties in the process and that the international system "creaked" on occasion, such as during the earlier-mentioned 1974 Herstatt crisis. Yet on the whole there was considerable faith in the markets, and they were seen to have functioned amazingly well even under stress. As a former governor of the Bank of England remarked after his assessment of the problems in 1974 and 1975 in the euromarkets: "My main reason for optimism lies in what I believe to be the market's own strength."[17]

After the 1974/1975 crisis there was a substantial acceleration of the accumulation of debt in Latin America and elsewhere. However, conventional logic on bank lending was lineal: lending to LDCs had essentially been on a sound basis and the banking system was therefore capable of sustaining adequate financing and the countries were capable on the whole of servicing their obligations. This was the message of analysts such as Beek, Biem, Brittain, Sargen, Smith, Solomon, and van B. Cleveland, to mention just a few.[18]

The mystique of the market grew to such proportions that even the

[16] Ibid., p. 345. Kindleberger subsequently adopted a less sanguine view of the functioning of private financial markets, pointing to overexpansion and crisis. See *Manias, Panics, and Crashes* (New York: Basic Books, 1978), p. 23.

[17] Lord O'Brien, "The Prospects for the Euromarkets," *Euromoney*, September 1975, p. 69.

[18] David Biem, "Rescuing the LDCs," *Foreign Affairs* 55 (July 1977): 717–731; David Beek, "Commercial Bank Lending to Developing Countries," *Federal Reserve Bank of New York Quarterly Review* 2 (Summer 1977): 1–8; Harold van B. Cleveland and W. H. Bruce Brittain, "Are the LDCs in over Their Heads?" *Foreign Affairs* 55 (July 1977): 732–750; W. H. Bruce Brittain, "Developing Countries' External Debts and Private Banks," *Banca Nazionale del Lavoro Quarterly Review*, December 1977, pp. 365–380; Nicholas Sargen, "Commercial Bank Lending to Developing Countries," *Federal Reserve Bank of San Francisco Economic Review*, Spring 1976, pp. 20–31; Gordon Smith, *The External Debt Prospects of the Non-Oil-exporting Developing Countries* (Washington, D.C.: Overseas Development Council, 1977); and Robert Solomon, "The Perspective on the Debt of Developing Countries," *Brookings Papers on Economic Activity*, no. 2 (1977), pp. 479–510.

IMF—the traditional disciplinarian in the adjustment process of LDCs—became increasingly perceived by some as somewhat superfluous. In 1976 one of the largest and most influential institutions in the international financial community commented:

> [I]t is incumbent on banks to improve further their competence in appraising borrowing countries' economic and financial policies. The Fund [IMF] generally will be involved only in the critical cases where the necessity for internal adjustment is clearcut. But, in the less-than-critical cases, bank credit decisions also involve a judgment on the way an economy is managed and on the prospects for the balance of payments. In deciding whether to extend credits, and in setting the terms and conditions for loans, banks can influence the nature and timing of borrowing countries' policies. This is a heavy responsibility, and admittedly one which is difficult to carry out, particularly in the face of competitive pressures. However, from the viewpoint of the borrower, *the discipline of the marketplace can be an important bearing on whether sound economic and financial policies are taken on a timely basis* [emphasis added].[19]

While actual events were to prove that the market actually did need the assistance of the IMF during periods of adjustment, faith in the invisible hand prevailed almost right up to the debt crisis in 1982. As late as May 1981 the IMF could state in an occasional paper:

> [T]he overall debt situation during the 1970s adapted itself to the sizable strains introduced in the international payments system and, in broad terms, maintained its relative position vis-à-vis other relevant economic variables. Though some countries experienced difficulties, a generalized debt management problem was avoided, and in the aggregate the outlook for the immediate future does not give cause for alarm.[20]

Of course, with the advent of the credit crisis in 1982 there was some modification of positions on the part of the advocates of the market's inherent efficiency. The IMF even began to consider the possibility of contagion effects in private markets.[21] Nevertheless, as I have pointed out, most attention both inside and outside the banking community re-

---

[19] Morgan Guaranty Trust Company, *World Financial Markets* (New York, May 1976), p. 9.

[20] Bahram Nowzad et al., *External Indebtedness of Developing Countries*, Occasional Paper No. 3 (Washington, D.C.: International Monetary Fund, 1981), p. 11.

[21] Paul Mentré, *The Fund, Commercial Banks, and Member Countries*, Occasional Paper No. 26 (Washington, D.C.: International Monetary Fund, 1984), p. 9.

garding the cause of the problem was overwhelmingly on LDC government deficit spending and/or adverse conjunctural factors, not on bank-lending behavior itself.

The Pricing and Volume of Loans: Rationality and Profit Maximization under Uncertainty

In a perfect economic world, where there are atomistic and complete credit markets, constant returns to scale, certainty, insurance for future contingencies,[22] no information or transaction costs, honesty, and a zero profit condition, economic agents are price takers and borrowers face an interest rate equal to the opportunity cost of funds for the lenders. Countries could then borrow and finance all investment that generates income streams with a positive present value at the prevailing rate of interest. Countries could also maximize satisfaction by equalizing their marginal utility for present and future consumption. Moreover, no economically productive investment would go unfinanced by creditors, and any decision to raise domestic savings would simply lead to transfers of funds abroad.

In this idealized picture of the functioning of financial systems loans could be bought and sold in auction markets much like any other commodity. This classic notion of competitive efficiency seems, at least in some sense, to have underpinned much of the optimism surrounding the expansion of international banking in the 1970s. But one cannot push the analogy too far since mainstream economics recognizes that the world of perfect capital markets exists only in the classroom and that informational costs and uncertainty may introduce distortions in the allocation of credit. In particular, the postwar literature stresses that markets may not be cleared by prices, such that supply may not equal demand and projects with positive present value income streams will not necessarily receive financing. Broadly speaking, the phenomenon is termed "credit rationing." There is a growing body of analysis in this area, with imaginative and sometimes quite complex models on diverse aspects of rationing.[23] But the message is similar: creditors are cautious

---

[22] Insurance for future contingencies is more formally known as an Arrow-Debreu contract that covers specified goods in specified states of nature. In reference to financial markets Tobin terms the availability of these contracts as full insurance efficiency. See James Tobin, "On the Efficiency of the Financial System," *Lloyds Bank Review* 153 (July 1984): 2–3.

[23] Some of this literature is Dwight Jaffee, *Credit Rationing and the Commercial Loan Market* (New York: John Wiley & Sons, 1971); Dwight Jaffee and Thomas Russell, "Imperfect Information, Uncertainty, and Credit Rationing," *Quarterly Journal of Economics* 90 (November 1976): 651–666; Dwight Jaffee and Franco Modigliani, "A Theory

and rational profit maximizers, and in the face of uncertainty this induces them to ration credit to borrowers. The general thrust of the analysis can be summarized in a relatively simple way.

Credit Rationing   Creditors lend on the assumption of repayment because obviously failure to service debt induces losses. Loan transactions take place in a world of uncertainty.[24] Potential insurance coverage is incomplete. Thus lenders attempt to maximize their expected return on loans subject to the risk of loss-inducing nonpayment by borrowers.

Creditors will lend even in the face of a positive probability of default if they can be compensated with risk premia. The risk of default generally increases with the quantity of loans; therefore, the supply schedule is upward sloping, that is, more lending will be forthcoming only at a rising premium over the opportunity cost of funds of the lender to compensate for the greater risk. In effect, in the conventional view the borrower is considered a quasi monopsonist; while it cannot affect the

---

and Test of Credit Rationing," *American Economic Review* 59 (December 1969): 850–872; Joseph Stiglitz and Andrew Weiss, "Credit Rationing in Markets with Imperfect Information," *American Economic Review* 71 (June 1981): 393–410; Kerry Vandell, "Imperfect Information, Uncertainty, and Credit Rationing: Comment and Extension," *Quarterly Journal of Economics* 99 (November 1984): 842–872; Jonathan Eaton and Mark Gersovitz, "Debt with Potential Repudiation: Theoretical and Empirical Analysis," *Review of Economic Studies* 48 (April 1981): 289–309; Jonathan Eaton and Mark Gersovitz, *Poor Country Borrowing in Private Financial Markets and the Repudiation Issue*, Princeton Studies in International Finance, No. 47 (Princeton, N.J.: Princeton University, Department of Economics, 1981); David Folkerts-Landau, "The Changing Role of International Bank Lending in Development Finance" (Washington, D.C.: International Monetary Fund, December 1984); Jeffrey Sachs, "Theoretical Issues in International Borrowing," Working Paper 1189 (Cambridge, Mass.: National Bureau of Economic Research, August 1983); Jeffrey Sachs, "LDC Debt in the 80s: Risks and Reforms," in *Crises in the Economic and Financial Structure*, ed. Paul Wachtel (Lexington, Mass.: Lexington Books, 1982), pp. 197–243; and Jack Guttentag and Richard Herring, "Credit Rationing and Financial Disorder," *Journal of Finance* 39 (December 1984): 1359–1382.

[24] The conventional notion of risk is the standard deviation of an expected return in a world with more than one outcome per event. In a world of perfect certainty there is perfect foresight so the probability of an outcome is zero or one with no risk. In a world of relative certainty the probability of an outcome takes on a value between zero and one and is known with complete confidence. In a situation of relative uncertainty agents can calculate subjective probabilities and risk and there is disagreement over the likelihood of an outcome. In perfect uncertainty, economic agents cannot even calculate subjective probabilities and risk. It is generally considered that banks operate in an environment of relative uncertainty. See Jack Guttentag and Richard Herring, "Uncertainty and Insolvency Exposure by International Banks" (University of Pennsylvania, Wharton School of Business, n.d.), pp. 1–3.

overall market rate, its marginal cost of borrowing is greater than its average cost because more loans are available only at a higher rate of interest.[25] Moreover, the relationship between the volume of lending and the interest rate is not monotonic. At some point credit limits must be imposed because at a loan volume sufficiently large the probability of default obtains a value of one. Other things being equal, once this point is reached payment of a higher interest rate will not elicit new lending.

The literature points to several potential sources of default. An obvious one is where the present value of the future income stream of the borrower (including the possible liquidation of attachable assets) is less than the present value of future debt service (interest and amortization). In this case the borrower is insolvent. Lenders would always want to limit lending to below the point of insolvency.

A second source of payment problems is illiquidity: a borrower may not be insolvent, yet in the short term the present value of its income stream may fall short of the upcoming present value of scheduled debt service. Alternatively, illiquidity could occur in the short term if there were adequate domestic resources for debt service but an inability to honor external claims due to a scarcity of foreign exchange. In this case (and assuming no significant reserve cushions), the present value of the potential short-term trade surplus that generates foreign exchange would be below the present value of the short-term scheduled debt service in foreign currency.

A third source of repayment problems is related to the willingness to pay, which introduces a probability of default even in the absence of insolvency or illiquidity problems. With ever greater emphasis the literature has relied on cold rationality as the underlying determinant of borrower behavior. In this framework all borrowers are deemed to be semidishonest; they will repay loans only when the cost of nonpayment exceeds the benefits.[26] The benefit of nonpayment is the present value of future income derived from not servicing the debt; the cost of nonpayment is the loss of income derived from sanctions—deprivation of new finance, interruption of trade, seizure of assets, et cetera—imposed by disgruntled creditors and perhaps their governments. A lender therefore

[25] Arnold Harberger, "Comentarios del Profesor Arnold Harberger" [Comments of Professor Arnold Harberger], in *Estudios Monetarios VII* [Monetary Studies VII] (Santiago, Chile: Central Bank of Chile, 1981), p. 187: and Sachs, "LDC Debt in the 80s," p. 211.

[26] The most pure use of the rationality postulate in determining borrower behavior is in Vandell, "Imperfect Information: Comment"; and in Eaton and Gersovitz, "Debt with Potential Repudiation." For a model which assumes that some borrowers are honest see Jaffee and Russell, "Imperfect Information, Uncertainty, and Credit Rationing."

would always want to keep lending below the level for which it was beneficial for the borrower to default.

In a world of perfect information a lender could always calculate the points of insolvency, illiquidity, and repudiation. But the world is uncertain. The future investment returns and income of the borrower—hence repayment capacity—are stochastic events. Moreover, a creditor cannot easily ensure that a borrower's ex ante commitments to certain risk-reducing behavior with regard to the use of the funds will be honored ex post after the credit is granted. This latter problem is especially pertinent for loans to sovereign governments where negative covenants and collateral arrangements are difficult to enforce. Finally, a creditor would have difficulty knowing in advance the exact costs that could be imposed on a borrower through sanctions.

The complicating factor of uncertainty enjoys a further specification in the literature under the heading of adverse selection.[27] This phenomenon arises because risk is influenced not only by the size of the loan but also by the level of the interest rate.

The fundamental proposition that underpins the concept of adverse selection is that lenders' and borrowers' interests may not coincide. Suppose a borrower finances a project entirely with a bank loan. The gross revenue, or return, on the project is a random variable. The borrower's net return on the project is the gross revenue generated by the venture less the service of the debt that originally financed the project (interest payments and amortization). As depicted in Figure 3.1, the borrower's net returns on the project do not begin to appear until after the gross revenues exceed a contractual debt service $(1 + r)D$. In this way the borrower's returns are a convex function of the gross revenue of the project, as illustrated by segment OAB in the figure.

The lender, on the other hand, encounters returns from the project up to the limit of required debt service; once the project generates gross revenue sufficient to repay the debt, the lender ceases to gain from further increments of gross revenue. Hence the creditor's returns from the project are a concave function of the gross revenue of the project, as depicted in segment OCL of Figure 3.1.

It becomes evident that the borrower and lender have different perspectives on the riskiness of project development. The lender sets an interest rate commensurate with the perceived risk of the project. However, for the borrower all revenue above debt service requirements is retainable and hence its net return can rise with an increase in the riski-

---

[27] The best treatment of this can be found in Jaffee and Russell, "Imperfect Information, Uncertainty, and Credit Rationing"; and Stiglitz and Weiss, "Credit Rationing."

FIGURE 3.1. Borrower and Creditor Returns.

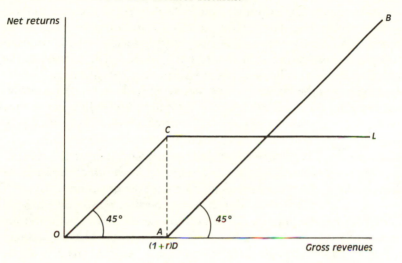

SOURCE: Derived from Joseph Stiglitz and Andrew Weiss, "Credit Rationing in Markets with Imperfect Information," *American Economic Review* 71 (June 1981): 396.

SYMBOLS: B = borrower
  L = lender
  D = debt owed to bank
  r = rate of interest
  $(1 + r)D$ = debt service in the form of interest and amortization

ness of project development. Thus, the borrower can have an incentive to alter its behavior after the loan is made in such a way that the project's riskiness rises. The lender, of course, is only concerned that gross revenue be adequate to service the debt; any alteration of project development that raises risk above that which was originally contemplated lowers the creditor's expected return.[28]

The lender will attempt to control the borrower's behavior through the contractual terms of the credit for the project, although, as mentioned, such control is difficult to realize. Given the difficulty of controlling behavior, the lender will tend to lump the borrower's diverse projects together and evaluate the average risk of that portfolio.

[28] The underlying proposition is a very technical one which shows that as the riskiness of a project increases, the expected value of a convex function of a random variable rises while the expected value of a concave function of a random variable falls. The rigorous treatment and proofs appear in Michael Rothschild and Joseph Stiglitz, "Increasing Risk: 1. A Definition," *Journal of Economic Theory* 2 (1970): 225–243. The proposition is applied to credit markets in Stiglitz and Weiss, "Credit Rationing."

The creditor will also want to avoid taking action that will encourage behavior on the part of the borrower that will raise the average riskiness of its loan portfolio. The creditor knows that for any given level of the interest rate, a borrower must assume a given level of risk in order to generate a gross return sufficient to pay back the debt. Hence, as the interest rate rises, relatively lower risk project development may be squeezed out of the market, raising the average riskiness of the portfolio and lowering the creditor's expected rate of return.[29] In other words, the raising of the rate of interest can bring an adverse selection of projects from the standpoint of the creditor.

The theory of adverse selection adds a backward slope to the conventional upward-sloping supply curve of credit. As the creditor raises the interest rate in the face of the risk of lending, the direct effect is an increase in expected revenue. But the direct positive effects on expected revenue of a higher interest rate are offset at some point by the indirect negative effects of adverse selection. Thus, as shown in Figure 3.2, there will be some interest rate $(^*r)$ that maximizes returns; any rate above that would not appear because it would reduce the expected returns of the creditor.

A bank's willingness to lend is assumed to be commensurate with a rise in expected earnings. From this and the insight of adverse selection a conventional view of the supply curve is drawn in Figure 3.3; it is upward sloping and backward bending. At point E, supply equals demand and the interest rate clears the market. But the literature places its emphasis on the possibility of rationing; for example, in Figure 3.3 when the demand curve intersects supply at T there is rationing equivalent to FG. The interest rate (r_1) that would clear the market never appears because the same loan supply could be obtained at a lower rate.

Thus the more technical literature on banking presents a credit market that is disciplined, cautious, rational, and profit maximizing. In the face of uncertainty, banks coldly evaluate the risk of credit applicants at the margin and charge appropriate premia. Credit, however, is often subject to rationing and therefore is not a normal product for which a sufficiently high price will always elicit a supply. It is important to note that, in effect, according to the prevailing technical literature, the major distortion in credit markets *biases the system toward underlending*.[30]

[29] Stiglitz and Weiss, "Credit Rationing," p. 401.

[30] One could extend the notion of credit rationing beyond one borrower to many borrowers grouped into distinct classes. Some class of borrower may experience no rationing over the relevant range of borrowing, while others may be rationed out of the market altogether. But here again the system is biased to underlending because some classes of borrowers cannot secure any credit at any price. Folkerts-Landau, "The Changing Role of International Bank Lending," pp. 27–29, extends the notion of credit rationing to three classes of borrowers.

FIGURE 3.2. The Interest Rate and the Maximum Returns of the Creditor.

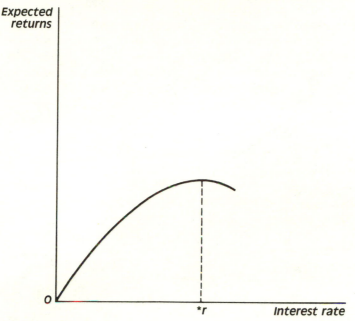

Source: Stiglitz and Weiss, "Credit Rationing," p. 394.

The Demand-Driven Nature of Indebtedness   Before examining how banks evaluated risk, we must refer briefly to what is another popular version of the nature of bank-lending behavior. This one came out of the banking industry itself. The basic proposition is that the rapid accumulation of private bank debt in developing countries was "demand driven."[31] This was presented as a strong assertion with little elaboration and therefore it is difficult to interpret clearly. At first blush one could be left with an impression that it is roughly comparable with the previous, more technical, argument: banks evaluate risk and ration credit cautiously, on a case-by-case basis, in response to the applications of borrowers. But implicit in the "demand-driven" argument is a supply schedule with a somewhat different shape. If interpreted strictly, a demand-driven argument would have to imply that the supply schedule is horizontal over a significant area; this is the only way loan volume could be unambiguously attributed to demand drives (as represented in Figure 3.4 by the shift in demand from D_0 to D_1). Moreover, for

[31] Friedman, *The Emerging Role of Private Banks*, p. 48; Irving Friedman, *The World Debt Dilemma: Managing Country Risk* (Philadelphia: Robert Morris Associates, 1983), p. 45; and Paul Watson, *Debt and Developing Countries: New Problems and New Actors* (Washington, D.C.: Overseas Development Council, 1978), p. 27.

FIGURE 3.3. Credit Rationing.

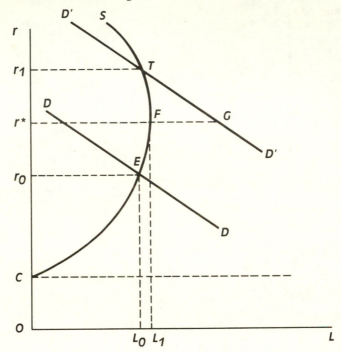

SYMBOLS:

D = demand schedule   L = loans
S = supply schedule   C = opportunity cost of funds for the
r = rate of interest   bank

demand-driven indebtedness to be a reality, credit rationing would not be a factor over the relevant range of credit decision making by borrower and lender; for example, in Figure 3.4 demand-driven indebtedness is possible only up until the vertical segment of the supply schedule.

Bankers stressed the demand-driven nature of LDC indebtedness with private banks to defend themselves against charges of loan pushing. We will see later that the demand-driven argument is one-sided and faulty, yet in some ways it provides more clues to the nature of lending in the 1970s than the more technical literature on banking outlined above.

Evaluation of Creditworthiness   We have just seen that banks were conventionally considered to be disciplined, cautious, and risk conscious; indeed, Irving Friedman has characterized the banks as "among

FIGURE 3.4. Demand-Driven Indebtedness.

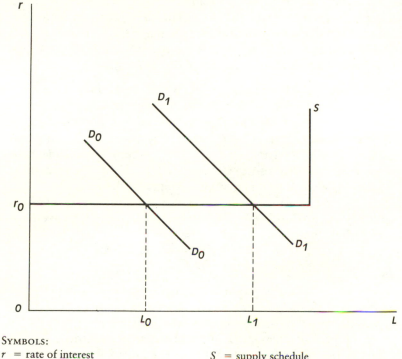

SYMBOLS:

r = rate of interest	S = supply schedule
L = loans	D = demand schedule

the most conservative and cautious sources of lending."[32] It remains to review the bankers' perception of country risk evaluation.

Private banks are profit-making institutions. They lend under the presumption of repayment; indeed, in their mind "the full and prompt servicing of debt to the lender has the highest priority in the usage of the foreign exchange resources of a country."[33] It is not surprising that private lenders are concerned about a borrower's capacity to service debt. If a borrower presents evidence of being able to meet past and future obligations promptly, it is deemed to be creditworthy by the banks.[34] Assessment of the creditworthiness of borrowers is called credit risk evaluation.

[32] Friedman, *The World Debt Dilemma*, p. 1.

[33] Irving Friedman, "The New Climate for Evaluating Country Risk," paper presented at the International Bankers Annual Roundtable, Cannes, France, 12–14 June 1980, p. 6.

[34] Watson, *Debt and Developing Countries*, p. 42.

Credit risk evaluation is as old as banking itself. Country risk analysis, a subset of credit risk, is not. Country risk occurs from cross-border lending between nations and has its origins in the fact that repayment depends not only on the conditions of the individual borrowing entity but also on factors that affect the general country environment. Country risk incorporates various major subcategories of risk:[35]

—Sovereign risk. This refers to the willingness and ability of a government to honor its debts. The risk is uniquely characterized by the fact that governments in practice can rarely be submitted to the laws of a foreign country. Thus the security arrangements, such as negative covenants (which restrict financial policy to certain guidelines) and collateral, that are traditionally in commercial loan agreements are less effective when dealing with governments.[36]
—Transfer risk. This reflects the possibility that borrowers will not be able to service debts due to a lack of availability of foreign exchange rather than an inability to pay per se.
—Political risk. This refers to disruption of debt service due to political instability or upheaval.

While banks have engaged in cross-border lending for many years, country risk evaluation did not become fashionable until the mid-1970s and was pioneered by Dr. Irving Friedman at Citicorp. In the 1960s lending was primarily between banks and industrial countries where little country risk was perceived. With the rise of lending to developing countries and public concern about OPEC recycling, country risk evaluation began to come into its own. Indeed, Citicorp deemed it necessary to publish a major exposé on its country risk evaluation procedures in its 1975 annual report.[37]

Country risk analysis is generally considered to be of paramount importance in the determination of portfolio development. While it would be beyond the scope of the study to enter into the detail of the various country risk assessment methodologies employed by a bank, a brief re-

---

[35] Friedman, *The World Debt Dilemma*, pp. 199–204.

[36] The problem arises from sovereign immunity. Governments frequently wave sovereign immunity in loan contracts, but there are still serious legal and practical obstacles in taking a sovereign to court. See Henry Harfield, "Legal Aspects of International Lending," in *Offshore Lending by U.S. Commercial Banks*, ed. F. John Mathis (Philadelphia: Robert Morris Associates, 1975), p. 86; and Lars Kalderén and Qamar Siddiqi, eds., in cooperation with Francis Chronnell and Patricia Watson, *Sovereign Borrowers: Guidelines on Legal Negotiations with Commercial Lenders* (London: Dag Hammarskjöld Foundation and Butterworths, 1984).

[37] Citicorp, *1975 Annual Report* (New York, 1976), pp. 18–19.

view is nevertheless merited to support later analysis. Friedman has classified systems of country analysis into three broad categories:

—delphi-expert opinion: a scorecard approach where expert opinions on elements of country conditions are weighted and scored;
—quantitative/econometric: a statistical evaluation focused on predicting balance-of-payments and transfer risk problems;
—structural/qualitative: a systematic qualitative and quantitative analysis focusing on balance-of payments outlook, likely capacity to respond to problems, and risks other than economic that may affect prompt debt service.[38]

A 1982 survey by the Group of Thirty found that the structural/qualitative approach was practiced by a majority of banks.[39]

What do banks look for when evaluating country risk and creditworthiness? According to the experts in this field, the overall criterion is "good management" of the economy, with special attention to the availability of foreign exchange for debt service.[40] Two country risk experts have made some observations as to what constitutes good management.[41] In terms of effective economic policies they include: (a) a structure of incentives that rewards risk taking for productive ends; (b) a legal structure conducive to free markets; (c) correction of market distortions at the source; and (d) simple and decentralized rules and regulations. Furthermore, a good development strategy is composed of certain characteristics: (a) open economies that follow the rules of comparative advantage; (b) reasonable investment coefficients and low ICORs of 2 to 3 (the worst-managed economies display ICORs of 6 to 10); (c) a declining ratio of fiscal expenditure to GNP; (d) monetary aggregates consistent with price stability; (e) positive real interest rates and minimal subsidized credit; and (f) a freely floating exchange rate that maintains parity between domestic and international prices. As examples of good policy/development strategy the experts cite South Korea and Taiwan, while Poland and Cuba are cited as countries suffering from bad management.

It also is worth noting the variables that attract the attention of the country risk analysts. The aforementioned Group of Thirty survey

[38] Friedman, *The World Debt Dilemma*, pp. 212–214.
[39] Group of Thirty, *Risks in International Lending* (New York, 1982), p. 41.
[40] Friedman, *The Emerging Role of Private Banks*, p. 2429; and Watson, *Debt and Developing Countries*, pp. 25–29.
[41] Sheila Trifani and Antonio Villamil, "Country Risk Analysis: Economic Considerations," in *The International Banking Handbook*, ed. William Baughn and Donald Mandich (Homewood, Ill.: Dow Jones-Irwin, 1983), pp. 109–112.

found that private banks used a diverse number of variables in their economic evaluation of borrowers. However, there emerged from their analysis a set of indicators that apparently were fundamental to the evaluation of the banks. They are the following:

—debt service ratio, or debt service/export earnings;
—the balance-of-payments position;
—the export growth trend;
—internal growth, or the change in GDP.[42]

Thus it is the above factors that the banks apparently scrutinized the most when evaluating to whom and how much they should lend. I will have more to say about these factors in this and the following chapter.

AN ALTERNATIVE VIEW OF INTERNATIONAL BANKING

The stylized picture of private bank lending presented in the previous pages is one of classically inspired efficient intermediation. The term efficiency is obviously used loosely here as even the most avid believers in free markets recognize that real-world distortions prevent the Pareto criterion of efficient resource allocation from being satisfied. Indeed, we saw that the emphasis on credit rationing in the mainstream technical literature involves a situation in which prices will not necessarily clear credit markets and therefore some productive investments may go unfinanced. But as mentioned, the conventional distortion importantly biases the system toward underlending and therefore reinforces the popular notion that private lenders are cautious and risk conscious and that the market imposes discipline on borrowers. This latter view prevailed in technical and policy circles at least up until the 1982 crisis, when, as I have noted, one can perceive the beginning of a shift to a somewhat more critical perspective on international lending. I myself had become somewhat skeptical of the evolving pattern of external finance of Latin America as early as the mid-1970s.[43] Here I want to further develop this concern in material that will explain why private financial markets in the 1970s had a tendency to overlend to developing countries. My analysis will employ an institutional perspective that is very different from that found in the popular view of banking. Nevertheless, as I mentioned earlier, the analysis has no pretentions of being

[42] Group of Thirty, *Risks in International Lending*, p. 37.
[43] This appeared in published form in Robert Devlin, "External Finance and Commercial Banks: Their Role in Latin America's Capacity to Import between 1951 and 1975," *CEPAL Review*, no. 5 (first half of 1978), pp. 63–98.

a complete theory of international banking. Rather, I more modestly propose to develop some perspectives on lending behavior that can broaden the understanding of the role of supply in the 1970s debt buildup in Latin America and other developing countries.

Modern International Banking

The conventional view of the arm's-length efficiency of international banking is more generally grounded in the assumption that loan supply has its determinants in an extension of modern portfolio theory.[44] In other words, banks impersonally allocate credit on the principle that the discounted expected return, appropriately adjusted for risk, is equal to the present value of risk-adjusted returns on other assets in the port-folio.[45] It is a view of a distant, arm's-length lender that coldly considers loan placements at the margin on the basis of differential returns and opportunity costs in competitive markets.

International investments of nonfinancial firms also had traditionally been evaluated in terms of differential rates of return and opportunity costs. It was Stephen Hymer's 1960 doctoral dissertation—so controversial that it was published only posthumously in 1976—that marked a break with the traditional approach. Hymer showed that portfolio theory could not be easily used as an instrument to predict international capital flows; in his own words, in the real world of uncertainty, risk, and administrative barriers "almost anything can happen" with regard to the movement of capital.[46] It is on the basis of the work of Hymer and subsequent analysts that we now know that transnational firms, which are vertically and horizontally integrated across the globe, can have criteria other than maximization of rates of return for undertaking new investments; factors such as control, market penetration and shares,

[44] See Jaffee, *Credit Rationing and the Commercial Loan Market*, p. 105; and Friedman, *The World Debt Dilemma*, pp. 248–249.

[45] Or in a portfolio with two types of assets:

$$PV_L = \sum_{t=0}^{n} EV_L/(1 + i + \lambda)^t = PV_A = \sum_{t=0}^{n} EV_A/(1 + i + \lambda)^t$$

where PV = present value
EV = expected value of the future income stream
L = loans
A = other assets
i = bank's cost of funds
λ = risk where $0 < \lambda < 1$

[46] Stephen Hymer, *The International Operations of National Firms* (Cambridge, Mass.: MIT Press, 1976), p. 7.

collusion, public image, rivalry, and so on can be important determinants of the timing and place of investments.

One can, in fact, use portfolio theory to interpret the international expansion of banking. As I have shown in the previous chapter, profits in regulated domestic markets were shrinking and banks saw higher differential profit rates in unregulated overseas markets. In effect, one could legitimately state that lending to LDCs in the 1970s was part of a stock adjustment of the loan portfolio after the forty-year retrenchment following the financial collapse of the 1930s.

While portfolio theory can probably tell us in broad terms why lending shifted from domestic to international markets and why credit flows went from the center to the periphery, it has more difficulty explaining why a credit was extended to one country and not another, the terms and conditions of lending, exposure levels, et cetera. Indeed, borrowing from Hymer's general insight, it may be appropriate to go beyond portfolio analysis and develop a more discriminating institutional theory to understand the lending behavior of the modern bank. The modern bank is transnational—diversified around the world with branches, subsidiaries, and affiliates that serve local and international markets at both the retail and wholesale levels. Services range from local checking accounts to commercial retail and wholesale loans, correspondent banking, currency exchange, underwriting, fiduciary accounts, specialized consulting, and financial services, all directed at vertical and horizontal integration.[47] Clients range from TNCs to the host governments of the TNCs and the common person walking the street. Thus it is probably excessively simplistic to look to only "indifferent" capital seeking out the highest rates of return as an explanation for bank lending to LDCs in the 1970s. Explanation can in fact be enriched and made more useful for policy making by adjusting theory to the institutional realities of the modern transnational bank.

In this regard Rae Weston offers some refreshing insights. He has observed that portfolio theory treats a bank as an individual investor and not as a firm.[48] Once a bank is viewed as a global firm, a foreign currency loan is just one dimension of a multidimensional business that may or may not be dedicated to long-term global profit maximization.[49] Thus,

[47] An examination of any annual report of Citicorp—probably the world's most international bank—confirms the diverse and global reach of a modern international bank.

[48] Weston, *Domestic and Multinational Banking*, p. 24.

[49] Profit maximization of course need not be a goal at all. Baumol, for instance, developed a hypothesis suggesting that firms can seek to maximize sales, or market share, constrained by a minimum level of profits. A variant of this comes from Galbraith, who has argued that modern firms are run bureaucratically and can sacrifice profits for stability

in practice, loan transactions to a country or group of countries can be motivated by factors other than optimal diversification, price, and profit maximization; indeed, according to Weston, the basic tenet of the rational investor is broken consistently by bankers.[50] Thus in the context of a global banking firm, deviations from the optimal allocation of world credit become possible for many reasons other than the miscalculation of an individual investor that is underscored in the literature on credit rationing. The discipline of the supply side of the market that seems inherent in the cold, rational investor should not be presumed.

The Bank and Its Product

Pursuing the analysis of the bank as a global firm is instructive because it can help us further understand how supply dynamics might have been a special contributing factor in the 1970s debt buildup in LDCs.

When a bank is considered a global firm, one must ask what it produces. There is considerable debate about this.[51] Some interpret the bank as a manufacturer; while the arguments vary, broadly speaking, deposits are viewed as inputs and loans and services as outputs. Weston, however, argues that banking activities do not fit easily into this scheme because there is really no transformation process in which inputs lose their identity and other goods and services are generated. In his judgment the bank can best be viewed as a retailer, a distributor of funds and related services.[52]

To Weston's "the bank as retailer" it is convenient to add "the bank as wholesaler" to account for the large international loans of the eurocurrency market. But what is important is that both functions come as subsets of marketing theory; indeed, "saler" is incorporated into the word "wholesaler." This is an important insight because the bank as a manufacturer and, above all, the bank as investor portray the banker as an impersonal arm's-length economic agent. This indeed is the image we all traditionally like to confer on our finance people, and it may be a bit shocking to put them into the same company with purveyors of used

---

and other objectives. Caves supports the notion that profits might be traded off for stability. William Baumol, *Business Behavior, Value, and Growth* (New York: Macmillan, 1959), pp. 45–57; John Kenneth Galbraith, *The New Industrial State* (New York: New American Library, 1968); and Richard Caves, "Uncertainty, Market Structure, and Performance: Galbraith as Conventional Wisdom," in *Industrial Organization and Economic Development*, ed. Jesse Markham and Gustav Papanek (Boston: Houghton Mifflin, 1970), pp. 283–302.

[50] Weston, *Domestic and Multinational Banking*, p. 24.

[51] Ibid., pp. 25–27; and Aliber, "Theory of International Banking," pp. 6–7.

[52] Weston, *Domestic and Multinational Banking*, p. 27.

cars, Coca-Cola, and cornflakes.[53] Bankers themselves abhor this image, in part explaining why some were so assertive in arguing that LDC lending was demand driven. But it cannot be escaped that salesmanship goes hand-in-hand with contemporary banking.[54] Thus one finds in a 1970s management text on commercial banking such statements as "no well-run bank can take a passive attitude toward lending"; "the outstanding successful banks in all parts of the country are those that have found the means to make more loans than their neighbors and to make some loans that their neighbors would not make at all"; and "in a competitive world, it is not enough to be a good fellow; one must aggressively seek business."[55]

We noted in an earlier chapter that the marketing concept in banking first blossomed in the United States in the 1950s. In domestic markets it had its manifestation in the rare sight of bankers offering gifts to depositors and borrowers.[56] In the international markets it had its manifestation in, among other things, the much-publicized eurocredit. We traditionally consider loans to be highly private affairs. But during the 1970s individual eurocurrency credits were splashed in full-page ads (nicknamed "tombstones" by the bankers) in major financial media. Moreover, it is well known that the banks participating in a syndicate could enter into long debates over where to position their names in the ad so as to be located in the most prominent area of the page.[57]

The aggressiveness of the salesmanship of the international bank is a matter of record. It began to take on a noticeable dimension around 1970.

> In the early years of the Eurodollar [*sic*] the raising of international loans was a sedate and gentlemanly business. The borrower, whether a corporation or a foreign government agency, would approach its customary bank or a specialised bank, which would then arrange the syndicate. But as it became more lucrative and competitive, the loan

---

[53] As Galbraith has observed: "Money is, to most people, a serious thing. They expect financial architecture to reflect this quality—to be somber and serious, never light or frivolous. The same, it may be added, is true of bankers. Doctors, though life itself is in their hands, may be amusing . . . [but] . . . a funny banker is inconceivable." See John Kenneth Galbraith, *Money* (Boston: Houghton Mifflin, 1975), p. 119.

[54] Delamaide characterizes modern bankers as "traveling money salesmen." See Darrell Delamaide, *Debt Shock* (Garden City, N.Y.: Doubleday, 1984), p. 43.

[55] Howard Crosse and George Hempel, *Management Policies for Commercial Banks* 2d ed. (Englewood Cliffs, N.J.: Prentice-Hall, 1973), pp. 207 and 280.

[56] Maurice Odle, *Multinational Banks and Underdevelopment* (London: Pergamon Press, 1981), p. 164.

[57] Anthony Sampson, *The Money Lenders* (New York: Penguin Books, 1983), p. 145.

officers of the banks began—around 1970—to solicit business, and to telephone or visit corporations and government agencies on their own initiative. Some of the banks were no longer acting simply as intermediaries between a surplus and shortage of funds: they were now actively selling loans."[58]

As the tone and intensity of salesmanship increased, those paid to observe market behavior on a daily basis made the appropriate assessments about the new style of banking. In the latter half of the 1970s the specialized financial magazine *Euromoney* coined the terms "Gunslingers," "Panthers," and "Sheep" to rank in corresponding order the aggressiveness of the banks in the market; it is telling that in 1978 47 percent of the institutions classified were Gunslingers and only 8 percent were Sheep.[59] Meanwhile, the *Wall Street Journal* at one point characterized creditor practices as a "glad-handed name your price approach."[60] These real-life images clearly do not square with the traditional picture of the bank as a passive arm's-length investor. Indeed, it will become more evident in this study that in Latin America during the 1970s banks often were not rationing credit but rather were marketing money like any other product. The "distortion" was not underlending but overlending.

The vision of the supply side of the market as arm's length and restrained is further eroded when we consider the nature of the service that is marketed. Selling a loan is not really identical to selling cornflakes. When cornflakes are sold, the exchange is a simultaneous one of money for the product. When banks market a loan, payment is in the distant future. Thus confidence and trust in the character of the borrower is a central factor, making banking an even more personal business than other types of marketing operations.

The personal nature of the business can make the modern bank an inherently forthcoming institution. First, since trust is built on information, a client relationship is an investment. Long-term relationships and market presence are a form of capital deepening that raise the productivity of the bank; it acquires continuous information at such low cost and high speed that it gains a competitive advantage over other institutions. Thus, once a bank establishes a relationship it is inclined to service the client's needs as much as possible; the reliable provision of ser-

---

[58] Ibid., pp. 145–146.

[59] *Euromoney* used the spreads and maturities on loans to rank the banks. See "Tracking the Lead Bank: Who's Competing Hardest," *Euromoney*, August 1979, pp. 14–30.

[60] *Wall Street Journal*, 12 March 1976, cited in Douglas Hayes, *Bank Lending Policies* (Ann Arbor, Mich.: University of Michigan, School of Business Administration, 1977), p. 49.

vices underscores the quality of the bank's products and helps the institution avoid losing the customer to other banks. Moreover, since the client relationship has a high fixed cost, servicing additional requests has lower marginal costs than dealing with new clients.[61]

Looked at from another angle, default risk—which underlies portfolio theory and the credit-rationing literature—on foreign currency lending is only one component in the overall aggregate risk of the global bank. A bank gains utility from a client relationship. A new loan may raise risk and lower expected profits, but not granting the loan to an established client may raise aggregate firm risk even more and lower expected profits in the short and long term. The argument is reinforced if the client is an important depositor.[62] Default risk may take on decisive weight in decision making only at a very advanced stage of a credit cycle. Even then this might not preclude new lending due to lock-in effects: that is, fresh credits generate positive externalities with regard to the solvency of old debt.

A second consideration is that the element of trust and confidence imparts economies of scale; according to Weston, uncertainties can be reduced by size on account of more comprehensive information flows.[63] (Later we will see that there are other factors that reward size.) Thus economies of scale explain in part the growth bias in the industry in the 1960s and 1970s and generate a logical concern for market shares.[64] This in turn means that a bank's decision to lend or not will not only be based on the default risk related to that transaction; there is an additional awareness of positive externalities from global operations and a consequent need to maintain a presence in the market. Meanwhile, new entrants will be concerned about attaining a minimum acceptable loan volume, without which their own viability—apart from any consideration of default risk—is in jeopardy.

[61] Grubel, "A Theory of Multinational Banking," pp. 352–353.

[62] The deposit relation can also induce a loan to a third party. There is evidence that an important corporate depositor wishing to sell equipment to a country can be a factor in a bank's extending a loan that it otherwise might not make due to concern for default risk. For a concrete example of this see S. C. Gwynne, "Adventures in the Loan Trade," *Harper's*, September 1983, pp. 25–26. The primary deposit relation is modeled in Edward Kane and Burton Malkiel, "Bank Portfolio Allocation, Deposit Variability, and the Availability Doctrine," *Quarterly Journal of Economics* 74 (February 1965): 113–134.

[63] Weston, *Domestic and Multinational Banking*, pp. 38–40. For a 1970s study on economies of scale see George Benston, "Economies of Scale of Financial Institutions," *Journal of Money, Credit, and Banking* 4 (May 1972): 312–341.

[64] Some studies recently have appeared which suggest that the prevailing notion of large economies of scale in banking could be exaggerated. What is not in dispute, however, is that bankers used (and still use) this notion to guide their portfolio strategy. See "Survey on International Banking," *Economist*, 26 March 1988, pp. 10–16.

Of course, much analytical work remains to be done on the transnational banking firm. But the above is already sufficiently suggestive and runs counter to the notion of a passive, arm's-length investor, which frequently dominates the conventional image of banking. The modern bank has diverse objectives, is forthcoming, is inclined to growth, and aggressively markets its services. It is not easy to understand why economically efficient credit allocation is the necessary outcome of the global financial firm's decision making, which furthermore is undertaken in a world of uncertainty.

The Structure of the Market

Domestic Markets   Further insight into the nature of credit supply in the 1970s can be gathered by examining the structure of the banking industry.

Virtually since its inception banking has been notoriously concentrated, with a handful of banks dominating the markets.[65] Today's domestic money markets are also concentrated. In the Netherlands banking is dominated by two firms, in France by four, in Canada by five, in Germany by three, Japan by thirteen, and Great Britain by eight to ten. The United States, with the enormous total of nearly fifteen thousand banking institutions, is generally considered to be one of the least concentrated markets. The top ten banks in the system control 18 percent of all assets and 15 percent of all domestic deposits.[66] The large number of banks reflects the effects of domestic banking regulation. But effective concentration is more than the numbers would suggest since U.S. banks are largely confined within state boundaries and New York banks are generally restricted to the city of New York.[67]

Domestic banking industries are considered to be loosely oligopolistic, with attempts at indirect collusion on deposit and loan rates. The Prime Rate convention used to price loans in the United States is a classic mode of indirect communication in an industry without a dominant price leader. The Prime Rate is a way to set up a simple and easily verifiable rate structure that objectively discriminates among borrowers

---

[65] Karl Born, *International Banking in the 19th and 20th Centuries*, trans. Volker Berghahn (New York: St. Martin's Press, 1983), pp. 59–102.

[66] Aliber, "Theory of International Banking," p. 6; Johann Wendt, "The Role of Foreign Banks in International Banking," in *The International Banking Handbook*, ed. William Baughn and Donald Mandich (Homewood, Ill.: Dow Jones-Irwin, 1983), pp. 47–70; and J. Andrew Spindler, *The Politics of International Credit* (Washington, D.C.: Brookings Institution, 1984), pp. 15–17 and p. 185.

[67] Benston, "Economies of Scale," p. 198. This situation is, of course, now gradually changing due to the recent trend toward deregulation of U.S. banking.

and thereby minimizes competitive underbidding of loan rates. The rate tends to move infrequently and to lag behind other market trends because the leaders need time and clear indications of need before attempting to modify the basic rate. A major signal to alter the Prime Rate is said to be a change in the Federal Reserve's Discount Rate.[68]

I mentioned earlier that the need for comprehensive information flows gives economies of scale to banking. But there are other (not wholly unrelated) factors that reward size and promote concentration. Benston points to technological considerations within the bank such as lower average skill (and hence wage) levels and indivisibilities in information processing.[69] Size also allows banks to cement customer relations (which lower information costs) by enabling them to provide a broad array of services. In addition, size can lower risk through greater opportunity to diversify. It can furthermore be argued that size reduces risk to the extent that bigness entitles banks to easy access to lender-of-last-resort facilities while smallness entitles them to only bankruptcy. Indeed, as represented in the bailout of Continental Illinois in 1984, supervisors tend to rescue bigger institutions rather than let them fail.[70]

Compared to manufacturing, banking has greater ease of entry and thus oligopolistic arrangements can more often be subject to competitive waves. Money is money and financial services are relatively standardized, so banks have difficulty in differentiating the products that they market. Customer loyalty depends on loan availability, price, and services. Since there are economies of scale, a main roadblock to entry is access to deposits. An institution that does not quickly capture a sufficient amount of deposits will have its scale limited and operate under higher average costs. It then may be subject to takeover by the larger banks. New entrants will manipulate price to obtain a foothold in the market; deposit rates will be set higher and loan rates set lower. Established banks attempt to dissuade entry by keeping deposit rates suffi-

[68] Jaffee, *Credit Rationing and the Commercial Loan Market*, pp. 104–107; and Weston, *Domestic and Multinational Banking*, pp. 38–43.

[69] Benston, "Economies of Scale," p. 338.

[70] For example, during the first eleven months of 1985 one hundred U.S. banks failed; all were small institutions. Swoboda argues that the big banks were aware that they were candidates for lender-of-last-resort facilities and that this influenced lending behavior. He may be right; on one occasion Citibank explicitly stated that central banks would not let big institutions fail. See Alexander Swoboda, "Debt and the Efficiency and Stability of the International Financial System," in *International Debt and the Developing Countries*, ed. Gordon Smith and John Cuddington (Washington, D.C.: World Bank, 1985), pp. 161–163; E. A. Brett, *International Money and Capitalist Crisis* (Boulder, Colo.: Westview Press, 1983, p. 223; and Nathaniel Nash, "Adjusting to 100 Failed Banks," *New York Times*, 17 November 1985, first page of business section.

ciently high, while competing with each other on loan volume and service but not price.

Market structure also raises attention about market shares. As mentioned earlier, a market share is both a customer relation and an investment in information that lowers average costs. Also, big banks traditionally follow a policy of stable dividends, which requires growth and protection of market shares.[71] A bank will thus be reluctant to accept an erosion of its share and indeed, if not involved in collusion or under regulatory restriction, will aggressively attempt to expand it. Given that the industry is dominated by a handful of large banks, shares are visible to all participants and can be monitored. This explains tendencies to collude as well as tendencies to compete aggressively when some institutions attempt to gain shares at the expense of others.

In sum, domestic markets are vulnerable to a process of short-term cutthroat competition and long-run concentration. This dynamic is dampened to the extent that the markets are regulated. Indeed, it is the industry's tendency to move between extreme stability and instability that has been one of the justifications for domestic banking regulation.[72]

International Markets: The 1960s   At the international level, banking had an unambiguously oligopolistic structure in the 1950s and 1960s. There is only limited published data for this period, but some simple indicators are reflective of the situation.

Beginning in 1970, the magazine *The Banker* began to rank banks worldwide by size according to the value of their assets. Although the internationalization of banking began in earnest in the late 1960s, 1970 can be used as an approximate benchmark for dividing the years of basically domestic banking from those where a predominantly international orientation took hold. Table 3.1 indicates that there was a strong degree of concentration in world banking before the boom: in 1970 the ten biggest banks held 17 percent of all assets, the top twenty-five a third of all assets, and the top fifty one-half.

Within this concentrated structure the United States had an overwhelmingly dominant position. Of the top ten banks worldwide, six were American and they accounted for 70 percent of all assets in this subgroup.[73] While data are not available on how the assets of the

[71] United Nations Centre on Transnational Corporations, *Transnational Corporations in World Development* (New York, 1988), p. 65.

[72] Odle, *Multinational Banks*, pp. 4–5; and Weston, *Domestic and Multinational Banking*, pp. 38–43. Of course, the major reason for regulation is that a bank's liabilities are considerably more liquid than its assets.

[73] Calculated from "The Top 300," *The Banker*, June 1971, pp. 663–684.

TABLE 3.1. Cumulative Distribution of the Value of Total Assets
of the Top 300 Banks Worldwide
(percentage of total value of assets)

Banks	1970	1975[a]	1980[a]
Top 10	17	17	17
Top 25	33	32	32
Top 50	51	52	51
Top 100	72	74	73
Top 300	100	100	100

SOURCE: Calculated from data in *The Banker,* "The Top 300" (June 1971), pp. 663–684; "The Top 300" (June 1976), pp. 653–697; and "The Top 500" (June 1981), pp. 153–181. *The Banker* converts all assets into dollars.
NOTE:
[a]Less contra accounts.

world's banks were distributed between domestic and international lending, it is well known that up until 1970 overseas operations were largely a U.S. domain. In effect, the dollar's privileged status as the only convertible currency in the years immediately after World War II and its relatively unchallenged position up until the late 1960s gave American banks an overwhelming advantage worldwide. Moreover, international operations were basically limited to a coterie of big banks from New York, Chicago, and San Francisco.[74] An idea of the degree of concentration of activity in a few American banks is given by the fact that in 1970 the nine major New York City banks accounted for 319 of a total of 550 foreign branch offices of U.S. banks and for more than 50 percent of all foreign branch deposits.[75]

Developing countries undoubtedly confronted an even tighter oligopolistic structure, since the then less familiar terrain of the developing periphery tended to be divided up according to historical, political, and economic links with the industrial Center. For instance, U.S.

[74] The banks were (a) New York—Chase Manhattan, Citibank, Chemical Bank, Morgan Guaranty, Manufacturers Hanover, Irving Trust, Marine Midland, and Bank of New York; (b) Chicago—Continental Illinois and First Chicago; and (c) San Francisco—Bank of America. Some of the non-U.S. banks with a significant international presence were Barclays and Lloyds of the United Kingdom, Bank of Tokyo of Japan, Bank of Nova Scotia and Royal Bank of Canada, Deutsche Bank of Germany, and Crédit Lyonnais of France.

[75] Frank Mastrapasqua, "U.S. Bank Expansion Via Foreign Branching," *Bulletin* 87–88 (January 1973): 27.

banks had a high profile in Latin America, the English-speaking Caribbean was an English and Canadian preserve, while French-speaking Africa was a natural market for French banks, and so on. As far as I know there is no systematic disaggregated data on the borrowing experience of LDCs with private banks during the 1960s. My case study work on Peru—one of the few Latin American countries with significant access to term loans from the banks prior to 1970—has, however, generated data that are suggestive of how the regional market might have been structured prior to the banking boom of the 1970s.[76]

During 1965 to 1970 Peru had only twenty-seven commercial bank lenders. Within this group, fourteen institutions were from the United States and they accounted for 86 percent of the $358 million authorized for the period (the next largest group was Canada with an 8 percent share lent out by three banks). The leading six lenders—Manufacturers Hanover, Citicorp, Bankers Trust, Chase Manhattan, Continental Illinois, and Bank of America—accounted for nearly three-quarters of total lending. All these principal lenders were American and they were all very big: four of them ranked in the top ten worldwide and all six were in the top twenty-five.[77]

This concentrated structure also evidenced more cooperation than competition as 68 percent of all authorizations came via what might be termed multibank, or club, agreements. These agreements represented an umbrella contract for credits from several banks and were a precursor of the loan syndicate of the 1970s. However, the participating banks were all of the same national origin. Furthermore, there was no official lead, or agent, bank, no organization fees, and disbursement/payments were effected on a bank-by-bank basis. Peru's principal creditors made use of this arrangement and were more frequently lending together than competing: 80 percent of the $257 million extended by the top six banks was via joint lending with each other.[78]

There is another case study worth mentioning that provides a partial view of the market's structure in a big Latin American country: Sánchez Aguilar's work on bank lending to Mexico in the 1960s.[79] The data base is different from that of my study on Peru; while I directly collected

[76] Robert Devlin, *Transnational Banks and the External Finance of Latin America: The Experience of Peru* (Santiago, Chile: United Nations, 1985).

[77] The figure on global authorizations is an unpublished one calculated from data provided by the Peruvian Ministry of Economy and Finance (MINFIN). The rest of the data appear in ibid., chap. 4.

[78] Calculated from unpublished data provided by the MINFIN.

[79] E. Sánchez Aguilar, "The International Activities of U.S. Commercial Banks: A Case Study of Mexico" (Ph.D. diss., Harvard University, 1973).

data on the universe of banks with term lending to the public sector, Sánchez Aguilar surveyed a sample of ninety-nine U.S. banks and covered their short- and medium-term lending to both public and private entities. Even though it is restricted to a sample of lenders, the study still suggests that even a big, and presumably attractive, market like Mexico confronted a concentrated financial market. The largest twenty-five U.S. lenders (ranked by assets) accounted for 80 percent of all lending in the sample. While the author does not provide a systematic disaggregation of these data, the study does reveal that just nine of these twenty-five banks—not ordered in any special way but including two of the three top lenders to Mexico—accounted for 40 percent of all the loans in the sample.[80]

While the two cases offer only a very limited view of the Latin American market, they are consistent with the notion that the periphery faced a concentrated financial market. The theory of concentration and oligopoly markets often stresses the characteristic of price stability as sellers avoid price competition in order to share the monopoly rents derived from their market power.[81] We have seen that in domestic markets, where direct collusion is prohibited, communication among leading banks is facilitated by the Prime Rate mechanism. Internationally, there were no such barriers to communication—indeed with multibank agreements communication was overtly direct—so that price stability among the handful of lenders was even easier to coordinate.

Another reason to expect price stability is related to what Okun refers to as the dynamics of customer markets.[82] According to him, when markets exhibit high shopping costs there is a greater tendency for client relationships to develop, which in turn causes sellers to face demand curves with relatively low price elasticity. This provides an incentive for stable prices. In the periphery during the 1960s there was only a limited number of loan transactions undertaken by a reduced number of banks. Presumably informational costs for inexperienced and low-volume borrowers like those in Latin America were high. This could have reduced random shopping and promoted Okun's customer relation. Peru's repeated visits to the same six banks is certainly suggestive of a country that did little shopping in the international market.

In any event, the two case studies are indicative of a degree of price

[80] Ibid., pp. 38, 100.

[81] For a concise survey of oligopolistic pricing see F. M. Scherer, *Industrial Market Structure and Economic Performance* (Boston: Houghton Mifflin, 1980), pp. 226–229 and 349–374.

[82] Arthur Okun, *Prices and Quantities* (Washington, D.C.: Brookings Institution, 1981), pp. 134–222.

stability. In the case of Peru a composite unweighted price incorporating the spread and maturity of fifteen variable-rate loans in 1965 to 1970 gave a coefficient of variation of 14 percent.[83] This is a pretty stable pricing pattern considering that over the period Peru evolved from a relatively calm setting to financial crisis under a civilian government, which in turn was followed by a military coup and a new self-declared revolutionary regime. In the case of Mexico it is not possible to make a similar calculation because Sánchez Aguilar's data mix short- and medium-term maturities and public and private sector borrowers. But his sample of variable-rate lending in eurodollars for 1965 to 1970 suggests relatively stable spreads of 1.75 to 2.0 percent, although by 1970 it was clear that margins were starting to fall sharply. His data do not permit any generalization about maturities except to say that in the 1960s they did not exceed six years.[84]

International Markets: The 1970s   Financial markets in the 1970s were not conventionally conceived as clubby. There were many banks actively involved internationally, estimated in total at well over a thousand.[85] These institutions encountered little or no restraint on their behavior, and prices and quantities appeared highly flexible and set competitively. LDCs contracted favorable terms, as spreads could be below 1 percent and maturities of ten years were quite common.[86] Loan volume was strong; as mentioned in the previous chapter, estimates of the expansion of bank lending to Latin America point to an average of around 30 percent per annum.[87]

[83] The coefficient of variation is s/x, where s is the standard deviation and x is the unweighted average of price on fifteen transactions. The index of price was calculated as M/A, where M is the margin and A is the period of amortization. Fixed-rate loans did show a high degree of variation, but many of these were not strictly commercial transactions; they were linked to home country export trade and some administrative bargaining related to the opening of new branch offices in Lima. All data are unpublished and were secured from the MINFIN. The price index employed is identical to that used by *Euromoney* (see "Tracking the Lead Bank" for more details).

[84] Sánchez Aguilar, "The International Activities of U.S. Commercial Banks," pp. 100, 108.

[85] Mentré, *The Fund and Member Countries*, p. 6. See also Diane Page and Walter Rodgers, "Trends in Eurocurrency Credit Participation, 1972–1980," in *Risks in International Lending* (New York: Group of Thirty, 1982), p. 57.

[86] As I noted in Chapter Two, data on the conditions of borrowing, itemized by country, were published regularly in the now discontinued World Bank publication *Borrowing in International Capital Markets*

[87] Also see Ricardo Ffrench-Davis, "External Debt, Renegotiation Frameworks and Development in Latin America," paper presented at a seminar on Latin American External Debt, Stockholm, May 1985, pp. 2–4.

It was this free-wheeling and seemingly atomistic environment that brought the aforementioned applause from many economists and policy makers. The ability of the banks to recycle petrodollars gave further impulse to the belief that free markets functioned efficiently. Moreover, as exemplified in the earlier statement of McKinnon, interpretations of the eurocurrency market were often modeled after the classic efficient arm's-length auction market found in the competitive parable of economic textbooks.

I think many of those who readily employed the classic competitive model perhaps fell victim to the mystique of free markets. A more fruitful approach to understanding events during the 1970s is to extend the oligopolistic framework of the 1960s. In effect, what happened in the 1970s is that the relatively tight oligopolistic structure of the previous decade was destabilized by brash new entrants. A classic price war broke out in a structure that remained essentially oligopolistic. The market was in severe disequilibrium for more than a decade, and this aggravated existing "distortions" stemming from the heightened uncertainty of a business that specializes in making exchanges in one period with payment in the distant future. Under the circumstances it is difficult to presume that the market allocated resources efficiently, even loosely defined.

The first step in clarifying this picture is to refer to the process of entry that destabilized the oligopolistic market. I mentioned earlier that the principal barriers to entry in banking are access to sufficient deposits and information as well as to the associated scale economies. At the international level these barriers declined dramatically in the 1970s due to some of the technological innovations alluded to in the previous chapter.

On the side of liabilities there was the large interbank market in dollars in the eurocurrency market. The market is a fast and informal one where banks deposit funds with each other. Credit checking among the banks was not rigorous, and most institutions could and did expect relatively automatic access to funds on a nondiscriminatory basis. Since banks could easily "purchase" deposits in this central market, they also could avoid the need to develop a costly international branching network and associated investments in deposit relationships. Indeed, net debtors in the interbank market were precisely those institutions that were excluded from international banking in the 1960s: small banks, institutions lacking international networks, and those without a strong dollar deposit base.[88]

---

[88] Bank for International Settlements, *The International Interbank Market* (Basel, 1983), pp. 7–8 and 32–38.

The existence of this informal interbank market obviously in and of itself lowered barriers to entry. But it must not be overlooked that the easy access and informality of the market was related in part to macroeconomic policy of the OECD economies, which promoted considerable growth of world liquidity. The preference of the OPEC countries for short-term investments also meant that a greater share of this liquidity was allocated to the banking system during the 1970s. These developments help explain why the interbank market grew from $160 billion in 1973 to nearly $700 billion by 1980.[89] If world liquidity had been tighter, this explosive growth might not have been possible. Banks in turn might have been more discriminating in their redepositing, and the bigger established banks would have had more ability to block entry.[90]

On the asset side of the ledger, informational barriers were seemingly reduced by the appearance of the syndicated loan. Banks could enter international lending without major investments in information by hopping onto a syndicated credit organized by other banks that had invested resources in information. We saw in the last chapter that since acceptable participations could be as low as $250,000, even small provincial banks could develop an international portfolio during the 1970s.

These two developments represented reductions in both costs and the minimum scale for international lending operations. This is exhibited in Figure 3.5. In the 1960s potential new entrants faced a situation whereby their entry could have driven prices below long-run average costs (AC), as shown by the fall in price from P_0 to P_1 in Figure 3.5. However, the aforementioned developments, coupled with others,[91] lowered perceived long-run costs and minimum scale, causing the average cost curve to shift downwards to AC'. This gave banks the margin and incentive they needed to enter and compete with the more established lenders via loan availability and price; as shown in Figure 3.5, the postentry price P_1 remains above the new average cost curve AC'. Market entry in the 1970s, of course, also was given further stimulus by the 1974 oil shock, which shifted the LDCs' demand curve to the right (not shown in the figure).

The reduction in barriers to entry on both the asset and liability side of the balance sheet, coupled with stagnation of domestic earnings, induced an incredible number of new entrants: estimates are that at a min-

[89] R. M. Pecchioli, *The Internationalization of Banking* (Paris: Organization for Economic Cooperation and Development, 1983), p. 30.

[90] I pointed out in the previous chapter that some analysts have linked the whole phenomenon of liquidity growth to capitalist crisis.

[91] Risks are also part of a bank's cost structure. Perceived risks of international lending apparently fell in the 1970s. This will be discussed in greater detail in the next subsection.

FIGURE 3.5. Effect of New Market Entrants on Price.

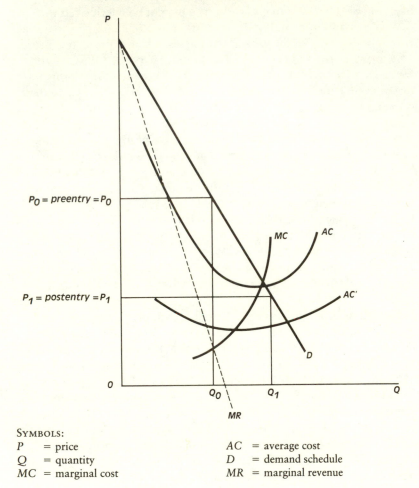

SYMBOLS:

P	= price	
Q	= quantity	
MC	= marginal cost	

AC = average cost
D = demand schedule
MR = marginal revenue

imum there was an average of sixty-six new entrants per annum over 1973 to 1980.[92] Table 3.2 breaks down new entrants by country of origin and divides them into a first phase (1973-1975) and a second phase (1976-1980). In the initial period the biggest burst of new entrants came from consortium (mixed capital) banks, U.S. institutions, and "other

[92] Page and Rodgers, "Trends in Eurocurrency Credit," p. 64. The data represent only a partial count of participants in loan syndicates and therefore underestimate new entrants.

TABLE 3.2. Annual Average Number of New Bank Entrants
to the International Market by Country of Origin

Country of Origin	1973–75	1976–80
Austria	1.7	2.4
Belgium	0.3	0.4
Luxembourg	0.7	2.2
Fed. Rep. of Germany	3.7	2.4
France	4.3	2.4
Italy	1.3	3.0
Netherlands	1.3	1.0
Spain/Portugal	4.0	3.4
Switzerland	1.0	2.8
United Kingdom	4.0	0.6
Other Western Europe	6.7	1.0
Canada	2.3	0.6
USA	10.7	7.0
Japan	1.7	1.8
Other countries	11.0	24.0
Consortia[a]	13.3	9.4
Total	68.0	64.4

SOURCE: Calculated from data in Diane Page and Walter Rodgers, "Trends in Eurocurrency Credit Participation 1972–1980," in *Risks in International Lending* (New
York: Group of Thirty, 1982), p. 64.
NOTE:
[a]Banks that are owned by two or more other banks.

countries." Banks from France, the United Kingdom, Germany,
Spain/Portugal, and other Western European countries also were active new entrants. In the second period the dynamic new entrants were
from other countries (mostly oil-rich Arab banks), consortia, and smaller U.S. institutions.

With such a large and sustained number of new entrants it is not surprising that vigorous price competition characterized the banking market in the 1970s. But as mentioned, the competition observed in the
market did not reflect the efficient functioning of an atomistic market,
but rather it was a cutthroat price war of an oligopolistic market unset-
tled by new participants. This becomes clear when one realizes that despite the large number of new entrants and the large number of active

TABLE 3.3. Top Ten in World Banking
(ranked by total assets)

Rank	1970	1975[a]	1980[a]
1	Bank of America (USA)	Bank of America (USA)	Citicorp (USA)
2	Citicorp (USA)	Citicorp (USA)	Bank of America (USA)
3	Chase Manhattan (USA)	Crédit Agricole (France)	Crédit Agricole (France)
4	Barclays Bank (UK)	Chase Manhattan (USA)	Group BNP (France)
5	National Westminster (UK)	Group BNP (France)	Crédit Lyonnais (France)
6	Manufacturers Hanover (USA)	Deutsche Bank (Germany)	Société Générale (France)
7	Banco Nacionale del Lavoro (Italy)	Crédit Lyonnais (France)	Barclays Bank (UK)
8	Morgan Guaranty (USA)	Société Générale (France)	Deutsche Bank (Germany)
9	Western Bancorp (USA)	Barclays Bank (UK)	National Westminster (UK)
10	Royal Bank of Canada (Canada)	Dai-Ichi Kangyo (Japan)	Dai-Ichi Kangyo (Japan)

SOURCE: *The Banker*, "The Top 300" (June 1971), pp. 663–684; "The Top 300" (June 1976), pp. 653–697; and "The Top 500" (June 1981), pp. 153–181.
NOTE:
[a]Excludes contra accounts.

participants in the eurocurrency market, the essential features of the loan market were determined in a concentrated structure.

THE NATURE OF CONCENTRATION: THE LENDERS.   Table 3.1 shows that there was a high and remarkably stable concentration of banking assets at the world level throughout the 1970s. The competition observed internationally was basically among giants as they pushed and shoved for growth and dominance. The basic pattern of the 1970s was that the big U.S. banks were challenged by the Europeans and Japanese. The struggle is displayed in the ranking of the top ten banks worldwide in Table 3.3: while in 1970 six of the top ten banks were from the United States, in 1975 there were only three U.S. institutions, and in 1980, only two. More generally, only four of 1970's top ten banks remained on the list in 1980.

Focusing on total assets has its limitations, however, because it includes domestic lending; for example, Crédit Agricole, the third largest bank in the world in 1980, is an institution that has little or no international exposure. The asset data also are distorted by the depreciation of the U.S. dollar during the 1970s; this inflated the value of the European and Japanese banks' domestic assets, which are expressed in U.S. currency in the rankings. Nevertheless, the limited data available on inter-

TABLE 3.4. International Exposure of U.S. Banks Ranked by Size, June 1982

Rank	World[a]	Developing Countries	Latin America
	Exposure as % of Total		
Top 9	59.1	62.2	59.4
Next 15	19.4	19.5	19.8
Next 143	21.5	18.3	20.8
Total 167	100.0	100.0	100.0
	Average Exposure in Billions of Dollars		
Top 9	21.5	8.6	5.3
Next 15	4.3	1.6	1.1
Next 143	0.5	0.2	0.1
Total 167	2.0	0.8	0.5

SOURCE: Calculated from data in the U.S. Federal Financial Institutions Examination Council, *Statistical Release* (Washington, D.C., 6 December 1982).
NOTE:
[a]Excludes offshore centers and lending to international organizations.

national exposure confirms concentration in the market: Mentré estimated that 20 large banks with international assets of more than $20 billion have accounted for 50 percent of the value of all international lending.[93] For U.S. banks, where more data are published, it can be found that just prior to the crisis of August 1982 the 9 largest banks controlled 60 percent of international lending and the top 24 accounted for 80 percent (Table 3.4). The average international exposure of the 9 largest was more than ten times larger than the overall average and forty-three times larger than the bottom 143 banks that represented 85 percent of the institutions surveyed. This is certainly not an atomistic market.

But the picture on concentration is not complete. The dynamics of market lending revolved around the syndicated credit. There were only a small number of institutions capable of consistently organizing these loans. The core group that formed the lifeblood of the system included

[93] Mentré, *The Fund and Member Countries*, p. 6.

only about twenty-five OECD area banks.[94] These lead banks searched for new markets, evaluated borrowers, negotiated terms, and invited other banks to participate in the syndicate. They also had a double-funding role. It was these banks that attracted deposits from the major surplus countries; thus they supported loan syndication not only by their direct participation but also by their redepositing in the interbank market that supplied funding to peripheral institutions entering into syndicated loans. The successful lead bank tended to be large because to compete it had to be able to directly or indirectly underwrite loans of huge value, and it needed broad international prestige, contacts, and informational networks to attract participants. Thus while any bank could lend internationally through participation in a syndicated loan, the traditional barriers of informational costs and scale economies confronted institutions wishing to gain the prestige and extra income that lead banks derive from syndication.[95]

Added to the core group were another two dozen banks that had pretensions of taking on a role as an important lead bank. But what is important is that concentration of power in this vital aspect of international lending was strong. Table 3.5 shows that in 1978 to 1981 the top ten lead banks mobilized roughly one-half of the publicized syndicated credit (in the tighter credit environment of 1975 to 1977 the top ten mobilized 80 to 90 percent). In the oligopolistic struggle banks displaced each other in the rankings. But Table 3.6 demonstrates that there was a core of eight to ten institutions that kept a high profile in the group of top ten lead banks in syndication. Moreover, it is here where one can appreciate that the U.S. banks lost less of their market power than appeared to be the case when examining data on assets: the institutions with the greatest frequency of appearances in the top ten were five U.S. lenders.[96]

---

[94] Ibid.

[95] The extra income came from front-end fees paid to the lead banks. These fees were attractive; they were paid up front, were riskless, and could represent up to one-fifth of the yield on a loan. See Pecchioli, *The Internationalization of Banking*, p. 48; Fabio Basagni, "Recent Developments in International Lending Practices," in *Banks and the Balance of Payments*, Benjamin Cohen in collaboration with Fabio Basagni (Montclair, N.J.: Allanheld, Osmun, 1981), p. 101; and "Buddy, Can You Borrow a Dollar?" *Euromoney*, May 1978, pp. 10–15. For a full description of the mechanics of loan syndication see Robert Bee, "Syndication," in *Offshore Lending by U.S. Commercial Banks*, ed. F. John Mathis (Philadelphia: Robert Morris Associates, 1975), pp. 151–165.

[96] Moreover, the big U.S. banks have been shown to be linked through interlocking directorates and reciprocal participation in each other's capital. See U.S. Congress, Senate, Committee on Government Operations, *Disclosure of Corporate Ownership*, 93d Cong., 2d sess. (Washington, D.C.: U.S. Government Printing Office, 1974); and U.S.

TABLE 3.5. Cumulative Distribution of the Value of Loan Syndications among the Top Lead Banks
(percentage)

Banks	1975	1976	1977	1978	1979[a]	1980	1981
Top 5	65	67	60	25	33	28	49
Top 10	86	90	79	44	50	47	64
Total	100	100	100	100	100	100	100
Number of banks listed	15	20	20	50	50	50	40

SOURCES: 1975, *International Herald Tribune*, 8 November 1976, p. 21. 1976–1977, *Euromoney*, April 1978, p. 85. 1978, *Euromoney*, February 1979, pp. 29–30. 1979–1980, *Euromoney*, November 1980, pp. 54–55. 1981, *Euromoney*, February 1982, pp. 65–67.
NOTE:
[a] January-September.

A stylized description of the competition among the lead banks in the syndicated loan market would be as follows. At the beginning of the 1970s the syndicated loan market was a domain of the big, traditionally international, U.S. banks.[97] In the early 1970s their international markets were challenged both by the big regional banks in the United States that previously were not interested in overseas lending and by European institutions. The newcomers gained an international footing by (a) offering to organize syndicated credits in new (and more risky) markets where the traditional lead banks had a weaker presence, (b) price cutting in crowded markets, and (c) inducing small banks interested in

---

Congress, Senate, Committee on Government Affairs, *Interlocking Directorates among Major U.S. Corporations*, 97th Cong., 2d sess. (Washington, D.C.: U.S. Government Printing Office, 1978).

At the country level concentrations could be even more notable. My case study work is illustrative. While Peru had 167 creditors, just five banks—Citicorp, Wells Fargo, Manufacturers Hanover, Dresdner Bank, and Bank of Tokyo—in their capacity as leaders in syndication, mobilized 75 percent of all loans. As for Bolivia, it had over 100 creditors, but just three lenders—Bank of America, Citicorp, and Dresdner Bank—organized nearly two-thirds of all syndicated loans. See Devlin, *Transnational Banks in Peru*, pp. 127–142, 156–159. For Bolivia see Robert Devlin and Michael Mortimore, *Los Bancos Transnacionales, el Estado, y el Endeudamiento Externo en Bolivia* [Transnational Banks, the State, and External Debt in Bolivia] (Santiago, Chile: United Nations, 1983), pp. 55–109.

[97] The first syndicate was organized by Bankers Trust in 1968. See "Syndicated Loans" (Special Supplement: World Banking Survey), *Financial Times*, 21 May 1979.

TABLE 3.6. Banks Ranked by Frequency of Appearance in the Group of Top Ten Lead Banks in Loan Syndication

Bank	1975	1976	1977	1978	1979	1980	1981
Citicorp	X	X	X	X	X	X	X
Chase Manhattan	X	X	X	X	X	X	X
Bank of America	X	X	X	X	X	X	X
Morgan Guaranty	X	X	X	X	X	X	X
Manufacturers Hanover	X	X	X	X	X	X	X
Lloyds Bank	X			X	X	X	X
Crédit Lyonnais	X	X			X	X	X
Bank of Montreal				X	X	X	X
Deutsche Bank			X	X	X		
Wells Fargo Bank	X			X			
Dresdner Bank		X	X				
Bank of Tokyo				X	X		
National Westminster						X	X
UBAF	X						
Creditanstalt	X						
Bankers Trust		X					
Iran Overseas Investment Bank		X					
First Chicago			X				
Morgan Grenfell			X				
Westdeutsche Landesbank				X			
Société Générale						X	
Crédit Suisse/First Boston						X	
Midland/Crocker National Bank							X
Royal Bank of Canada/Orion Royal							X

SOURCE: Calculated from the same sources as Table 3.5.

going international to participate in their syndicates. The big traditional lead banks reacted in a conventionally oligopolistic way: they did not give ground and competed with the newcomers by matching them on quantity and price in their established markets and by usually pursuing them into frontier markets, all with market shares in mind. The competition between the established and new lead banks in syndication contributed to the dramatic lowering of spreads, lengthening of maturities, and high volume of lending in Latin America in the early 1970s.

The Herstatt bankruptcy of mid-1974 served to temporarily concentrate power once again in the big, traditional lead banks. We saw in the previous chapter that the collapse rippled through the interbank market and stirred a crisis of confidence. Many newcomers dropped out of the market, and those that stayed had trouble obtaining deposits.[98] The banks that had been seeking to establish themselves as leaders found their position undermined, leaving the market in the hands of the big banks with an established international presence. The concentrated power is reflected in part in Table 3.5 for the years 1975 to 1977: only ten banks did the bulk of the loan syndication. With a tighter oligopolistic structure, LDCs confronted a marked increase in spreads and shorter maturities.[99]

As the crisis environment eased, banks began to return to the market in late 1977. Some institutions, such as those from Japan and Germany, returned with a full commitment to establish themselves as international leaders.[100] Their price cutting was so aggressive that the big, established U.S. banks—in a classic bid for communication and price leadership—*publicly* expressed their irritation and vowed to resist the fall in spreads.[101] They could not, although there is evidence that the bigger lenders this time gave ground to the newcomers by slowing down the pace of their own lending. This helps explain why the U.S. share of LDC lending fell from 53 percent in 1974 to about one-third in the early 1980s.[102] But the developing countries and Latin America did not notice the differences as aggressive lending by Europeans, Japanese, and U.S. regionals more than filled the gap. The displacement is exhibited in Table 3.7: notwithstanding a truly dramatic drop in the rate of expansion of lending to LDCs by U.S. banks in 1978, the overall rate of

[98] I mentioned in the last chapter that a minimum of 160 banks withdrew from the market.

[99] According to Ffrench-Davis, the average spread and maturity for a large sample of nonoil LDCs was 1.85 percent and 4.7 years in 1976, compared to the corresponding figures of 1.24 percent and 9.8 years in 1973. See Ricardo Ffrench-Davis, "International Private Lending and Borrowing Strategies of Developing Countries," *Journal of Development Planning*, no. 14 (1984), pp. 142–143.

[100] A good exposé on the Japanese expansion is found in Quek Peck Lim, "The Year of the Samurai," *Euromoney*, February 1978, pp. 10–18.

[101] In 1977 Citibank made public its intention not to lend below 1 percent. Big U.S. banks later publicly set 0.75 percent as a floor. The Europeans and Japanese would not go along. See "Buddy, Can You Borrow a Dollar?" *Euromoney*, May 1978, p. 5; and Pamela Clarke and Peter Field, "Boycott? No, They Just Won't Go Below ¾%," *Euromoney*, February 1978, p. 21.

[102] Rodney Mills, Jr., "U.S. Banks Are Losing Their Share of the Market," *Euromoney*, February 1980, pp. 50–62; and Michael Moffitt, *The World's Money* (New York: Simon & Schuster, Touchstone paperback, 1983), p. 104.

TABLE 3.7. Growth of Claims of U.S. and Non-U.S. Banks
on Developing Countries
(rates of growth)

Banks	1975–77	1978
U.S. banks	27.8	7.5
Non-U.S. banks	30.1	50.7
Total	28.9	29.7

SOURCE: Calculated from Rodney Mills, Jr., "U.S. Banks Are Losing Their Share of the
Market," *Euromoney,* February 1980, table 1.
NOTE: Information is for oil- and nonoil-exporting countries.

growth of loans to these countries remained practically identical to the
high average of 29 percent per annum recorded in 1975 to 1977. The
market, then, was certainly being deceptive, or at least not very transparent, from the borrower's perspective. In effect, even though the king-
pins of the system went into retrenchment, loan volume continued to be
extraordinarily high and spreads fell to levels similar to 1973. It was as
if nothing important had happened, when in fact the U.S. slowdown
reflected the beginning of serious exposure problems in the international financial system.

THE NATURE OF CONCENTRATION: THE BORROWERS.   Not
only were lenders concentrated but so were the countries that banks selected to lend to. Table 2.10 displays the distribution of bank exposure
in the Third World by region. Table 3.8 lists the top ten developing
country borrowers for 1975 and 1981. The former table revealed that
Latin America had absorbed almost two-thirds of the loans extended by
private banks to the developing world. Concentration also is found
when one examines the individual top borrowers. In 1975 and 1981 the
top five country borrowers absorbed 49 and 57 percent, respectively, of
all LDC exposure, while the top ten accounted for 62 and 69 percent.
Moreover, there is practically no displacement, as eight of the ten countries appeared in the top ten for both years.

After examining the two sides of a credit transaction, even a loosely
held notion of an arm's-length auction market falls apart. Borrowing
from an observation made by Jane D'Arista a number of years ago, the
private bank market in the periphery during the 1970s resembled more
of a "poker game" than textbook atomistic competition.[103] In such an

[103] Jane D'Arista, "Private Overseas Lending: Too Far, Too Fast?" in *Debt and Less
Developed Countries,* ed. Jonathan David Aronson (Boulder, Colo.: Westview Press,
1979), p. 80.

TABLE 3.8. Cumulative Participation of Top Ten Borrowers
in LDC Bank Debt, 1975 and 1981
(percentages)

1975		1981	
1. Brazil	19.1	1. Mexico	18.9
2. Mexico	36.5	2. Brazil	35.9
3. South Korea	40.8	3. Argentina	43.8
4. Argentina	44.9	4. Venezuela	51.3
5. Venezuela	48.7	5. South Korea	57.1
6. Indonesia	51.9	6. Chile	60.4
7. Peru	54.9	7. Philippines	62.8
8. Taiwan	57.5	8. Algeria	65.2
9. Philippines	60.1	9. Taiwan	67.1
10. Colombia	62.1	10. Colombia	68.7

SOURCE: Calculated from the tables in Bank for International Settlements, *International Banking Statistics 1973–1983* (Basel, April 1984).
NOTE: Excludes countries with offshore banking facilities. Also excludes Israel.

oligopolistic structure there is no reason to believe that unregulated activity will promote an efficient allocation of resources. On the contrary, a priori notions should lead one to suspect that when the market is stable underlending is occurring and the banks are using their market power to gain monopoly rents; alternatively, when the structure is destabilized by new entrants, price wars and overlending will break out and are stopped only by a crisis of some sort.

The Institutional Dynamics of Risk Evaluation

The conventional assumption of an upward-sloping supply curve for credit rests on the general theory of a cautious portfolio manager and the notion that bankers rationally evaluate risk at the margin. Furthermore, it means that the marginal cost of borrowing is rising and the market therefore imposes discipline on the borrower through appropriate price signals. As Harberger once pointed out while discussing bank lending to LDCs, the upward-sloping curve is "more plausible, more logical and more attractive" than a flat curve. According to him, this is so because it is the only way countries have an incentive to save internally and because it is consistent with a cautious international financial community that is continuously evaluating risks.[104]

However, a closer examination of the institutional dynamics of the transnational bank in the 1970s suggests that a flat curve was in fact

[104] Harberger, "Comentarios," p. 187.

plausible over at least part of a country's credit cycle. And in these circumstances a borrower would not encounter market discipline but rather permissiveness. It is here that we find the active link between country overborrowing and its necessary counterpart of bank overlending.

Risks, Prices, and Quantities   There is evidence that banks do in fact assess risk.[105] But it is interesting that when one surveys the literature of risk evaluation there is virtually no word of loan pricing.[106] Studies of what bankers actually do in practice confirm that pricing is not part of the process: the Blask survey of thirty-seven U.S. institutions found that "none of the banks in the survey use the country evaluation results in determining interest rates or fees."[107] This is a very curious situation since risks are an important component in a bank's cost structure. In effect, the evidence suggests that risk evaluation only translates itself actively into country limits, or rationing points. A bank establishes a quantitative credit ceiling for a country and then seeks to place loans within that limit.

But what about price? We saw earlier that banks sell loans in customer markets, so they are in principle price makers, not price takers.[108] Since banks do assess risks in order to establish country limits, they have some basis on which to rank potential borrowers. Logic and commercial common sense would demand that higher-ranked customers have their loans tagged with a lower price than that of more inferior-ranked clients. Since in a world of uncertainty the drawing up of fine lines among borrowers would require extraordinarily costly and time-consuming analysis of dubious accuracy, it can be expected that categories are broadly defined—formally or informally—into a few

---

[105] See Jerome Blask, "A Survey of Country Evaluation Systems in Use," in *Financing and Risk in Developing Countries*, ed. Stephen Goodman. Proceedings of a Symposium on Developing Countries' Debt sponsored by the U.S. Export-Import Bank, Washington, D.C., August 1977, pp. 77–82.

[106] Friedman, *The World Debt Dilemma*, pp. 204–282; Mentré, *The Fund and Member Countries*, pp. 7–11; Roger Anderson, "Bankers Assess Country Risks: Limits of Prudence," *Asian Finance*, 15 September 1977, pp. 46–47; "BOA Methodology," *Asian Finance*, 15 September 1977, pp. 46–47; Bruce Brackenridge, "Techniques of Credit Rating," *Asian Finance*, 15 September 1977, pp. 46–53; Stephen Goodman, "How the Big U.S. Banks Really Evaluate Sovereign Risks," *Euromoney*, February 1977, pp. 105–110; Group of Thirty, *Risks in International Lending*; T. H. Donaldson, *Lending in International Commercial Banking* (London: Macmillan Publishers, Ltd., 1983), pp. 37–52; and Jean-Claude García Zamora and Stewart Sutin, eds., *Financing Development in Latin America* (New York: Praeger, 1980).

[107] Blask, "A Survey of Country Evaluation," p. 82.

[108] Okun, *Prices and Quantities*, p. 192.

easily identifiable groups, for example, A, B, C, D, and E, in which A would be mostly OECD countries, B the relatively industrialized LDCs, C upper-income LDCs, D the poorer LDCs, and E the countries for which credit limits are zero and there are no loans to tag. The groups are sufficiently broad and obvious that there would be a considerable degree of symmetry in the implicit or explicit credit categories of different banks even if there were no communication among them. For instance, unless some bank had inside information, it could be reasonably expected that during the late 1970s it would have put Germany in A, Mexico in B, Chile in C, Haiti in D, and Grenada in E. This common-sense situation provides for a natural tiering of loan prices in the market and it is therefore not at all surprising that studies have found some correlation between country spreads and default risk, the latter defined in terms of proxy variables related to debt-servicing capacity.[109] Nevertheless, the notion of price is clearly weak and only passively linked to risk evaluation. The active link is found in credit ceilings and portfolio diversification.

In any event, to sell a loan a bank must tag its credit limit with an explicit or implicit reservation price. The price is unlikely to be written independently of what the competition is doing because most borrowers will shop a bit and compare tags on loans. The tighter the oligopolistic structure around the country's market, the more likely the bank will collude with others and price loans well above marginal costs (which include risk). If communication among the banks breaks down, or if new entrants destabilize the market, the banks' pricing decision becomes more complicated.

Assume we are in late 1973 and there are seven banks (denominated f through l) that have a willingness to establish exposure in a politically stable developing country with prospects of exporting oil and no previous borrowing experience in the eurocurrency market. In their risk evaluation the banks will actively derive their credit limits. Price is passively determined. The country is easily identifiable as a category C case which includes other borrowers that have established spreads in the market. Our new country borrower will be offered a spread that is somewhere between the highest charged for category B countries and

[109] Gershon Feder and Richard Just, "An Analysis of Credit Terms in the Eurodollar Market," *European Economic Review* 9 (1977): 221–243; Sargen, "Commercial Bank Lending," pp. 27–30; Monroe Haegele, "The Market Still Knows Best," *Euromoney*, May 1980, pp. 121–128; Laurie Goodman, "The Pricing of Syndicated Eurocurrency Credits," *Federal Reserve Bank of New York Quarterly Review* 5 (Summer 1980): pp. 39–49; and Sebastián Edwards, "LDC Foreign Borrowing and Default Risk: An Empirical Investigation," *American Economic Review* 74 (September 1984): 726–734.

the lowest charged for category D countries. Even though all the banks easily identify the new borrower as a member of category C, in the absence of communication there is no reason why their ex ante reservation price should be identical. But the common-sense tiering of risk across countries means that the price should not be too different either. This would hold true even if some banks had put the country into an adjacent category, because spreads in the market were notoriously thin: for example, during 1974 to 1981 the difference in average spreads between public borrowers in industrialized and nonoil-exporting developing countries was rarely above $1/2$ percent.[110]

The above situation is depicted in Figure 3.6 (A), where the seven banks establish the ex ante reservation price for their new credit limits. Although the banks do not entirely coincide, there is considerable bunching of prices P_0-P_3. Assuming that the banks are not fully aware of their competitors' credit limits, or of lending externalities,[111] the ex ante market supply curve will be the sum of the individual curves and form a step function that is relatively flat (Figure 3.6 [B]).

The ex ante market supply curve could be the ex post market supply curve if all banks stuck to their ex ante reservation price. This could be the outcome if demand were large enough to absorb the banks' credit limits as in DD of Figure 3.6 (B). But if supply were constrained by demand, as in the case of $D'D'$, sticking to an ex ante reservation price above P_0 would preclude a bank from occupying its credit limits. Thus, unless the country was badly informed, or a bank had a rock-solid client relationship, institutions h through l would have to compete and lower their price to P_0 or confront open credit limits and no loans.

During the 1970s, most banks would have been highly tempted to

[110] From data in table 4 of Folkerts-Landau, "The Changing Role of International Bank Lending."

[111] The assumption that the bank is unaware of lending externalities is reasonable. First, the data on external debt in developing countries suffered from many deficiencies during much of the 1970s. Data on public debt appeared with a one- or two-year lag. Little or no information was available on external debt in the private sector, and nobody knew what the accumulation of short-term debt was. Moreover, publicized eurocredit syndication did not cover all bank transactions. In my study on Peru I found that the World Bank's tapes on publicized credits missed 20 percent of the medium-term loans. Ricardo Ffrench-Davis has commented to me that in his study of bank lending to fourteen LDCs, World Bank tapes on publicized eurocredits captured only 30 percent of total lending (including short-term) in the late 1970s. Second, even as data improved the banks' credit decisions did not react quickly to evident debt buildups. A. Lamfalussy of the Bank for International Settlements attributes the banks' insulation from the data in part to competition and marketing considerations. See his "Monetary Reform," *Economist*, 26 October 1985, p. 6. I will examine this faulty transmission of data into credit decisions in the next section of the chapter.

FIGURE 3.6. The Market's Formation around a Borrower.

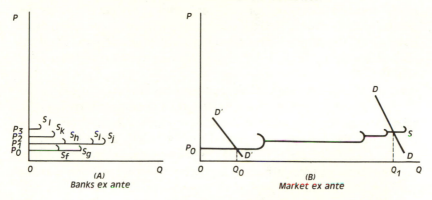

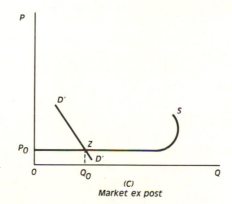

NOTE: The three graphs are not drawn on the same scale for reasons of space.
SYMBOLS:
S = supply schedule P = price
D = demand schedule Q = quantity

reduce their price to P_0. First, since the ex ante reservation price is not actively derived from risk evaluation, the whole notion of the "correct price" is somewhat vague to the lending institutions. Second, the difference between P_0 and P_{1-3} is seemingly not large. Third, in the case of new, virgin borrowers like our oil exporter, the bank has no significant outstanding claims on the country so that the risk of lending is minimal and the full burden of risk can easily be placed on the credit limit itself. Fourth, lack of definition about the correct price is fertile ground for marketing instincts to take over; it is well known that many banks during the 1970s had a tendency to see a country loan not as a financial instrument with a yield but as a market share.[112] Fifth, a bank could hardly rely on bad information or client loyalty to cement a deal. On the one hand, banks were aggressively soliciting loans so that shopping costs fell drastically for borrowers. On the other, countries did not display strong loyalty in the 1970s and were known to go for the cheapest deal.[113]

If the banks did decide to compete and match the price of banks f and g at P_0, our potential oil exporter would face a flat supply curve over the relevant range of borrowing as depicted in Figure 3.6 (C). Thus, when one moves away from an ahistorical general theory to a more institutional focus, it is clear that a flat supply curve may in fact be a more logical, plausible, and attractive depiction of the transnational credit market of the 1970s.

It is also interesting to note that our equilibrium price P_0 may not be stable. Even if banks h through l match f and g's price P_0, the market remains constrained by demand. If the banks are concerned about market shares, they will struggle to get a piece of terrain in OQ_0. Moreover, soliciting by the banks will lower the borrower's shopping costs and make the country's demand curve more elastic. The incentive to cut price is very strong and the supply curve shifts downward, causing price to fall, while loan volume rises.

This is a plausible explanation of what happened to many LDCs during the 1970s when they entered the eurocurrency market for the first time as virgin borrowers. The framework is particularly suitable for small and medium-sized countries. This is because in the 1970s banks f through l were loan syndicates instead of individual institutions. It is clear that in an aggressive market the amount of resources that could be mobilized for a country via this mechanism was enormous compared to its absorptive capacity. With potential supply well in excess of its immediate needs, a country could receive deceptive price signals as the marginal cost of borrowing was constant or falling. And as Henry Wallich of the U.S. Federal Reserve has pointed out, when countries receive money that easily, they can't help but think that their economic policies are "not all that bad."[114]

Thus, through much of the country's credit cycle the market's signals could be permissive, or at best ambiguous. Moreover, if a bank began to perceive problems in the debtor country it had no incentive to "blow the

---

[112] Henry Wallich, "Professor Wallich Presents a Perspective on the External Debt Situation," *Press Review* (Bank for International Settlements), 14 January 1985, p. 4.

[113] "Buddy, Can You Borrow a Dollar?" *Euromoney*, May 1978, pp. 11–12.

[114] Wallich, "Professor Wallich on External Debt," p. 3.

whistle." To the contrary, individual rationality would dictate that it remain quiet; this is because the bank's exposure reduction is facilitated if less-informed new entrants come into the country market to take its place. The market, then, seems to have been capable of giving clear warnings and imposing discipline only when the borrower approached the credit limits of *the banking system as a whole* (the positive sloped portion of the supply curve in Figure 3.6 [C]). But by this time the credit cycle could be mature and dependence on debt could be excessive; the sudden, unexpected rise of prices and restriction of loan volume could thus set off a debt crisis and socially inefficient forced adjustment. I will elaborate considerably on this issue in the next chapter.

My framework is strongly underpinned by the notion that when Latin American countries initiated their credit cycle with private banks they were not rationed. In other words, credit markets were constrained by demand rather than supply. All evidence points in this direction.

Rationing cannot be measured directly because it requires information about ex ante demand functions. But Jaffee has suggested a proxy that can be modified and used for my analysis. According to him, there is a positive relation between the degree of credit rationing and the proportion of total credit granted to risk-free prime customers.[115] For our purposes developed countries can be considered to be prime borrowers. According to Table 3.9, there was a generalized trend of sharply declining shares for industrialized countries in total bank lending during the 1970s.[116] This indicates that market dynamics were not in the direction of rationing.

Second, rationing generally means that the price charged for credit should be relatively high and stable; that is, it won't fall because demand is pushing against credit limits and it won't rise much to clear the market in order to protect against adverse selection.[117] In contrast, Ffrench-Davis's analysis of a sample of fourteen LDC borrowers of diverse size and resource endowments (oil and nonoil) showed great movement of spreads (and maturities) over the period 1972 to 1980. In the borrower's market of 1972 to 1974 average spreads evolved from 1.43 percent to 1.17 percent. They then rose to as high as 1.72 percent in the lender's market of 1975/1976, only to dip to under 1 percent in the borrower's market of 1977 to 1980. Maturities showed similar

[115] Jaffee, *Credit Rationing and the Commercial Loan Market*, pp. 83–88.

[116] Please note that Table 3.9 uses a different source from that for Table 2.9 of Chapter Two, which explains the discrepancies in the estimates.

[117] This cannot be pushed too far, however. Spreads also move with the level of base interest rates and their variation. See Laurie Goodman, "Pricing of Syndicated Credits," p. 46.

TABLE 3.9. Distribution of Eurocurrency Loans by Economic Region (millions of dollars)

Region	1970	1971	1972	1973	1974	1975	1976	1977	1978	1979	1980	1981	1982
Industrialized countries	4246	2601	4097	13783	20683	7231	11254	17201	28952	27248	39100	86022	42571
Developing countries	446	1286	2414	7288	7318	11098	15017	20852	37290	47964	35054	45264	41519
Other countries and inter-national organizations	38	76	285	779	1262	2662	2577	3584	3927	7600	3238	2093	925
Total	4730	3963	6796	21851	29263	20992	28849	41637	70169	82812	77392	133379	85015
Memorandum item: %													
Industrialized/total	90	66	60	63	71	34	39	41	41	33	51	65	50
Developing/total	9	32	36	33	25	53	52	50	53	58	45	34	49

SOURCE: Morgan Guaranty Trust Company, *World Financial Markets*, 1970–1977: March 1978, p. 4; 1978–1980: July 1981, p. 12; and 1981–1982: January 1985, p. 15.

TABLE 3.10. Average Spreads and Maturities for Fourteen LDCS

Variable	1972	1973	1974	1975	1976	1977	1978	1979	1980
Spreads (%)									
Total 14 countries	1.43	1.15	1.17	1.69	1.72	1.55	1.17	0.83	0.86
Oil exporters	1.39	1.09	1.05	1.61	1.58	1.36	1.05	0.79	0.66
Oil importers	1.44	1.24	1.26	1.80	1.85	1.72	1.30	0.87	1.01
Maturities (years)									
Total 14 countries	6.7	9.8	8.7	5.5	5.1	6.2	8.3	9.0	7.9
Oil exporters	6.3	9.8	8.9	5.5	5.7	6.5	7.8	8.0	7.6
Oil importers	7.1	9.8	8.5	5.5	4.7	5.9	9.0	10.0	8.2

SOURCE: Ricardo Ffrench-Davis, "International Private Lending and Borrowing Strategies of Developing Countries," *Journal of Development Planning*, no. 14 (1984), pp. 142–143.
NOTE: The fourteen LDCs are Algeria, Argentina, Brazil, Chile, Colombia, Costa Rica, Ivory Coast, Malawi, Mexico, Morocco, Niger, Philippines, Republic of Korea, and Yugoslavia.

movement, reaching highs of nearly ten years in the borrower's market and lows of five years in the lender's market (Table 3.10).

It is also revealing to note that spreads and maturities showed practically no tightening in the face of the historic rise of oil prices in late 1973 that initiated petrodollar recycling.[118] Moreover, the dramatic tightening of terms and shift to a lender's market in mid-1974 was set off not by reduced global liquidity, or by problems in developing countries, but rather by the crisis in the interbank market related to the poor foreign exchange currency speculation and subsequent bankruptcy of Bankhaus Herstatt of Germany and Franklin National of the United States.

Another sign that rationing is not taking place in markets is when banks begin to do things that they traditionally profess not to like to do. The traditional preferences have been well summarized by Aronson: "Banks prefer lending for cash flow-generating projects which will allow borrowers to meet their obligations. They prefer not to finance consumption and infrastructure, are uneasy about financing payments deficits, and would rather not refinance previous loans."[119]

[118] Ibid., p. 44.
[119] Jonathan David Aronson, *Money and Power* (Beverly Hills, Calif.: Sage Publications, Inc., 1977), p. 177. A commercial banker makes a similar observation; see Donaldson, *Lending in Commercial Banking*, p. 45.

It is difficult to examine this dictum carefully because there is very little disaggregated data available on bank lending to LDCs. But it is well known that in their urge to grow and gain a worldwide presence, banks often abandoned their stated principles of conservative banking. This to some extent is demonstrated by the eagerness with which they undertook balance of payments financing. In the next chapter I will offer concrete evidence of how banks during the 1970s pursued financing that they traditionally professed to dislike.

Finally, we turn to some anecdotal evidence that nevertheless pretty much summarizes the situation. Angel Gurría, the long-time head of Mexico's Office of Public Credit, has observed the following concerning bank lending to his own country before the crisis:

> The banks were hot to get in. All the banks in the U.S. and Europe and Japan stepped forward. They showed no foresight. They didn't do any credit analysis. It was wild. In August 1979, for instance, Bank of America planned a loan of $1 billion. They figured they would put up $350 million themselves, and sell off the rest. As it turned out they only had to put up $100 million themselves. They raised $2.5 billion on the loan in total.[120]

The general thrust of Gurría's statement has been echoed much too often by other serious Latin American authorities to be dismissed.[121] In effect, whether big or small, rich or poor, once a country attracted the attention of the bankers it could become overwhelmed with offers of credit. For a significant number of LDC borrowers it is likely that an upward-sloping supply curve was not to be found until it was too late; the market was capable of imposing discipline only when the situation had already become critical.

Some general indication of the problem can be observed in Table 3.11, which displays the positions of Latin American countries in the creditworthiness rankings of *Euromoney*. The rankings are based on the price (spread and amortization period) charged by the banks to borrowers for loans in the eurocurrency market; the lower the price, the higher the creditworthiness ranking. It can be seen that just before the explosion of the debt crisis only three countries (Brazil, Panama, and Venezuela) had been receiving clear and unambiguous price signals concerning deterioration in their image of creditworthiness; most of the

---

[120] Cited in Joseph Kraft, *The Mexican Rescue* (New York: Group of Thirty, 1984), pp. 19–20.

[121] Several interesting quotes to this effect can be found in "Do the Bankers Take the Risks?" *Latin American Weekly Report*, 25 September 1981, pp. 10–11.

TABLE 3.11. *Euromoney* Country Risk Ratings
(ranks)

Country	1979	1980	1981	Change in Creditworthiness 1981/1979
Argentina	37	24	38	− 2.7%
Bolivia			63	
Brazil	47	53	62	− 31.9
Colombia	40	21	26	35.0
Costa Rica	48	55		
Cuba			45	
Chile	41	38	34	17.1
Ecuador	50	42	39	22.0
Mexico	34	13	27	20.6
Panama	43	52	56	− 30.2
Peru	64	55	47	26.6
Uruguay	53	36	33	37.7
Venezuela	22	51	61	−177.3
Total countries in survey	58	69	69	

SOURCE: *Euromoney,* February 1981, pp. 66–79, and February 1982, pp. 46–51.
NOTE: *Euromoney* rates countries on the basis of spreads and maturities contracted in international loan syndication. The lower the rank, the higher the evaluation of creditworthiness; thus a rank of 1 is the highest score.

countries had been encountering signals indicative of enhanced credit-worthiness in the market.

The Quality of Risk Assessment   We saw that the only active link with risk evaluation was found in the development of credit limits. But even this link was weak, making loan volume very elastic.

One general problem was that the banks' willingness to lend often exceeded their actual capacity to evaluate risks. Lending to developing countries had taken off long before country risk evaluation became a household word in banking. Indeed, country risk evaluation only came into vogue in the mid-seventies as a response to congressmen's and bank shareholders' concern about a "LDC debt problem" following petro-dollar recycling. Thus, while loan volume was already soaring, most banks were still groping to find the fundamentals of the art of country creditworthiness analysis.

The problem was exacerbated by the fact that so many lenders were internationally inexperienced new entrants. Many of these banks felt compelled by competition to lend abroad yet were in no position to invest in information and therefore were thinly staffed.[122] Indeed, they often lent to countries they had never seen or visited.[123] As mentioned earlier, the inexperienced tried to overcome these bottlenecks by relying on the information provided by the lead banks of loan syndicates, which had invested in information. But the "placement memorandum" prepared by the lead banks for potential participants was little more than a sophisticated tourist guide prepared as a sales document rather than a serious analytical statement on the country.[124] Most participants in fact joined the syndicate basically on the good name and prestige of the lead bank, which they presumed had done its own in-house confidential analysis.

This might seem like an efficient arrangement involving specialization: a big bank invests in information and for a fee organizes a syndicate that other banks of less international stature can join. One obvious drawback, however, is that independence of decision making—a fundamental requisite for efficient resource allocation—breaks down and there is greater likelihood of herd instincts developing. The problem of "following the crowd" was further enhanced by the concentration in the market of lead banks. As Sampson has pointed out, syndication depends on about one hundred people in London who all know each other and hate to be left out.[125]

Another drawback related to specialization is that the lead bank's own decision to lend could often be a muddled one. First, in the 1970s, data on country debt, the balance of payments, et cetera, came with lag time of a year or two. As Guttentag and Herring have pointed out, in the absence of reliable information there was a tendency to look to what

[122] For instance, one relatively large East Coast regional bank had a significant exposure in Latin America, but only one economist was responsible for analyzing borrowers. It was frequent even in big internationally oriented banks to have one economist covering several of the institution's country clients. This thin coverage contrasts with an international organization such as the World Bank, which assigns one economist to each country in which it does business. The information is based on interviews.

[123] Gwynne's article ("Adventures in the Loan Trade") provides good documentation of just how awkward a small bank's insertion into the international arena could be.

[124] Christine Bogdanowicz-Bindert and Paul Sacks, "The Role of Information: Closing the Barn Door?" in *Uncertain Future: Commercial Banks and the Third World*, ed. Richard Feinberg and Valeriana Kallab (London: Transaction Books, 1984), p. 71.

[125] Sampson, *The Money Lenders*, p. 145.

one's peers were doing.[126] "Staying in the pack" also protected a bank from criticism of its bank supervisors because in the 1970s few ever dared to question the "judgment of the market."[127] Moreover, if something bad should happen to a bank, it would have lots of company and this would likely induce bailout measures by public authorities. Mexico is a good example of where this strategy paid off.[128]

Second, the banks could have been excessively cavalier about the risks of lending due to a fashionable argument during the 1970s to the effect that, unlike corporations, sovereign governments cannot legally go bankrupt and therefore are always around to pay their debts. But as Kuczynski has correctly observed, while countries are always around to pay, there is no guarantee that they will pay, a lesson the banks are learning today.[129]

Third, as I pointed out earlier in this chapter, a large transnational bank's decision about where and how much to lend goes beyond a narrow default risk-return calculus on that transaction. Market shares are an important decision variable for a bank, and the certain loss of a market today may outweigh the uncertain loss of a default tomorrow. Also, a medium-term loan is only one facet of the bank's business in a specific country market and therefore can be treated as a "loss leader."[130] The big banks' credit allocation also is influenced by home government foreign policy.[131] This latter dimension was seen in Peru when the big U.S. banks cooperated with the Nixon administration's boycott of the Velasco regime. We will see later that, when the U.S. administration made peace with Velasco in 1974, it was these same banks that organized syndicated loans for Peru to help it finance the compensation of nationalized U.S. firms that was stipulated in the bilateral agreement

[126] Jack Guttentag and Richard Herring, "Commercial Bank Lending to Developing Countries: From Overlending to Underlending to Structural Reform," in *International Debt and the Developing Countries*, ed. Gordon Smith and John Cuddington (Washington, D.C.: World Bank, 1985), p. 134.

[127] Lawrence Brainard, "More Lending to the Third World?: A Banker's View," in *Uncertain Future: Commercial Banks and the Third World*, ed. Richard Feinberg and Valeriana Kallab (London: Transaction Books, 1984), p. 35.

[128] For details of the rescue see Kraft, *Mexican Rescue*.

[129] Pedro-Pablo Kuczynski, "Latin American Debt," *Foreign Affairs* 61 (Winter 1982/1983): 352.

[130] Pecchioli, *The Internationalization of Banking*, pp. 49–50; and Christopher Korth, "The Eurocurrency Markets," in *The International Banking Handbook*, ed. William Baughn and Donald Mandich (Homewood, Ill.: Dow Jones-Irwin, 1983), p. 32. Specifically, in my study of Peru I found that some foreign currency bank loans to the government at low rates were linked to the opening of new branch office networks in Lima. See Devlin, *Transnational Banks and Peru*, pp. 174–184.

[131] See Spindler, *Politics of Credit*, for the case of Japanese and German banks.

between the two governments. Finally, a bank also may help organize or participate in a syndicate simply to maintain ongoing relationships with other friendly banks.[132]

Fourth, the big banks often were not structured in a way to effectively translate risk evaluation (however deficient) into their credit decisions. For instance, the Blask survey found that banks did not check their country risk evaluation against actual experience and tended not to subject ongoing creditworthiness analysis to independent evaluation within or outside the institution.[133] This lack of follow-up reinforced internal incentive systems geared toward management's preoccupation about growth, in which successful loan placement was rewarded more than successful prediction of loan repayment. High mobility in a fast-growing industry where product exchange and payment are not simultaneous also allowed bankers to avoid accountability: by the time a loan went bad the individual would be a manager in another institution.[134] Accountability was further diffused by most banks' efforts to decentralize in order to make fast credit decisions and thereby not lose a deal.[135] The general institutional inability to translate risk evaluation into credit exposure and prices is well captured by Alexander's observation that "some bankers were so afraid of missing out that during lunch hours they even empowered their secretaries to promise $5 million or $10 million as part of any billion-dollar loan package for Brazil or Mexico."[136]

Fifth, a lead bank's motives for promoting a syndicate were not necessarily symmetric with those of the participants, which relied on the leader's assessment. As noted earlier, at least one-fifth of a lead bank's return on a loan came from fees that were paid up front and risk free. This provided an incentive to churn loan volume.[137] Furthermore, the lead bank's ability to negotiate fee income was strongest in the less-attractive markets. While the greater fee income could have covered the greater risk for the lead bank, the participants in the syndicated loan assumed the same risk without benefit of the fee. Another consideration is that the big lead banks often were heavily committed in their markets;

---

[132] Group of Thirty, *Risks in International Lending*, pp. 8–9.

[133] Blask, "A Survey of Country Evalaution," p. 80.

[134] Gwynne's story ("Adventures in the Loan Trade") lends credibility to these points.

[135] Donaldson, *Lending in Commercial Banking*, p. 90.

[136] Charles Alexander, "Jumbo Loan, Jumbo Risks," *Time*, 3 December 1984, p. 33. Dalamaide discovered the same phenomenon, which he called "receptionist banking" (*Debt Shock*, pp. 44–45).

[137] When spreads are falling, all banks have an additional incentive to raise volume in order to maintain earnings growth.

thus new loans generated positive externalities for them that were not enjoyed by the less-committed banks that were invited to participate in the syndicate.

Sixth, should the loans turn bad, the big banks enjoyed certain advantages not available to their smaller counterparts. On the one hand, they had the implicit security of the lender-of-last-resort facilities. On the other, they could buy the smaller banks' loans at large discounts; this could come about either through purchases in secondary markets or takeover bids in the event that the smaller institution encountered financial difficulties.[138]

Finally, it is possible that the market's whole perception of risk during the 1970s was miscalculated. This is what Guttenberg and Herring have called "disaster myopia."[139] They argue that defaults are low-frequency events and can be assessed at best by subjective probabilities. Borrowing from psychology, they point out that individuals tend to formulate their subjective probabilities from the events easiest to recall, giving their expectations an "availability bias."[140] In times of prolonged prosperity banks can thus sharply lower their subjective probabilities of problems or default. Likewise, when defaults do appear, they can overreact.[141]

The problem is further complicated by the tendency of individuals to establish thresholds in which in practice they at some time give a low-frequency event a probability of zero. This can cause neglect of potential hazards that in fact can be identified. Moreover, even when these hazards become so obvious that they cannot be neglected, an individual

[138] William Darity, Jr., "Loan Pushing: Doctrine and Theory," International Finance Discussion Papers, No. 253 (Washington, D.C.: U.S. Federal Reserve Board, February 1985), p. 47.

[139] They have developed this rather extensively in Guttentag and Herring, "Commercial Bank Lending to Developing Countries," pp. 132–134; and Guttentag and Herring, "Credit Rationing and Financial Disorder," pp. 1360–1364.

[140] A good example of this is the March 1985 earthquake in Chile. This country is prone to quakes. However, a long hiatus in quakes, coupled with new technology, gave rise to the construction of many high-rise apartment towers. After the 1985 earthquake there was a virtual halt in the construction of high rises, and the more traditional three-story apartment dwellings began to reappear in the market as the favorite new format. By 1987, however, high-rise towers were once again back in vogue with the upper income groups as memories of earthquake damage faded.

[141] Keynes also has referred to the availability bias without calling it that in his analysis of firms' investment decisions. See John Maynard Keynes, The General Theory of Employment, Interest, and Money (London: Harvest/HBJ, 1964), p. 45. Minsky has taken the general Keynesian framework and applied it to his development of the hypothesis about financial instability. See Hyman Minsky, Can "It" Happen Again? (Armonk, N.Y.: M. E. Sharpe, Inc., 1982).

may effectively ignore them because they show that past decisions were incorrect. (Technically this is termed "cognitive dissonance.")

While only a hypothesis, there is enough circumstantial evidence to make Guttentag and Herring's arguments plausible. There was a long postwar expansion in which economic recession and defaults dropped into the background. The potential availability bias in the assessment of risk was enhanced by the retirement of managers who had lived through the Great Depression and their replacement by young executives who had grown up in prosperity. At the macrolevel bankers overlooked the arguments of a number of analysts that pointed to a structural slow-down in world economic growth in the 1970s, which simultaneously contributed to debt accumulation and undermined the prospects of it ever being repaid.[142] At the microlevel we will find in the next chapter that bankers could overlook deterioration in key economic performance indicators of their country clients and continue lending eagerly until a crisis of major proportions was inevitable. Bankers also overlooked the fact that much of the finance in Latin America was to some extent similar to that of a speculative Ponzi unit: many countries depended on new loans to pay interest. If the rollover of debt service were broken by a crisis of confidence, payments would depend on the political feasibility of imposing a deep recession on the debtor countries. When criticized about their lending patterns in LDCs, bankers invariably pointed to the relatively small loan losses on international banking.[143] This, of course, was not a very good argument given that lending to LDCs was a relatively new phenomenon and there are long time-lags between disbursement and repayment of debt.

Some have argued contrary to the availability bias hypothesis and insisted on the existence of entirely rational markets. Folkerts-Landau has recently posited that banks did lower their perceptions of risk in the 1970s, but this was a rational response to developments in the market that made reschedulings rather than default the likely outcome of repayment problems.[144] There is clearly some truth in Folkerts-Landau's argument, but it cannot explain the remarkable compression of spreads

[142] See, for instance, Ernest Mandel, *The Second Slump*, trans. Jon Rothschild (London: New Left Books, Verso edition, 1980); Bank for International Settlements, *Forty-Eighth Annual Report* (Basel, 1978); and W. Arthur Lewis, "The Slowing Down of the Engine of Growth," *American Economic Review* 70 (September 1980): 555–564.

[143] See Friedman, *The Emerging Role of Private Banks*, p. 55; and G. A. Costanzo, "Statement" before the Subcommittee on Financial Institutions Supervision, Regulation, and Insurance in the U.S. House Banking, Finance, and Urban Affairs Committee, 6 April 1977, p. 7.

[144] Folkerts-Landau, "The Changing Role of International Bank Lending," pp. 7–10.

between countries and their overall fall to levels that sometimes put into doubt the coverage of administrative costs. In effect, countries today rarely default on loans, but the ability to reschedule doesn't mean that banks necessarily will be repaid. We have seen this already; despite reschedulings, the value of bank shares quickly fell in the initial years of the crisis to discount future losses.[145] Moreover, by 1987 those losses began to appear: with Latin American loans trading in secondary markets at deep discounts, many banks were obliged to aggressively increase loan loss reserves on their Latin debt, with a consequent hit on earnings.

SUMMARY AND CONCLUSIONS

I observed in earlier chapters that there are many ways to interpret the developments on the supply side of the international banking market during the 1970s, and they are not all necessarily incompatible with each other. In fact, one can turn to traditional portfolio theory to understand events: banks pursued higher differential profit rates on overseas lending as compared to their domestic markets. The differential arose out of many developments, such as:

—the rise of the unregulated euromarkets, where there were no required reserves, lower tax rates, wholesale scale economies, et cetera;
—lower perceived risks due to technical innovations, such as floating rate loans, which passed interest risk on to the borrower; syndicated credits, which allowed banks to freely communicate with each other and lend in bloc; cross-default clauses, which prevented selective default on the part of the borrowers; and improved communication and computation systems;
—strong postwar expansions of world trade and investments;
—crisis in the center, which lowered rates of return in domestic markets and contributed to growing world liquidity through the response of anticyclical fiscal and monetary policy;
—OPEC policy that increased the demand and supply of finance for borrowing countries.

All these points are important and relevant to our problem. But they abstract from market structures and institutional considerations. Ex-

---

[145] Kyle and Sachs have found a correlation between the evolution of U.S. bank shares and exposure in LDCs. See Steven Kyle and Jeffrey Sachs, "Developing Country Debt and the Market Value of Large Commercial Banks," Working Paper No. 1470 (Cambridge, Mass.: National Bureau of Economic Research, September 1984).

amination of these latter factors can enrich the analysis and also aid policy prescription.

We found that portfolio theory could not capture all the dimensions of lending in the 1970s. In particular, it focuses on the short-term default risk-return calculus of a cold and standoffish investor. It can explain the phenomenon of overlending only by faulty risk perception on the part of an individual investor.

However, the modern bank does not fit comfortably into the traditional mold of a portfolio investor. A bank is much more of a "firm" than an investor. Banks are not arm's-length price takers but rather price makers, as most of their business is done in customer markets where the client relationship is important. In effect, the banking firm actively markets financial services at the retail and wholesale level; in contrast to the distant portfolio investor, personal salesmanship and marketing expertise are key components of modern banking. The traditional vision of a reserved banker sitting at his or her desk awaiting loan applications for assessment is simply not a proper reflection of postwar banking ethos.

The idea of an arm's-length portfolio investor also does not properly capture the dynamic of the client relationship on which customer markets thrive. And the banker's client relationship is probably the most intimate of any economic agent because the loan is an unusual product for which exchange takes place long before payment is realized. Thus firsthand knowledge about, and trust of, the borrower is paramount. Looked at from another angle, a client relationship is an investment that enters into the profit equation of a bank. Therefore, not lending to an established client may often in fact have costs that meet or exceed the costs of default risk should the loans be made. In all but a very mature credit cycle the bank is inclined to lend because the certain loss of an established client will probably outweigh the possible and uncertain costs of default in the distant future. In essence, for valued customers, banks are inherently forthcoming.

But information gathering also enjoys externalities and economies of scale. The value of a client relation goes beyond that relation itself and extends into a systemwide network designed to assess profit opportunities. Thus banks are interested in maintaining a market presence, or share. Through much of a credit cycle, then, a concern for market presence can override the costs of default risk.

In sum, it may be that the modern bank cannot afford to behave like a classical portfolio manager guided primarily by concern for default risk. Except in the mature part of the credit cycle, default risk is usually not an immediate threat. The more immediate threat may be that if the bank does not grow in response to its clients' needs and external economies of scale, it may find its commercial viability in jeopardy because of a takeover by a more aggressive competitor. Slow growth also may eliminate it from eligibility for lender-of-last-resort facilities.

The popular view of the bank as portfolio investor also was often accompanied by the notion that unregulated international banking approached the classic efficiency of textbook atomistic markets. But the modern bank is not an atomistic specialized institution. Rather it is a global firm that is highly diversified around the world with multiple products and objectives. A loan placement in any given market at any given time does not necessarily conform to economically efficient credit allocation but rather is tied up in the global business strategy of a transnational bank. A credit in and of itself may be a loss leader, protecting other interests in the market concerned, or interests even outside that market. Nor is there even conclusive evidence that banks are global profit maximizers, as competing theories related to alternative goals of market stability, bureaucratization, sales maximization, et cetera could be employed to explain lending strategies in the 1970s.

The frequent notion of the 1970s that unregulated international banking markets approached textbook efficiency was indeed seriously misplaced. The economies of scale in banking reward size, and market dynamics—notwithstanding the hundreds of lenders in the international market of the 1970s—were determined in a relatively concentrated industry. Oligopoly is in fact the market structure of international banking, and the expansion of the 1970s must be viewed through this optic and not that of atomistic economic agents.

The industry was concentrated in the 1960s with a handful of big U.S. money-center banks dominating international credit flows. During the 1970s the rapid growth of liquidity fueled the expansion of the eurocurrency market's interbank market. Access to this informal market became very easy and helped banks overcome one of the major barriers to entry into the international market: access to dollar deposits to support asset growth. The advent of the syndicated credit reduced another barrier: investments in information. In effect, smaller and/or inexperienced banks found that they "could avoid" this investment by relying on lead institutions to provide what they felt to be the necessary information for lending decisions. Syndication, cross-default clauses, floating-rate loans, et cetera also lowered perceived risks and hence the costs of international operations. In effect, the average cost curve of the industry fell sharply, permitting the entry of new lenders that competed with the club of U.S. banks that had controlled the international market in the 1950s and 1960s. But even with the new entrants the basic features of the market remained concentrated and oligopolistic.

In this perspective one would evaluate the 1970s phenomenon of rising credit volume and falling credit prices not as the reflection of healthy competition in an atomistic market but rather as the outcome of an oligopolistic price war between the giant established international banks and newcomers from the United States, Japan, Europe, and the Arab world. In a destabilized oligopolistic market there is no reason to presume a priori that credit was being allocated efficiently. This, of course, is aside from the other considerations outlined above.

What difference does it make whether the international banking market was atomistic or oligopolistic? In equilibrium, the major difference is that price is higher than marginal costs. But given the economies of scale in banking, a dynamic assessment may make oligopoly a more socially desirable outcome in any event. In other words, overall welfare may be improved with some degree of concentration in banking.

Both atomistic and oligopolistic markets are subject to crisis and overlending. But the magnitude of crisis may be larger in the latter structure. On the one hand, there is more interdependence of decision making in oligopoly, which can make the industry more prone to herd instincts and concentration in certain markets that are considered "safe" by the industry leaders. On the other hand, given the size and diversification of the transnational bank, "mistakes" can perpetuate themselves for a longer period of time because the big bank is more capable of covering losses in one activity with profits from another activity and because the big institutions can count on bailouts from their governments should the losses become unmanageable. In sum, when the market is destabilized by price competition among established leaders, or by new entrants, both the magnitude and temporal length of a disequilibrium can be enormous.

In contrast, in an atomistic market banks would be more accountable for their short-run decisions, and mistakes might be manifest sooner, bringing more timely corrective responses in the market. It is unlikely that an atomistic market would have generated the concentration ratios of the early 1980s, where loans outstanding to some Latin American countries were 20 to 50 percent of the capital of lending institutions. However, once a crisis appears, an atomistic market would be much less able to manage it. Comparing the 1980s with the 1930s shows that an oligopolistic market is more adroit at creditor coordination, which helps to avoid, or at least postpone, technical defaults and open capital losses. But at the same time we will see in a later chapter that in rescuing themselves, the big banks pass a disproportionate amount of the cost of the problem on to the debtors and the international public sector.

On balance, it would seem that the problem of the 1970s was not the oligopolistic structure per se but excess liquidity, coupled with the lack of banking regulation that permitted uncontrolled entry and cutthroat competition on loan pricing and volume. It may be that international markets should be modeled more after domestic markets and not vice versa.[146]

We have seen that the modern transnational bank has many concerns, of which default is only one. Evidence suggests that through much of the 1970s default risk and its assessment was only a latent input in credit decisions, as other objectives held more sway within the institutional hierarchy of the banks. It therefore would not be at all surprising if the market did not give borrowers clear signals and did not impose discipline on them. The technical literature stresses that markets are rationed. When markets are rationed there is systematic underlending, at least to some borrowers. The literature does not give much attention to what happens to unrationed borrowers, but if some borrowers are underlent to, then it could be suspected that others might be overlent to.

Indeed, by examining how banks institutionally examine risk and price loans, we found that unrationed borrowers may face a flat rather than the conventionally assumed upward-sloping supply curve. In these circumstances a borrower encounters constant marginal costs for loans and has less incentive to save internally. Moreover, in a demand-constrained market with an unstable oligopolistic structure, equilibrium is hard to obtain as the banks compete for shares in the constrained market. Thus, through much of the credit cycle a country can encounter falling marginal costs and rising credit volume. It is only when the credit cycle is well advanced that default risk becomes an active ingredient in credit decisions and an upward-sloping supply curve is unambiguously experienced; but by then the country can be highly dependent on debt and the sudden rise in price and restricted loan volume can generate crisis.

Evidence suggests that Latin America was not rationed in the 1970s, and therefore during part of the credit cycle some countries could have faced flat supply curves that were shifting downwards. In these circumstances the debt buildup for the countries would be entirely too easy. Moreover, credit prices/volume could signal that their macroeconomic

---

[146] It could be argued that unregulated markets and international banks allocate resources efficiently only over the long term. This is certainly plausible. But it also begs the issue of the costs of the market's short-term mistakes and who is to bear them. Indeed, the market's supposed long-term efficiency is small consolation to Latin American debtors or northern taxpayers who are gradually being forced to assume more of the costs of the problem. The whole purpose of modern public policy is to assuage the inherent tendency of private markets to push themselves to extreme limits and crisis.

policies were being viewed well by the market, even if the countries pursued development strategies that were inconsistent with sustained access to private bank loans. Indeed, the market generally would not be able to signal problems until a crisis was nearly inevitable.

We also found that the banks' risk evaluation itself left much to be desired. Sovereign risk evaluation was new to the banks, and most of the lending to LDCs was undertaken when these institutions were still groping for the fundamentals of assessment. Banks also could have suffered from "disaster myopia," which induced them to systematically underestimate the risks of international lending. Even when the internal risk evaluation was effective, many banks were not structured internally to absorb the assessment into their credit decisions.

All the preceding analysis points to a credit system in the 1970s that was prone to lend too much to Latin America from the standpoint of traditional criteria of economic efficiency. This does not mean that banks were foolish; indeed, their international lending has proven to be highly profitable to them. But for society as a whole, and for Latin America in particular, it is not clear that welfare was raised by the great banking expansion of the 1970s. A manifestly positive event—the revitalization of private capital markets and their incorporation of Latin American countries—was abused by the lenders, their governments, and the borrowers, so that the whole system became overextended. It is in this light that my analysis can perhaps begin to provide some technical foundation to the Latin American's intuitively correct argument of coresponsibility in the debt crisis.

Finally, it must be mentioned that the concentration of the debt crisis in Latin America may not be unrelated to market structure. The leaders in the oligopolistic market—especially in the initial phase of the 1970s expansion—were U.S. banks. These institutions have traditionally been most comfortable in Latin America. To the extent that the credit market was subject to interdependent decision making and follow-the-leader psychology, Latin America may have been the developing region subject to the most intensive marketing pressures of the banks. This externally generated permissive environment did not mix well with the region's own internal permissive instincts, giving rise to the crisis we know so well today.

CHAPTER FOUR

The Expansive Phase of
an LDC Credit Cycle

IN THE PRECEDING CHAPTER we saw that, contrary to conventional assumptions, the modern bank can be a very forthcoming lender. Moreover, when the market is forming itself around a new borrower, there is reason to believe that the conventional logic of an upward-sloping supply curve for credit may not be immediately relevant. Indeed, when one examines how banks institutionally translated risk assessment into credit decisions, a flat, or horizontal, curve becomes more plausible over a significant stretch of the credit cycle. And, of course, with a flat curve the traditional notion of discipline in the marketplace can break down.

The above proposition is general for the international credit markets of the 1970s. In this chapter I will attempt to channel the analysis more directly into the context of a bank-borrower relationship in a developing country for the same period. My intention is to illustrate the transmission of bank lending into developing-country overborrowing; that is, how supply can contribute endogenously to an overaccumulation of debt. This will be done through the development of an analytical framework patterned after the experiences of Peru and Bolivia in the 1970s, which I have had an opportunity to study in considerable detail.[1] The analysis, while abstract, is contextually linked to the two countries in a specific historical setting. There are obvious limits to the generalization of such a framework, but this is an issue that I will address more thoroughly in the conclusions to the chapter.

The chapter will begin with a presentation of the analytical framework of the articulation between LDC borrowers and bankers during the 1970s.[2] This will be illustrated from two angles: one that stresses

---

[1] The studies, cited earlier, are Robert Devlin, *Transnational Banks and the External Finance of Latin America: The Experience of Peru* (Santiago, Chile: United Nations, 1985); and Robert Devlin and Michael Mortimore, *Los Bancos Transnacionales, el Estado, y el Endeudamiento Externo en Bolivia* [Transnational Banks, the State, and External Debt in Bolivia] (Santiago, Chile: United Nations, 1983). See the Appendix for a description of the methodology underlying the data bases of the study.

[2] This further elaborates and modifies a framework I published in *El Trimestre Económico* 51 (July-September 1984): 559–589, entitled "Banca Privada, Deuda, y Capacidad Negociadora de la Periferia: Teoría y Práctica" [Private Banks, Debt, and Negotiating Capacity of the Periphery: Theory and Practice].

the permissive nature of the supply side and another that lays stress on how the borrowers could have dealt with the permissive environment to their advantage. This relatively abstract analysis will be followed by an overview of the concrete experiences of Peru and Bolivia, which inspired the framework and lend it credibility.

MARKET SIGNALS AND DEBT MANAGEMENT

Some General Considerations

The new articulation of private banks with a developing country in the 1970s put new demands on economic management because as a financial instrument bank loans carried many idiosyncracies as compared to more traditional sources of finance. Indeed, bank credits were truly a double-edged sword, offering many advantages but also many potential dangers.

In the first place, banks are very agile lenders and could, in any given period, mobilize enormous sums that dwarfed those available from more traditional sources such as governments, multilateral lenders, and suppliers of equipment. The more elastic source of finance was certainly a welcome event for capital-scarce developing countries, but their private risk/profit orientation in principle put more demands on public authorities to manage resources efficiently.

Second, the cost of commercial loans was significantly higher (by about 50 percent) than that of credit granted by official agencies, such as the World Bank, and also was considerably higher than the cost of supplier credits.[3] Given their commercial costs, bank loans are strictly compatible only with activities that generate a commercial rate of return. Countries must be careful, then, because many of the financial requirements of the state—the principal borrowing agent—are for projects that may generate a high social rate of return but not necessarily a high commercial one.

Third, the cost of bank credit is based on variable interest rates, meaning that should the interest rate rise, not only can the price of marginal borrowing undergo a radical and unexpected increase (as could be the case even with traditional creditors that lend at fixed rates) but the higher interest rates are transmitted to the entire stock of the debt as well, potentially making previously profitable investment decisions

---

[3] This can be confirmed by examining the data on Latin America in the World Bank, *World Debt Tables* (Washington, D.C., 1981 and 1982). I have traced the differential cost of credits from different sources for Peru in Robert Devlin, *Transnational Banks and Peru*, figure 2.

very unprofitable. Also, the rise in interest costs increases debt service and current account deficits. This in turn can raise bankers' perceived risk and adversely affect their disposition to lend, precisely at the moment when new credits are needed to finance the increased deficit. Variable rates also mean that debtor countries lose—except for very brief periods—a traditional mechanism of debt relief: real devaluation of liabilities via inflation. In effect, when inflation rises, so eventually do interest rates, which maintains the real value of payments.[4]

Fourth, important parts of the direct and indirect costs (the spread, amortization period, fees, fines, restrictive clauses, et cetera) are subject to negotiation, instead of being institutionally given as in the case of official lenders. While this situation offers countries greater opportunities to determine the cost of their credit, it also places greater demands on the authorities in terms of loan negotiations and awareness of the lending practices of the many banks operating in private international capital markets.

Fifth, amortization periods on bank loans can be half or less of that offered by official lenders and fall short of the fifteen to twenty years needed for payback on even most commercial capital investments.[5] Thus, when borrowing from banks, authorities must accelerate "debt activity," that is, the entering into the market to contract new loans to pay off old ones. This absorbs the time of scarce technical manpower and also makes the countries more vulnerable to the changing disposition of banks to lend.

Sixth, since banks are private, profit-making institutions, their lending patterns can tend to be procyclical, expansive on the upside of the economic cycle and restrictive on the downside, thus accentuating economic fluctuations. This behavior is what led to a popular joke during the years of the Great Depression that characterized private credit as "an umbrella which a man is allowed to borrow as long as the weather is fine, but which he has to return the moment it starts raining."[6] Official lenders, in contrast, have a public risk perception and are usually willing to lend in economic circumstances that might unnerve a private lender.

Lastly, commercial bank loans, while organized rapidly, are accompanied by little or no technical assistance, in contrast to the technical support systems associated with official loans, supplier credits, and di-

[4] The World Bank gives a numerical example of this in *World Development Report 1985* (Washington, D.C., 1985), p. 25.

[5] World Bank, *World Debt Tables*.

[6] Ragnar Nurske, *Problems of Capital Formation in Underdeveloped Countries* (New York: Oxford University Press, Galaxy Books, 1967), p. 135.

rect foreign investment. This difference is an important consideration for the less-industrialized developing countries that have less capacity to plan and implement projects.

In sum, then, both quantitatively and qualitatively, commercial bank loans represented a radically new and unfamiliar financial instrument for developing countries. The access to a new source of credit was certainly a positive event, but it also introduced new sources of potential instability and problems. A credit market that would give clear price signals and that would impose a certain amount of discipline on a country borrower would in these circumstances be a welcome complement to national management of the debt and the economy. But during the 1970s, this was not the case. We saw in the previous chapter that the basic assumptions underlying the conventional notion of discipline in the marketplace were undermined by the dynamics of an emerging modern transnational bank credit market. The environment of the 1970s was in reality very permissive. I will use this insight to show how the private banks could be a misleading source of finance that helped to bias the system in the direction of overindebtedness, which is, of course, just the other side of overlending. The pattern is illustrated below.

Supply-Led Indebtedness

I noted in the previous chapter that banks can be attracted to "virgin borrowers," that is, countries that meet some minimum standard of creditworthiness but that have little or no exposure with the lending institution. I also pointed out that for the bank, a decision to lend under these circumstances is a relatively easy one. Due to portfolio diversification, the cost of running the risk of a new loan is nominal. Meanwhile, the profitability of the loan can be considerable, since new borrowers often pay stiff premiums on their loans because of inexperience in negotiation or because their recognition factor in the market is still too low for competition among the banks to flatten out the price structure of credit. But the mere presence of some banks in a developing country market attracts the attention of other banks that are concerned about global presence and market shares. The supply curve can quickly begin to flatten out, elongate, and shift downwards. In these circumstances the borrower objectively is in the driver's seat.

Contracting loans with the banks becomes extremely easy: the borrower encounters constant or declining marginal costs and more available loan volume than it might even have initially contemplated possible. It finds the supply of loans so abundant that debt service is more than covered by new credits. All things being equal this easy environment can persist for several years. But as the borrower's participation in the portfolio of the bank rises, the lender can and does become more conscious of exposure considerations, and enthusiasm for new loans shifts into greater degrees of reticence. In these circumstances the market can begin to enforce discipline on the borrower and bargaining power shifts to the lender: as the eagerness to lend becomes relatively less pronounced, the eagerness to borrow is on the rise, if for no other reason than to roll over the exponentially growing debt service to the banks. The country now falls into a potential debt trap. The terms of indebtedness can become more severe and volume more restricted, involuntarily lowering the net transfer from the banks, or even making it negative. As the transfer wanes, the country is threatened with a cutoff of the automatic rollover of debt service. Once the rollover ceases to be automatic the burden of debt becomes onerous for the first time and the country is more vulnerable to crisis. These exposure considerations—and the consequent erosion of bargaining power and increased vulnerability—can be accelerated if and when the banks perceive a deterioration in the borrower's image of creditworthiness. Alternatively, the problem can be postponed by an improved image of creditworthiness or by an expanded supply of deposits in the international financial markets, which lower costs and encourage new entrants. But the credit cycle always faces limits in the capital and reserve structure of the banks.

These considerations are generalized and are illustrated in Figure 4.1. The figure shows both how demand for foreign funds might be generated in the short to medium term and the response of the banks. Here we will simplify and assume for the moment that in the initial periods the borrower finances all of its real investment externally and that a certain number of commercial banks are the sole available source of foreign credit. As we saw in the previous chapter, based on considerations of risk, there is some minimum price at which loans become available to the borrower. Moreover, given the great difference in scale between the borrowing country and international capital markets, as well as the banks' reluctance to be left out of the pack, after a brief trial period in the market a new borrower can face a horizontal supply curve over the initial phases of its credit cycle, as depicted in quadrant 1. Under these supply conditions a point nevertheless will be reached where the supply curve turns up sharply—eventually becoming perfectly inelastic—as exposure considerations make the banks increasingly reluctant to lend additional resources even at a higher price. This is when credit rationing begins to set in. Under the stated assumptions, the country's supply curve for capital in quadrant 2 is identical to the supply curve for bank funds.

While the precise sources of demand for finance in a developing country are many and complex, to illustrate the present argument it is suffi-

FIGURE 4.1. The Demand and Supply of Foreign Bank Loans in an LDC Market.

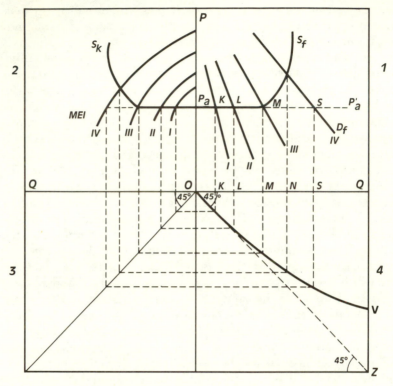

SYMBOLS:

S_k = supply schedule of capital
S_f = supply schedule of bank finance
MEI = marginal efficiency
  of investment
I = net investment

D_f = demand schedule for bank finance
P = price of bank finance
Q = quantity supplied of bank finance
  or capital

cient for the moment to focus on demand as such and limit its determinants to two simple and basic categories: the marginal efficiency of investment (*MEI*), which reflects investment opportunities given an optimal capital stock, and the need to roll over upcoming debt service payments, assuming, as usually is the case in practice, that the developing country borrower does not want to repay its debt and thereby undergo a net outflow of resources.[7] The *MEI* is initially very inelastic, reflecting

---

[7] When new loans cease to cover interest and amortization, the borrower must turn its trade deficit into a trade surplus. If the new loans do not even cover amortization, the

the absorption problems regarding efficient project identification and implementation that are common to most developing countries. However, if investment is carried out wisely, and labor supply is relatively elastic, the *MEI* curve should shift out and gradually turn flatter as economic growth proceeds over time. This is seen in quadrant 2 over phases *I* to *IV*. Quadrant 4 displays the second source of demand that stems from the desire to refinance debt service with new loans. This latter demand is expressed by the difference between the diagonal *OZ* and the sloping curve *OV*. The two curves increasingly diverge as debt service becomes due and refinance credits are demanded. The demand for finance stemming from investment and the refinance of debt service grows exponentially over time, and thus this curve for bank finance shifts to the right over the described phases (quadrant 1).

In phase *I*, at equilibrium price P_a, the quantity demanded, P_aK, is much less than the amount that the banks are willing to lend, that is, P_aM. We assume for the moment that the banks are passive and accept the demand constraint, which permits a stable equilibrium. During the succeeding phases, the borrower's demand for loans at the given prices is still less than the available supply. Moreover, until phase *IV* the market does not signal that borrowing is in any way affecting future supply. That is, as we saw in the last chapter, both because of lags in data availability and an institutional structure that gave creditworthiness evaluation a back seat to marketing departments, banks in practice did not observe the negative externalities of each other's lending. Thus, the country encountered all the loan volume it needed at a constant marginal cost.

In these circumstances a country could become hooked on easy credit through points *K* through *M* and thus mistakenly project the future supply curve as P_a-P_a'. It would formulate its investment requirements accordingly, perhaps setting P_aS as a borrowing target, based on requirements for investment and the refinance of debt service. But at the prevailing price of the loan (P_a), the planned borrowing cannot be undertaken because exposure and risk considerations make the banks willing to extend new loans only at a higher price. The borrower must therefore scale back its investment program and growth and reevaluate its debt service capacity. Thus, conditions that were initially favorable to the borrower can gradually shift in favor of the lender.

---

borrowing country must generate a current account surplus, or external dissavings. When loans do not cover amortization and a country has little reserves, it frequently seeks a rescheduling or enters into default.

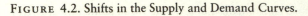

FIGURE 4.2. Shifts in the Supply and Demand Curves.

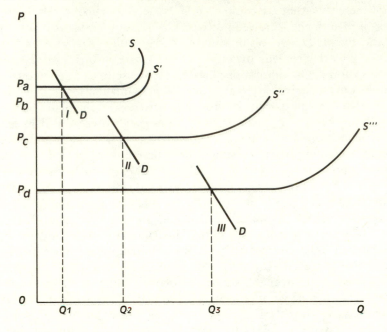

The dynamics of lending/borrowing in fact could be much more explosive than the relatively pastoral setting of Figure 4.1.

First, we pointed out in the earlier chapter that in the competitive environment of the 1970s banks were unlikely to accept the constraint of demand. They would compete to enter into the demand-constrained market via price competition. This would drive the supply curve down from S to S', as depicted in Figure 4.2. Thus, rising loan volume was encountered simultaneously with a falling negotiated price for credit.

Second, the presence of some major banks in the market attracted others. This had the effect of elongating the flat portion of the supply curve and aggravating the demand constraint, which put even more pressure on prices and caused further downward shifts of the supply curve (S'' and S''').

Third, the competition could cause some banks to relax their original credit limits in order to preserve market shares. Alternatively, as bank loans fueled economic growth in the country and the accumulation of foreign exchange reserves, the borrower could appear more creditworthy to some, especially inexperienced institutions, causing them to loosen their credit limits. Either way, the inelastic portion of the curve, which signals that credit limits are approaching, flattens, providing for an even more permissive environment.

Fourth, in some loose sense supply could generate its own demand, inducing the demand curve to shift to the right at a highly accelerated pace. This in turn promoted a massive buildup of debt over a short period of time and reduced even more the possibility that the banks would perceive the negative externalities of their loans before the debt buildup reached critical proportions.

Elaborating on the fourth point, it can be seen in figures 4.1 and 4.2 that price cutting can overcome the demand constraint only in a limited way. Demand in any period is constrained by investment activity and refinance requirements, and the first of these is not very responsive to price changes in the short term. Thus, by cutting prices, loan sales are won more by displacement of other lenders than by absorption of new resources. But banks found that they could overcome this constraint by untying loans from efficient investment activity (or, alternatively, economic adjustment programs[8]).

In effect, banks discovered that they could break into a market by offering free-disposition credits. These are loans that are extended without any conditions and can be used for any purpose. By delinking loans from efficient investment activity the banks effectively made the demand curve potentially highly elastic, raising a country's ability to contract loans in any given period. If loans were linked to efficient investment activity, the ability of a country to accept credit offers would be restricted by its real absorptive capacity, that is, its ability to formulate commercially viable projects (or specific economic programs).

The phenomenon is simplified and illustrated in Figure 4.3. A country's demand curve for finance, as related to real absorptive capacity, say, in the short to medium term might be the "kinked" curve DAD. In other words, after point A, the effective demand for the finance of efficient investment activity is assumed to become perfectly inelastic due to absolute human/physical bottlenecks with respect to the efficient deployment of resources. However, given that banks are prepared to lend considerable amounts of free-disposition resources that are not in any way linked to absorptive capacity, the effective demand curve for contraction of finance becomes the straight line segment DAD'. When a borrower has only limited access to bank credit, the supply curve will intersect with the solid portion of the demand curve DAD' as shown for the first two supply curves in Figure 4.3 (a). However, should the banking system as a whole become attracted to the borrower, the supply curve will quickly shift to the right and flatten out, becoming horizontal

---

[8] One could alternatively speak of economic adjustment programs in which finance was linked to specific investment and economic reforms designed to improve international competitiveness and creditworthiness.

FIGURE 4.3. Free Disposition Loans and the Absorptive Capacity of the Borrower.

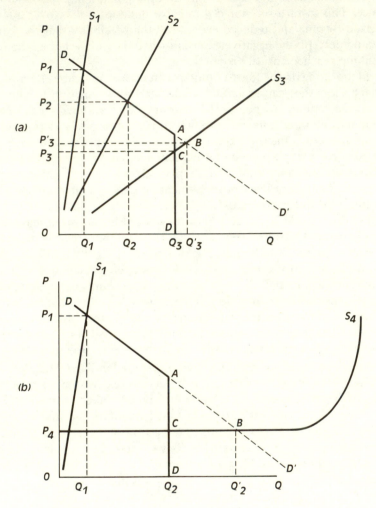

over an extended area, as shown in Figure 4.3 (*b*). Here one can notice that the economy can only efficiently absorb resources equivalent to OQ_2, but authorities—engulfed by the intense marketing pressures of the banks—have been able to contract OQ'_2 in new loans.

Loan quantity $Q_2Q'_2$ represents potential problems for a country. If the country is not highly disciplined and does not have a priori notions about how to deploy the resources efficiently, quantity $Q_2Q'_2$ can end up in activities that are unable to support the commercial cost of the resources. When the loans are not linked to economically efficient investment or deliberate macroeconomic reform programs, there is a great risk that they will be channeled into consumption, corruption, ill-conceived and overscaled projects, capital flight, et cetera that do not generate returns sufficient to service the debt.

This, of course, is not a necessary outcome since authorities in a borrowing country could always sterilize the foreign exchange brought in via free-disposition loans until such time that the resources could be deployed efficiently. The stated strategy would require, among other things, the availability of economic technicians instilled in the principles of conservative demand management as well as a national political leadership with a disposition to integrate anticyclical economic policy into their political program. One simply cannot assume such a happy set of circumstances, however. Unfortunately, in practice, a developing country's authorities can often be prone to many of the same shortcomings that I outlined in Chapter Three for the private banks. In effect, the unconditional availability of bank loans could generate a demand to contract them and disburse the resources.

A developing country is not a *homo economicus*, making cold cost-benefit calculations at the margin. Rather it constitutes a complicated class structure where there are different social groups with divergent and conflicting interests.[9] Political processes moreover are usually not very institutionalized, creating what Chalmers calls the "politicized state."[10] In the politicized state—which manifests itself in the developing world in *both* authoritarian and democratic regimes—the coalition of classes underpinning a national political structure is especially delicate and shifting. Thus political decision making is short-term in its horizon and geared to survival:

> In the politicized state the chief executive must constantly build and rebuild his political support to meet the threat of attempts to overthrow him. His support must be exceptionally broad and flexible. . . . The chief executive is compelled to build a "maximum winning coalition" to protect himself. There is a strong inclination to expand his support as much as possible and a strong tendency for his supporters to jump on the bandwagon of an apparently successful opponent.[11]

[9] An overview of theories of class and social structure can be found in Richard Wolff and Steven Resnick, "Classes in Marxian Theory," *Review of Radical Political Economics* 13 (Winter 1982): 1–18.

[10] Douglas Chalmers, "The Politicized State in Latin American," in *Authoritarianism and Corporatism in Latin America*, ed. James Malloy (Pittsburgh: University of Pittsburgh Press, 1977), pp. 23–45.

[11] Ibid., pp. 31–32.

The divergent interests of groups and classes are magnified in an environment of economic stagnation, where decisions of economic agents are more likely to represent a zero-sum game. Coalitions are difficult to build and exceptionally fragile in this environment. In contrast, economic growth helps to mask the divergent interests of society as it provides a positive-sum game where all actors can benefit simultaneously (of course, some more than others).

Authorities in politicized states can therefore find the offer of easy credit from the banks exceptionally attractive as it is a very effective instrument in coalition building: growth can be stimulated and without the cost of unpopular and divisive short-term political decisions related to taxes, exchange rates, interest rates, et cetera that might have to be confronted in the absence of available foreign finance.

Of course, by postponing such decisions, the country can become overly reliant on debt and suffer an erosion of its servicing capacity, which would eventually undermine its access to credit and threaten a crisis. But developing country authorities, like the banks, often had their decisions influenced by the unique qualities of the product we call a loan: they could buy the loan today and worry about the payment tomorrow. The benefits were thus immediate, while the future costs were problematic and perhaps would not even appear during the political life of the regime.

Potential problems were intensified by two other factors, one related to the country, the other related to the banks.

With regard to the former, there was a significant probability that free-disposition credits would be channeled into less than efficient activities, in part because in the 1970s a developing country was likely to have no effective institutional system to control the contraction of credits and their deployment in the economy.

A Latin American country was accustomed to the slow and laborious process of loan contraction from official agencies, where controls were imposed externally through evaluation of projects or economic programs. The overriding problem was to secure credits, not control their inflow. When bankers began to approach a country with offers of massive loans without any conditions whatsoever, the country could be unprepared institutionally to screen the borrowers and lenders to ensure that loans were contracted on the best possible terms and deployed efficiently. Even if a country did establish an institutional mechanism to control the national interface with the banks, it could have serious flaws or be undermined by internal political dynamics that were influenced by the general permissiveness of the decade. In other words, there could be a big gap between systematic institutional control on paper and control in practice.

The international banking system could aggravate the situation. As mentioned in the last chapter, many banks were either not good at evaluating creditworthiness or had difficulty in translating their analysis into credit decisions. Once credit momentum built up around a borrower, loan access became nearly automatic. Thus a country could find credit volume high and terms improving, even while important indicators of creditworthiness were deteriorating. If some banking institution became concerned and tried to impose discipline on the borrower by withholding credit, there always was a new entrant willing to take its place. This deceptive forward momentum in the credit cycle was encouraged by a fact mentioned in the last chapter: that should a bank discover a serious problem in the country's management, it had no incentive to "blow the whistle." On the contrary, it had a reason to hide the information because the bank's withdrawal from the market was facilitated by new lending from less-informed competitors.

Looked at from another angle, supply again could generate its own demand. The slackening of economic discipline in the country—which, all things being equal, raises the need for finance and shifts the demand curve to the right—was possible only if it was validated by available finance. That is, deficits could not occur unless there was first finance. And that finance was eagerly placed at the country's disposal by an expanding international banking market.

In effect, during the 1970s the market unwittingly gave authorities a green light for their economic policies, even though they may not always have been sustainable. The market could react and impose discipline on the borrower only with a big and deceptive lag, when the credit cycle was well advanced and the disequilibrium so large that it couldn't possibly be ignored. But by that time a country would be highly dependent on debt, so that the banks' withholding of finance inevitably brought with it a disruptive and socially costly adjustment process.

A Restatement of the Framework

Here I will turn the framework around a bit and restate it more directly from the viewpoint of the borrower's policies. I want to do this to reinforce the fact that a debt crisis can never be one-sided. The dynamics of supply, or the dynamics of demand, standing in isolation are a necessary, but not sufficient, condition for crisis. In the end supply and demand interact and the two sides of the Marshallian scissors cannot be separated.

Figure 4.4 illustrates the evolution of the bargaining power of a developing country over its credit cycle with the banks. The figure presents "snapshots" ([a] and [b]) of two potential points in the cycle. Through-

FIGURE 4.4. Bargaining Power and the Credit Cycle of an LDC.

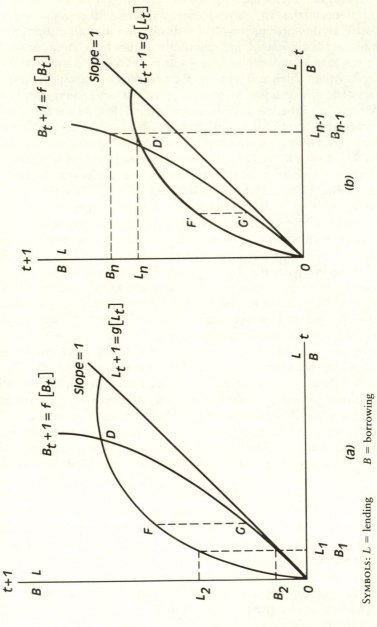

SYMBOLS: L = lending   B = borrowing

out the credit cycle it is assumed that the number of lenders, international liquidity, and perceptions of creditworthiness are unchanged.

On the horizontal axes there is borrowing (B) by the country and lending (L) by the banks in period $t(B_t = L_t)$; on the vertical axes are the borrowing requirements and loan availability for the country in the subsequent period $t+1$. In conditions where $L_t = B_t$ there is an equilibrium price for credit; at this given price future borrowing and lending becomes a function of the previous period's borrowing and lending. The second derivative of the borrowing function is positive, reflecting the fact that there is an increasing propensity to borrow due to expanding absorptive capacity in the country and requirements for the refinancing of old debt. For the banks, however, the second derivative is negative, reflecting exposure and risk considerations as the country's position in the banks' loan portfolio rises.

Segment (a) of Figure 4.4 depicts an early phase in the credit cycle. In period t the country has borrowed B_1 and the banks have lent an identical amount L_1, the transaction being cleared at a given market price. For reasons similar to those elaborated on earlier, at the given price banks are able to lend in period $t+1$ considerably more than what the country is able to effectively demand as demonstrated by the fact that $L_2 > B_2$. However, the situation cannot be depicted as stable; as mentioned, private commercial banks are very concerned about their market position vis-à-vis competing institutions. They will seek to gain a footing in the demand-constrained credit flow. Thus, in the initial periods of borrowing where $L_2 > B_2$ the country can affect the terms of credit (both the price and nonprice components) even given the large asymmetry of scale between the borrower and capital markets. In these circumstances there are opportunities to force a shift downwards in the supply curve while simultaneously expanding borrowing. In other words, the country's bargaining position is potentially very strong. To the extent that there are new entrants to international lending (as was the case in the 1970s), the bargaining power of the borrower is further enhanced.

All things being equal, the borrower's situation can deteriorate as the demand for credit rises. Segment (b) of Figure 4.4 displays a potential position in an advanced stage of the borrowing cycle. Here the demand for credit has been pushed beyond point D', and negotiating power has decisively shifted in favor of the lenders as future borrowing needs exceed available loans. The terms of credit (both price and nonprice) can now severely deteriorate for the borrower simultaneously with a restriction in supply.

In view of the foregoing, a possible strategy for the borrower during the course of a credit cycle is to locate itself in or around the area $F'G'$—

the maximum divergence between demand and available supply of credit, and hence the strongest bargaining position—and still maintain an adequate growth of the flow of credit for investment and finance needs.

One possible policy (now introducing the possibility of substitution) is to assuage the growth of the demand for foreign credit via increased domestic savings, thus shifting curve ODB_{t+1} downward and to the right and enhancing overall bargaining power. But there is also a "dividend" to such a strategy: raising domestic savings will probably improve the image of creditworthiness and shift curve ODL_{t+1} upwards and to the left. The net effect, then, is a broadening of the opportunity for new borrowing under favorable terms. Indeed, any policy that provides a better image of creditworthiness should help to shift curve ODL_{t+1} upwards and to the left.[12]

What is being posited here is what might be termed a "defensive" borrowing strategy with the banks. Even in the face of a rapidly expanding supply of foreign bank loans, a country's public authorities should attempt to keep the banks "on the hook" by controlling domestic demand, pressing hard to raise domestic savings and exports, minimizing unnecessary foreign content in projects, maximizing the use of subsidized official credit, efficiently allocating resources, and establishing extremely controlled interface with commercial creditors. Essentially what is being exploited here is the principle that private banks are most eager to lend to borrowers that do not need the resources!

Unfortunately, a developing country often did not pursue this type of policy. Governments correctly viewed the availability of bank loans as a new and timely instrument to support their objectives yet did not treat them as an instrument that cuts two ways, which, when employed carelessly, would be capable of undermining an entire political program. Instead of establishing a carefully planned defensive relationship with the banks, public authorities, in moments of objective bargaining strength, all too often let themselves become engulfed by the forces of the market, accepting offers of credit from the banks regardless of whether the resources could be deployed efficiently or not. The economies soon became vulnerable and excessively dependent on the banks' willingness to

---

[12] The curve ODL_{t+1} also could shift upwards due to the growing liquidity in international markets and/or new entrants to international lending.

From the standpoint of the earlier analysis using traditional supply and demand curves, one would want to keep the demand curve on the flat portion of the supply curve. Moreover, an improving image of creditworthiness would help to ensure a lengthening of the elastic portion and a flattening of the inelastic portion.

roll over payments to service the debt. Any reluctance of the banks to do so brought on a crisis.

Why would the authorities become engulfed in the market forces instead of establishing a cautious interface with the banks? One can posit various factors, some of which are interrelated:

—The aforementioned fragile class coalitions made it politically difficult to introduce appropriate economic policy and easier to substitute hard decisions with easy foreign credit;
—The market gave positive signals to policies that were unsustainable in the medium term and only altered these signals when the economy was in a critical state;
—Many borrowers were in the market for the first time and through inexperience may have accepted the favorable signals of the market at face value. After all, the conventional wisdom in the North—which presumably should have known better—was that "the market knows best";[13]
—The financial ethos in development circles during the 1970s conventionally viewed the growing indebtedness with private banks as good policy.[14]

THE CASES OF PERU AND BOLIVIA

The two countries' relationship with the private banks during the 1970s has been analyzed in depth in the separate publications by Devlin and Devlin and Mortimore I cited earlier. Here I will only highlight the developments that are most pertinent to the aforementioned analytical framework. Unless otherwise indicated, the information presented here and relevant documentation can be found in the two studies.

Virgins Defrocked

Prior to their respective credit cycles with the banks in the 1970s, Peru and Bolivia were reliant on nonbank sources of finance, as was for that

[13] See, for example, Monroe Haegele, "The Market Knows Best," *Euromoney*, May 1980, pp. 121–128.

[14] Moreover, this covered the political spectrum. See Carlos Díaz-Alejandro, "The Post-1971 International Financial System and Less Developed Countries," in *A World Divided*, ed. G. K. Helleiner (New York: Cambridge University Press, 1976), pp. 190 and 193; Walter Robichek "Some Reflections about External Public Debt Management," in *Estudios Monetarios VII* [Monetary Studies VII] (Santiago, Chile: Central Bank of Chile, December 1981), pp. 170–183; and Arghiri Emmanuel, "Myths of Development vs. Myths of Underdevelopment," *New Left Review* 85 (1974): 63.

TABLE 4.1. Peru and Bolivia: Distribution of Public Medium- and Long-Term Debt by Source of Finance
(percentages)

Year	Private				Official		
	Suppliers	Banks	Bonds	Others	Multilateral	Bilateral	Total
1965							
Peru	33	12	6	. . .[a]	25	24	100
Bolivia	9	2	. . .	. . .	12	78	100
Latin America	20	12	7	1	23	37	100
1970							
Peru	36	13	2	. . .	20	29	100
Bolivia	10	3	12	14	10	50	100
Latin America	17	19	6	2	24	31	100
1975							
Peru	17	41	. . .	. . .	8	34	100
Bolivia	8	18	5	4	21	45	100
Latin America	11	42	4	1	20	22	100
1980							
Peru	14	35	. . .	. . .	12	39	100
Bolivia	4	31	2	. . .	29	33	100
Latin America	6	55	7	. . .	17	14	100

SOURCE: Inter-American Development Bank, *External Public Debt of the Latin American Countries* (Washington, D.C., July 1984).
NOTES: Percentages may not add up to one hundred due to rounding.
[a](. . .) = zero or not large enough to quantify.

matter most of Latin America. But when the countries gained access to the eurocurrency market there was a dramatic change in the structure of their debt. This can be observed in Table 4.1, which breaks out the composition of public medium-term debt, the only type of data for which one can find a significantly longtime series.

In the mid-1960s commercial banks accounted for only 12 percent of Peru's public term debt and only 2 percent of Bolivia's. For Peru, foreign suppliers and official lenders were important as sources of finance, while for Bolivia—one of the poorest countries in Latin America—the main supplier of foreign credit was official bilateral institutions.

Peru's entrance into the eurocurrency market occurred in early 1972, and by the time its credit cycle ended in crisis in mid-1976 over 40 percent of the public medium-term debt was in the hands of private banks. Adding in short-term and private sector debt, I estimate that the banks' participation in the total national external debt at the end of 1976 was roughly 60 percent.[15] As for Bolivia, its credit cycle began in 1974 and ended in crisis in 1979. By then nearly a third of its public medium-term debt was in the hands of the banks. When short-term and private sector debt is considered, the participation rises only slightly, to 35 percent.[16]

Both countries were for all practical purposes virgins when they entered the market. As noted in the previous chapter, Peru had done some borrowing from a handful of banks in the 1960s, mostly from the United States. However, the 1968 coup by General Juan Velasco brought with it nationalistic policies that soon met opposition from U.S. firms and the Nixon administration. Peru's U.S. creditor banks participated in a financial blockade, orchestrated by the Nixon administration, and began to run down their exposure. On the eve of its entrance into the eurocurrency market the international banking system had only a small exposure in that country and it was held by just a few institutions. As for Bolivia, its exposure with the banks prior to 1974 was practically nonexistent. The country was notorious for its political instability, manifested in an accumulation of more governments than years of independence. Its debt payment record was poor, exemplified by the fact that in the 1970s the government still had outstanding some bonds that it had defaulted on in the 1930s. It also exhibited acute problems in designing projects and absorbing resources, which partly explains the low participation of multilateral lenders in the country's debt profile.[17] In sum, Bolivia was not a country where private banks had shown much interest.

When the banks did decide to turn their attention to these two markets, debt activity rose dramatically. As mentioned, the banks entered the Peruvian market in 1972 after having lent practically nothing the previous year. In just the first year of penetration, gross lending, or debt

[15] To make a rough calculation I used data for Peru published by the United Nations Economic Commission for Latin America and the Caribbean in their *Economic Survey of Latin America and the Caribbean 1984* (Santiago, Chile, 1986), vol. 1, table 20, of the study on Peru. Of the total debt of $7.4 billion, I incorporated into the banks' share $2.5 billion of public medium-term debt, $300 million of medium-term Central Bank debt, three-quarters of the medium-term private sector debt, and three-quarters of the short-term debt (less Central Bank obligations).

[16] This estimate is based on data provided to me by Ricardo Ffrench-Davis, who had access to unpublished data of the World Bank and the Bank of International Settlements.

[17] Multilateral lenders are very strict in tying their loans to sound project formulation.

TABLE 4.2. Peru and Bolivia: Gross Value of Term Loans to Public Sector Authorized by Private Banks (millions of dollars)

Variable	1971	1972	1973	1974	1975	1976	1977	1978	1979
				Peru					
Gross loan authorizations	1.5	213.0	568.1	429.6	431.4	556.7	213.3	327.6	167.2
Exports[a]	1067.2	1153.0	1343.5	1841.2	1688.9	1744.2	2131.0	2400.6	4101.1
Loans/exports	0.1	18.5	42.3	23.3	25.5	31.9			
				Bolivia					
Gross loan authorizations	197.8	19.4	32.3	92.7	109.4	221.7	213.3	327.6	167.2
Exports[a]		222.5	286.9	593.4	485.7	623.4	695.0	703.4	854.6
Loans/exports		8.7	11.3	15.6	22.5	35.6	30.7	46.6	19.6

SOURCES: Loan data Peru—Ministry of Economy and Finance; loan data Bolivia—Central Bank; export data—ECLAC, Division of Statistics and Quantitative Analysis.

NOTES: Term loans exclude short-term credits and also loans related to national defense.

[a] Goods and services.

activity, was equivalent to nearly 20 percent of that year's export earnings (Table 4.2). In the second year of the credit cycle gross lending
more than doubled and was in excess of 40 percent of the country's export sales. In the last three years of the cycle new loans ranged between
20 and 30 percent of export earnings.[18] By 1975 Peru was ranked among
the top seven clients of the banks in the group of nonoil-exporting developing countries.

The Bolivian case has some similarities. In the three years preceding
1974 credits from private banks—which were equivalent, on average,
to roughly 10 percent of export earnings—were for specific transactions related to OECD export promotion and the indemnization of nationalized firms, and not part of an overall sustainable trend. But when
Bolivia did gain access to the eurocurrency market in 1974, the volume
of loans rose sharply: by the second year of the cycle new credits were
equivalent to 23 percent of exports, rising to between 30 and 47 percent
of foreign sales during the next three years (Table 4.2). Moreover, the
volume at the very beginning of the cycle would perhaps have been
higher if it were not for the 1974/1975 minicrisis in the eurocurrency
interbank market, which caused many banks to withdraw temporarily
from international lending.

When the banks penetrated the markets, they also dwarfed all other
sources of finance during the expansive phase of the credit cycle. While
data in figures 4.5 and 4.6 are not wholly compatible with each other, or
with Table 4.2, they do demonstrate that the banks' credits outstripped
all others during the respective cycles of the countries during the
1970s.[19]

The Dynamics of Market Penetration

Why did banks decide to enter these countries when they did? We have
already seen that the 1970s was a decade of general expansion into Latin America. The factors that converted a specific country into a center of
bank-lending activity were complex. But while admittedly over-

---

[18] In the beginning of the cycle gross lending can approximate net lending due to grace
periods, which postpone repayments. As the cycle progresses, grace periods expire and
gross lending can become progressively less in net terms as payment obligations rise.

[19] Figures 4.5 and 4.6 are based on separate sources of data, where definitions and cov-
erages are different. My data on Peru are unpublished estimates that were provided by the
Ministry of Economy and Finance. They are for medium- and long-term transactions and,
with the exception of direct foreign investment, pertain to the public sector. Transactions
related to national defense are excluded. The unpublished data for Bolivia are calculated
from the World Bank's debt reporting system and include only public transactions of a
medium- and long-term nature. Meanwhile, both figures 4.5 and 4.6 present net flows,
whereas Table 4.2 presents the banks' gross loan authorizations.

Figure 4.5. Peru: Net External Flows by Source, 1965–1976.

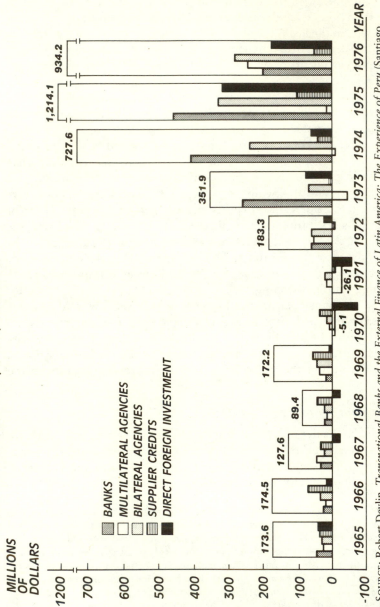

SOURCE: Robert Devlin, *Transnational Banks and the External Finance of Latin America: The Experience of Peru* (Santiago, Chile: United Nations, 1985), p. 64.

NOTE: With the exception of direct foreign investment, all flows relate to medium- and long-term public sector flows.

FIGURE 4.6. Bolivia: Net External Flows by Source, 1966–1979.

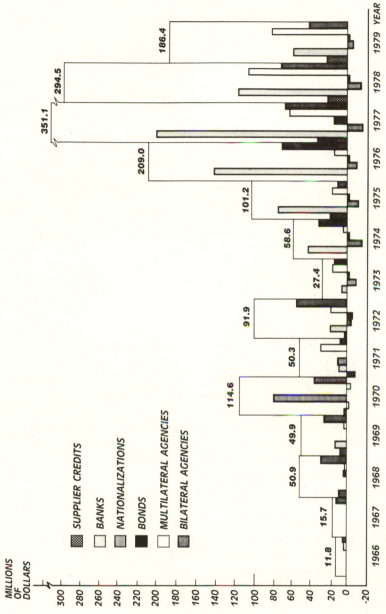

SOURCE: Robert Devlin and Michael Mortimore, *Los Bancos Transnacionales, el Estado, y el Endeudamiento Externo en Bolivia* [Transnational Banks, the State, and External Debt in Bolivia] (Santiago, Chile: United Nations, 1983), p. 44.

NOTE: Medium- and long-term flows to the public sector.

simplifying, the situation was as follows. Although Peru was being blockaded by the U.S. banks that had lent to it in the 1960s, other new entrants to international lending became interested in the market because of rumors, beginning in late 1971, of very large oil deposits in the Amazon. Oil, credible economic adjustment and stabilization programs in 1969 to 1971, and the stability of a relatively popular military government made Peru seem like a good market opportunity, notwithstanding the self-proclaimed revolutionary credentials of the Velasco regime.

Bolivia, the pariah of the international bankers during most of the postwar period, was courted by the banks in the 1970s for several reasons. Its image as a politically unstable country was attenuated by the consolidation of the strong-arm rightist military government of General Hugo Banzer, which came into power by way of a coup in 1971. He had introduced an IMF program, openly favored private capital, national and foreign, and through coercive measures of one type or another quelled Bolivia's traditionally cantankerous labor unions and other socially dissident groups. These factors were joined by the historic OPEC price hike, which gave more value to the country's export of 30,000 B/D of petroleum. But more importantly, seventeen foreign firms had been exploring for oil and gas, and some banks conjectured that by 1980 the country would be producing 200,000 B/D of the former mineral and 550 million cubic feet of the latter. Finally, the banks became disposed to lend to Bolivia also in part because other more established LDC clients that were net oil importers suddenly became less attractive with the advent of OPEC's new pricing policies.

The New Entrants   It was noted in the earlier chapter that when a country became a focal point of attention of the banks, it could bring with it a massive number of new entrants, which destabilized the market and brought a rash of competitive bidding for market shares. Tables 4.3, 4.4, 4.5, and 4.6 display new entrants both according to the country of origin and the size of the bank.

In the case of Peru the entry was clearly quite explosive. There were no new entrants into the Peruvian market in 1969 to 1971, but once the banks focused their attention on the country, the change was dramatic: an average of forty-one new lenders per annum were registered in the first two years of the cycle and twenty-seven and twenty, respectively, in the next two years. In the case of Bolivia, in the first year of the cycle there were seventeen entrants (compared to seven the year before), with roughly nineteen in each of the next three years. While Bolivia's experience with new entrants was less intense than Peru's, the country is con-

TABLE 4.3. Peru: Banks with First-Time Loans According to Country of Origin (number of institutions)

Origin	1965	1966	1967	1968	1969	1970	1971	1972	1973	1974	1975	1976
United States	2	7	3	2	...[a]	...	...	8	11	6	3	...
Japan	...	...	...	1	...	...	...	10	12	2	...	1
Canada	...	1	...	2	...	...	...	1	1	1	...	...
United Kingdom	...	1	1	1	...	...	...	3	1	1	1	2
Germany	...	...	1	...	...	...	...	2	1	3	2	2
France	...	...	...	...	...	...	...	5	1	1	...	...
Italy	...	1	...	...	...	...	...	3	2	1	...	...
Switzerland	...	...	...	...	...	...	...	4	...	1	...	2
Consortium	...	...	...	2	...	...	...	4	5	7	4	1
Other	...	...	...	...	...	...	...	3	3	4	10	1
Unknown	...	1	1	1	...	...	...	...	1	...	...	...
Total	2	11	5	9	...	...	...	43	38	27	20	9

SOURCE: Calculated from data of the Ministry of Economy and Finance of Peru.
NOTES: Institutions are quantified after consolidating subsidiaries into the parent. The credits granted involve medium-term loans without a guarantee of the home country government.
[a] (. . .) = zero or not large enough to quantify.

TABLE 4.4. Peru: Banks with First-Time Loans According to Size of Institution (number of institutions)

International Rank[a]	1965	1966	1967	1968	1969	1970	1971	1972[b]	1973[b]	1974	1975	1976
1–10	2	3	1	...[c]	...	...	...	3	2	1	1	...
11–46	...	3	2	3	...	...	...	13	6	4	...	...
47–91	...	2	1	3	...	...	...	5	6	2	3	1
92–147	...	1	...	...	...	...	...	3	5	3	3	2
148–263	...	...	...	...	...	...	...	7	6	2	4	2
264–300	...	...	...	...	...	...	...	1	...	...	...	...
>300	...	2	1	3	...	...	...	11	12	15	9	4
Total	2	11	5	9	...	...	...	42	37	27	20	9

SOURCE: Calculated from data of the Ministry of Economy and Finance of Peru.
NOTES: See Table 4.3.
[a]Ranked according to an annual survey published in the June issue of The Banker. For years prior to 1970 the data pertain to 1969, the first year for which data were published.
[b]One bank was not ranked and therefore does not appear in this statistical summary.
[c](...) = zero or not large enough to quantify.

TABLE 4.5. Bolivia: Banks with First-Time Loans According to Country of Origin
(number of institutions)

Origin	1970	1971	1972	1973	1974	1975	1976	1977	1978	1979
United States	1	...[a]	1	...	3	6	12	3	2	2
Japan	...	...	1	3	1	...	1	3	...	...
Canada	...	...	...	1	1	3	1	1	...	...
United Kingdom	...	...	...	2	1	2	1	...	1	...
Germany	...	...	...	...	2	2	1	3	...	1
France	...	...	...	...	2	...	...	...	...	2
Italy	...	...	...	...	2	...	...	...	...	...
Switzerland	...	...	1	...	1	...	1	1	1	...
Consortium	...	...	...	1	2	3	2	3	2	7
Other	...	...	1	...	1	3	...	3	2	2
Unknown	...	...	...	...	1	...	...	1	...	1
Total	1	...	4	7	17	19	19	18	8	15

SOURCE: Calcuated from data of the Central Bank of Bolivia.
NOTES: See Table 4.3.
[a] (. . .) = zero or not large enough to quantify.

TABLE 4.6. Bolivia: Banks with First-Time Loans According to Size of Institution (number of institutions)

International Rank[a]	1970	1971	1972	1973	1974	1975	1976	1977	1978	1979
1–10	1	. . .[b]	1	1	1	1	. . .	. . .	. . .	1
11–46	. . .	. . .	3	1	8	3	5	3	1	1
47–91	. . .	. . .	. . .	2	2	7	2	3	1	1
92–147	. . .	. . .	. . .	. . .	1	1	1	1	1	2
148–263	. . .	. . .	. . .	. . .	. . .	2	7	. . .	1	1
264–300	. . .	. . .	. . .	1	. . .	. . .	1	. . .	. . .	. . .
>300	. . .	. . .	. . .	2	5	5	3	11	4	9
Total	1	. . .	4	7	17	19	19	18	8	15

SOURCE: Calculated from data of the Central Bank of Bolivia.
NOTES: See Table 4.3.
[a]Ranked by assets according to the annual survey published in the June issue of *The Banker*.
[b](. . .) = zero or not large enough to quantify.

TABLE 4.7. Peru and Bolivia: New Entrants per Million Inhabitants

Country	1970	1971	1972	1973	1974	1975	1976	1977	1978	1979
Peru	. . .[a]	. . .	3.1	2.6	1.8	1.3	0.6			
Bolivia	0.3	. . .	0.9	1.5	3.5	3.9	3.8	3.5	1.5	2.7

SOURCES: Tables 4.3 and 4.5 and population data provided by ECLAC's Division of Statistics and Quantitative Analysis.
NOTE:
[a](. . .) = zero or not large enough to quantify.

siderably smaller and so the reduced number of new entrants was in fact, relatively speaking, very high. This is illustrated in Table 4.7, which scales new entrants to the size of the two markets.

In the case of Peru the penetration was led by U.S. and Japanese banks and to a lesser extent the consortium institutions (Table 4.3). For Bolivia, U.S. banks stand out above the rest (Table 4.5). This latter phenomenon is explained in part by the fact that Bolivia's cycle was initiated in the years when the interbank market was in crisis and many institutions (especially non-U.S.) had temporarily retired from active international lending.

It also is interesting to note that when new entrants are organized according to size, there was an evident tendency for the size of the entrant to decline as the market matured (tables 4.4 and 4.6). This is suggestive of a leader-follower dynamic among lenders, whereby new opportunities are first exploited by the larger institutions, the presence of which validates the creditworthiness of the country and attracts other smaller, less-informed lenders.[20]

[20] Alternatively, it could also be indicative of an "insider-outsider" dynamic of crisis. That is, better informed insiders seek new opportunities, while uninformed outsiders—eager to participate in the observed profit making—hop on late in the cycle, often when the insiders have slowed down their new commitments due to a reevaluation of the situation. This is a principal ingredient in what Kindleberger terms a financial mania, or bubble, which is a prelude to crisis. There is a concrete example of this in the case of Bolivia. In February 1978 Citicorp apparently became concerned about the situation in Bolivia, especially regarding the prospects for petroleum and gas. The bank at this time was Bolivia's principal lender and closely in touch with developments in the country due to its established bank branch operations in La Paz. It decided to quietly wind down its exposure as a precautionary measure. But even though the principal lender had reevaluated the situation, authorities still faced a buoyant market as other banks and new lenders eagerly took Citicorp's place. See Charles Kindleberger, *Manias, Panics, and Crashes* (New York: Basic Books, 1978), pp. 16–20; and Devlin and Mortimore, *Los Bancos Transnacionales y Bolivia*, pp. 98–100.

The Terms of Lending   Once the markets were penetrated by the banks, both countries experienced easy access to a large loan volume on improving terms.

PERU   During early 1972, in the years of the Nixon blockade, Peru secured only a few refinance credits from its traditional bank lenders, basically because they wanted to avoid default. Terms were tough: 2.25 percent over LIBOR for five-year maturities. Moreover, the banks refused to grant fresh credits, that is, loans beyond the need of refinancing.

By mid-1972 some nontraditional international lenders from Japan, the West Coast of the United States, and Europe began to show some interest in Peru, for reasons outlined earlier. Loans were extended on highly lucrative terms—2.25 percent over LIBOR for 4.5- to 6.5-year maturities—because Peru was a new entity in the market, perhaps inexperienced in negotiations, and eager to break out of the straitjacket of the Nixon blockade. However, in the last quarter of the year Wells Fargo headed a $40 million syndicate for 7.5 years at 2 percent over LIBOR and Dresdner Bank headed a $40 million loan for 7 years at 1.75 percent over LIBOR. The Wells Fargo loan probably had the greatest impact on market psychology because, while the Dresdner syndicate was for a project—which will be shown later to be a preferred form of finance of many banks—the Wells Fargo credit was for what could be considered a relatively less attractive refinance operation. Moreover, while there was a degree of geographic dispersion for the banks participating in both syndicates, Wells Fargo's loan incorporated twenty-nine banks versus fourteen for Dresdner (Table 4.8). The larger number of banks in the former loan surely had a greater psychological impact on the market.

After the Wells Fargo and Dresdner credits in late 1972 other lenders reacted defensively and moved to match terms; the market tugged back and forth between spreads of 1.75 and 2 percent over LIBOR, with maturities ranging between 6.5 and 7 years. Then in April 1973 Wells Fargo led a $100 million loan involving sixty-one banks; although the spread of 2 percent did not break new ground, the maturity of 8 years for a free-disposition loan was the longest yet received on a syndicated credit. Then in the same month Wells Fargo, alone, extended $35 million for refinance at 1.75 percent over LIBOR and the unprecedented maturity of 10 years. These two credits again altered the market as other banks reacted defensively to match terms; soon thereafter it became common for bank loans to carry a maturity of 9 to 10 years.

Some slippage in the prevailing LIBOR spread occurred in September 1973 when a twenty-four-bank syndicated credit headed by Manufacturers Hanover and Citicorp—two of Peru's traditional lenders from

TABLE 4.8. Peru: A Comparison of Syndicated Credits Headed by
Wells Fargo and Dresdner Bank in 1972

Country of the Participating Banks	Wells Fargo		Dresdner Bank	
	Number of Participating Banks	Percentage of Credit	Number of Participating Banks	Percentage of Credit
United States	8	38.8	. . .[a]	. . .
Japan	8	23.7	5	30.0
Canada	3	11.2	2	13.3
United Kingdom	2	6.2	. . .	. . .
Germany	. . .	. . .	2	23.3
Italy	3	7.5	1	10.0
Switzerland	. . .	. . .	1	13.3
Other	2	3.7	1	3.3
Consortium	3	8.7	2	6.6
Total	29	100.0	14	100.0

SOURCE: Robert Devlin, *Transnational Banks and The External Finance of Latin America: The Experience of Peru* (Santiago, Chile: United Nations, 1985), p. 158.
NOTE:
[a](. . .) = zero or not large enough to quantify.

the 1960s—provided a $130 million loan at a split interest margin averaging 1.6 percent over LIBOR. However, it again was Wells Fargo that led the next fundamental break in the market's treatment of Peru. In December this bank organized a thirty-one-bank, $80 million loan at 10 years and a spread of only 1.25 percent over LIBOR.

In early 1974 Morgan Guaranty Trust, until now a bank with an obviously very restrained attitude toward the revolutionary government, headed the famous $76 million credit associated with the U.S.-Peruvian settlement of some ongoing investment disputes. It carried an unusually low spread of only 1 percent over LIBOR. Although the credit clearly was of a political nature, its economic significance, its relatively low price, and the fact that it was headed by one of the most conservative and most respected banks in the industry all made for a large psychological impact on the market.[21] Major loans followed with 10-year matu-

---

[21] With the loan, most of the remaining holdouts among the traditionally established international banks—e.g., Chemical Bank and First Chicago—began to lend to the government.

rities and spreads as low as 1.13 percent over LIBOR. Subsequent lending by Wells Fargo and Dresdner Bank heavily supported the trend toward a lowering of interest margins on eurocurrency credits.

In 1975 there was a general rise in spreads and a shortening of maturities. However, it is difficult to pinpoint which banks may have led or resisted the trend because the overall market conditions were highly unstable and mere access to credit, let alone cost, was a real preoccupation. The situation was further complicated by the fact that the economy began to show open signs of strain that year and General Velasco was deposed in August by the more moderate General Francisco Morales Bermúdez. Nevertheless, the volume of lending was quite buoyant in 1975. It wasn't until 1976 that the expansive phase came to a decisive halt. In midyear the government and its lead creditors would have to arrange a $380 million emergency refinance operation with the banks to avoid open default.

From the preceding one gains an idea of how banks can create inflection points in the market's terms of credit. One also obtains more evidence of the special character of Wells Fargo's participation in Peru's external finance. Its marketing strategy in Peru certainly did lead to more favorable loan-pricing trends and, occasionally with the help of Dresdner Bank, also was important in augmenting the volume of credit.[22] It may be added that as lead banks, Crocker National Bank and the Bank of Tokyo often reinforced trends created by Wells Fargo.

It is interesting to note that in forming their syndicates the upstart banks relied heavily on the participation of other relatively inexperienced banks. For instance, Wells Fargo drew heavily on Japanese banks, which contributed approximately one-third of the funds raised in syndication by this institution. Small- and medium-sized U.S. regional banks also had a high profile in this California bank's syndicates. Wells Fargo— as well as other upstart lead banks—also had a tendency to develop market power by establishing a working relationship with certain newcomers, repeatedly drawing them into its syndicates. The big, internationally established banks, in contrast, rarely developed relationships in their formation of syndicates, and to the degree that they did, it was with each other.[23]

BOLIVIA   Before 1974 Bolivia had little access to bank loans, except for guaranteed export credits and the like. But in early 1974 Bank

[22] It also is interesting to note that a high-level executive in Wells Fargo's international loan office was an ex-Peruvian central banker during the first Belaúnde administration. This illustrates how personal contacts are so important in banking.

[23] This is illustrated in table 40 of Devlin, *Transnational Banks and Peru*.

of America (BOA)—then the world's largest bank, and better-informed about Bolivia due to a branch office in La Paz—organized a $25 million syndicate for the government in which there was the participation of twelve other institutions. The biggest shares, after BOA, were taken up by Bank of Montreal, First Chicago, and Banco do Brasil—all mega-banks, and with the exception of the latter, well established internationally. The terms were very stiff for this period, 1.875 percent over LIBOR and a commission of 2 percent for a maturity of eight years. The authorities were willing to pay the high price for their first syndicated loan because they viewed it as a way to establish themselves in the market.

And this is exactly what happened. The BOA loan was followed by the organization of another syndicate of twelve banks for $24 million, headed by Dresdner Bank of Germany and having Citicorp and Banca Nazionale de Lavoro as comanagers.[24] This was a competitive operation, reflected in the better terms: a margin of 1.81 percent and commissions of 1.1 percent for an eight-year maturity.

Bolivia's maiden voyage into the eurocurrency market was disrupted by the Herstatt crisis in Europe, and no major credits were contracted for the rest of the year and into early 1975. However, in mid-1975 BOA organized another syndicate, of $35 million, for the state oil company. There were fourteen banks participating, and some of them were those of earlier syndicates such as Citicorp, First Chicago, and Dresdner. The market at this time was evidently quite uncompetitive due to the withdrawal of many institutions, as evidenced by the virtual absence of the once aggressive Japanese banks from Bolivian syndication that year.[25] As one might expect in a tight oligopolistic market, the institutions that remained interested in international lending competed more in loan availability than in price, as reflected in the 2.14 percent margin and seven-year maturity for the BOA syndicated credit. Nevertheless, the willingness of these big, mostly well-established international lenders to award finance in a tight market to little-appreciated Bolivia obviously raised the country's stature in international banking circles.

Indeed, thereafter Bolivia's reception in the market steadily improved. The period June to September 1976 was one of exceptional success for the authorities. At midyear BOA led the then-largest syndicate ever for the country: with seventeen banks it mobilized $50 million. The

[24] Both Dresdner and Citicorp had offices in La Paz. The Bolivian minister of finance was the ex-general manager of Citicorp's local branch in the country. Once again, there is the evidence of the importance of personal contacts in bank-lending behavior.

[25] The Japanese minister of finance had prohibited the country's banks from lending overseas.

loan was expensive (2 percent over LIBOR for five-year maturities) but incorporated prestigious banks that never before had lent to Bolivia, such as Chemical Bank and Deutsche Bank. A few months later Citicorp—BOA's principal competitor both in the Bolivian market and worldwide—organized an even bigger loan for $75 million on similar terms. Moreover, it too brought in new prestigious banks as participants, for example, Morgan Guaranty and Bank of Tokyo.

And so it went—terms improved the next couple of years, while loan volume was high. The country's expansive credit cycle, however, ran into difficulty during the course of 1978. The economic situation had begun to show obvious deterioration and General Banzer was ousted in midyear by another general. In 1979 access to credit was finally halted and the economy collapsed. Debt was eventually rescheduled in 1981. However, that agreement was quickly broken by the government as the crisis deepened and the country drifted into an indefinite moratorium.

What distinguishes the penetration of the Bolivian market is that it was a relatively more controlled and protracted process, the dynamics of which were more influenced by the big, internationally established banks than by the newcomers. This had its origins in the restricted nature of the interbank market at the outset of banks' penetration and, perhaps, Bolivia's notoriously poor reputation as a borrower, which the big banks were in a better position to overcome. But it also is less than coincidental that the country's main lead institutions had offices in La Paz and were in a better position than other banks to be affected by the optimism of the Banzer regime.

Further Information on the Terms of Lending   We just reviewed some of the dynamics of competition surrounding the penetration of the Peruvian and Bolivian markets. Tables 4.9 and 4.10 provide more insight on the trends. Table 4.9 displays loan volume and the negotiated cost, or price, of credit—margin, amortization period, and commission—for loans to Peru and Bolivia. The table also allows one to compare the negotiated cost with Mexico, the premier Latin American borrower during the 1970s. Table 4.10 converts the data into comparative indexes over the respective credit cycles. The indexes of the negotiated cost of credit have moreover been given two dimensions: one is an absolute index of the terms granted Peru and Bolivia, respectively, while the second is a relative index of those terms, which tracks their evolution as compared to those of Mexico. The use of Mexico as a benchmark allows us to discriminate—admittedly quite imperfectly—between trends in credit terms for the two countries and overall market trends.

It can be seen that Peru received a large volume of loans throughout

TABLE 4.9. Peru, Bolivia, and Mexico: Loan Volume, Margins over LIBOR, Amortization Periods, and Flat Commissions on Syndicated Loans

Year	Peru				Bolivia				Mexico		
	Loans[a]	Margin[b]	Amort.[c]	Comm.[d]	Loans[a]	Margin[b]	Amort.[c]	Comm.[d]	Margin[b]	Amort.[c]	Comm.[d]
1972	148.2	2.08	6.3	0.28	. . .[e]	. . .	. . .	. . .			
1973	412.0	1.68	8.9	0.44	. . .	. . .	. . .	. . .	0.65	11.3	
1974	315.0	1.13	9.7	0.29	52.5	1.87	7.8	1.51	0.83	7.9	
1975	382.4	1.79	5.7	0.95	85.3	2.17	6.2	0.81	1.50	4.8	
1976	403.9	2.19	5.0	1.42	161.0	2.02	5.0	1.63	1.50	5.7	
1977					128.0	1.86	6.8	1.19	1.67	6.8	
1978					207.2	1.57	7.0	0.74	1.09	8.2	
1979					108.1	1.43	6.2	0.73	0.69	8.4	

SOURCES: Peru—Ministry of Economy and Finance; Bolivia—Central Bank; Mexico—World Bank, *Borrowing in International Capital Markets* (Washington, D.C.), various numbers.

NOTES: Information is for syndicated loans that are based on the LIBOR (London Interbank Offer Rate) and that do not have the guarantee of export credit agencies.

[a] Millions of dollars of medium- to long-term loans.

[b] Weighted average of points over LIBOR.

[c] Weighted average amortization period, in years.

[d] Weighted average of flat commissions, expressed as a percentage of the total face value of the loan.

[e] (. . .) = zero or not large enough to quantify.

TABLE 4.10. Peru and Bolivia: Loan Volume and Price Indexes (1974 = 100)

Year	Peru Loan Volume[a]	Peru Price[b] Absolute[c]	Peru Price[b] Relative[d]	Bolivia Loan Volume[a]	Bolivia Price[b] Absolute[c]	Bolivia Price[b] Relative[d]	Absolute Price with Commission[e] Peru	Absolute Price with Commission[e] Bolivia
1971	...f	...		...	...		...	...
1972	47	283		...	...		282	...
1973	131	162	296	...	...	...	163	...
1974	100	100	100	100	100	100	100	100
1975	121	270	91	163	146	49	287	140
1976	128	376	150	307	169	67	414	177
1977				244	114	49		113
1978				395	94	74		90
1979				206	96	123		94

SOURCES: Same as Table 4.9.

NOTES: Loan volume and price indexes are for syndicated loans based on the LIBOR that do not have guarantees of export credit agencies.

[a]Gross loans valued in dollars.

[b]Index developed from the margin over LIBOR and the amortization period where for each year the average margin is divided by the average amortization period. Averages are weighted by the value of the loans.

[c]$= [(Mi/Ai)/(Mo/Ao)] \times 100$, where M = margin, A = amortization period, i = ith year, o = base year.

[d]$[(Mxi/Axi)/(Mmi/Ami)] \times 100$, where x is Peru or Bolivia and m is Mexico. Converted to a 1974 base.

[e]A price index that incorporates the commission: $P = \{[(Ci/Ai + Mi)/Ai]/[(Co/Ao + Mo)/Ao]\} \times 100$, where C = average commission.

[f]$(...)$ = zero or not large enough to quantify.

the credit cycle. On an absolute basis terms improved until 1975, when there was a sharp deterioration. But the deterioration that year reflects the tight market due to the Herstatt crisis; on a relative basis its negotiated price of credit continued to improve right up until 1976, the year of a critical payments crisis with the banks.

As for Bolivia, the conditions of credit in absolute terms underwent a deterioration in the second and third years of the cycle, yet this was due again to the Herstatt crisis. Viewed relatively, there was a general trend of favorable conditions up until 1978, when one notes a reversal. But although relative conditions underwent a deterioration, the absolute conditions—reflecting the overall shift to a borrower's market—continued to improve in 1978 and underwent practically no change in the crisis of 1979, the last year of regular market access. This illustrates quite well the point made in the earlier chapter in which banks price loans passively on the basis of a ranking system rather than on any explicit or active calculation of a risk-price relationship.

Credit Rationing

I pointed out in Chapter Three that credit rationing cannot be measured directly. However, indirect measures suggest that during much of the credit cycle Peru and Bolivia did not experience rationing. On the contrary, supply was abundant and apparently in excess of what could be deployed productively.

As I mentioned earlier, one sign that rationing is not taking place is when banks begin to do what they profess not to like to do. The quote from Aronson in the previous chapter (p. 109) lays out the traditional preferences. Basically, banks prefer to lend for commercially viable projects or specific programs and are uncomfortable with refinance loans and general lending, which erodes their ability to control the use of credit. Yet in their respective credit cycles in the 1970s a high proportion of credits went into exactly the types of lending that the banks profess to dislike. In the case of Peru, 49 percent of the lending was to refinance old loans, 28 percent was of free disposition (totally untied), and only 15 percent was directly linked to projects or capital goods imports. In Bolivia, 18 percent of the lending went to refinance loans, 43 percent were of free disposition, and 33 percent were linked to projects or capital goods imports (tables 4.11 and 4.12).

The free-disposition loans are exceptionally illustrative of the dynamics of abundant supply. As I have repeatedly noted, banks were attempting to break into demand-constrained credit markets. If all their lending were tied to real activity, the constraint would have been nearly binding. However, the aggressive banks cleverly offered the borrowers free-disposition loans, which instantly made the demand curves more elastic and reduced the constraint on market penetration. A very poor country such as Bolivia, with a notoriously low ability to absorb resources, could be accommodated to market supply only by selling "do-as-you-like" loans. This, of course, raised the risk of the resources ending up in unproductive uses—which we will see often happened—but it apparently was not a concern of many creditors at the time.

Refinance loans could serve the same purposes, but not always. These credits are an instrument of market penetration; a bank offers to refinance another bank's loan at a cheaper price. This type of sales promo-

TABLE 4.11. Peru: Bank Loans by Type, 1972–1976
(percentages)

Type	1972	1973	1974	1975	1976	Entire Period
Goods imports	3.0	4.1	1.2	0.1	1.9	2.1
Refinance	74.6	23.1	65.6	14.9	78.1	48.6
Free disposition	. . .[a]	69.1	4.0	39.1	6.1	27.8
Projects	22.3	0.5	5.7	45.8	7.6	14.7
Nationalizations	. . .	2.8	19.1	. . .	6.3	6.1
Other	0.1	0.4	4.4	0.1	. . .	0.7
Total	100.0	100.0	100.0	100.0	100.0	100.0

SOURCE: Calculated from data provided by the Ministry of Economy and Finance of Peru.
NOTES: Information is for loans without export credit guarantees.
[a](. . .) = zero or not large enough to quantify.

tion, of course, is attractive to the borrower as well because an old expensive loan can be traded in for a new, less expensive one. The granting of refinance loans also can be motivated by a desire to avoid default, however, and in this sense are somewhat forced on the banks. The latter type of refinance occurs only at, or near, the crisis phase of the cycle. For instance, the large percentage of refinance loans offered in 1976 to Peru was due to the banks' efforts to avoid default in a country that could no longer honor its obligations.

Project loans in contrast are only a limited instrument for market penetration because their volume is restrained by the ability of the country to formulate investment ventures. But even project loans can have an undesirable marketing component if the banks willingly finance poorly designed or overdimensioned investments. This issue by its nature is difficult to evaluate, but there is some evidence of easy finance for ill-conceived projects, especially in Bolivia.[26]

The degree of aggressive nontraditional lending behavior was found not to be uniform among the banks.[27] For instance, the Japanese, Ital-

[26] Devlin and Mortimore, *Los Bancos Transnacionales y Bolivia*, chapter 7.

[27] In the two cases, I ranked the relative aggressiveness of the banks grouped by country of origin. The ranking was based on the distribution of loans by type and sectorial preference. Nontraditional loans were those that were for free disposition and refinance (type) and had a noncommercial sectorial preference (sector). The distributions were converted into standardized variables and scored. The step-by-step calculations and scores are pub-

TABLE 4.12. Bolivia: Bank Loans by Type, 1970–1979 (percentages)

Type	1970	1971	1972	1973	1974	1975	1976	1977	1978	1979	Entire Period
Goods imports	. . ᵃ	. . .	. . .	. . .	5.1	8.9	0.5	9.7	2.1	0.3	3.8
Refinance	. . .	. . .	. . .	. . .	. . .	. . .	3.7	3.5	63.9	. . .	18.2
Free disposition	. . .	. . .	. . .	. . .	68.0	23.5	79.7	21.2	25.9	59.2	43.2
Projects	100.0	. . .	47.4	100.0	26.9	61.6	16.1	65.6	8.1	40.5	32.7
Nationalizations	. . .	. . .	. . .	. . .	. . .	. . .	. . .	. . .	. . .	. . .	0.6
Other	. . .	. . .	52.6	. . .	. . .	6.0	. . .	. . .	. . .	. . .	1.5
Total	100.0	. . . .	100.0	100.0	100.0	100.0	100.0	100.0	100.0	100.0	100.0

SOURCE: Calculated from data provided by the Central Bank of Bolivia.
NOTES: Information is for loans without export credit guarantees.
ᵃ(. . .) = zero or not large enough to quantify.

ian, and consortium banks were the relatively most unorthodox lenders in the case of Peru. British and German banks, on the other hand, tended to stay more within the traditional norms of banking outlined by Aronson. In the case of Bolivia the most unorthodox lenders were Canadian and U.S. banks, while the most traditional behavior was recorded by Japanese, German, and "other" banks, the latter being a residual category that incorporated largely small countries and small banks. The strikingly different rating for Japanese institutions in the two cases reflects the fact that these banks were exceptionally conservative for a couple of years following the Herstatt crisis.[28]

There is other evidence of unrationed markets and abundant supply. In 1973 to 1974 Peru's loan syndications were frequently oversubscribed, meaning that the banks at the moment of syndication offered more money than the government and its lead banks had solicited.[29] A good sign of oversupply in Peru was the banks' participation in a loan syndicate in 1974, which was part of the financial package for a highly controversial and evidently overdimensioned $1 billion trans-Andean oil pipeline.[30] There is similar evidence of oversubscriptions in Bolivian syndicates beginning in 1976. Particularly revealing is an incident in which Chase Manhattan was so eager to lend to the country that it broke ranks with the tradition of creditor solidarity and entered into a syndicate even though the government was in default on some turn-of-the-century bonds that had been underwritten by Chase. The bank's legal advisers were horrified by the marketing department's lack of discretion. The legal department eventually won the battle, but as Chase withdrew from the syndicate there was another institution willing to replace it.

---

lished in Devlin, *Transnational Banks and Peru*, pp. 159–174; and Devlin and Mortimore, *Los Bancos Transnacionales y Bolivia*, pp. 100–106 and 258–268.

[28] A similar, but less-marked, behavior was found for other banks. During Peru's credit cycle, Italian, consortium, and "other" banks on balance were relatively unorthodox lenders. But during Bolivia's cycle these same banks—under the influence of the interbank crisis—behaved relatively more conservatively. The different behavior also reflects changing market conditions.

[29] Drawn from conversations with negotiators in COFIDE, the Banco de la Nación, and the Ministry of Economy and Finance.

[30] The technical merits of the pipeline were apparently quite weak. The U.S. Export-Import Bank refused to finance the project on the grounds that studies on proven reserves were dubious and did not justify such a massive investment. The refusal was not an easy one since at this time the U.S. administration was actively attempting to improve its image in Peru after having settled a six-year investment dispute that had involved a financial blockade of the country. The bank's evaluation subsequently proved correct as the level of reserves could not justify the scale of the pipeline.

Other evidence running counter to the notion of rationing was that neither country's public sector confronted demands for collateral or escrow accounts during the periods of intense expansion, nor were loans conditioned by the presence of the IMF. The only security required was a general guarantee from the state, which was a pro forma demand of the banks everywhere.[31]

Finally, we turn to some anecdotal evidence that echoes Angel Gurría's remark of the last chapter. Questioned on the environment in Lima during the development of the credit cycle in the early 1970s, one local banker remarked, "Foreign bankers wanted to give us the money before we asked for it." Meanwhile, an official from COFIDE, a Peruvian state development bank mandated to contract foreign loans for the public sector, has commented that during the 1970s, "the banks were eager to lend and would lend for anything."[32]

Creditworthiness

At the Outset of the Credit Cycle   There is little doubt that Peru and Bolivia merited access to bank credit. Prior to entering into their respective credit cycles, both countries had undertaken adjustment and stabilization programs, which were in some ways successful. Bearing in mind the creditworthiness criteria of the banks that were outlined in Chapter Three, we can briefly review the state of the economies at the outset of the respective credit cycles.

PERU   The Velasco regime took power in late 1968 amidst President Belaúnde's economic crisis. Through the inheritance of the civilian administration's emergency economic measures of June of that year, through its own emergency policy, and through a windfall improvement in the terms of trade in 1969 to 1970, the government managed to stabilize the domestic economy and balance the crisis-ridden external accounts. Moreover, the ordering of the domestic economy—done without the IMF—was accompanied by very respectable growth rates (tables 4.13 and 4.14). On the political side the regime was stable and enjoyed considerable support in the popular segments of society.

[31] During the 1960s, Peru had to arrange escrow accounts on some loans. Bolivia had to do this on certain credits contracted prior to 1976. During a period of active market penetration no bank can demand special security because there will always be a competing institution willing to do the same loan without such arrangements.

[32] The first quote is from Everett Martin, "Peru's Economic Woes Are Worrying Bankers Who Aid Third World," *Wall Street Journal*, 1 September 1977, p. 1; the second is from Deborah Riner, "Borrowers and Bankers: The Euromarket and Political Economy in Peru and Chile" (Ph.D. diss., Princeton University, 1982), p. 203.

TABLE 4.13. Peru: Selected Economic Indicators (I)

	Growth Rates (%)							As Percentage of GDP									
				Exports[d]		Imports[d]			External Sector[e]		Fiscal[f]					
								Fixed			Income		Expenditure		Deficit	
Year	Prices[a]	Money[b]	GDP[c]	Value	Vol.	Value	Vol.	Investment	Exports	Imports	(I)	(II)	(I)	(II)	(I)	(II)
1968	19.0	10.9	-0.3	13.0	11.1	13.3	-13.2	12.7	15.4	11.7	16.2		17.9		2.6	
1969	6.3	8.4	3.9	5.2	-4.2	-1.5	-1.6	12.6	14.2	11.1	16.3		16.5		2.1	
1970	5.0	25.8	5.4	16.5	4.4	8.5	5.9	13.3	14.3	11.2	16.1		17.5		3.8	
1971	6.8	19.0	5.0	-12.8	-8.6	4.5	1.0	13.8	12.3	10.7	15.7		18.7		6.1	
1972	7.2	17.0	1.7	8.0	7.8	8.7	-2.9	14.0	13.0	10.3	15.5		14.1		6.7	
1973	9.5	24.3	4.3	16.5	-14.7	34.6	17.7	17.0	10.6	11.6	14.9	36.1	18.8	45.0	8.3	8.9
1974	16.9	26.1	7.5	37.1	-2.6	64.6	54.3	20.2	9.6	16.6	15.3	39.3	18.5	49.8	6.7	10.5
1975	23.6	26.0	4.5	-8.3	-3.1	24.4	6.9	20.9	8.9	17.0	15.8	34.8	21.3	51.8	7.8	12.0
1976	33.5	14.3	2.0	3.3	-1.0	-13.6	-16.3	17.6	8.7	13.9	14.5	28.6	20.8	50.9	8.4	12.3

SOURCES: Prices, money, and reserves—IMF, *International Financial Statistics Yearbook 1985* (Washington, D.C., 1986), lines 54, 82, 106; GDP, exports, imports, ICOR—ECLAC data; fiscal data—Banco Central de Reserva del Perú, *Memoria* (Lima), various number; external debt—Inter-American Development Bank, *External Public Debt of the Latin American Countries*, tables 1 and 57, and Banco Central de Reserva del Perú, *Memoria 1983* (Lima, 1984), p. 129; interest rates—Vincent Galbis, "Inflation and Interest Rate Policies in Latin America, 1967–1976," *Staff Papers* 26 (June 1979): 334–366; exchange rate—Devlin, *Transnational Banks and Peru*, table 6.

NOTES:

[a] Consumer prices.

[b] M_2.

[c] Real (1970 = 100).

[d] Goods and services.

[e] Expressed in 1970 dollars.

[f] (I) is central government and (II) is consolidated public sector.

Referring to the four key indicators of creditworthiness of the banks, Peru would have fared reasonably well. The public debt service ratio of 16 percent in 1971 was relatively low.[33] The balance of payments position was strong, as international reserves were nearly five months' import requirements, well above the three months that is traditionally considered the safe minimum. While the value of exports had declined in 1971, the export performance in the three preceding years was reasonably strong; moreover, the government and foreign oil companies were promising new exports of oil on a large scale. Finally, Peru's internal rate of growth during 1969 to 1971 was relatively high (Table 4.13).

The country fares less well when we compare Peru's economic policies with those described in Chapter Three as indicative of good economic management from the banker's point of view. These include:

—*A structure of incentives that rewards risk taking for productive ends.* Peru did give considerable tax breaks for private investment, but its positive effects were eroded by strong ideological differences with the business community and a 1970 law that introduced a phased program of workers' control of private enterprises. The regime was relatively hostile to foreign investors;

—*A legal structure conducive to free markets.* Peru's regime was skeptical of free markets and indeed blamed the country's traditional liberal economic policy for the conditions of dependence and underdevelopment;

—*Correction of market distortions at the source.* The regime actively relied on price controls, subsidies, and tariffs to direct economic activity;

—*Simple and decentralized rules.* Peru's regime was statist and favored bureaucratization and planning;

—*Open economies that follow the rules of comparative advantage.* The regime vigorously rejected this type of strategy; indeed, Peru had traditionally followed the policies of open economy and this was blamed for the country's underdevelopment;

—*Reasonable investment coefficients and low ICORs of 2 to 3.* Peru's investment coefficient in 1969 to 1971 was relatively modest, 13 to 14 percent, reflecting stabilization efforts and the Nixon financial blockade. The ICOR was reasonable, at 3 (Table 4.14);

—*A declining ratio of fiscal expenditures to GNP.* Central government expenditures were held relatively constant during 1969 and 1970 but

[33] Some have argued that a safe maximum overall coefficient is 40 percent. See Eduardo Sarmiento, *El Endeudamiento en Economías Fluctuantes y Segmentadas* [Debt in Fluctuating and Segmented Economies] (Bogotá: Fondo Editorial CEREC, 1985), p. 110.

TABLE 4.14. Peru: Selected Economic Indicators (II)

Debt	Debt[a] ÷ Exports		Public Debt Service[a] ÷ Exports	Reserves[b]	Exchange Rate[c]	ICOR[d]	Real Interest Rates[e]
	Public	Total					
1968	1.0		14.6	1.5	93.0		−11.8
1969	1.0		11.9	2.2	89.6	3.4	−1.2
1970	0.9		11.7	4.2	87.0	2.6	0.0
1971	1.2		15.9	4.6	86.7	2.9	−1.7
1972	1.3		15.9	4.9	86.3	8.9	−2.2
1973	1.8		29.7	3.8	85.4	4.2	−4.6
1974	1.9	2.8	23.5	3.9	86.7	2.9	−11.6
1975	2.4	3.7	26.1	1.6	83.1	4.8	−20.9
1976	3.2	4.2	26.1	1.3	91.1	8.9	−27.7

SOURCES: See Table 4.13.
NOTES:
[a]Excludes short-term debt.
[b]Expressed as months of imports.
[c]Index of the real value of the exchange rate based on differential rates of inflation between Peru and the United States (1964 = 100).
[d]Incremental capital output ratio ($I/\Delta Y$).
[e]On savings deposits.

showed a significant rise in 1971 (Table 4.13). Given government nationalizations of private firms, total public sector expenditure had to be rising sharply in the early 1970s;
— *Positive real interest rates and minimal subsidized credit.* Real interest rates were negative in 1969 to 1971, but the negative rate was much less negative than that prevailing in 1968 (Table 4.14). Subsidized interest rates were common. The government nevertheless had the stated goal of promoting investment with internal savings;
— *A freely floating exchange rate that maintains parity.* The regime had a strong commitment to a fixed rate. The exchange rate was unchanged since 1968, a year in which there was a 26 percent devaluation.

In sum, on policy Peru violated most of the bankers' tenets of good economic management. It is evident that what attracted the bankers' attention was the immediacy of the relatively strong liquidity in the external sector, the promises of an oil bonanza, and political stability.
    BOLIVIA   The country had entered into a Fund stabilization program in 1972 to 1973. The revolutionary measures of the previous re-

gime of General Juan-José Torres were rolled back by General Banzer, and, as mentioned earlier, the new government strongly favored private capital, both national and foreign.

On the basis of the banks' key creditworthiness indicators, Bolivia did fairly well. Even though the country had a large debt (nearly three times export earnings in the early 1970s), the debt service ratio was not alarmingly high due to the basically concessionary sources of finance (tables 4.15 and 4.16). The rise in oil prices (and commodity prices in general) in 1973 and 1974 dramatically boosted export earnings, reducing the debt service coefficient further and raising reserves to a record level of five months of import requirements. In addition to a liquid external sector, growth was strong in the early years of the Banzer regime. And as I said before, the regime was seemingly stable.

Turning to policy, Bolivia's program would have been looked upon favorably by most bankers. It incorporated:

—*A structure of incentives that rewards risk taking for productive ends.* The Banzer regime blatantly favored the private sector and wanted to reorient Bolivia's massive public sector (which accounted for more than 40 percent of the official GNP) in a way that would be supportive of private sector activity;

—*A legal structure conducive to free markets.* Since the 1952 revolution Bolivia has had a state-dominated economy. The Banzer regime was committed to shifting the country to a private market-oriented economy;

—*Correction of market distortions at the source.* There was a commitment to "get the prices right." The regime removed, or substantially reduced, subsidies on popular food items and services, while taxes and tariffs were lowered or abolished to facilitate the free flow of private capital;[34]

—*Simple and decentralized rules.* Again a commitment to this policy, but the regime inherited a highly bureaucratized economy and continued to support a planning apparatus;

—*Open economies that follow the rules of comparative advantage.* The regime opened the economy to foreign capital and imports and wanted to promote commodity exports, particularly private sector agrobusiness from the Santa Cruz area;

—*Reasonable investment coefficients and low ICORs of 2 to 3.* In 1972 and 1973 investment coefficients were at an intermediate level of 15 to 16 percent. The ICOR was about 3 (Table 4.16);

—*A declining ratio of fiscal expenditures to GNP.* In the early 1970s

[34] Details can be found in James Dunkerley, *Rebellion in the Veins: Political Struggle in Bolivia, 1952–1982* (London: New Left Books, Verso edition, 1984), pp. 210–219.

TABLE 4.15. Bolivia: Selected Economic Indicators (I)

| | Growth Rates (%) | | | | | | | | As Percentage of GDP | | | | |
| | | | | Exports[d] | | Imports[d] | | | External Sector[e] | | Fiscal[f] | | |
Year	Prices[a]	Money[b]	GDP[c]	Value	Vol.	Value	Vol.	Investment	Exports	Imports	Income	Expenditure	Deficit
1970	3.8	12.0	5.2	7.9	-6.0	-16.6	-19.8	14.5	14.9	13.1	8.9	9.5	1.5
1971	3.7	14.9	4.9	-3.3	13.5	6.2	3.6	15.2	16.2	12.9	8.3	9.8	2.3
1972	6.5	23.5	5.8	12.5	9.2	14.4	8.2	16.0	16.7	13.2	8.7	12.3	4.8
1973	31.5	33.2	6.7	29.0	5.4	21.7	6.0	14.7	16.5	13.1	9.2	9.9	1.5
1974	62.8	40.6	5.1	106.8	5.3	67.2	36.2	15.2	16.5	17.0	12.8	12.9	1.2
1975	8.0	30.6	6.6	-18.2	-9.7	39.6	23.9	17.1	14.0	19.7	12.8	13.2	1.6
1976	4.5	33.2	6.1	28.4	21.5	6.5	1.6	16.9	16.0	18.9	13.4	14.8	2.8
1977	8.1	40.2	4.2	11.5	-4.3	15.3	4.6	17.2	14.7	19.0	13.0	17.9	5.7
1978	10.4	18.4	3.4	1.2	-8.0	24.6	13.4	18.2	13.1	20.8	12.5	16.1	4.4
1979	19.7	11.8	1.8	21.5	3.1	14.3	-2.6	15.8	13.3	19.9	10.3	17.3	8.2

SOURCES: Prices and money—IMF, *International Financial Statistics Yearbook 1985*, lines 82, 106; GDP, exports, imports investment—ECLAC data; fiscal data—Banco Central de Bolivia, *Memoria*, various numbers; external debt—Inter-American Development Bank, *External Public Debt of the Latin American Countries*, tables 1 and 57; interest rates—Galbis, "Inflation and Interest Rates"; exchange rate—Michael Mortimore, "The State and Transnational Banks: Lessons from the Bolivian Crisis of External Public Indebtedness," *CEPAL Review*, no. 14 (August 1981), pp. 127–151, table 10.

NOTES:

[a]Consumer prices. Note that consumer prices were subject to price controls.

[b]M_2.

[c]Real (1970 = 100).

[d]Goods and services.

[e]Expressed in 1970 dollars.

[f]Central government.

TABLE 4.16. Bolivia: Selected Economic Indicators (II)

Year	Public Debt[a] ÷ Exports	Public Debt Service[a] ÷ Exports	Reserves[b]	Exchange Rate[c]	ICOR[d]	Real Interest Rate[e]
1970	2.7	11.2	3.1		2.9	5.9
1971	3.2	12.1	3.5		3.3	6.2
1972	3.4	17.9	3.3		2.9	3.3
1973	2.7	16.0	3.3	100.0	2.3	−16.4
1974	1.6	11.5	5.1	75.3	3.4	−32.4
1975	2.6	15.4	3.4	76.7	2.8	1.9
1976	2.6	17.3	3.2	73.6	2.9	4.3
1977	2.9	22.6	3.7	68.7	4.3	
1978	3.4	50.5	2.5	67.2	5.6	
1979	3.3	31.5	2.3	65.8	8.8	

SOURCES: See Table 4.15.
NOTES:
[a]Excludes short-term debt.
[b]Expressed as months of imports.
[c]Index of the real value of the exchange rate based on differential rates of inflation between Bolivia and the United States.
[c]Incremental capital output ratio ($I/\Delta Y$).
[d]On savings deposits.

the central government's expenditures were equivalent to 10 to 12 percent of GNP (consolidated public accounts are unavailable). There was a marked drop in the relative magnitude of the fiscal deficit (Table 4.15);

—*Positive real interest rates and minimal subsidized credit.* Interest rates were positive in real terms prior to the unexpected inflationary boom of 1973 to 1974, brought on in part by high external prices for exports and imports. In 1975 positive real rates were restored (Table 4.16). The government subsidized credit for some activities, for example, agriculture. There was a stated goal to finance the bulk of investment with internal savings;

—*A freely floating exchange rate that maintains parity.* After a devaluation of 68 percent at the end of 1972, the authorities pursued a fixed exchange rate policy.

In sum, Bolivia's declared intentions were all very closely allied with the bankers' perception of good management. In practice, the economy was highly state-run, however, reflecting the heritage of the previous twenty years. Beginning in late 1973 the external sector was very liquid, and this, given that 90 percent of exports were generated by the state, buoyed the fiscal accounts. Moreover, the government and foreign oil drillers promised more oil and gas exports in the future.

During the Credit Cycle   It has been noted that banks were conventionally conceived as enforcers of discipline in borrowing countries. Their caution was supposed to encourage an economic policy that enhanced both creditworthiness and development. Just prior to initiating their credit cycles with the banks, both countries had indeed pursued credible stabilization and adjustment programs, which improved their image of creditworthiness. This, coupled with favorable external prices, put the economies in reasonably good shape. As for policy instruments, Bolivia had stated intentions that were mostly consistent with the bankers' notion of good management; Peru did not. Both countries offered the banks the promise of lucrative petroleum exports.

What is interesting is that upon gaining access to bank credit, many key economic variables ceased to improve and indeed drifted into deterioration. In other words, rather than enforcing discipline, the bank loans allowed the discipline that the countries initially displayed to unravel. Moreover, the international banking system as a whole did not react to the situation until the magnitude of disequilibrium was very large and a crisis of major proportions was difficult to avoid.

One key variable to note is exports. The relatively good export performance of the countries was to a large extent due to exogenous price effects; the volume of exports turned down almost immediately with the initiation of the countries' respective credit cycles. By the end of the credit cycles the respective export coefficients (exports/GDP) were well below the levels registered at the outset of the cycle—29 percent lower for Peru and 19 percent for Bolivia (tables 4.13 and 4.15). In the case of Peru the decline was particularly severe and marked the persistence of a trend that had begun before the arrival of bank finance. In sum, the seemingly solid export growth was built on highly uncertain exogenous price effects. When the commodity price boom ended in 1975, export performance was no longer a strong feature of the economies.

The slippage in the performance of exports was to at least a significant degree linked to economic policy. In the case of Peru there never was a strong vocation for exports, as suggested by a demagogic policy stance on the exchange rate, maintaining it fixed between 1968 and 1975.[35] As seen in Table 4.14, the exchange rate had lost competitive-

---

[35] Peru had a tradition of political "machismo" regarding the exchange rate. Devaluation was interpreted as a sign of political weakness. This has been confirmed in the case of General Velasco. In an interview with Deborah Riner, a former director of the Central

ness since its last adjustment in 1968.[36] The government also chose to pursue a vigorous program to reorder its relations with private capital, which adversely affected investment, especially in the all important export-oriented mining sector.[37] Moreover, those investments that were undertaken had extremely long gestation periods.

Bolivia, in turn, was not a dynamic exporter, also in part due to policy. We will see later that state enterprises were taxed to such an onerous degree that they had difficulty investing in new capacity, while existing capacity was often of low productivity and reliant on high world prices for commercial viability. Meanwhile, the promotion of exports in the private sector often was for speculative activities related to high world commodity prices; when prices collapsed, so did the exports. The policy of maintaining the exchange rate fixed between 1972 and 1979 further aggravated the problem and inhibited development of more sustainable nontraditional exports.

On the side of imports the trend was quite the opposite. The two countries went on an import binge, and import coefficients rose dramatically during the credit cycles of both the countries (tables 4.13 and 4.15). Some increase was of course essential in view of ambitious investment programs, but there also was fat in the import structure. In Peru the military government indulged in an extravagant military arms purchase program;[38] it subsidized food imports while doing little conducive to boosting stagnant local food production, and durable goods imports—cheapened by the fixed exchange rate—rose nearly sixfold between 1971 and 1975.[39]

Bank revealed that the military president felt that a devaluation would destroy his political program (Riner, "Borrowers and Bankers," p. 180).

[36] Moreover, the devaluation in 1968 had still left the exchange rate parity 7 percent below that registered in 1964. See Devlin, *Transnational Banks and Peru*, table 6.

[37] Peru also suffered from the ecological disappearance of the anchovy in the early 1970s. This was a major export product of the country. Some have said that the disappearance was related to overfishing.

[38] Some estimates have put the foreign purchases of arms as high as the equivalent of 30 percent of export earnings in 1973 to 1975. See José Encinas del Pando, "The Role of Military Expenditure in the Development Process: Peru, a Case Study, 1950–1980," *Ibero-Americana, Nordic Journal of Latin American Studies* 12 (1983): 85. Also, it has been commented to me on occasions that some big investment projects were motivated more by military geopolitical considerations than commercial viability. For what it is worth, some have said that the large and expensive irrigation projects on the north and south coasts of Peru were largely motivated by a perceived need to establish population buffer zones on borders with Ecuador and Chile. Meanwhile, some have commented that the military opted for the $1 billion trans-Andean pipeline because the alternative— barging oil down the Amazon River through Brazil—violated strategic considerations.

[39] From $20 million to $115 million. Banco Central de Reserva del Peru, *Memoria 1976* (Lima 1977), p. 182.

As for Bolivia, it also engaged in an import binge: purchase of consumer durables rose nearly eightfold between 1973 and 1978, while illegal imports were nearly as massive.[40] When the agriboom collapsed, many entrepreneurs turned to imports of materials for speculative real estate ventures.

On the fiscal front one also finds deterioration. Governmental tax pressure (tax income/GDP) stagnated during the upswing of the credit cycle, while expenditure jumped. The consequence was rising fiscal deficits (tables 4.13 and 4.15).

Also during the credit cycle money aggregates in both countries expanded very rapidly, feeding growth in domestic demand and imports. Inflation was delayed by price controls, subsidies, and a buoyant supply of imported goods but eventually reared its head during the credit cycle (tables 4.13 and 4.15).[41] Meanwhile, Peru's interest rates were increasingly negative during the cycle (Bolivia's were positive).

The debt indicators also deteriorated during the cycle. Debt service ratios (debt service/exports) rose steadily in both countries, though reaching alarming levels only for Bolivia in 1978 and 1979.[42] Debt-to-export ratios also rose in both countries, and these were more indicative of potential problems; ratios above 2 are frequently considered excessive from the standpoint of commercial credit relations. Bolivia's ratio was above this and rising from the initial stages of the credit cycle. Peru's medium- and long-term public debt did not double exports until 1975, but data on total debt for 1974 suggest that the 2:1 ratio was in fact breached earlier in the cycle.

What about positive performance? Investment coefficients rose and growth was strong during the credit cycles of both countries. Peru's ICOR increased uncomfortably, but this was to be expected during an investment program, especially one like Velasco's, which was biased to long-term payouts. The ICOR for Bolivia was remarkably low during the cycle. The international reserve situation was solid for both countries until the last two years of the credit cycle, when the import cover fell below three months.

---

[40] Legal durable consumer goods imports rose from $11 million in 1973 to $85 million in 1978. Estimates of illegal imports were $70 million annually. United Nations Economic Commission for Latin America and the Caribbean, *Economic Survey of Latin America 1978* (Santiago, Chile, 1979), p. 89.

[41] Uriarte has recently empirically linked the bank loans to inflation in Peru. See Manual Uriarte, "Transnational Banks and the Dynamics of Peruvian Foreign Debt and Inflation" (Ph.D. diss., The American University, 1984).

[42] The debt service ratios underestimate the burden because they exclude short-term obligations and private sector debt. (The latter was not important in either country.)

TABLE 4.17. Peru and Bolivia: The Internal and External Finance
of Investment
(percentages)

Year	Peru[a]		Bolivia[b]	
	Internal	External	Internal	External
1970	64.6	35.4	88	12
1971	76.6	23.4	80	20
1972	77.8	22.2	82	18
1973	71.2	28.8	92	8
1974	53.2	46.8	132	−32
1975	56.0	44.0	72	28
1976	59.6	40.4	84	16
1977			76	24
1978			56	44
1979			51	49

SOURCES: Peru—Hugo Cabieses and Carlos Otero, *Economía Peruana* [The Peruvian
Economy] (Lima: Centro de Estudios y Promoción del Desarrollo, 1977), p. 209;
Bolivia—Robert Devlin and Michael Mortimore, *Los Bancos Transnacionales, el
Estado, y el Endeudamiento Externo en Bolivia* (Santiago, Chile: United Nations,
1983), p. 126.
NOTES:
[a]Public sector.
[b]Entire economy, but investment was largely a public sector activity.

Those few positive indicators could have attracted a disproportionate amount of the bankers' attention. Indeed, they were to some extent
part of an elaborate mirror show, because the investment and growth,
as well as reserve situation, were increasingly linked to foreign borrowing. In Table 4.17 it can be seen that over the cycles investment was increasingly reliant on foreign funds.

As for the reserve situation it too was underpinned by loans. Peru ran
growing trade and current account deficits, so reserve accumulation
was facilitated by bank finance, not the autonomous generation of resources. Bolivia's reserve accumulation in 1973 and 1974 did have an
autonomous component as oil prices permitted the country to run trade
and current account surpluses. But thereafter the accounts ran into deficit and reserve levels were supported by an ability to borrow abroad.

How did the market react? It generally did not clearly signal a problem until the credit cycle was well advanced. Peru's access to credit was relatively easy until late 1975 and its credit conditions improved in absolute and relative terms up through 1974 (Table 4.10). An absolute deterioration in conditions was registered in 1975, but this could have been interpreted as a general market trend; indeed, as shown in Table 4.10, there was a slight improvement in the relative conditions of borrowing. Only in late 1975 and in 1976 were the bankers clearly signaling distress by a reluctance to extend new loans without reforms and by demanding stiff terms.

In the case of Bolivia there were no clear signs of problems with the bankers until early 1978. Before then authorities received as much finance as they considered necessary—and more. As for credit conditions, they worsened in absolute terms as a consequence of the tight international market. But in relative terms there was a trend of improvement up through 1977. In 1978, although relative terms deteriorated, on an absolute basis they actually improved because Bolivia benefited from a general softening of conditions in the eurocurrency market.

In sum, the market's signals were not very transparent until the situation had deteriorated sharply. Why? The answer is necessarily speculative. Some banks perhaps did not notice the deterioration. Other banks maybe noticed it but were unable to translate this institutionally into credit policy. Others, such as Citicorp in the case of Bolivia, evidently noticed a deterioration and translated it into a restrictive credit policy. Yet it apparently tried to disguise its withdrawal so that less-informed banks would fill the gap and thereby facilitate Citicorp's exposure reduction.[43]

The banking system's overall tolerance also undoubtedly was influenced by expectations of oil and gas discoveries in the two countries. Indeed, the bankers' signaling of difficulties more or less coincided with their eventual "discovery" that expectations about new hydrocarbon deposits were greatly exaggerated. But why did the banks lend so much on a promise? The market certainly could have served a useful disciplinary function by being more skeptical of the reports on oil until such time as confirmed quantities for export were available. As it was, the market did not temper the authorities' optimism but rather reinforced it in a procyclical way. Indeed, one senses the presence of casino instincts rather than discipline in the market's behavior.

---

[43] See Devlin and Mortimore, *Los Bancos Transnacionales y Bolivia*, p. 99, for details.

The Borrowers' Control of Debt

The Debt Control System   While the behavior of the borrowers is not central to the analysis, a brief review will help round out the story and reinforce some points made earlier about bank behavior.

Both Peru and Bolivia had been accustomed to capital scarcity. Both countries responded to changing events in world credit markets by eventually establishing internal institutional controls on foreign borrowing. The control apparatus was within a broader context of national planning. The systems provided for an elaborate procedure to approve projects, approve a financial package, and approve the terms of borrowing. Specialized offices or organizations were created to evaluate proposals and negotiate the amounts and terms of finance.

I refer the reader elsewhere for a detailed analysis and evaluation of how these systems and their respective agencies functioned bureaucratically.[44] The basic conclusion is, however, that they didn't work. At their best the respective systems were an ex post stamp of approval of decisions taken outside established channels. At their worst the systems were bypassed altogether.

The problems were legion. The new control agencies were not equipped to process and store such a large volume of credit flows generated by so many decentralized government agencies.[45] Thus they were overwhelmed by paper work and manpower was absorbed by filing rather than monitoring debt contraction and payment. Responsibilities were divided among different offices, making coordination difficult and fueling the rivalries to which large bureaucracies are so prone. The agencies also suffered from the fact that they did not have the political leverage to confront large state enterprises, which take pride in their autonomy, and generals who covet the prerogatives of the chain of command.

---

[44] Ugarteche has a very detailed analysis of the Peruvian debt control system during the Velasco period. See Oscar Ugarteche, "Mecanismos Institucionales del Financiamiento Externo del Perú: 1968–1978" [Institutional Mechanisms of External Finance in Peru, 1968–1978] (Santiago, Chile: United Nations Economic Commission for Latin America and the Caribbean, Joint Unit CEPAL/CET, E/CEPAL/L.205, September 1979). The study is summarized in Devlin, *Transnational Banks and Peru*, pp. 45–46, 54–56. Riner, "Borrowers and Bankers," chapter 3, also presents useful analysis on the Peruvian system. For an exhaustive study of the Bolivian system see Juan Villarroel and Tanya Villarroel, "Control Institucional de la Deuda Externa en Bolivia" [Institutional Control of the Bolivian External Debt] (La Paz, Bolivia, May 1981). The study's findings have been summarized in Devlin and Mortimore, *Los Bancos Transnacionales y Bolivia*, chapter 6.

[45] In the case of Bolivia I found that many loans were not filed and therefore I had to spend a good deal of time searching for contracts.

The latter problem was perhaps a central one and explains why only 10 percent of Bolivia's public projects passed through the formal planning system.[46] As for Peru, the behind-the-scenes process is captured in a remarkable comment of a Central Bank official:

> Loans were approved by the President although they were not profitable or could not generate any income to repay them. It was done by shouts. If a project wasn't approved, you went to the President. He shouted "yes" and the contract was presented to the Dirección General de Crédito Público [General Office of Public Credit] who had no choice but to approve it.[47]

The Dynamics of Indebtedness   Why the permissive environment? It was possibly because easy access to debt was an expedient for consolidating political power. At least this is the conclusion of some studies of the two experiences.

Riner has directly addressed this issue in Peru. She found that easy access to credit gave power to the "spenders" in Peruvian bureaucracy and undermined the position of "controllers." Moreover, the spenders served the regime's immediate political interests because spending gave legitimacy to the government and consolidated power with its two main constituencies: the generals and the popular masses. In effect, foreign loans financed arms purchases and facilitated the subsidization of consumer items. The availability of foreign exchange also helped Velasco pursue his uncomfortable alliance with the private sector and the middle class. Riner's analysis found support in the following observation made by a Central Bank official:

> Foreign borrowing was the way Velasco maintained his position. Ministries were the fiefdoms of the generals who headed them. Each general did whatever he wanted. There was a lot of borrowing for corruption's sake: the generals wanted their kickbacks. They received their percentage from the contract regardless of the merits of the project, so they borrowed for anything. Generals got rich from the projects and banks wanted to lend; the merits of the project were unimportant. By giving the generals free rein, Velasco retained his position.[48]

---

[46] Eduardo Arze Cuadros, *La Economía de Bolivia: Ordenamiento Territorial y Dominación Externa, 1492–1979* [The Economy of Bolivia: Territorial Order and External Domination, 1492–1979] (La Paz: Editorial Los Amigos del Libro, 1979), pp. 474–475.

[47] As quoted in Riner, "Borrowers and Bankers," p. 183.

[48] Ibid., p. 179.

Of course, a policy of massive indebtedness had built-in risks. But the market did not signal these risks until late 1975; before then, what was being done could have been legitimately interpreted as having fit into the bankers' notion of good management. Indeed, at the end of 1974 General Velasco felt comfortable enough to tell his nation that Peru had avoided the crisis that was afflicting the rest of the world.[49] That day he was secure and he would tackle tomorrow when it came. But Velasco was toppled in mid-1975 by a controller—his general heading the Ministry of Finance—as the latent crisis exposed itself. It certainly is ironic that a regime with the declared intention of reducing external dependence, and which vigorously "Peruvianized" major foreign enterprises, ended up having its existence partly determined by banks in New York. This same development also is indicative of how favorable signals from the banking community lulled the regime into a false sense of security.

In Bolivia the Banzer regime had its constituency in the generals and the private business community, especially in the new frontier area surrounding Santa Cruz. Mortimore argues that Banzer imposed an elitist regime on Bolivia's traditionally populist state.[50] The new role for the state—which traditionally had a sectorial or entrepreneurial role—was to mediate the expansion of the private sector. Internal credit was reallocated to the private sector; state banks subsidized loans, especially for Santa Cruz's often speculative agriculture; taxes and tariffs were reduced, and state enterprises often were restricted from pursuing commercial pricing.

Mortimore shows that these policies were supported by financially draining state enterprises, which were exceptionally attractive for milking given the high world prices for petroleum and minerals. As a somewhat perverse form of compensation for the raid on their own resources, Banzer let state enterprises randomly go to the eurocurrency market to borrow commercially expensive resources, that is, they exchanged export revenue for debt.

The effect on resource allocation of this program was tragic. According to Mortimore, the state enterprises felt threatened by Banzer's new mediatory role and attempted to protect their traditional sectorial function by using the foreign loans to invest as quickly as possible in fixed assets. As a consequence, investments were often ill-planned and over-

---

[49] His statement is famous and readily recognized by most any Peruvian.

[50] Michael Mortimore, "The State and Transnational Banks: Lessons from the Bolivian Crisis of External Public Indebtedness," *CEPAL Review*, no. 14 (August 1981), pp. 127–151.

scaled.[51] Meanwhile, the private sector was overwhelmed by the resources available to it and increasingly drifted into speculation and conspicuous consumption.[52] The international financial market, of course, did not signal its displeasure with these developments until late 1978, when for the first time it became difficult to secure credit and the relative terms of borrowing began to deteriorate.

As mentioned earlier, the underlying problem here is that politicized states are prone to short-term decision making designed to broaden coalitions. Credit is an exceptionally attractive instrument for this purpose because the benefits of a loan are immediate, while its costs are in the future. But even an institutionally mature state can be prone to similar behavior: witness President Ronald Reagan's willingness to make the United States a net debtor in lieu of tackling the problem of the fiscal deficit. Of course, the United States' vulnerability is much less than that of any Latin American regime, but the example does illustrate how indebtedness is all too often a political rather than technical decision.

Conclusions

The preceding analytical framework is historically rooted in the concrete experiences of Peru and Bolivia during the 1970s. Its generality is, strictly speaking, limited to these two countries and can be expanded only if a similar thematic is observed in other case study work designed to explore the precise articulation between international banks and borrowers in a developing country.

The dynamics of the framework center on an abundant and aggressive supply of credit pitted against the limited capacity of the borrower to absorb resources efficiently. In Chapter Three I derived the existence of a flat supply curve for the relevant range of borrowing from the institutional mechanics of the modern transnational bank during the 1970s. I then showed that the circumstances necessary to reproduce this particular supply dynamic were present during part of the credit cycles of Peru and Bolivia during the 1970s. It was in this context that I could illustrate more specifically the transmission of abundant supply into overindebtedness. It is in this sense that the banks were active agents in the crisis.

[51] For a detailed examination of the investments of state enterprises, see Devlin and Mortimore, *Bancos Transnacionales y Bolivia*, chapter 7.

[52] Private sector investment collapsed after 1975 and interests shifted to nonproductive activities. The classic case of misallocation was the speculative boom and bust of cotton production financed by the state agricultural bank. For details on this and other fiascos, see ibid.; and Dunkerley, *Rebellion*, pp. 219–230.

It should be stressed that I do not pretend to "prove" or "falsify" any theory. It is well known that data will never permit one to prove or disprove most aspects of supply and demand analysis because such analysis can be organized only around a broad and rather awkward counterfactual, that is, the *ceteris paribus*.[53] Indeed, there is absolutely no proof of the existence of the upward-sloping supply curve that has long underpinned conventional credit analysis.[54] The plausibility of the conventional parable rests on the assumption of the rational portfolio investor in an atomistic market. We saw that when analysis is adjusted to take into account that the bank of the 1970s was a transnational firm in a destabilized oligopolistic global market, a flat curve becomes more plausible over an important range of the credit cycle. McKinnon, a strong advocate of the conventional parable, may now think so too. In a recent brief comment on the collapse of the Southern Cone economies he suggests that borrowers did not face the "normal" upward-sloping supply curve for credit. This in turn constituted a market failure that contributed actively to overindebtedness.[55]

While I cannot yet claim generality for the framework, I strongly suspect that it has a broader application. As a working hypothesis, I would suggest that this central dynamic could be found in its purest form in the experiences of small- and medium-sized borrowers, for example, Jamaica, Costa Rica, Uruguay, and Chile. On the other hand, a big and highly dynamic economy such as Brazil's could probably mitigate the dynamics of aggressive supply through its enormous capacity to absorb resources into productive projects.[56] However, the plight of Mexico suggests that even big economies could confront a credit supply in excess of productive possibilities.

But abundant and aggressive supply is only one component of overin-

[53] The old problem is that in observing data one never knows whether movement is along a curve or the result of a curve shifting. See Peter McClelland, *Causal Explanation and Model Building in History, Economics, and the New Economic History* (Ithaca, N.Y.: Cornell University Press, 1975), pp. 184–193.

[54] See Jeffrey Sachs, "LDC Debt in the 80s: Risks and Reforms," in *Crises in the Economic and Financial Structure*, ed. Paul Wachtel (Lexington, Mass.: Lexington Books, 1982), p. 211.

[55] But unfortunately he may have derived the right conclusion for mostly the wrong reason. He still abstracts from credit institutions and blames the failure on public sector guarantees. See Ronald McKinnon, "The International Capital Market and Economic Liberalization in LDCs," *The Developing Economies* 22 (December 1984): 478.

[56] Brazil did, however, seem to have such a voracious capacity to absorb loans that it began to run up against the prudential exposure limits of the banking system in the late 1970s. Thus, before the crisis it found rationing setting in and the terms of indebtedness deteriorating. (See Table 3.11.)

debtedness. The borrower's internal political disposition to utilize resources efficiently is another major determinant. A medium-sized borrower such as Colombia had, until 1980, an active policy of resisting the bankers' overtures. This reflected a tradition of cautious demand management in that economy. Bankers were frustrated by their inability to penetrate the Colombian market, and the country, having the bankers "on the hook," was able to achieve major concessions on its loans. It even gained a reputation in financial circles as the "prickliest" borrower in the developing world.[57] In other words, it practiced the defensive strategy outlined earlier in the text. During the early 1980s the emergence of some neoliberal economic policies (in northern terminology, neoconservative monetarist policy) during the Turbay administration brought a relaxation of the defensive strategy. Nevertheless, the country avoided a debt problem as such, and its post-1982 difficulties with debt service are largely the result of the negative market externalities brought on by the debt crises of neighboring Latin American countries.

The bigger and more industrialized the borrowing country the greater the weight one must give to internal political factors in any apparent inability to absorb bank resources efficiently. But economic policy is as much political as it is technical, and if bank-lending behavior stimulates the more permissive instincts of a society, there nevertheless is a problem that merits serious attention.

[57] The frustration of the banks to break into the Colombian market was so large that the banks made the rare concession of not insisting on the waiver of sovereign immunity by the government. See Richard Ensor, "Latin America's Prickliest Borrower," *Euromoney*, June 1978, pp. 98–101.

CHAPTER FIVE

The Crash and the Political Economy of Rescheduling

LATIN AMERICA'S credit boom of the 1970s ended in mid-1982, when practically all the significant clients of the banks (except Colombia)[1] began one by one to enter into de facto default and multiple reschedulings.[2] But it is important to note that problems in servicing bank debt were not new in Latin America: Peru, Bolivia, Jamaica, Guyana, and Nicaragua all went through one or more restructuring exercises with the banks prior to the great crash (Table 5.1).[3]

The emergence of the earlier credit problems that led to the restructurings of the 1970s and the very first years of the 1980s was rooted in a complex causal structure related to the unique historical circumstances of those countries. It would be beyond the scope of my analysis to examine these and other cases in detail, but a common feature to all of them is that once the banks' concern about the creditworthiness of their client became sufficiently heightened, they as a group became reluctant to effect an automatic roll over of debt service payments. This helped to raise the effective debt service burden to unsustainable levels. A rescheduling/forced refinancing eventually followed.[4]

---

[1] Even so, Colombia has found access to credit extremely difficult due to the "neighborhood" problem.

[2] I will use the terms rescheduling, refinancing, and restructuring interchangeably. While rescheduling and refinancing are technically distinct, the difference is a cosmetic one. In the first, the loan agreement is amended to extend the maturities. In the second, banks extend new loans to cover payments that otherwise would not be made. Banks have sometimes preferred the latter approach because it is "quieter" and calls less attention to the problems in the portfolio. See David Biem, "Rescuing the LDCs," *Foreign Affairs 55* (July 1977): 723–724.

[3] Costa Rica also had announced its intention to reschedule debts in January 1981, while falling into arrears. Argentina fell into arrears during the Malvinas War in April to June 1982. See David Dod, "Restricción del Crédito de la Banca Comercial en Situaciones de Crisis de la Deuda Internacional" [Restriction of Bank Credit in Situations of International Debt Crisis], *Monetaria 6* (April–June 1983): 160; and Paul Mentré, *The Fund, Commercial Banks, and Member Countries,* Occasional Paper No. 26 (Washington, D.C.: International Monetary Fund, 1984), pp. 11–12.

[4] For an examination of bank behavior before and after a crisis in a selected number of countries see Dod, "Restricción del Crédito de la Banca Comercial," as well as William Gasser and David Roberts, "Bank Lending to Developing Countries: Problems and Prospects," *Federal Reserve Bank of New York Quarterly Review 7* (Fall 1982): 18–29.

TABLE 5.1. Latin America: Some Bank Debt Restructuring Agreements That Predate the 1982 Mexican Crisis

Year and Country	Maturities Rescheduled (years)	Amounts (millions of dollars)	Terms			Commissions[b]
			Total Amortization Period (years)	Grace Period (years)	Spread over Base Interest Rate[a] (%)	
1976						
Peru	1.0	430	5.0	2.0	2.25	1.5
1978						
Peru	0.5	186				
	2.0	200	5.0–6.0	2.0	1.88[c]	0.5
Jamaica	1.0	63	5.0	2.0	2.0	
1979						
Jamaica	2.0	149	5.0	2.0	2.0	
1980						
Peru[d]	1.0	340	5.0	2.0	1.25	
Nicaragua	2.0	240	12.0	5.0	1.0–1.75[e]	. . .[f]
1981						
Jamaica	2.0	89	5.0	2.0	2.0	1.5
Bolivia	2.0	244	5.0–6.0	2.0	2.25	1.125
Nicaragua	1.7	180	10.0	5.0	1.0–1.75[e]	. . .
1982						
Nicaragua	1.0	55	10.0	5.0	1.0–1.75[e]	. . .
Guyana	1.0	14		0.6	2.5	

SOURCES: Robert Devlin, *Transnational Banks and the External Finance of Latin America: The Experience of Peru* (Santiago, Chile: United Nations, 1985), pp. 212 and 254; Robert Devlin and Michael Mortimore, *Los Bancos Transnacionales, el Estado, y el Endeudamiento Externo en Bolivia* [Transnational Banks, the State, and External Debt in Bolivia] (Santiago, Chile: United Nations, 1983), p. 49; Richard Weinert, "Nicaragua's Debt Renegotiation," *Cambridge Journal of Economics* 5 (June 1981): 187–192; Quek Peck Lim, "The Borrower's Trump Card is His Weakness," *Euromoney*, October 1982, p. 37; E. Brau et al., *Recent Multilateral Debt Restructurings with Official Bank Creditors* (Washington, D.C.: International Monetary Fund, 1983), pp. 30–43.
NOTES: Restructuring excludes agreements concerning the elimination of arrears.
[a]LIBOR.
[b]As a percentage of the face value of loan agreement.
[c]For 1979 maturities.
[d]Peru prepaid 1979 debt service and renegotiated the terms of the 1980 agreement.
[e]The spread gradually rose from 1 to 1.75 percent during the period in which the agreement was in force, with an average spread of 1.5 percent. Nicaragua paid a maximum rate of 7 percent; the difference between this and the actual market rate was capitalized.
[f](. . .) = zero or not large enough to quantify.

A clear pattern for the restructurings emerges from Table 5.1. It can be seen that the banks used a short horizon to deal with the problem as only one to two years of upcoming maturities were rescheduled. Amortization and grace periods were very short; the margin over the base LIBOR rate was very high, and commissions (where information is available) were lucrative for the creditors.

The only agreement that departed sharply from the general pattern was that of Nicaragua in 1980. While only two years of maturities were rescheduled, the amortization period applied to them was unusually long (twelve years), the margin over LIBOR was comparatively moderate (a backloaded 1.5 percent average with an interest rate cap of 7 percent), and it was the only agreement for which no commissions were charged. At the time, the Nicaraguan agreement was quite novel because it was the first rescheduling on terms that, although ostensibly commercial, were designed around the requirements of growth and development.[5]

The 1980 Nicaraguan package was, however, very controversial. The bankers had agreed to it only grudgingly due to the tough negotiations of the revolutionary Sandinista regime and its apparently embarrassing information about irregularities in the contraction and use of the debt by the deposed Somoza government.[6] When more reschedulings came up the following year in Bolivia and Jamaica, the banks were able to reestablish the status quo with its onerous credit terms.

But these earlier exercises were a minor challenge compared to what the banks were to encounter later. Beginning in mid-1982 the banks faced a systemwide crisis. As was mentioned earlier on in the study, by the beginning of 1983 more than twenty-five countries in the periphery and Eastern Europe had begun negotiations to reschedule debts, which amounted to half of the foreign currency portfolio of the banks in those areas.[7] Latin America was, of course, the focal point of problems since fully seventeen countries were in trouble, including Brazil and Mexico, the two biggest debtors in the developing world.

Once again the precise causes of the current crisis are extremely com-

[5] Richard Weinert, "Nicaragua's Debt Renegotiation," *Cambridge Journal of Economics* 5 (June 1981): 187–192. Bankers traditionally prefer strict criteria of financial discipline to design a rescheduling. For a review of the general principles bankers employ in these exercises see United Nations Economic Commission for Latin America and the Caribbean (ECLAC), *External Debt in Latin America: Adjustment Policies and Renegotiation* (Boulder, Colo.: Lynne Rienner, 1985), pp. 72–76.

[6] To my knowledge this information has never been published; it was brought to my attention in conversations with people close to the negotiations.

[7] Morgan Guaranty Trust Company, *World Financial Markets* (New York, February 1983), pp. 1–2.

TABLE 5.2. Latin America: Rescheduling of Bank Debt, 1982–1987 (millions of dollars)

	First Round 1982/83			Second Round 1983/84			Third Round 1984/85			Fourth Round 1986/87		
	Restructured Maturities		New Loans	Restructured Maturities		New Loans	Restructured Maturities[a]		New Loans	Restructured Maturities[a]		New Loans
Country	Amount	Years	Amount	Amount	Years	Amount	Amount	Years	Amount	Amount	Years	Amount
Argentina	13000[b]	82–83[b]	1500[b]	N[c]	N	N	16500	82–85	3700	29600	86–90	1550
Bolivia	N	N	N	N	N	N	N	N	N	N[d]	N[d]	N[d]
Brazil	4800	83	4400	5400	84	6500	16300	85–86	...[m]	N[e]	N[e]	N[e]
Costa Rica	650	82–84	225	N	N	N	440	85–86	75	N	N	N
Cuba	130	82–83	...	103	84	...	82	85	...	N	N	N
Chile	3424	83–84	1300	...	...	780	5700	85–87	714; 371[f]	12490	88–91	...[g]
Ecuador	1970	82–83	431	...	...	...	4800	85–89	...	N	N	N
Honduras	121	82–84	...	...	...	...	220	85–86	...	N	N	N
Mexico	23700	82–84	5000	12000[b]	82–84	3800	48700	85–90	...	43700	85–90	7700[i]
Nicaragua	...[j]	...[j]	...[j]	...[j]	...[j]	...[j]	N	N	N	N	N	N
Panama	80	83	100	N[k]	N[k]	N[k]	603	85–86	60	N	N	N

Peru	400	83	450	662	84–85	...	N	N	N	N	N	N
Dominican Republic	568	82–83	...	N	N	N	790	84–89	...	N^k	N	N
Uruguay	630	83–84	240	...	...	N	1700	85–89	45^l	1780	86–91	...
Venezuela	N^k	N^k	N^k	N^k	N^k	N^k	21200	83–88	...	20450	86–88	...

SOURCE: ECLAC, Division of Economic Development.

NOTES: Information includes the values of rescheduled medium-term maturities as well as fresh medium-term credits that were awarded as part of the rescue package. Excludes the English-speaking Caribbean.

^{a}In some cases the banks included maturities that were rescheduled in earlier rounds.

^{b}The agreement was rejected by a new democratic government; the debt was eventually incorporated into the agreement of the third round.

^{c}N = no agreement.

^{d}In 1987 Bolivia established a donor fund to finance a buy back of its debt with the banks.

^{e}In early 1988 Brazil indicated that it was on the verge of reaching an agreement to reschedule its debt with the banks.

^{f}Corresponds to loans for 1985 and 1986, respectively. Includes $150 million that is guaranteed by the World Bank.

^{g}No new loans were awarded. However, Chile negotiated a one-time switch from half-yearly to yearly interest payments which was estimated to save $450 million in 1988.

^{h}Private sector.

^{i}Includes $1.700 millions in contingency loans.

^{j}See agreement in the previous table.

^{k}The country continued to service interest payments on a normal basis.

^{l}Forms part of a cofinancing with the World Bank.

^{m}(...) = zero or not large enough to quantify.

TABLE 5.3. Latin America: Conditions in the First Round of Reschedulings, 1982/1983

Country	Margin over LIBOR		Amortization Period (years)		Grace Period (years)		Commission[a]	
	R	NL	R	NL	R	NL	R	NL
Argentina	2.13	2.50	7.0	5.0	3.0	3.0	1.25	1.25
Bolivia	N	N	N	N	N	N	N	N
Brazil	2.50	2.13	8.0	8.0	2.5	2.5	1.5	1.5
Costa Rica	2.25	1.75	8.0	3.0	4.0	2.0	1.0	0.5
Cuba	2.25		7.0		2.5		1.25	
Chile	2.13	2.25	7.0	7.0	4.0	4.0	1.25	1.25
Ecuador	2.25	2.38	7.0	6.0	1.0	1.5	1.25	1.25
Honduras	2.25		7.0		1.0		1.38	
Mexico	1.88	2.25	8.0	6.0	4.0	3.0	1.0	1.25
Nicaragua[b]								
Panama	2.25	2.25	6.0	6.0	2.0	2.0	1.5	1.5
Peru	2.25	2.25	8.0	8.0	3.0	3.0	1.25	1.25
Dominican Republic	2.25		6.0		2.0		1.25	
Uruguay	2.25	2.25	6.0	6.0	2.0	2.0	1.38	1.50
Venezuela	N	N	N	N	N	N	N	N

SOURCE: ECLAC, Division of Economic Development.
NOTES: Symbols are as follows: R = rescheduled principal; NL = new loans; N = no agreement.
[a]Expressed as a percentage of the face value of the loan. Based on public information and therefore may underestimate the actual fee that was paid.
[b]Continued with the terms of the 1980 agreement.

plex and will not be analyzed here.[8] But a common feature was that the banks became concerned about the creditworthiness of their clients and suddenly demanded effective payment, as reflected in the dramatic appearance of a negative transfer of resources to Latin America in 1982

[8] I have argued in earlier chapters that the causes are, generally speaking, rooted in borrower policy, bank behavior, and events in the OECD economies. For more on this see Robert Devlin, "Deuda, Crisis, y Renegociación: El Dilema Latinoamericano" [Debt, Crisis, and Renegotiation: The Latin American Dilemma], in *América Latina: Deuda, Crisis, y Perspectivas* [Latin America: Debt, Crisis, and Perspectives], ed. the Instituto de Cooperación Iberoamericana (Madrid: Ediciones Cultura Hispánica, 1984), pp. 67–83.

TABLE 5.4. Latin America: Conditions in the Second Round
of Reschedulings, 1983/1984

Country	Margin over LIBOR		Amortization Period (years)		Grace Period (years)		Commission[a]	
	R	NL	R	NL	R	NL	R	NL
Argentina	N	N	N	N	N	N	N	N
Bolivia	N	N	N	N	N	N	N	N
Brazil	2.0	2.0	9.0	9.0	5.0	5.0	1.0	1.0
Costa Rica	N	N	N	N	N	N	N	N
Cuba	1.88		9.0		5.0		0.88	
Chile		1.75		9.0		5.0		0.63
Ecuador								
Honduras								
Mexico		1.50		10.0		6.0		0.63
Nicaragua[b]								
Panama	N	N	N	N	N	N	N	N
Peru	1.75		9.0		5.0		0.75	
Dominican Republic	N	N	N	N	N	N	N	N
Uruguay								
Venezuela	N	N	N	N	N	N	N	N

SOURCE: ECLAC, Division of Economic Development.
NOTES: Symbols are as follows: R = rescheduled principal; NL = new loans; N = no
agreement.
[a]Expressed as a percentage of the face value of the loan. Based on public information
and therefore may underestimate the actual fee that was paid.
[b]Continued with the terms of the 1980 agreement.

(Table 2.1). The countries were in no position to fully service the debt
once the roll over mechanism was broken, and this initiated the crisis
and the rescheduling exercises.

The reschedulings that began in mid-1982 have been multiple. In a
way this follows earlier patterns; as seen in Table 5.1, the reschedulings
of the 1970s also were often multiple. The current rescheduling exercises can be divided into four rounds. Tables 5.2 through 5.6 summarize
the amounts involved and the terms for each of the four exercises.

Since very detailed accounts of the four rounds of reschedulings are

TABLE 5.5. Latin America: Conditions in the Third Round
of Reschedulings, 1984/1985

Country	Margin over LIBOR		Amortization Period (years)		Grace Period (years)		Commission[a]	
	R	NL	R	NL	R	NL	R	NL
Argentina	1.38	1.63	12.0	10.0	3.0	3.0	. . .[b]	0.58
Bolivia	N	N	N	N	N	N	N	N
Brazil	1.13		12.0		5.0		. . .	
Costa Rica	1.63	1.75	10.0	7.0	3.0	1.5	1.0	1.0
Cuba	1.50		10.0		6.0		0.38	
Chile	1.38	1.63	12.0	12.0	6.0	5.0	. . .	0.50
Ecuador	1.38		12.0		3.0		. . .	
Honduras	1.58		11.0		3.0		0.88	
Mexico	1.13		14.0		. . .		. . .	N
Nicaragua	N	N	N	N	N	N	N	N
Panama	1.38	1.63	12.0	9.0	3.5	3.0	. . .	0.5
Peru	N	N	N	N	N	N	N	
Dominican Republic	1.38		13.0		3.0		. . .	
Uruguay	1.38	1.63	12.0	12.0	3.0	3.5	. . .	. . .
Venezuela	1.13		12.5		. . .		. . .	

SOURCE: ECLAC, Division of Economic Development.
NOTES: Symbols are as follows: R = rescheduled principal; NL = new loans; N = no
    agreement.
[a]Expressed as a percentage of the face value of the loan. Based on public information
    and therefore may underestimate the actual fee that was paid.
[b](. . .) = zero or not large enough to quantify.

published elsewhere,[9] I will limit myself to sketching the broad outline
of the pattern.

Mexico's crisis in mid-1982 shook the financial world both because
of the magnitude of the bank debt (at the time nearly $60 billion) and

[9] See United Nations Economic Commission for Latin America and the Caribbean
(ECLAC), *Economic Survey of Latin America and the Caribbean 1982* (Santiago, Chile,
1984), 1: 74–84; United Nations Economic Commission for Latin America and the
Caribbean, *Economic Survey of Latin America and the Caribbean 1983* (Santiago, Chile,
1985), 1: 66–72; United Nations Economic Commission for Latin America and the
Caribbean, *Economic Survey of Latin America and the Caribbean 1985*, (Santiago, Chile,
1987), pp. 55–61; United Nations Economic Commission for Latin America and the

TABLE 5.6. Latin America: Conditions in the Fourth Round of Reschedulings, 1986/1987

Country	Margin over LIBOR		Amortization Period (years)		Grace Period (years)		Commission[a]	
	R	NL	R	NL	R	NL	R	NL
Argentina	0.81	0.88	19.0	12.0	7.0	5.0	. . .[b]	0.38[c]
Bolivia	N	N	N	N	N	N	N	N
Brazil	N	N	N	N	N	N	N	N
Costa Rica	N	N	N	N	N	N	N	N
Cuba	N	N	N	N	N	N	N	N
Chile	1.0		15.0		6.0		. . .	
Ecuador	N	N	N	N	N	N	N	N
Honduras	N	N	N	N	N	N	N	N
Mexico	0.81	0.81	20.0	12.0	7.0	4.0	. . .	. . .
Nicaragua	N	N	N	N	N	N	N	N
Panama	N	N	N	N	N	N	N	N
Peru	N	N	N	N	N	N	N	N
Dominican Republic	N	N	N	N	N	N	N	N
Uruguay	0.88		17.0		3.0		. . .	
Venezuela	0.88		14.0		. . .		. . .	

SOURCE: ECLAC, Division of Economic Development.
NOTES: Symbols are as follows: R = rescheduled principal; NL = new loans; N = no agreement.
[a]Expressed as a percentage of the face value of the loan. Based on public information and therefore may underestimate the actual fee that was paid.
[b](. . .) = zero or not large enough to quantify.
[c]For banks signing on to the new loan agreement before 17 June 1987.

the suddenness with which it appeared.[10] A panic similar to, but much more intense than, that of the 1974 Herstatt crisis appeared in the inter-bank market. This in turn set off a wave of negative externalities within

Caribbean, *Estudio Económico de América Latina y el Caribe 1986* [Economic Survey of Latin America and the Caribbean 1986] (Santiago, Chile, 1988), pp. 55–71; and United Nations Economic Commission for Latin America and the Caribbean, "Preliminary Overview of the Latin American Economy 1987" (Santiago, Chile, December 1987), sec. II.4.

[10] Mexico was already in trouble at the outset of 1982, but its difficulties were hidden from observers (including apparently many banks) behind a veil of short-term loans that were contracted to roll over medium-term obligations. However, the short-term debt

the financial community.[11] In effect, problems in one country adversely affected the bankers' perception of risk in other countries.[12] The externalities were extremely potent in Latin America, where, as was illustrated in Chapter Two, the bankers had the bulk of their Third World loans. As a country was increasingly perceived as "just another one of the half-collapsed economies of Latin America," new loans became scarcer, the maturity shortened, and the cost rose, all of which undermined the roll over process. With access to new loans difficult, most countries found themselves unable to service the debt, and one by one they slipped into technical default. Some, like Chile and Peru, tried desperately to distance themselves from their faltering neighbors, but by early 1983 they too had to admit defeat and request a restructuring.[13]

In the second semester of 1982 and the first semester of 1983 the banks, in conjunction with their home governments and the IMF, attempted to rescue the loan portfolio in the region. The general formula worked out among all the parties is by now relatively well known. In exchange for agreeing to enter into an austerity program with the IMF, the debtor country received a restructuring of its bank debt falling due in 1982/1983 and in some instances those maturities pertaining to 1984. In coordination with the Fund's adjustment programs the banks also agreed to extend, as an integral part of their rescue package, new

---

buildup soon made matters worse, and the situation exploded in August. For a revealing analysis of the Mexican crisis see Joseph Kraft, *The Mexican Rescue* (New York: Group of Thirty, 1984).

[11] Prior to the Mexican crisis the market was receiving unsettling news on other fronts. High interest rates had adversely affected the payment capacity of some former blue-chip firms such as International Harvester. Several bankruptcies, such as Penn Central and Banco Ambrosiano, occurred. Meanwhile, as mentioned in footnote 3, the Malvinas War also had undermined Argentina's ability to service the debt. See Mentré, *The Fund and Member Countries*, pp. 11–12.

[12] Anthony Saunders has shown this empirically. See his "An Examination of the Contagion Effect in the International Loan Market" (Washington, D.C.: International Monetary Fund, December 1983).

[13] Interestingly, the initiative for a restructuring in Peru came from the banks and not the government. During the second half of 1982 the country had tried to avoid default, but the loans it contracted to roll debt over were on increasingly onerous terms. It was also rapidly losing short-term lines of credit. Peru's two biggest creditors, Citicorp and Chase Manhattan, "counseled" government authorities to call a temporary moratorium on debt service. They wanted to stop smaller institutions from pulling out of Peru, which would have left the big banks "holding the bag." By calling the moratorium on payments, the smaller lenders became locked into the country's fate. See Robert Devlin and Enrique de la Piedra, "Peru and Its Private Bankers: Scenes from an Unhappy Marriage," in *Politics and Economics of External Debt Crisis*, ed. Miguel Wionczek in collaboration with Luciano Tomassini (Boulder, Colo.: Westview Press, 1985), pp. 409–410.

TABLE 5.7. Latin America: Credit Conditions Prior to the 1982
Mexican Crisis
(January 1980–June 1981)

Country	Margin over LIBOR	Amortization Period (years)	Commissions[a]
Argentina	0.67	7.5	1.09
Bolivia			
Brazil	1.62	8.5	2.01
Costa Rica	1.13	6.0	1.23
Cuba	1.00	5.0	0.88
Chile	0.91	7.6	0.81
Ecuador	0.74	8.0	0.97
Honduras	1.40	6.7	0.97
Mexico	0.65	7.6	0.70
Nicaragua			
Panama	1.09	8.0	1.00
Peru	1.12	8.2	1.07
Dominican Republic	1.30	8.1	0.91
Uruguay	0.98	9.1	0.90
Venezuela	0.68	6.9	1.67

SOURCE: Calculated from data in World Bank, *Borrowing in International Capital Markets* (Washington, D.C.), various numbers.
NOTE:
[a]Expressed as a percentage of the face value of the loan. Based on public information and may underestimate the actual fee that was paid.

loans for the calendar year 1983. The general formula worked out between the banks and the IMF was that the private creditors would expand their portfolio (via what was termed involuntary lending) by 7 percent that year. According to the IMF and the creditor governments this scheme contained the two central pillars of a solution to the crisis: adjustment in the debtor countries and the financing needed to support that effort.[14]

Since the first round rescheduling packages were almost uniformly tied to an IMF adjustment program,[15] and needed the approval of hun-

[14] See ECLAC, *External Debt in Latin America*, p. 77.
[15] The exception was Cuba (not a member) and revolutionary Nicaragua, which never accepted IMF intervention.

dreds of creditors, negotiations were awkward and protracted. To bridge the time gap, unprecedented emergency short-term loans were awarded (mostly to the big debtors) by the U.S. Treasury and the Bank for International Settlements to tide the countries over until the rescue packages were approved by the commercial banks.[16] OECD governments also supported the crisis management by rescheduling the region's bilateral official debts through the Paris Club.[17]

Even with the intense efforts of the banks, the IMF, and OECD governments to avoid defaults through rescheduling packages some countries failed to reach agreements. Bolivia, which had overt debt service problems since late 1979, was not able to honor its 1981 rescheduling with the banks both because of the unrealistically severe commercial terms of that accord and domestic political instability. When the Mexican crisis broke out in mid-1982, the country had already been accumulating arrears, and a rapid succession of governments had made it impossible to negotiate any sustainable agreement. In Venezuela the government never accepted the bankers' terms for a rescheduling. With nearly $8 billion in reserves it had enough leverage with its creditors to stonewall and repeatedly negotiate temporary three-month moratoria on principal, even while keeping interest payments current.

The banks' conditions for rescheduling in the first round were onerous, as they had generally been in the precrisis restructurings. Typical conditions for rescheduled maturities and new loans included a margin over LIBOR of 2.25 percent, an amortization period of six to eight years, and commissions of 1.25 percent. When these negotiated terms—alternatively denominated the negotiated price of credit—of the first round are compared with those prevailing in normal credit markets before the crisis, it can be seen that the debtor countries often suffered a deterioration of between 100 and 250 percent (Table 5.8). Even the pure financial cost (interest rate plus commission) rose sharply: ECLAC calculated that for most debtors the financial cost of credit in real terms during the first round of reschedulings was 20 percent or more above that prevailing before the crisis.[18] In addition to these onerous financial

[16] For information on the amount of these loans, by borrower, see ECLAC, *Economic Survey of Latin America and the Caribbean 1982*, and *1983*, 1: 75 and 67, respectively.

[17] The bulk of Latin American debt is with the private banks and for this reason I will not examine Paris Club negotiations. Nevertheless, it must be noted that some of the smaller debtors relied heavily on bilateral financing, giving greater importance to Paris Club negotiations. For details on the Paris Club exercises see Eduard Brau et al., *Recent Multilateral Debt Restructurings with Official and Bank Creditors*, Occasional Paper No. 25 (Washington, D.C.: International Monetary Fund, 1983).

[18] United Nations Economic Commission for Latin America and the Caribbean used the formula $LIBOR + C/A + M$, where LIBOR is the base interest rate in real terms (5

TABLE 5.8. Latin America: Evolution of the Terms of Indebtedness with Private Banks
(index {1980/1981 = 100)[a]

Country	1st Round 1982/83	2d Round 1983/84	3d Round 1984/85	4th Round 1986/87
Argentina	319		114	40
Brazil	144	107	43	
Costa Rica	151		82	
Cuba	148	93	65	
Chile	250	151	89	50
Ecuador	335		107	
Honduras	152		65	
Mexico	280	160	83	44
Panama	274		79	
Peru	197	134		
Dominican Republic	235		61	
Uruguay	349		98	44
Venezuela			68	47

SOURCE: ECLAC, Division of Economic Development.
NOTE:
[a]Based on an index of the components of the cost of credit that are subject to negotiation: $\{[(Ci/Ai + Mi)/Ai]/[(Co/Ao + Mo)/Ao]\} \times 100$, where C = commission, A = amortization period, and M = margin over LIBOR. The subscript i refers to the conditions existing in the respective rescheduling rounds and the subscript o refers to the terms prevailing in the normal, precrisis credit market of 1980/1981. All the elements of the formula refer to rescheduled debt and/or new credits and are weighted by the dollar values of the transactions.
The index does not capture other nonprice costs such as ex post public guarantees of private sector debt, required IMF programs, etc.

conditions the countries also had to adhere to the tough standards of IMF-sponsored adjustment programs and the demands of the banks that the governments guarantee, directly or indirectly, previously unguaranteed debt in the often bankrupt private sectors of their countries.

During 1983 a second round of negotiations emerged, even while some countries had not finalized the agreements of the first round. Some debtors that had rescheduled only 1983 maturities had to contact their

percent in both the pre- and postcrisis periods), C is commissions, A the amortization period, and M the margin over LIBOR. See table 48 of ECLAC, *Economic Survey of Latin America and the Caribbean 1982*, vol. 1.

creditors for a restructuring of 1984 payments of principal. A number of these same countries, as well as those that had restructured 1984 maturities in the first round, also needed to negotiate new credits to support the 1984 balance of payments.

It can be seen in Table 5.4 that the negotiated commercial terms for the second round were softened somewhat: margins fell by about one-half a point, amortization periods were lengthened by one to two years, and commissions were reduced by one-quarter to one-half a point. Nevertheless, the terms were still severe compared to precrisis levels (Table 5.8).

Note can be taken in Table 5.2 that some countries were outside the banks' program in the second round. Bolivia's newly emerged democratic government failed to arrive at an agreement with the banks. Meanwhile, Argentina's new democratic government rejected the agreement reached between the previous military regime and the banks and sought a more favorable accord. Panama, Costa Rica, and the Dominican Republic also had problems complying with the terms of the agreement in the first round, while Venezuela continued to stonewall.

In mid-1984 a third round of reschedulings got underway. Here one notes a rather dramatic switch in the pattern. In many cases the reschedulings went beyond two years; the longest horizon was set in Mexico, where maturities were restructured for the period 1985 and 1990. Moreover, the negotiated terms of indebtedness, though still at commercial levels, were substantially improved, as margins were again compressed, amortization periods were extended up to fourteen years, and flat front-end commissions fell, in some cases to zero (Table 5.5). Indeed, Table 5.8 demonstrates that in most cases the negotiated price of credit actually fell *below* that contracted by the debtors in the normal credit market of 1980/1981. On the other hand, in the third round one notices a marked falloff of new involuntary lending by the banks.

Even with the dramatic softening of the commercial terms of the reschedulings, some countries remained outside the banks' program. Bolivia still could not reach an agreement, while Brazil, Peru, and Nicaragua became new entrants into the problem club. On the other hand, two big debtors, Argentina and Venezuela, finally did reach agreements after protracted negotiations with their creditors.

In mid-1986 yet another rescheduling round emerged in Latin America. Following the pattern of earlier rounds, it was Mexico that initiated the new set of restructuring exercises. In this, the fourth round of reschedulings, the negotiated terms continued to soften. Mexico's spread fell below 1 percent, the amortization period reached twenty years, and again no commissions were charged (Table 5.6). But the major novelty of this round was a new loan package of $7.7 billion from the banks that was explicitly linked to a 3 percent target rate of growth in Mexico for 1986/1987. In other words, for the first time the creditors made the economic growth of a debtor an explicit and integral part of the rescheduling and adjustment processes.

The explicit growth guarantee and related financing grew out of a new policy focus introduced by U.S. Treasury Secretary James Baker during the IMF/World Bank Joint Annual Meetings in Seoul, South Korea, at the end of September 1985. His "Program for Sustained Growth" (more popularly known as the "Baker Plan") promised a conceptual shift in the international management of the crisis from emphasis on belt tightening to emphasis on structural adjustment with growth. He promised to mobilize $29 billion of new loans over three years for fifteen problem debtors, of which $20 billion would be involuntary lending by private banks and the rest official commitments. The bank lending represented an expansion of the loan portfolio equivalent to $2^{1/2}$ percent per annum.

The private creditors' concern about precedent resulted in the commercial loan package for the pilot Mexican case being formally linked to growth only indirectly; thus, bank financing was set to rise and fall according to the evolution of the price of Mexico's principle export, petroleum.[19] Nevertheless, the growth target was explicitly there, and for the first time a debtor country's output became, at least in principle, an endogenous variable in the adjustment process.

During 1987 Argentina, Chile, Uruguay, and Venezuela joined Mexico in a fourth round of reschedulings. None, however, was able to reproduce the explicit growth guarantee afforded to Mexico, and only Argentina mobilized a significant amount of new money from the banks.[20] On the other hand, all four countries continued to improve their negotiated commercial terms of indebtedness (Table 5.6).

In September 1987 at the joint annual meetings of the IMF and World

[19] The total financial package for Mexico totalled a record $13.7 billion. The banks' contribution of $7.7 billion included $1.7 billion of contingency loans. The remaining $6 billion of financing came from multilateral and bilateral lenders. In the agreement Mexico's access to funds depended on the evolution of the price of petroleum through the end of 1987; if oil prices fell below $9 a barrel, the contingency financing would automatically become available, while if they rose above $14 a barrel, base-level financing would be automatically withdrawn. Apart from this, if growth in early 1987 failed to be consistent with the annual target rate, Mexico had the option to draw on a $500 million fund to stimulate public investment.

[20] Chile, however, won a "retiming" of interest payments for one year from a semiannual to annual basis. This reportedly would save $450 million in interest payments for 1988. See ECLAC, "Preliminary Overview of the Latin American Economy 1987," p. 8.

Bank in Washington, D.C., U.S. Treasury Secretary Baker unveiled yet another new twist in the international management of the debt crisis called the "Market Menu Approach." Its key feature involved a downplaying of involuntary lending by the banks in the international debt strategy and the raising to the forefront of nonlending options—principally debt-equity swaps and different forms of securitization—that the banks could draw upon and deploy in their negotiations with problem debtor countries.

The official strategy placed major stress on the fact that all instruments in the menu must be based in private markets and come out of the case-by-case voluntary responses of the banks. Formally included in the market menu of options are trade and project loans; on-lending (the rechanneling of part of the bank loans to the debtor country's private sector); the emission of new money bonds; exit bonds; debt-equity swaps; debt-charity swaps; limited and specific capitalization of interest; and involuntary balance of payments loans, which pointedly always appear last on the official list. Formally excluded from the market menu are schemes of debt forgiveness and unilateral debtor initiatives to limit debt service because, in the words of Secretary Baker, the debtor countries' "course into the twenty-first century must be built upon increasing their trade and financial linkages with the rest of the world, not undermining them."[21]

Perhaps the most striking characteristic of the fourth round of rescheduling, however, is the small number of countries participating in it. As illustrated in Table 5.2, the majority of the debtor countries of the region had by the end of 1987, for diverse reasons, still failed to reach an agreement with the banks. Moreover, the failure to arrive at an agreement usually meant an accumulation of arrears in principal and interest payments with the banks and other creditors. We will see later that this was one manifestation of serious strains in the international management of the region's debt crisis.

AN EVALUATION OF RESCHEDULING PRACTICES

The Economic Justification for the Cost of Credit

In this section I will focus my attention on the early polemics surrounding the pricing of the rescheduling operations. While a rescheduling has a wide range of other characteristics, an examination of its price is a

---

[21] James Baker, "Statement" to the Joint Annual Meetings of the Board of Governors of the World Bank and International Monetary Fund, Washington, D.C., 30 September 1987, pp. 4–6.

good vehicle for revealing the central dynamics of the political economy of rescheduling.

It has already been noted that in the first round of rescheduling the negotiated price of credit underwent a massive rise. This was not unusual, however, because banks customarily jacked up the price of credit upon rescheduling debts. The practice is reflected in the high cost of those few restructuring operations that preceded the general crisis of 1982. During the management of the current crisis I saw at least four arguments coming out of creditor circles to justify the phenomenon. None of them holds up well under scrutiny.

Positive Price Elasticities   During the early rounds of the rescheduling exercises one frequently encountered the observation that the increase in the negotiated price of credit was necessary to facilitate the financing of adjustment. For example, in their analysis of the cost of rescheduling Gasser and Roberts commented: "Clearly the more attractive the terms of restructured or rescheduled debt, the more willing will be the participation of all banks and a reasonably early resumption of lending will be more likely."[22]

There is, however, no empirical evidence to support the notion that a bank's willingness to reschedule debt is linked to a higher negotiated price of credit. It is almost self-evident that banks reschedule not to make profits but to avoid the losses that would result if the borrower fell into open default.

As for new net credit, studies[23] have shown that the habitual reaction of banks to reschedulings—even when the negotiated price has risen sharply—is to cut back exposure, not expand it.[24] This should come as no surprise. We have seen that banks ration credit. When a crisis breaks out, creditors quickly adjust their rationing points; prices cannot clear the market, and access to autonomous credit flows will depend on the creditors fundamentally changing their perception of the debtors' capacity to service debts.

[22] Gasser and Roberts, "Bank Lending to Developing Countries," p. 28.

[23] See Dod, "Restricción del Crédito de la Banca Comercial."

[24] Peru was one of the few developing countries that rescheduled in the 1970s and was eventually able to gain regular access to bank credit. During 1976 to 1978 the country was in a bitter struggle with its creditors, in which month-to-month and day-to-day roll overs were granted by the banks to avoid defaults. At the end of 1978 Peru finally arrived at a rescheduling agreement. Toward the end of the following year banks began to show renewed interest in the country, and this initiated another credit cycle, which collapsed with the rest of Latin America in 1982/1983. The basic reason the banks became interested in Peru was the unexpected sharp rise in petroleum prices in 1979. The high price, coupled with an exportable surplus of oil (due to the modest discoveries in the Amazon and depressed domestic demand), gave a sharp boost to the country's external accounts.

TABLE 5.9. Latin America: Ratio of Total Interest Payments to Exports
of Goods and Services
(percentages)

	1979	1980	1981	1982	1983	1984	1985	1986	1987[a]
Latin America	17.6	20.4	28.0	41.0	36.2	35.7	35.2	36.0	30.5
Oil-exporting countries	15.7	16.8	22.6	35.6	31.4	32.5	32.2	35.3	25.2
Bolivia	18.6	25.0	34.6	43.4	39.9	50.0	46.8	42.6	40.0
Ecuador	13.6	18.3	22.8	30.3	27.4	30.7	27.0	30.9	31.1
Mexico	24.5	23.3	29.0	47.2	37.5	39.0	36.0	37.9	27.9
Peru	15.5	18.4	24.1	25.1	29.8	33.2	30.0	26.7	22.4
Venezuela	6.9	8.1	12.7	21.0	21.7	20.1	26.2	32.8	26.3
Nonoil-exporting countries	19.3	23.9	33.8	46.8	41.0	38.7	37.8	36.3	33.0
Argentina	12.8	22.0	35.5	53.6	58.4	57.6	51.1	53.0	56.2
Brazil	31.5	34.1	40.4	57.1	43.5	39.6	40.0	41.4	34.5
Colombia	9.9	11.8	21.9	25.9	26.7	22.8	26.3	19.7	25.2
Costa Rica	12.8	18.0	28.0	36.1	33.1	26.7	27.3	21.2	19.3
Chile	16.5	19.3	38.8	49.5	38.9	48.0	43.5	38.6	26.7
El Salvador	5.7	5.9	7.8	11.9	12.2	12.3	12.9	12.5	13.2
Guatemala	3.2	5.3	7.6	7.8	8.7	12.3	14.9	16.5	16.3
Haiti	3.2	2.1	2.7	2.4	2.4	5.2	7.4	3.4	4.6
Honduras	8.6	10.6	14.4	22.4	16.4	15.8	16.2	15.5	16.5
Nicaragua	9.7	24.3	37.4	41.8	45.3	11.9	13.3	8.9	69.9
Paraguay	10.7	13.5	14.8	13.5	14.3	10.2	8.3	18.5	14.8
Dominican Republic	14.3	19.9	19.1	22.7	24.5	18.1	15.4	19.0	19.6
Uruguay	9.0	11.0	12.9	22.4	24.8	34.8	34.3	24.7	24.0

SOURCE: ECLAC, "Preliminary Overview of the Latin American Economy 1987" (Santiago, Chile,
December 1987), table 17.
[a]Preliminary.

Now it is true that banks have extended new loans during the four
rounds of rescheduling exercises. This represented a break with the
past, since banks typically rejected requests for new lending during the
pre-1982 rescheduling exercises, limiting their relief to the restructuring
of principal. But this new attitude responded to the banks' own interests, as it allowed them to avoid considerable losses and possible collapse. In effect, the awarding of new credits during the debt restructurings represented a disguised rescheduling of interest payments, which
had reached unsustainable levels.

As shown in Table 5.9, at the outbreak of the crisis in 1982 interest payments averaged an unprecedented 41 percent of export earnings. For many important debtor countries the coefficient was much higher: Brazil, 57 percent; Argentina, 54 percent; Chile, 50 percent; Mexico, 47 percent; et cetera. Faced with these unsustainable interest burdens, the creditors urgently needed to find a way to avoid technical defaults.[25] Most did not want to reschedule interest charges. On the one hand, there was a tradition in banking circles of not altering the payment of interest as a way of enforcing discipline on the errant borrowers.[26] On the other, for some banks (especially in the United States), under prevailing rules of domestic bank accounting a rescheduling of interest would have meant losses. Thus the banks opted for new loans, which had the same effect of postponing the payment of interest but were not automatically challenged by bank accounting regulations.[27]

Strictly speaking, the so-called new credits, introduced with so much fanfare in the first round of reschedulings, were a forced, emergency administration of loans already authorized in earlier periods, making it impossible to discriminate in practice between the new loans and the old debt. In other words, if the banks had not authorized the new debt, interest on old debt would have failed to accrue, bringing losses.[28] At

[25] It should be noted that a significant part of this problem was related to the arrival of floating interest rates in international markets. When banks decided to substitute fixed rates with floating rates, they successfully passed the interest rate risk from themselves to the borrower. But in doing so they transformed the former interest rate risk into a commercial risk of borrower default. Also, as Taylor points out, when floating rates were introduced, the covariance of returns on loans increased among borrowers, eroding the benefits of diversification. That is, if LIBOR rises, it rises for everyone, and commercial risk increases simultaneously for all borrowers (at different rates, of course). See Lance Taylor, "The Theory and Practice of Developing Country Debt: An Informal Guide for the Perplexed," mimeographed (Cambridge, Mass., Massachusetts Institute of Technology, Department of Economics, 1985), p. 17.

[26] Group of Thirty, *Risks in International Lending* (New York, 1982), p. 14. But it has been done; for example, in 1980 Nicaragua negotiated a 7 percent interest rate cap on its rescheduling. Any difference between the cap rate and a higher market rate was capitalized and amortized over 1986 to 1990.

[27] A loan is generally considered bad when scheduled interest is not fully accrued. Accounting regulations often punish direct admission of this (e.g., rescheduling interest) but are more lenient of indirect actions that have the same effect. Thus in accounting terms a bad loan is revealed as bad when interest is rescheduled but can be disguised as a good loan if interest is refinanced. For analysis of U.S. accounting rules see Karin Lissakers, "Bank Regulation and International Debt," in *Uncertain Future: Commercial Banks and the Third World*, ed. Richard Feinberg and Valeriana Kallab (London: Transaction Books, 1984), p. 57.

[28] This would have appeared as reduced earnings through nonaccrual of interest and the setting aside of reserves for loan losses. Depending on the attitude of regulators, the

the same time the banks, in conjunction with the IMF, designed the new loans around what was, in practice, necessary to avoid technical default in the debtor countries.[29] Since the new loans (via the aforementioned 7 percent formula) covered only approximately one-half of the interest payments, the countries effected a large transfer of resources to the North in economic circumstances that were objectively adverse.

Now it is true that at the outbreak of the crisis there were a number of latecomers (mostly smaller lenders) to the credit cycle, with relatively more modest exposure in Latin America. Hence, they were less subject to the previously mentioned lock-in effects regarding forced lending. In contrast to the bigger lenders, which were quite committed (in the sense that their loans represented a high percentage of capital and reserves) in the region, these smaller institutions admittedly often had less built-in incentives to refinance interest payments with new loans.

On the one hand, the group of smaller lenders could have seen its own lending as individually unimportant to the success or failure of the new loan packages. Therefore the institutions could perceive an opportunity to act as what William Cline has termed "free-riders."[30] A free-rider essentially thinks it can sneak out unnoticed from the new lending package and have the debtor's obligations covered by the bigger, more committed creditors, which do have strong built-in incentives to lend in order to avoid technical defaults on old debt and damaging losses. On the other hand, in the face of unwanted costly and protracted negotiations with a problem borrower a bank with smaller exposure might be willing to risk the losses involved in a failure to arrange the said new loans. This is because the possible devaluation of its loan assets, stemming from a lack of refinance for the borrower and consequent default, could in the last instance be absorbed and would not threaten the viability of the bank. Indeed, a write-down of asset values is a classic way to sanitize a

---

bank also might have had to actually write down the loan. American banks—under more public scrutiny than other institutions—are highly sensitive to reports of reduced earnings. European banks are often less sensitive, in part because they are legally less subject to public accountability, receive more favorable tax treatment, and can draw on what is termed "hidden reserves" in their accounting balances, which allow them to smooth the earnings flow in bad times. See Graeme Rutledge and Geoffrey Bell, "Facing Reality on Sovereign Debt," *Euromoney*, November 1984, p. 105; and "Provided the Banks Stand," *Economist*, 8 September 1984, p. 82.

[29] As mentioned earlier in the chapter, the 7 percent formula arose in conjunction with the IMF adjustment-stabilization programs. These programs had no specific growth targets and had an outcome based on the domestic authorities' willingness to accept belt tightening.

[30] William Cline, *International Debt: Systematic Risk and Policy Response* (Washington, D.C.: Institute for International Economics, 1984), p. 75.

loan portfolio and could often be preferred to new lending by a bank able to absorb the resulting losses.[31]

A retreat of smaller lenders in the early rounds of reschedulings could have had severely disruptive consequences for the big banks. With their departure the big lenders would have had to extend new loans to cover the payments of interest on not only their own loans but those of the free-riders—or confront the possibility of losses.[32] This is because banks are legally linked with each other through cross-default clauses that appear in most loan contracts. Simply stated, the clause makes a default on one bank equivalent to a default on all the banks. If a smaller bank were to go unpaid, it could declare a default that would in practice force unwanted declarations of default on the bigger creditors. It is in the context of this problem that some analysts argued that the higher margins, commissions, et cetera were necessary in order to ensure the participation of the smaller creditors in the new loan package.[33]

But a higher price of credit in the situation of high uncertainty that characterizes a rescheduling is not an important factor in the cooperation of the smaller lenders. Again, this is because if there were freedom of action the supply curve would be at its point of absolute rationing and no price would freely elicit a supply of credit. In other words, observing Figure 5.1, for a country with problems, the smaller bank would be at point D, the perfectly inelastic point of the offer curve. The only way to freely induce new voluntary lending would be for the creditor to perceive that with the new credit the borrower has fully restored its true capacity of repayment, or creditworthiness. But if the banks perceived such a happy set of events, the flow of new credit could be secured at a lower price, since in the face of restored creditworthiness the supply curve would have displaced itself downward and to the right. Indeed, the raising of the price in the middle of a crisis could be absolutely counterproductive since it increases the debt burden and can therefore further erode the prospects of autonomous repayments. As illustrated in

[31] The matter also can be examined from the standpoint of client relationships. The big banks wanted to avoid a break with a borrower because of their preoccupation about client relationships and market shares over the long term. The smaller banks, confronting the crisis, simply wanted to abandon international lending altogether. As one banker from a small institution remarked, "We feel that we are far too small a fish in the great big world pond for any government to care what we do." See Erik Ipsen, "After Mexico, the Regionals Are in Retreat," *Euromoney*, January 1983, p. 65.

[32] Data on loan exposures are notoriously poor. However, data on U.S. banks indicate that in June 1982 smaller banks had about one-fifth of the banking system's $83 billion exposure in Latin America. U.S. Federal Financial Institutions Examination Council, "Statistical Release," (Washington, D.C., 6 December 1982).

[33] For example, see Cline, *International Debt*, p. 81.

FIGURE 5.1. The Supply of Credit and Rationing.

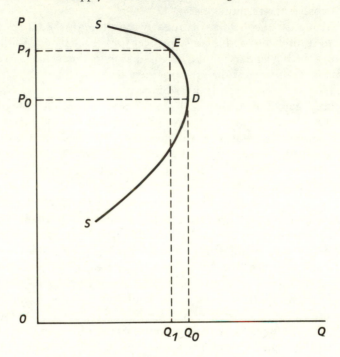

Figure 5.1, if the smaller banks were at their rationing points, the higher price would in fact give them more incentive to reduce credit commitments and flee. Indeed, in practice the smaller lenders did attempt to escape no matter how attractive the price of the loan package.[34]

The true manner in which the small banks were kept in the new credit packages was by introducing nonprice incentives.[35] In effect, the big

[34] See "U.S. Regional Banks Cut Lending to Latin America," *Press Review* (Bank for International Settlements), 27 February 1984, p. 6.

[35] Fernández comes up with a similar conclusion in a model designed to critique Cline, although he assumes a price elastic supply curve. Price increases *will* attract new credit from the smaller banks, but the price would have to increase each time a new loan was needed, which according to him is unsustainable. Therefore, direct coercion and not price increases is the effective way in which smaller banks are kept in the loan packages. However, as I mentioned earlier, evidence suggests that bank supply curves are inelastic and collapsing during a crisis, explaining why the creditors' typical voluntary reaction to a rescheduling is to reduce new credit even in the face of a much higher offer price. The only banks willing to lend semivoluntarily are the bigger creditors that are locked in due to overextensions of their commitments, and in this case a higher price is not the decisive factor in decision making. Indeed, as shown in Table 5.2, Mexico received a record vol-

banks had to ensure that the potential cost for the smaller creditors of not participating in the rescue package was larger than that directly at stake in the value of their loan portfolio with the problem debtor country. For example, one important measure was direct moral suasion by the big banks, which are net depositors in the interbank market and also are important international and national correspondent institutions for the smaller lenders. Another form of pressure—and a very effective one—was a call from the smaller creditor's central bank authorities, who actively supported the international management strategy; they monitor the entire operation of the bank and can make life difficult for it if they want to. And, of course, pressure from the IMF, and even the debtor country, helped to keep the smaller lenders in the rescue packages.[36]

Greater Risk   Another argument frequently raised by the banks and some analysts to justify the sharp rise in the cost of the debt in the first rounds of reschedulings was that it compensated the banks for the greater risks they assumed.[37] In effect, in a rescheduling the creditors agree to stretch out the maturity beyond the original contract dates. This accordingly raises risk.

However, we must remember that when an efficient bank authorizes a credit in a competitive market, the creditor covers risk by loan portfolio diversification and by the charge of a premium over base interest rates. Thus, an efficient bank evaluates the risk *before* awarding the loan and charges appropriate premia. If and when a borrower is unable to pay, the efficient bank is presumably in a position to absorb the loss.

This is indeed the classic market solution. When a loan turns bad and a country defaults, those who evaluated risk well can absorb the loss, while those that evaluated it poorly may go bankrupt. As is often the case in the classic parable of competition, there is a sense of justice. Here we have risk sharing. The country pays a premium over the lender's op-

---

ume of new loans in the fourth round of rescheduling with prices at record lows. See Javier Fernández, "Crédito Bancario Involuntario a Países" [Involuntary Bank Credit to Countries], *Coyuntura Económica*, December 1983, pp. 198–210.

[36] The importance of all these direct pressures is quite evident in Joseph Kraft's detailed account of the Mexican rescue; see Kraft, *Mexican Rescue*, pp. 48–55. Also see Miguel Wionczek, "Mexico's External Debt Revisited: Lessons of the 1985 Rescheduling Arrangement for Latin America," paper presented at a seminar on Latin American External Debt, Stockholm, May 1985. More generally, Vinod Aggarwal specifically analyzes the subject of bank cooperation during the crisis. The measures used to ensure the participation of the small banks were all coercive; price is never mentioned. See Aggarwal, "Cooperation in the Debt Crisis" (Berkeley, Calif:, University of California, September 1985).

[37] As an example, see again Cline, *International Debt*, p. 81.

portunity cost of funds to compensate for risk. If the country should be unable to pay, this induces losses for the creditor, which it should be able to absorb, assuming risks have been properly evaluated and priced. The country receives debt relief via the default, which temporarily releases the debtor from payments, and by the consequent market-induced devaluation of the creditor's assets to levels that are more closely aligned to their real underlying worth.[38] However, by jointly rescheduling debts in 1982/1983 the private banks were able to effectively elude the operation of the market mechanism.

Banks and some analysts argued during the initial rounds of rescheduling that creditors faced *additional* risk that the debtors had to compensate them for. But rigorously speaking, banks did not encounter additional risk, just the materialization of the risk that they had already evaluated, and the country had paid a premium for, at the moment of signing the original loan contract. Indeed, the situation was just the opposite of what the banks claimed, since the rescheduling actually reduced risk; without it the formal default and losses would have materialized with certainty. Moreover, risk was further reduced by other factors, for example, the debtor states generally agreed to guarantee the previously unguaranteed obligations of the country's private sector as well as to enter into IMF adjustment programs.[39] It is thus hard to justify the rise in the cost of credit by the claim of new risk.

Moral Hazard   During the first two rounds of restructurings another very fashionable argument used to justify the high cost of the rescheduling was the claim to moral hazard. This essentially means that the higher price upon rescheduling represented a penalty for bad behavior

---

[38] The default causes debt paper to trade at a large discount. The countries can repurchase the debt at a discount or renegotiate the terms with the creditor in such a way that part of the discount is passed on to the debtor. We saw in Chapter Two that this is what happened to Latin American debts during the interwar period.

[39] The banks put enormous pressure on the debtor countries to guarantee private sector debts. However, the insistence on ex post guarantees had no justification from the standpoint of conventional economic criteria. The banks supposedly evaluated the risk of default of lending to private entities without public guarantees and charged the appropriate premiums when they originally authorized the loan. To demand a guarantee after that risk materialized was entirely arbitrary, unless the banks paid the state guarantor an insurance premium. And this insurance premium would have had to be quite high—indeed infinite in some cases—because many of the private sector debts were quite simply bad. The banks generally did not pay premiums for the state guarantees, although a token fee was granted to the government of Chile in its third round of debt rescheduling in 1985, when it reluctantly renewed its guarantor status on private debts.

on the part of the debtor and as such served to discourage similar action in the future.[40]

The concept of moral hazard is related to the literature on health insurance.[41] The original health insurance problem is as follows. Upon buying health insurance an individual would face zero marginal costs for medical attention. With health care "free" after the initial purchase of the insurance, the insurer faces the risk that the client will behave in ways that might actually alter ex post the demand for medical attention. For instance, with zero marginal costs for health care the client might be more inclined to risk his or her good health by smoking, drinking, dressing improperly in winter weather, et cetera. Thus to avoid this moral hazard, insurance companies habitually make the insured person pay a deductible on health care, under the assumption that with positive marginal costs their client will be less likely to behave in ways that would increase the demand for health services.

But it is important to note that the notion of charging a premium against moral hazard is derived in a competitive market environment in which the forces of supply and demand operate. An insurance company cannot arbitrarily charge a premium but must subject it to the competitive forces in the marketplace. To the extent that creditors charge for moral hazard, it too must be incorporated into the original loan agreement, which was subject to the forces of the market. To charge for this risk ex post is not a premium for moral hazard but an arbitrary surcharge that is equivalent to informing a patient of the cost of health care after the patient falls sick.

Furthermore, in the finance literature (reviewed in Chapter Three) it is well known that the jacking up of the price of credit—especially when borrowers are under economic stress—can increase moral hazard, not reduce it. On the one hand, when the price rises, borrowers must undertake more risky behavior to meet the higher service charges.[42] On the other hand, if a borrower is dishonest, and weighing the costs of default versus the benefits, the higher price can simply raise the benefits of not paying.[43]

[40] Cline, *International Debt*, p. 81, once again is a good example.

[41] Kenneth Arrow has made important contributions in this area. One of his more interesting statements is "The Economics of Moral Hazard: Further Comment," *American Economic Review* 58 (June 1968): 537–539.

[42] Joseph Stiglitz and Andrew Weiss, "Credit Rationing in Markets with Imperfect Information," *American Economic Review* 71 (June 1981): 401–402.

[43] Eaton and Gersowitz have an excellent analysis of the dishonest borrower; see Jonathan Eaton and Mark Gersowitz, "Debt with Potential Repudiation: Theoretical and Empirical Analysis," *Review of Economic Studies* 48 (April 1981): 289–309.

But more importantly, the price of credit is never the true incentive for good behavior on the part of a debtor. No country wants to end up in circumstances that require a rescheduling because it means an interruption of external flows of credit, which generally can have a high rate of return in the developing country's economy. Of course, a country could conceivably be in a situation in which the benefits of default on old debt exceed the costs in terms of lost new credit. But, as just pointed out, if the country were dishonest and willing to act on this narrow calculation, a price increase would merely reinforce the decision to default.

Indeed, the whole preoccupation about moral hazard was probably unnecessarily exaggerated. As Arrow has pointed out, the action of any agent can never be controlled simply by economic incentives.[44] One of the characteristics of a successful economic system is that there is sufficient trust between the principal agent and the subordinate that the latter will not act in bad faith even if it were rational to do so. In other words, in an efficient and integrated economic system one cannot assume a pure *homo economicus*, which bases all action on cold cost-benefit calculus.

It is in this light that one can appreciate the strong integration of Latin America into the world capitalist system during the postwar era. Moreover, what started largely as an economic process has evolved into a political one as well, as manifest by the emerging democracies in the region. This trend towards integration has been partly behind the great responsibility with which most authorities honored their obligations at the outset of the crisis. In effect, there is no evidence that authorities contemplated default, even though, as we will see a bit later, this could have been an exceptionally appropriate bargaining tactic. While the costs of default may have been on the minds of the authorities, their unwillingness to use default even as a bargaining chip and their willingness to accept the high economic and social costs of the international management of the crisis suggest that they shared the values of financial orthodoxy.[45]

Equity   The fourth and last argument that appeared during the early rounds of reschedulings to justify the high cost of credit was based on a

[44] Arrow, "The Economics of Moral Hazard," pp. 537–539.

[45] As Peter Montagnon of the *Financial Times* observed concerning Latin debtors: "There is an astonishing degree of moral purpose even in the seemingly most helpless cases. Their finance ministers will still tell you emphatically that default is wrong and against their national pride." Peter Montagnon, "What To Do About Countries Which Cannot Settle Their Debts," *Financial Times*, 9 March 1985, p. 16.

loose notion of equity.[46] The argument begins by noting that the spreads and commissions on loans fell to absurdly low levels in the 1970s. This in turn was brought on by the "ferocious competition" among the banks in that period. Hence, the increase in price demanded by the creditors during the reschedulings was simply a way to adjust the price to normal levels after having been unjustifiably low during the expansive phase of the international money market.

This normative argument interestingly comes closer to the reality of things than the more technical propositions advanced earlier. It also helps to better understand at least one aspect of the creditors' strategy. In effect, it is possible that the risk premia charged in the 1970s were excessively low, which would mean that the banks were really not in a position to fall back on them when their loan portfolio turned bad in 1982/1983.[47] However, this unfortunate situation was not the product of the intense competition in the market but rather the consequence of deficient risk evaluation, or deficient institutional translation of that evaluation into credit decisions. Thus, the increase of the price of credit upon rescheduling the debt in 1982 and 1983 was in reality a successful attempt to pass the cost of a weakly developed loan portfolio on to the debtor countries.

Looked at from another angle, the ex post facto rise in the cost of debt at the moment of the first round of rescheduling had all the appearances of a monopoly rent. In other words, it constituted an income above economic costs generated by the ability of the banks to join together en bloc to not only reschedule debt but additionally to do it on terms highly lucrative to them. In other words, a rent is any payment above that which is necessary for any agent to do what it has done. In this instance the banks charged more for an administrative operation—the rescheduling of debt—necessary in any event to avoid the large losses that would come with a formal default. The additional income was a super-profit and created the anomaly that banks could report robust profits from Latin America in the middle of their worst financial crisis since the 1930s.[48] Thus for the first time in history a debt crisis became good

[46] This argument came to my attention in a closed-door conference statement by a London banker who is one of the leading personalities on the LDC debt issue. The conference was held at the Economic Commission for Latin America and the Caribbean in Santiago, Chile, in early 1983.

[47] The price of credit was sometimes felt even to have fallen below administrative costs. See Fabio Basagni, "Recent Developments in International Lending Practices," in *Banks and the Balance of Payments*, Benjamin Cohen in collaboration with Fabio Basagni (Montclair, N.J.: Allanheld, Osmun, 1981), pp. 98–100.

[48] See R. Lambert, "New York Banks Show Strong Gains," *Financial Times*, 19 January 1983, p. 32; R. Banner, "Banks Gain from Fees by Altering Latin Debt," *New York*

business for the creditors. The nature of the rents and how banks managed to generate them will become clearer in the pages that follow.

The Correct Framework: Competitive or Monopolistic?

One might suspect "ad hocery" when four separate arguments simultaneously emerge to justify the single phenomenon of a skyrocketing price of credit upon rescheduling a debt. Indeed, scrutiny of the arguments has shown all of them to be flawed. Moreover, all but the last justification are rooted in concepts related to the operation of a competitive market; that is, the rise in price could be interpreted as a mere shift of the supply curve upwards and to the left.

This type of market-oriented argument is illustrated in Figure 5.2. There one can observe a demand curve DD that has a perfectly inelastic slope RT and a normal slope TD. These are in fact parts of "two" demands for credit, OQ_o^r and $Q_o^r Q_o$. The first demand for credit is simply to refinance the amortization of old debt, while the second is for net credit.[49]

One could expect inelastic demand on the part of the borrower for the refinance of amortization payments, either because of a reluctance to default in face of a shortage of foreign exchange or because of a desire to avoid negative external savings through the obligatory generation of a current account surplus to effect the payment.[50] Nevertheless, there would be a third segment of the curve (DR), where the price of credit would be too high to justify the refinance operation. In this latter case the country would opt either to generate the required current account surplus or to enter into default. Finally, the segment where net credit appears $(Q_o^r Q_o)$ presents the conventional inverse relation between price and quantity demanded.

In this context in normal circumstances the equilibrium price would be P_o for the quantity of credit Q_o. But when a country falls into pay-

---

Times, 10 January 1983, p. D3; J. Plender, "Of Profits and Imprudence," *Financial Times*, 18 February 1983, p. 5; and Max Wilkinson, "Banks Greedy over Third World," *Financial Times*, 31 March 1983, p. 10. According to Wellons, the problem Latin American countries became "luminous profit centers" for the banks in their darkest hour. See Philip Wellons, *Passing the Buck* (Boston: Harvard Business School Press, 1987), p. 253.

[49] To simplify the exposition, I will assume that the payment of interest is zero and therefore there is no concern about refinancing this obligation. However, if one wanted to incorporate interest payments into the analysis, they could be joined with the inelastic demand for the refinance of OQ_o^r.

[50] The surplus could be avoided if debt were amortized through a drawdown of external reserves. But this also is not an attractive option since bankers typically use reserve levels as an indicator of creditworthiness (Group of Thirty, *Risks in International Lending*, p. 45).

FIGURE 5.2. A Competitive Framework for Prices and Quantities.

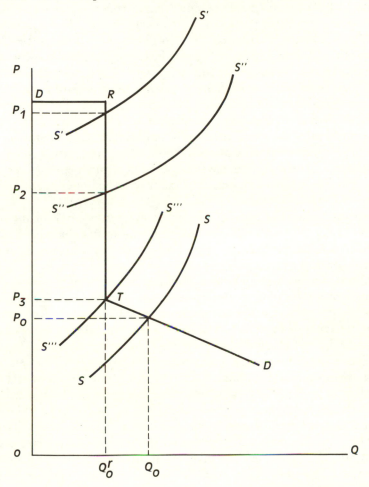

ments problems the supply curve shifts upwards and to the left (S to S') as a consequence of the bankers' increased perception of risk and moral hazard. Thus, with the existing demand curve, credit operations are limited to the refinance of amortization at the much higher price P_1. However, it is important to observe that in this type of interpretation the elasticity of the supply curve is positive, and therefore net credit is available, although only at an even higher price. This then would explain analytically what came to pass in the first round of the rescheduling exercises.

According to the creditors' arguments, the slight softening of the conditions of indebtedness in the second round of these exercises was due to the better economic performance of the borrowers and consequent lower risk. In other words, on the basis of this more optimistic evaluation of the creditors the supply curve began to shift itself downwards and to the right again,[51] arriving at S'', with the more moderate equilibrium price P_2. Similarly, in the third round of negotiations the bankers perceived more progress in the debtors' situation, giving rise to a further downward shift of the supply curve to S''', in which the price approaches that which prevailed prior to the crisis. In sum, drawing on the theoretical concepts employed by the creditors in the early rounds of rescheduling, one could conclude that the prices and quantities appearing in the restructuring exercises were determined once again by the logic of the marketplace.

The preceding illustration, inspired by market forces, is highly stylized but demonstrates how the creditors' arguments could be reasonably interpreted, and perhaps were interpreted, by the borrowers at the outset of the crisis. However, the market-oriented justifications of the creditors—which have persisted in various forms throughout the four rounds of reschedulings—clearly mask the options open to the countries. As pointed out earlier, if a competitive market were in fact operating, the bankers would have had to absorb a much larger share of the costs of the crisis than they actually have to date.

The ex-president of the Brazilian Central Bank, Carlos Langoni, captured the underlying contradiction early on when he observed that the bankers were "taking a market-oriented view of a situation to which market forces no longer apply."[52] He clearly was right.[53] The rescheduling of debt and the refinance of interest payments does not constitute a market transaction, where there is a price for a determined quantity. This type of exercise takes place outside of a competitive market and falls within the framework of a bilateral monopoly in which debtor and creditor sit down to administratively decide how to share the losses on a weak portfolio. The outcome is theoretically imprecise and depends on the negotiating power of the two parties. To the extent

---

[51] For the sake of simplicity I have not shifted the demand curve in Figure 5.2. But in the second round the amount of maturities rescheduled was different from that of the first round.

[52] Carlos Langoni, "The Way Out of the Country Debt Crisis," *Euromoney*, October 1983, p. 26.

[53] For analytical support of Langoni's assertion see Robert Devlin, "Renegotiation of Latin America's Debt: An Analysis of the Monopoly Power of Private Banks," *CEPAL Review*, no. 20 (August 1983), pp. 101–112.

FIGURE 5.3. A Framework of Bilateral Monopoly.

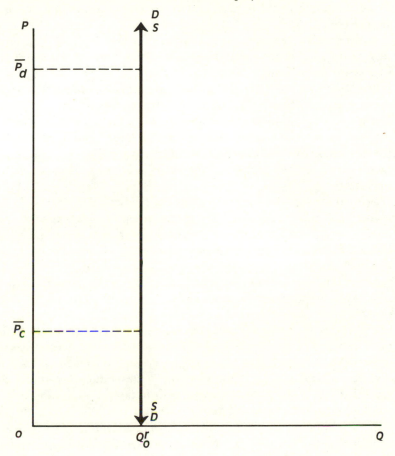

SYMBOLS:

$\bar{P}_d$ = maximum price accepted by the debtor to avoid default

$\bar{P}_c$ = minimum price accept by the creditor to avoid default

Q_o^r = credit to refinance/reschedule capital that is unpayable

S = supply schedule

D = demand schedule

that the bank manages to impose a rescheduling with conditions that allow it to escape the losses and consequent devaluation of assets that would result in a competitive market environment, it obtains rents. These rents both in theory and practice can be captured by the debtor.

The Rescheduling of Capital   The alternative framework of a bilateral monopoly is presented in Figure 5.3. For the moment I will assume that there is only a rescheduling of amortization that otherwise would be in default. Also, we want to abstract from externalities, or "demonstration effects."

In the graph we can observe that in the framework of a bilateral monopoly the supply and demand curves are superimposed upon one another over the amount of debt that is subject to rescheduling, Q_o^r. The curve DD is perfectly inelastic because the debtor is not entirely sensitive to the price of credit in its effort to refinance debt and avoid default. For its part the creditor is also not precise about the price of a rescheduling because it wants to elude default, market forces, and the losses that would appear in the absence of the restructuring. For this reason the creditor also has a wide range of prices that are acceptable to effect the operation.

Nevertheless, at the outset the debtor will have a maximum price $\bar{P}_d$ above which it will be preferable to abandon negotiations and enter into default. At the same time the creditor will have a minimum price $\bar{P}_c$ below which it would be preferable to call a default. Thus there is a range of possible prices $\bar{P}_c$ to $\bar{P}_d$ for which an acceptable agreement can be reached. The final result does not depend on supply and demand as such—which offers no precise solution—but on the relative bargaining power of debtor and creditor.

One might ask how far $\bar{P}_d$ could be pushed down if a debtor had adequate bargaining power or, alternatively, what is the lowest price acceptable to the banks ($\bar{P}_c$) after which it is viewed convenient by them to declare a formal default? In the absence of externalities it would be the price that would induce losses just inferior to the alternative losses that would appear in the event of an open default.

If the valuation of bank loans had been subject to market forces ("marked to the market"), $\bar{P}_c$ would have been well below the price recorded in the first four rounds of rescheduling; indeed, it undoubtedly would have had to reflect a negative rate of return.[54] However, current

---

[54] As an example, suppose a bank had $100 million outstanding and is forced to declare a default. It could enter into a secondary market to trade the paper. While there is really no highly developed secondary market for LDC loans, there has been informal trading, which can give us a conservative idea of the discounts banks might face. (It is conservative because with open default discounts might be larger.) At the outset of the crisis the discount on Latin American paper was around 20 percent. With a cost of funds of 10 percent, the loss for the bank would be 20 percent of principal ($20 million) plus 10 percent ($10 million). The return on the loan would be −30 percent [$100(1 + x) = 70$]. Thus in this case any rescheduling accord offering a return superior to −30 percent could be attractive to the creditor. If the bank secures a price above this inferior limit it obtains a rent. It is also worth noting that more recently discounts have widened considerably; by 1987 many Latin American debt documents were circulating at a discount of 50 percent

domestic banking regulations insulate banks from market forces.[55] Any devaluation of assets would be administratively determined in conjunction with banking supervisors according to the diverse accounting practices of the OECD governments. It is, moreover, difficult to accurately anticipate the reaction of regulatory authorities since accounting rules can be broadly interpreted and "massaged" by political considerations. In most cases, even in the worst of circumstances initial write-downs of the debt would undoubtedly be partial and phased over a number of years. Nevertheless, nonpayment by the borrowers would bring direct or indirect write-downs of some sort and losses for the banks.

The introduction of externalities also greatly complicates the analysis. Without considering the action of other debtors the creditor might be very willing to accept a price well below a commercial rate. But the creditor will always fear that a nonmarket price for one debtor will bring demands from others for equal treatment. In other words, the acceptable losses of one rescheduling in practice could be multiplied to an unviable amount by the reaction of other debtors. In light of this, $\bar{P}_c$ is in all likelihood much higher than in any situation that artificially assumes away externalities. One can only speculate whether $\bar{P}_c$ is below the price registered in the fourth round of reschedulings. But it may well be since many borrowers are in practice paying much less and avoiding declarations of default.[56]

The New Loans   The same framework of bilateral monopoly serves to analyze the range of possibilities with respect to the administratively organized new loans that refinance interest payments. We mentioned earlier that these loans have appeared in order to avoid arrears, making them part of a disguised rescheduling of interest. The flow of credit consequently has little to do with price but rather is directly related to the bargaining power of the debtor.

For a bank, a new loan, in the middle of circumstances that require a rescheduling, is clearly an undesirable cost. If there were acceptable alternatives the bank would certainly not authorize the credit. But a borrower can have enough leverage to forcibly extract new loans. This is because the new credit has a decisive impact on the value of the bank's

---

or more. See Eugenio Lahera, "The Conversion of Foreign Debt Viewed from Latin America," *CEPAL Review*, no. 32 (August 1987), p. 106.

[55] Jack Guttentag and Richard Herring, *The Current Crisis in International Lending* (Washington, D.C.: Brookings Institution, 1985), pp. 11–21.

[56] In 1987 Bolivia, Brazil, Cuba, Ecuador, Peru, Costa Rica, Panama, Honduras, Nicaragua, and Paraguay had protracted arrears on their debt payments. See ECLAC, "Preliminary Overview of the Latin American Economy 1987," p. 7.

TABLE 5.10. Loans as a Percentage of Bank Capital for Selected U.S. Institutions

Bank	Argentina	Brazil	Mexico	Venezuela	Chile	Total	Capital[a]
Citibank	18.2	73.5	54.6	18.2	10.0	174.5	5,989
Bank of America	10.2	47.9	52.1	41.7	6.3	158.2	4,799
Chase Manhattan	21.3	56.9	40.0	24.0	11.8	154.0	4,221
Morgan Guaranty	24.4	54.3	34.8	17.5	9.7	140.7	3,107
Manufacturers Hanover	47.5	77.7	66.7	42.4	28.4	262.8	2,592
Chemical	14.9	52.0	60.0	28.0	14.8	169.7	2,490
Continental Illinois	17.8	22.9	32.4	21.6	12.8	107.5	2,143
Bankers Trust	13.2	46.2	46.2	25.1	10.6	141.2	2,895
First National Chicago	14.5	40.6	50.1	17.4	11.6	134.2	1,725
Security Pacific	10.4	29.1	31.2	4.5	7.4	82.5	1,684
Wells Fargo	8.3	40.7	51.0	20.4	6.2	126.6	1,201
Crocker National	38.1	57.3	51.2	22.8	26.5	196.0	1,151
First Interstate	6.9	43.9	63.0	18.5	3.7	136.0	1,080
Marine Midland		47.8	28.3	29.2			1,074
Mellon		35.3	41.1	17.6			1,024
Irving Trust	21.6	38.7	34.1	50.2			996
First National Boston		23.1	28.1				800
Interfirst Dallas	5.1	10.2	30.1	1.3	2.5	49.2	787

SOURCE: William Cline, *International Debt: Systematic Risk and Policy Response*, table 2.2. Copyright © 1984, Institute for International Economics, Washington, D.C. Reprinted by permission from *International Debt: Systematic Risk and Policy Response* by William R. Cline.
NOTE:
[a]In millions of U.S. dollars.

existing portfolio: a rescheduling of amortization loses its commercial viability if interest is not accrued on those postponed capital payments. In other words, if in the absence of new lending the borrower ceases to pay all or part of the interest due, the bank faces reduced income and direct or indirect write-downs even if the debt is rescheduled.

At the outbreak of the crisis some banks were quite susceptible to forced new lending. On the one hand, for many of them loans to certain Latin American countries were a shockingly high percentage of the institution's capital, making direct or indirect write-downs potentially very costly and destabilizing (Table 5.10). On the other hand, some banks, but particularly big U.S. institutions, were (and are) very reluctant to report the reduced earnings that would come about from non-accrual of interest.[57] This introduced a vulnerability in the system that debtors could initially exploit.

To be more precise, I can expand the focus of a formula originally worked out by William Cline.[58] In effect, a bank will be disposed to award a new loan to refinance interest and avoid default to the extent that (a) the reduction in the probability of default (or extended moratorium) achieved by the new loan, multiplied by the value of the existing stock of debt, is greater than (b) the probability of a default (or extended moratorium) after the new loan multiplied by the value of that loan.[59] Thus (a) is the benefit of the new loan for the bank, while (b) is its cost.

It is evident from this framework that two variables which are important in obtaining new loans are the probability of default and the size of the bank's portfolio (relative to capital) in the country. If the country is a relatively large debtor and there is a strong likelihood of default in the absence of some amount of new lending to refinance interest, the possibilities of securing new loans should be good.[60] Alternatively, it is ironic that if a debtor is totally cooperative with a creditor and shows an unlimited disposition to compress imports to generate foreign exchange for debt payment, it is less likely to be able to secure new loans. This suggests that it might not be a good bargaining tactic for a debtor country to discard unilaterally the possibility of a default, or even direct cooperation with other debtor countries.

[57] While I cannot examine bank regulatory practices in detail here, it is worthwhile to briefly summarize a general procedure in the United States. As long as interest arrears are less than 90 days, a bank can continue to account interest payments as accrued income. When arrears exceed 90 days, loans are classified as "nonperforming" and interest can be accrued as income only on a cash basis. Earnings are thus immediately reduced. If arrears go beyond 180 days, the loan can be classified as "value impaired." This then requires the banks to additionally charge off, or set aside in nonreversible reserves, a percentage of the face value of the loan (10 percent minimum the first year). All of the above, of course, has an adverse impact on earnings. A loan also eventually may be classified as a loss and written off the books as an asset. See C. Fred Bergsten, et al., *Bank Lending to Developing Countries: The Policy Alternatives* (Washington, D.C.: Institute for International Economics, 1985), pp. 25–32; Robert Bennett, "The Intricacies of Bank Accounting," *New York Times*, 2 July 1984, p. D3; and Lissakers, "Bank Regulation and International Debt."

[58] Cline, *International Debt*, p. 72.

[59] As Cline points out, it is worthwhile to extend a new loan to the extent that $(P_0 - P_1)D > P_1 L$, where D is the existing stock of debt in the bank's portfolio, P_0 is the probability of default before the new loan (L) is extended, and P_1 is the probability of default after the loan.

[60] This partially explains why most of the new lending went to relatively big debtor countries.

Adjustment efforts are also relevant. While a high probability of default is an incentive for a bank to lend, that probability must fall sharply after the new loans are extended. This requires that the country have some capacity to adjust and move the economy in the direction of renewed creditworthiness. It is in this light that one understands why new forced lending is more easily induced for debtors suffering from a problem perceived as illiquidity. A state of clear insolvency is obviously less conducive to new lending because the probability of default after the loan is likely to fall only very transitorily and the fictitious nature of accounting is more blatant.[61]

Nevertheless, a bank may be willing to lend to a big insolvent borrower. On the one hand, the new loan can postpone the day of reckoning and permit current bank administrators to pass the problem on to their successors or, more positively interpreted, allow them to prepare the bank and its stockholders for the ultimate write-down. The bank also may take into account externalities related to market presence or the negative demonstration effects a default of a big debtor might have on the behavior of other countries.

Finally, the disposition to lend depends very much on the collective action of the banks because in the face of cross-default clauses no bank would be willing to lend on its own.

THE DYNAMICS OF NEGOTIATION

I will now employ the framework of bilateral monopoly in order to gain richer insights into the evolution of the international debt crisis than can be found in the competitive market concepts so frequently observed in the creditors' interpretations of the management of the crisis.

The First Round

The crisis broke out very suddenly. Northern banking systems were extremely vulnerable to nonpayment. That systemic vulnerability is well illustrated by the fragile condition of the U.S. institutions: at the outset

---

[61] The concepts of illiquidity and insolvency are technically commercial concepts and not strictly applicable to a sovereign debtor. Nevertheless, the terms are frequently employed in the literature on debt to distinguish between cases where adjustment and a return to creditworthiness can be achieved in a reasonably short period and cases where such a process can be expected to be very protracted and succeed only after a structural overhaul of the economy. I will use these same terms often in the study even though some economists would frown upon the practice. See for instance Larry Sjaastad, "International Debt Quagmire: To Whom Do We Owe It?" *The World Economy* 6 (September 1983): 305–324.

TABLE 5.11. United States Banks' Exposure in Latin America
as a Percentage of Their Primary Capital
(percentages)

	June 1982			December 1987		
	Top 9	Rest	Total	Top 9	Rest	Total
Latin America	180.0	85.4	124.0	96.7	31.8	57.7
Oil exporters	87.0	44.2	61.8	40.2	16.1	25.7
Nonoil exporters	93.0	41.2	62.2	56.5	15.7	32.0
Memorandum Item						
Primary Capital	27.1	39.1	66.2	51.5	77.7	129.1

SOURCE: Calculated from data of the U.S. Federal Financial Examination Council,
   Statistical Release (Washington, D.C.), various editions.

of the payments crisis they had loans outstanding in Latin America
equivalent to 124 percent of their primary capital. Moreover, the region's payment problems were led by three big debtors (Argentina, Brazil, and Mexico) whose loans alone represented over 80 percent of the
U.S. banking systems' capital. The situation of the nine big money center banks—the heart of the U.S. system and a kingpin in global financial
markets—was even more critical because their loans to the region absorbed 180 percent of primary capital (Table 5.11). Facing this situation, bankers did what bondholders could not do in the 1930s: they coordinated effectively to confront the problem debtor countries in order
to avoid defaults and an immediate devaluation of their assets. This historically unique outcome of a systemic international payments crisis
was facilitated by a set of special circumstances.

Unlike bondholders, private banks had at their disposal the coordi-
nating mechanism of an "advisory (or steering) committee" with a
track record of success in dealing with problem debtor countries during
the 1970s. The committee—typically made up of the ten to fourteen
biggest lenders and broken down along geographic lines[62]—is en-

[62] The committees usually have the biggest creditors from each region, typically the
United States, Canada, Japan and Europe. The country's biggest single bank creditor is
normally named the chairman of the advisory committee. For a list of the members of the
advisory committees for selected LDC problem debtors see John Reed, "The Role of External Private Capital Flows," in *Growth-Oriented Adjustment Programs,* ed. Vittorio
Corbo et al. (Washington, D.C.: International Monetary Fund and World Bank, 1987), p.
427.

charged by a country's creditor banks (which for a big debtor could exceed five hundred) to negotiate a rescheduling and its terms with the problem borrower. Advisory committees can be quickly formed because, in contrast to anonymous and disbursed bondholders, bankers work out of the clubby oligopolistic confines of New York and London; they know each other and their approximate market shares. Moreover, while in domestic markets communication among banks is often legally restricted due to concerns about collusion, in unregulated international markets there is unbridled communication. Indeed, communication among banks became institutionalized by the two-tiered market structure in which the very big banks—in their capacity as lead institutions in syndication—managed many aspects of international lending for their small- and medium-sized brethren. Also facilitating communication and coordination among the banks are the legal incentives deriving from cross-default clauses that accompany almost all international loan agreements.

Formally, the banks present their committee structure as a public good, that is, an innocent mechanism of coordination among the hundreds of lenders, which facilitates the rescue of the borrower. Given the large number of lenders and free-rider problems in private international markets, the committee could indeed perform a valuable public goods function by promoting socially efficient collective solutions. But there is a potentially dark side to the committee structure as well: it can facilitate collusion and the formation of an effective cartel geared to skewing the distribution of the costs of a problem.

On the one hand, by joining together in a committee operated by the world's largest banks the creditors can create a formidable negotiating bloc against a single debtor. On the other hand, by virtue of the fact that there is no meaningful alternative to bank finance, in practice the commercial lenders have a monopoly over credit flows. Noncooperation with the banks would threaten to alienate the capitalist system's biggest lenders, which control medium-term loans as well as the short-term credit that moves day-to-day import and export trade.

The bargaining strength of the committees formed during the current crisis was moreover reinforced by several other factors.

First, the steering committees enjoyed strong support from the OECD governments and the IMF. During the 1980s many governments of the industrialized countries—and in particular the United States—were especially strident in promoting private markets, unfettered by public intervention. However, when the crisis broke in Latin America, ideology took a back seat to the pragmatic need to rescue domestic and international financial systems from the collapse that could have possibly occurred if multiple defaults appeared in the region.[63] In effect, OECD governments—led by the United States in whose sphere of influence Latin America fell—rapidly mobilized the decentralized international lender-of-last-resort facilities that had evolved out of postwar global political and economic cooperation.[64]

Both because of the urgency of the crisis and the opportunity to reassert its international role after being marginalized by the great banking expansion of the 1970s, the IMF immediately agreed to insert itself between debtors and creditors. It allowed the banks to tie their rescheduling packages directly to a Fund adjustment program, which helped them squeeze foreign exchange out of the economies and thereby keep to a minimum the finance required to roll over interest payments and avoid default. In addition to making the elimination of arrears a condition of its adjustment programs, the IMF supported, or at least never questioned, the onerous commercial terms that the banks demanded to effect the reschedulings.[65] The IMF and OECD governments also helped the big banks overcome free-rider problems by cajoling reticent lenders—especially the smaller ones—to participate in the rescue packages.[66] Meanwhile, the U.S. government organized official bridge financing for cooperative debtor countries to avoid defaults while the steering committee and the IMF haggled with the LDC and marginal lenders. Finally, bank regulatory authorities in the U.S. and elsewhere were usually tolerant of the creative accounting of the banks; this insulated the lenders from a market valuation of their problem loans in the region and assuaged potential dissension among institutions with different abilities to write down their assets.

[63] The exmanaging director of the IMF, Jacques de Larosière, formally observed that the debt problem represented "a very serious threat to the international financial and trading system." *IMF Survey*, 9 January 1984, p. 4.

[64] There is tacit agreement among creditor governments that leadership in the mobilization of lender-of-last-resort facilities falls to the government with a claim to a sphere of influence over the problem debtors. See Wellons, *Passing the Buck*, p. 245.

[65] There is no evidence that the Fund questioned the terms. Conversations with Latin American negotiators at that time confirm that the IMF at least tacitly supported the bankers' stringent terms for a rescheduling. The Fund, which was in a position to influence the conditions, essentially ignored advice from conventional development circles that had long argued that reschedulings be done on soft terms. See the Pearson Commission, *Partners in Development* (New York: Praeger, 1969); Gamani Corea, "The Debt Problems of Developing Countries," *Journal of Development Planning*, no. 9 (1976), pp. 53–78; and Brandt Commission, *North-South: A Program for Survival* (Cambridge, Mass.: MIT Press, 1980).

[66] Banks are not a homogeneous group. Some of them—even big ones—were not initially happy with the IMF's use of moral suasion to keep them in the loan packages. The irritation came largely from the ethos in banking circles that "the market knows best."

Second, the bankers had precedent on their side. Their demands as well as the market-oriented justifications for them were neither more nor less than what the bankers had established as normal practice in the 1970s (with Nicaragua the lone exception). The people who initially negotiated with the bankers were central bankers and ministers of finance who largely shared the bankers' paradigm.

Third, the bankers, their governments, and the IMF strongly insisted on a case-by-case approach to the problem under the pretext that each country's situation was very different.[67] This discouraged the joint action by the borrowers that could have, at least in principle, counterbalanced the power of the committee.

Fourth, notwithstanding the case-by-case approach that the creditors imposed on the rescheduling process, the countries initially had a relatively passive bargaining strategy. As mentioned, there was little or no talk of moratorium, nor did the debtors attempt to pursue the logic of a bilateral monopoly and cooperate among themselves; indeed, during the first round of rescheduling the Latin American debtors competed vigorously with each other to appear as the most creditworthy client of the banks.[68]

One important factor in this initially passive stance was the aforementioned observation that most of the authorities in the debtor governments shared the prevailing values of the capitalist system. This produced an appreciable degree of empathy with the creditors' objectives of avoiding defaults and destabilization of financial markets through a cooperative international strategy as well as patience with the banks' insistence on onerous terms to compensate for risk, et cetera. But there were also undoubtedly more narrow incentives at work. Creditors promised that a quick adjustment of the debtors' economies would restore their creditworthiness and access to credit markets. There also existed the implicit threat that default would ostracize debtors from those credit markets and bring costly sanctions.[69] Thus conventional wisdom

[67] See, for instance, Karl Otto Pöhl, "Herr Pöhl Elucidates the Deutsche Bundesbank's Views on the International Debt Situation," *Press Review* (Bank for International Settlements), 4 February 1985, p.1.

[68] The environment is partly captured by developments in Brazil. After the Mexican crisis of August, Delfim Neto, Brazil's minister of finance, refused to consider a debt rescheduling, even though the country's access to credit was waning. A call by opposition economist Celso Furtado for the formation of an "OPEC for the indebted" was dismissed out of hand. Meanwhile, conservative economist Roberto Campos rejected debtor cooperation or rescheduling and suggested Mexico's problems would work in Brazil's favor by eliminating a major competitor for credits. See "Debate Rages over Renegotiation," *Latin American Weekly Report*, 13 August 1982, pp. 2–4.

[69] The conventional threats for uncooperative debtors are found in Cline, *International Debt*, pp. 86–93. Chapter Six will broach the question of sanctions in somewhat more detail.

based on a rational economic calculation of self-interest justified cooperation: assuming markets are efficient, it was entirely plausible that the present discounted value of future flows of private credit, less the actual cost of short-term adjustment, would be greater than the present discounted value of debt service saved by default less the lost income derived from sanctions.

Fifth, an important global factor that contributed to the strength of the committee's positions in the earlier rounds of reschedulings was the widely accepted diagnosis that the debtor countries suffered from problems of illiquidity—as opposed to insolvency—and therefore would be quickly pulled out of trouble by the then expected sustained recovery of the world economy.[70] In these circumstances it became that much more rational for banks to cooperate with the committee in the attempt "to lend" the creditor institutions out of trouble and for the debtor countries to accept the short-term costs of the banks' demands for rapid adjustment and commercial terms on the rescheduled debt.

In sum, circumstances and objective conditions tended to strongly consolidate the bargaining power of the block of private banks, while the debtors, reacting passively and independently, further enhanced that power. It is well known from neoclassical theory that when a monopolist confronts economic agents that act as if they were competitors, the likely outcome can be the exploitation of the latter.[71] Here we have a theoretically more solid foundation on which to explain the extraordinarily high cost of credit in the first round of the reschedulings.

The Second and Third Rounds

The second round began in late 1983 and drifted into 1984. The bankers received some criticism for the onerous terms of the rescheduling exercises. Opposition parties in the debtor countries, some northern press, and even the U.S. Congress complained about the severe terms of the restructurings.[72] Meanwhile, the borrowing country authorities began to express a feeling that they were being overcharged. As already mentioned, the newly elected Alfonsin government rejected the agreement that the bankers had reached with the military in the first round, and Venezuela stonewalled because it found the bankers' terms unac-

---

[70] See Cline, ibid., for an influential analysis that underpinned the popular notion of illiquidity in the debt crisis.

[71] In the neoclassical sense of the extraction of excess profits.

[72] See Wilkinson, "Banks Greedy over Third World"; Celso Furtado, *Não à Recessão e ao Desemprego* [No to Recession and Unemployment] (Rio de Janeiro: Editorial Paz e Terra, 1983); and Organization of American States, "Extract of Public Law 98–181 of the Congress of the United States Entitled: Law of National Housing and International Recovery and Financial Stability" (Washington, D.C.: OAS/SERH/XIV/CEFYC/4 January 1984).

ceptable. Moreover, the seeds of cooperation were being sown; in January 1984 President Hurtado of Ecuador convoked a high-level regional governmental meeting in Quito on debt and the crisis. The conference's final declaration condemned the harsh and one-sided distribution of the costs of the management of a crisis, which had its cause in factors that were partly out of the region's control. Among the measures proposed were the limiting of debt service to a "reasonable" percentage of export earnings; drastic reductions of margins, fees, and commissions; longer maturities; and the *exchange of information and technical assistance among the Latin American debtors.*[73] All this pressure induced the banks to soften somewhat the terms in the second round. As the magazine the *Economist* observed: "The cheaper loans are being given because everybody is telling the banks that they overcharged last year."[74]

But the pressure on the creditors increased. Argentina remained recalcitrant, as the region's third-largest debtor seemed to recognize its relative power in the game of bilateral monopoly.[75] It accumulated arrears and insisted that they be liquidated with new bank loans rather than by the use of the country's growing international reserves.[76] The rise in world interest rates in early 1984 provoked alarm even in the most cooperative debtors: in May 1984 the presidents of Brazil, Mexico, Colombia, and Argentina made a joint declaration condemning the high level of world interest rates and calling for "adequate repayment and grace periods, reduction of interest rates, margins and commissions and other financial charges."[77]

At midyear the situation became more tense. The new democratic government in Bolivia declared that it planned to limit debt service to 25 percent of exports. Meanwhile, the aforementioned joint declaration of the presidents gave rise to a ministerial meeting of eleven debtors in Cartagena, Colombia, in June 1984.

The Cartagena meeting was a very moderate affair. The participants rejected any notion that they were interested in forming a "debtors' cartel," and Bolivia's attempt to persuade other participants to support

[73] See "Latin American Economic Conference," *CEPAL Review*, no.22 (April 1984), pp. 39–52.

[74] "Rescheduling," *Economist*, 18 February 1984, p. 71.

[75] Aldo Ferrer, a distinguished Argentine economist, had published a book arguing that the Argentine economy was relatively self-sufficient and could confront the bankers and any sanctions they might impose. See Aldo Ferrer, *Vivir con Lo Nuestro* [Living on Our Own] (Buenos Aires: El Cid Editor, 1983).

[76] "Argentina Cries All the Way to Its Bankers," *Economist*, 31 March 1984, p. 77.

[77] "Presidents Publicly Toughen Regional Stance on Debt Issue," *Latin American Weekly Report*, 25 May 1984, p. 1.

its 25 percent rule was ignored.[78] Even so, the creditors and governments feared that a cartel could coalesce. It was this fear that caused the creditors to offer the radically more favorable conditions of the third round.[79]

The more generous terms were flashed initially at Mexico and Brazil, the two biggest debtors. The bankers and their governments justified the new terms on the grounds of "the important gains" of the debtors in the official adjustment program[80] (again implicitly referring to market concepts of risk). The creditors gave the new, visibly more generous scheme first to Mexico in August 1984. A clear message emerged: Mexico was the most cooperative of Latin debtors and these new terms would be available to others that followed Mexico's good example.[81]

But the decision to enter into a new framework had little to do with improvement in the debtors' situation. It is more instructive to view the more generous conditions in the context of a game theoretic, in which creditors selectively passed "side payments" to the debtor countries in order to defuse the growing cooperation among them.[82] Moreover, the strategy paid off; with the new package awarded to Mexico the debtor countries were quickly silenced and Argentina became totally isolated in its attempt to break the creditors' cartel management of the crisis. Moreover, subsequent meetings of the eleven Latin American ministers (now dubbed the Cartagena Consensus) in Santo Domingo and Mar del Plata were extraordinarily dull affairs.

The above suggests that market forces had little to do with the softening of terms in rounds two and three of the reschedulings. Moreover, the evolution of terms gives us some empirical indications of the monopoly rents captured by the banks in the first round. In that initial round, despite all the bankers' expressed concern about the individuality of the borrowers' problems and the need for a case-by-case approach, the terms were remarkably similar for all countries (Table 5.3).

[78] Hugh O'Shaughnessy, "Debtors' Conference Divided on Strategy for Service Payments," *Financial Times*, 21 June 1984, p. 4; and "Cartagena Conference of 11 Latin Nations Rejects Debtors' Cartel, Proposes Reforms," *IMF Survey*, 2 July 1984, pp. 201–202.

[79] Leonard Silk, "Acting to Avert Debtor Cartel," *New York Times*, 20 June 1984, p. D2.

[80] Kenneth Noble, "Volcker Sees Eased Debt Terms," *New York Times*, 9 August 1985, p. D3.

[81] "Plazos Más Largos para Pagar Deudas Externas" [Longer Periods for Payment of External Debts], *El Mercurio*, 31 August 1984, p. B1.

[82] O'Donnell uses game theory to explain the lack of cooperation in the region. See Guillermo O'Donnell, "External Debt: Why Don't Our Governments Do the Obvious?" *CEPAL Review*, no. 27 (December 1985), pp. 27–33.

We have seen that in subsequent rounds the bankers uniformly softened the terms for all the debtors, when only a few countries had shown any sign of some improvement in creditworthiness that might have merited such treatment; indeed, some of the beneficiaries of the softer conditions had been accumulating arrears.[83] Moreover, in the third round terms fell to levels *below* those that the countries had been contracting when they were ostensibly creditworthy and able to secure autonomous loans in the eurocurrency market (Table 5.8). In effect, then, even though their objectives were limited, the countries, through better use of their bargaining power, managed to secure the same administrative roll over of their debts at progressively less cost to them.

The Fourth Round

The new initiative on debt announced by U.S. Treasury Secretary James Baker in September 1985 must be viewed in the same light. At the outset of 1985 there was a sense of satisfaction in certain circles of the North about the success of the orthodox management of the crisis. Indeed, many thought the crisis had ended.[84] The strong growth in the United States had helped to boost Latin American exports by 11 percent in 1984.[85] The third round of rescheduling was being quietly implemented. Mexico continued to be a model debtor and announced that it would need no new forced credits. There was even an expectation that in late 1985 or early 1986 the country might reenter the voluntary eurocurrency market in a limited way in a "showcase loan" orchestrated by the steering committee. Dissident Venezuela and Argentina had been brought into the bankers' program. Although Brazil was having some difficulties complying with its IMF program, all expectations were that its new democratic government would be cooperative.

However, in March Fidel Castro held a lengthy, but well thought-out, interview with the Mexican newspaper *Excelsior*, in which he "demonstrated" that the Latin American debt was unpayable, even at concessionary rates of interest. He proposed that the OECD countries forgive the debt and cover the cost by reducing military expenditures. This would be one component in a package that reinstated the princi-

---

[83] "Rescheduling," *Economist*, 18 February 1984; and "The Mood Is Gloomy," *Latin American Weekly Report*, 7 October 1983, pp. 8–9. In addition, the arrears themselves were eliminated by new loans from the banks.

[84] See Gary Hector, "Third World Debt: The Bomb Is Defused," *Fortune*, 18 February 1985, pp. 36–50.

[85] Brazil was the main beneficiary of the buoyant U.S. market and thus strongly influenced the average rate. The data are from United Nations Economic Commission for Latin America and the Caribbean's Division of Statistics and Quantitative Analysis.

ples of the New International Economic Order.[86] Then Castro, with his characteristic flamboyance, attempted to renew debt as a regional issue.[87] He eventually invited eminent people from all over the region to discuss the debt problem with him in two separate meetings in July in Havana.[88] Meanwhile, in April Alan García and his APRA party had won a spectacular election victory in Peru, in which he had placed at the center of his campaign platform a promise not to submit the country to an IMF austerity program or let debt interfere with the legitimate aspirations of his people for a reactivation of the economy.[89] In his inaugural address in July, García reiterated his stance on the IMF and announced a unilateral limitation of medium- and long-term public debt service payments to 10 percent of exports.[90]

Shortly after García's inauguration problems in Brazil deepened. In August President Sarney began discussing foreign debt with his neighbors in preparation for his upcoming speech before the U.N. General Assembly in September. He was reported to be adopting a position "parallel to Cuba's" and promoting the idea that debt cannot be paid with recession. Suddenly, in September, Sarney's cooperative minister of finance and Central Bank president resigned in a power struggle with the minister of planning, who had been pushing for a more aggressive stance on the debt issue. The new economic team made it known that it planned to deal more aggressively with the issue of foreign debt and make the crisis the centerpiece of Sarney's address to the United Nations.[91]

Finally, even Mexico, the North's model student in the orthodox ad-

[86] Fidel Castro, *How Latin America's and the Third World's Unpayable Foreign Debt Can and Should Be Cancelled and the Pressing Need for the New International Economic Order: Interview Granted to the Mexican Daily Excelsior* (Havana: Editora Política, 1985).

[87] As one observer reported, "Castro has managed to turn, since March, every major public speech and every interview with a foreign newspaper into an occasion to present his views on the debt problem" ("Castro Escalates Debt Diplomacy," *Latin American Weekly Report*, 26 July 1985, p. 10).

[88] Ibid.

[89] As a high-level APRA party official commented: "We have decided first to feed our people, then pay the debt. This does not mean that we refuse to pay. In order to make payment possible we have to stimulate development" ("APRA's Government Priorities," *Latin American Weekly Report*, 28 June 1985, p. 6).

[90] Alan Riding, "Downcast Peru Is Given Lift by the New Leader," *New York Times*, 3 September 1985, p. A1.

[91] "Sarney Turns to His Neighbors," *Latin American Weekly Report*, 23 August 1985, p. 8; "Funaro Vows Fight against Inflation," *Latin American Weekly Report*, 6 September 1985, p. 4; and "Funaro Selects a New Team," *Latin American Weekly Report*, 13 September 1985, p. 4.

justment process, began to send out disturbing signals. The country apparently felt growing political isolation on the debt issue and was beginning to have problems with the orthodox program because falling oil prices and more expansive public policy were contributing to noncompliance with IMF targets. Moreover, Mexican authorities had held a "secret" meeting—quickly leaked—with Latin American leaders in Oaxtepec in July to discuss debt and new ways to press OECD governments to help ease the debt crisis. This marked a beginning in a shift of Mexico's position as well.[92] Later in the year the country would openly fail the performance criteria agreed to in its adjustment program with the IMF.[93]

It was these developments that contributed to Baker's announcement in the October annual meetings of the IMF/World Bank in Seoul that debt management would shift its focus from austerity to growth. The modest scale of the Baker Plan's financing scheme (roughly $10 billion annually, or less than what Mexico alone borrowed from the banks in 1982), coupled with clear signs that the new scheme was highly improvised, suggest that its real intent was to silence the few big debtors that could have access to the limited amount of funds and thereby isolate the more strident critics such as President García of Peru.[94] Or in the game theoretic of O'Donnell the plan can again be interpreted as one more "side payment" to selective debtors designed to defuse the growing appearances of regional solidarity on the debt issue.[95] Indeed, a Baker trip to then dissident Brazil to discuss the country's economic policy almost made explicit the game theoretic underlying the plan: "The Treasury official said Mr. Baker had not decided which debtor country would be the test case for his plan, preferring instead to work with those nations restoring their economies."[96]

Baker's tactic, though improvised, was easily the boldest initiative to appear in the management of the crisis. Yet at the same time it ironically marked the beginning of signs of serious cracks in the creditor cartel.

[92] "Mexico: Hush-Hush Meeting," Latin American Weekly Report, 19 July 1985, p. 7.

[93] "Earthquake Comes at Worst Time for Cash-Strapped Mexico," Latin American Weekly Report, 27 September 1985, p. 1.

[94] A former Treasury official confirms the underlying motives of the Baker Plan. See Robin Broad, "How about a Real Solution to Third World Debt?" New York Times, 28 September 1987, p. A25.

[95] Guillermo O'Donnell, "External Debt: Why Don't Our Governments Do the Obvious?" CEPAL Review, no. 27 (December 1985).

[96] "Baker to See Brazil Aide," New York Times, 26 November 1985, p. A32.

The Creditors   The banks' vulnerability to default was a common feature that galvanized the formation of a unified front vis-à-vis the debtor countries. Keeping most of the Latin American portfolio current bought the banks time to bolster primary capital (equity and loan loss reserves) and thereby reduce their vulnerability to default. Yet the strengthening balance sheets progressively drove a wedge into the banking community and made it much more difficult for these institutions to maintain a coordinated position with which to confront the problem debtors. As illustrated in table 5.11, the small- and medium-sized lenders in the United States had made more progress than their bigger brethren in bringing down their relative exposure in the region. For them new lending became that much less attractive and indeed was even perceived as a drag on their strategies to compete with the big banks in the increasingly deregulated home market.[97] The still vulnerable large U.S. lenders therefore found it increasingly more difficult to corral the less committed banks into rescheduling and new loan packages; thus the U.S. steering committee members realized that any new agreement and concessions granted a dissident borrower would require proportionately bigger contributions from them.

A further rift developed between the big U.S. banks and European institutions. The latter, often more conservative in their accounting practices, had generated relatively larger reserves (hidden or otherwise) against their Latin loans.[98] Moreover, their bank regulatory authorities often found the creative accounting favored by the big U.S. banks (extending new loans to pay old ones) unacceptable, forcing them to reserve one dollar for every new dollar lent. This evidently made new lending proportionately more expensive; therefore their initial spirit of solidarity gradually gave way to self-interest and the need to search for alternative formulas to deal with the problem borrowers.[99] In other words, the disparate reserve levels, regulatory and tax requirements, as well as portfolio strategies among the banks began to impinge adversely on their initial cartel-like behavior.

[97] The effect of provisioning on the incentive to lend is analytically derived in Jack Guttentag and Richard Herring, "Provisioning, Charge-Offs and Willingness to Lend" (Washington, D.C.: International Monetary Fund, June 1986).

[98] Richard Evans, "New Debts for Old—and the Swapper Is King," *Euromoney*, September 1987, p. 72.

[99] An appreciation of how the European banks began to distance themselves from the conventional rescheduling strategy can be seen in Herve de Carmoy, "Debt and Growth in Latin America: A European Banker's Proposal," Working Paper No. 9, Institute of European-Latin American Relations, Madrid, 1987.

Also undermining the common front of the banks was the realization that the OECD economies could not sustain the 5 percent real rate of growth recorded in 1984 and indeed even the 3 percent growth popularly considered to be the minimum threshold rate needed to reestablish the debtors capacity to pay.[100] With real interest rates persistently high, the debtors' terms of trade persistently low, and Latin America's indicators of debt burden worsening or showing no real signs of improvement,[101] the perception of a short-term liquidity problem in the region gave way to concern for a protracted crisis and potential insolvencies.[102] Moreover, the underlying problems could no longer be swept under the carpet by new lending and creative accounting because a budding secondary market began to impose embarrassingly high discounts on those Latin American loans subjected to the fresh air of a competitive trade (Table 5.12).

Further weakening a joint approach was the growing split between the banks and the lender-of-last-resort. The IMF's insertion into the crisis had given the banks an indirect handle with which to control the debtors' behavior. Viewed from the narrow perspective of current account balances, Latin America and the Caribbean adjusted in spectacular fashion: a deficit of $41 billion in 1982 fell to nearly zero by 1985. However, the adjustment was achieved at the expense of investment and growth in the debtor countries, causing adjustment fatigue to set in. For many debtor countries the IMF became a serious political liability.

By mid-1985 the Fund's grip on the Latin American and Caribbean adjustment process had clearly begun to weaken. Only a few problem debtors had been able to consistently comply with its targets. Indeed, a growing number of countries had made it a matter of public policy to eschew the IMF entirely, or accept only partial and indirect contact through Article IV consultations. Thus, the role of the Fund as a referee in the negotiations between debtor and creditor faltered. Moreover, with a growing number of standby programs paralyzed the IMF's net transfer of resources to the region declined and turned negative in

[100] This popular formulation was promoted by Cline, *International Debt*. The problems of the world outlook are seen in International Monetary Fund, *World Economic Outlook* (Washington, D.C., October 1987).

[101] See data on debt indicators in ECLAC, "Preliminary Overview of the Latin American Economy 1987," and "Preliminary Overview of the Latin American Economy 1986" (Santiago, Chile, December 1986).

[102] John Reed, "New Money in New Ways," *The International Economy*, October/November 1987, p. 52; and the Institute of International Finance, Inc., "Restoring Market Access" (Washington, D.C., June 1987), p. 10.

TABLE 5.12. Latin America: Market Value of Foreign Debt Notes
by Country
(100 = nominal value)

	1985	1986			1987			1988
	June	Jan.	June	Dec.	Jan.	June	Dec.	Jan.
Argentina	60	62	63	62	62	58	35	36
Bolivia			7			11		
Brazil	75	75	73	74	74	61	45	45
Costa Rica				40				
Chile	65	65	64	65	65	68	60	56
Colombia	81	82	80			85	67	65
Ecuador	65	68	63	63	63	51	34	32
Mexico	80	69	55	54	54	57	51	53
Peru	45	25	17	16	16	14	7	6
Uruguay			64					
Venezuela	81	80	75	72	72	71	49	55

SOURCE: *International Financing Review* (London), various numbers.

1986.[103] Ironically from the banks' perspective the Fund had become a
free-rider, which created another obstacle in organizing the rescheduling packages.[104]

The Fund, for its part, also became troubled by its growing isolation
in Latin America. In effect, when the Fund permitted a direct link to be
established between the commercially based rescheduling demands of
the private banks and its macroeconomic standby programs, it unwittingly allowed a major contradiction to emerge: an international public
good (the Fund and its adjustment programs) became a partial hostage
of the short-term private logic of profit-driven banks. The Fund programs, being designed around the sparse financing and uniformly tough
commercial terms demanded by the private creditors, could not—

[103] Richard Feinberg and Edmar Bacha, "When Supply and Demand Don't Intersect:
Latin America and the Bretton Woods Institutions in the 1980s," paper presented at a
conference on Latin America and the World Economy, sponsored by Sistema Económico
Latinoamericano, Caracas, May 1987.

[104] This sentiment is expressed in Institute of International Finance, "Restoring Market Access," p. 7.

despite professing a case-by-case approach—possibly accommodate the desperate situation of most borrowers. The inability of the countries to meet the resulting unrealistic macrotargets of the Fund and/or the onerous terms of the banks' repayments schedule often was enough to abort an entire adjustment program. Such a development clearly was unfortunate since in a crisis public goods generally are expected to rise above short-term private criteria if they are to maximize social benefits and minimize social costs. Consequently the relationship between the Fund and the private banks, while perhaps functional to a lender-of-last-resort role, was very damaging to the social efficiency of the adjustment process. The pretense of being an honest broker in the adjustment process therefore became increasingly more difficult to sustain, ultimately reducing the Fund's attractiveness for creditors and debtors alike.

Under its new managing director, Michel Camdessus, the Fund began in 1987 to attempt to restore its image and role in the crisis.[105] Camdessus eventually announced that the Fund would begin to consider a longer time path of adjustment, the introduction of more comprehensive contingency financing for debtor countries, and a reduction of the number of variables employed in the application of conditionality.[106] Camdessus also began a difficult campaign to raise the quotas of the Fund, which represented a sine qua non if that organization was to take on a more independent and socially efficient role in promoting adjustment.[107] In October 1987 the Fund moreover announced a new $65 million standby agreement with Costa Rica in which it did not require the government to reach agreement with the private banks concerning its arrears with them. The new IMF accord—which was not well received by the private lenders—represented an important sign that the Fund might be prepared to formally delink its adjustment programs from the crisis management of private bank assets.[108]

There also was increasing tension between the banks and the U.S. government over new lending commitments and the softening negoti-

[105] Hobart Rowen, "IMF Seeks to Improve Image in Third World," *Washington Post*, 26 June 1987, p. D1.

[106] Michel Camdessus, "Statement" to the Board of Governors of the International Monetary Fund and the World Bank (Washington, D.C., 29 September 1987), p. 11.

[107] "Camdessus Calls for Doubling of IMF Quotas," *Morning Press* (Washington, D.C.: International Monetary Fund, 10 March 1988). We will see in Chapter Six that the marriage in 1982 between the Fund and the private banks partly grew out of the former institution's weak resource base.

[108] Organization of American States, *Despachos de Agencias Noticiosas* [News Agency Dispatches] (Washington, D.C., October 1987), p. 8.

ated terms of indebtedness. Consequently, the Baker Plan's growth-oriented adjustment process had a very difficult takeoff. Indeed, the pilot rescheduling in Mexico came about only after extremely protracted and tense negotiations and because of a last-minute emergency intervention of the chairman of the U.S. Federal Reserve Board. In effect, to stave off an impending Mexican declaration of moratorium, U.S. authorities literally "informed" the private banks of their participation in the $13.7 billion financing package for that country.[109]

By the last quarter of 1986 Chile, Venezuela, Argentina, and Uruguay had already knocked on their bankers' doors asking for "the Mexican treatment." Bankers, however, let it be known that the Mexican rescheduling was a special case; indeed, Citibank publicly went on record to declare that it opposed any more concessions for the debtor countries.[110] Thus, an expansion of the fourth round of rescheduling was stalled until a surprise declaration of a moratorium by Brazil in February 1987. This, coupled with an earlier moratorium in Ecuador in January, caused the bankers to back pedal. Attempting to isolate Brazilian authorities and discourage copycats, the banks fired off a rapid series of new rescheduling agreements (or side payments in O'Donnell's terminology) with the four above-mentioned countries.[111] The new accords in fact closely approximated the softer negotiated terms granted Mexico the year before. However, the banks avoided awarding growth guarantees, and with the exception of Argentina—the country showing the most disposition to follow Brazil's example—new money allocations were not exactly generous.

Another defensive move was fired by the banks when on 20 May 1987 Citicorp surprised the financial world with an announcement that it would raise loan loss reserves by 150 percent, to $5 billion, or enough to cover 25 percent of its developing country loans.[112] Regarding the cartel-like behavior of the banks, the move proved significant in at least two respects. First, it spawned even more tension within the bank cartel; the unilateral decision to raise reserve allocations forced Citibank's unsuspecting U.S. competitors to grudgingly follow suit, bringing the decade's first wide-scale reporting of annual losses in the banking sys-

[109] For details of the Mexican negotiations see ECLAC, "Preliminary Overview of the Latin American Economy 1986," sec. II.5.

[110] "Till Debt Us Do Part," *Economist*, 28 February 1987, p. 85; and "Hernan Somerville: La Negociación por Dentro" [Hernan Somerville: Inside the Negotiation], *El Mercurio*, 1 March 1987, p. B1.

[111] Peter Truell, "Chile and Banks Reach a Pact on Global Debt," *Wall Street Journal*, 27 February 1987, p. 6.

[112] "Citicorp Comes Clean on Third World Debt," *Economist*, 23 May 1987, p. 83.

tem.[113] Second, the reserves drove a bigger wedge in between the banks and the U.S. government, which had committed itself to a new lending program. Indeed, for some the Citibank strategy marked a death blow for the Baker Plan and the creditors' coordinated management of the crisis.[114]

The Borrowers   A final factor that undermined the creditor cartel was the debtors' behavior. With time their perceptions changed about the management of the crisis and about the options available to them to reduce the burden of payments.

First, the debtor countries continued to question the distribution of the costs of the crisis management. As we will see in Chapter Six, this generated a large outward transfer of resources from Latin American to creditor countries. The official strategy also validated the private banks' claim to commercial interest margins and fees on the restructuring exercises. The marked contrast between the lenders' robust profitability up through 1986 and the borrowers' depressed economies was too striking to be overlooked by the latter. This created resentment in the debtor countries and induced them to press much more aggressively for lower interest margins and the elimination of fees. Indeed, margins and fees gained a life of their own and became a symbolic test of burden sharing in the debt restructurings.

Second, the debtor countries' initial perception of a transitory crisis changed when it became evident that the medium-term outlook involved sluggish world economic growth, depressed commodity prices, protectionism, and high real international interest rates.

Third, private credit markets failed to fulfill their promise to respond to adjustment efforts with renewed lending. In effect, Latin American countries had made serious efforts to adjust and generate large trade surpluses. Moreover, countries such as Brazil, Mexico, and Venezuela had by 1984 generated—albeit at great social cost—large enough trade surpluses to finance all of the interest payments without the help of involuntary loans from the banks. In 1984 Mexico and Venezuela even agreed to begin a modest amortization of the debt. However, the debtors found that the cooperative approach and the renouncing of involuntary loans did not bring forth voluntary lending; rather it only became a vehicle to accelerate the banks' pullout from the region.

[113] "Citicorp Sharply Lifts Loss Reserves, Putting Its Rivals on the Spot," *Wall Street Journal*, 20 May 1987, p. 1.

[114] Anne Swardson, "Citicorp Move Brings New Era," *Washington Post*, 21 May 1987, p. D1.

The market's failure to respond with new lending clearly represented a degenerative influence on the creditor cartel's ability to control events. As mentioned earlier, illiquid borrowers will naturally be inclined to accept the relatively high short-term costs of adjustment and commercially priced restructuring packages. This is because underlying internal rates of return on capital are high; after a relatively brief period of adjustment the borrowing country expects to gain access to foreign loans that could be deployed to exploit the high rate of return. Thus, the net of foregone income today and the present discounted value of future income from new loans is positive. This cooperative spirit, however, can change when markets fail to respond to positive developments. The illiquid borrower can gradually perceive that it is in its interest to behave like an insolvent borrower, even though he may not be one. The insolvent borrower, of course, calculates the net of foregone income today and the present discounted value of future income generated from new loans as negative. Thus the best way for an insolvent borrower to maximize the present discounted value of future resource flows from private markets is to negotiate debt forgiveness, or enter into full or partial moratorium.

This latter conclusion was reinforced by a fourth factor. With experience, the debtor countries realized that the creditors' threats of dramatic sanctions for noncooperative behavior were greatly exaggerated. In practice, the major cost of de facto default was rather subtle: more difficult access to short-term credit lines. While the loss of short-term credit is undoubtedly troublesome, we will see later that its negative impact can be controlled by countervailing strategies in the debtor countries.

Finally, as we have seen, the debtor countries gradually perceived the bilateral monopoly framework for negotiations and advantages derived from cooperation. The debtors employed cooperative tactics only very timidly; indeed, they always disavowed intent to form a debtors' cartel and all too often exploited regional initiatives for individual advantage in the rescheduling negotiations. However, the strong a priori logic supporting a debtors' club, coupled with the permeability of the debtor countries regarding the countervailing side payments by the creditors, did make the cooperative efforts a factor in the changing face of the reschedulings exercises at least up through 1985.[115]

[115] The last strong initiatives of the Cartagena Consensus were the Declaration of Montevideo in December 1985—which among other things showed that the debtors were not impressed by the Baker Initiative—and a communiqué in February 1986 by a working committee which expressed the countries' support of any member that found it necessary to take unilateral action on the debt. The Consensus' forceful tone was closely linked to Mexico's tough negotiations with the creditors in the last half of 1985 and early

CONCLUSIONS

As we enter the seventh year of the crisis, it can be observed that during the four rounds of reschedulings the debtors have gradually gained ground at the expense of the creditors' monopoly rents. The relatively coherent cartel-like behavior of the banks that characterized the early rescheduling exercises has given way to a more disparate creditor response to the crisis in the problem debtor countries. Indeed, the most recent twist in the official creditor strategy—the market menu approach—appears less like a side payment to salvage monopoly power than a tacit recognition by the banks and their governments of the centrifugal forces at play in the crisis that have the lending institutions increasingly going their own way and cutting their own deals.[116] The other side of the coin, of course, is that the Latin American countries find themselves somewhat less pressed by their creditors and with additional degrees of freedom to manage their debt payments.

At the outset of 1988 the situation in the region began to display some remarkable parallels with the debt crisis of the 1930s. As we saw in Table 5.2, in the fourth round of reschedulings only a few countries maintained a regular payments status with their creditors; the majority of debtors in fact were, in one form or another, in a state of arrears even on rescheduled debt service. Moreover, secondary market prices for traded Latin American bank loans displayed big discounts. At the top of the rung one found the long-time maverick Peru (94 percent) and problem-plagued Bolivia (89 percent). But even those debtors ostensibly current on their debt service witnessed a large divergence between nominal and market values: for example, heavy discounts showed on loans of such

---

1986. However, by then the creditors seemed less convinced about the debtors' ability to form a cartel, an opinion that was reinforced when Mexico abandoned the Consensus to negotiate bilaterally with the creditors. Subsequently, the Cartagena Consensus lost its momentum, giving rise to more ad hoc regional formulations on the debt. The latest was the declaration of eight Latin American presidents contained in "Acapulco Commitment to Peace, Development, and Democracy, Signed on November 29, 1987, at Acapulco, Mexico" (Washington, D.C.: Organization of American States, 1 December 1987).

[116] Symptomatic of this situation was the decision of Midland Bank and First Interstate Bank to bypass Peru's Steering Committee and bilaterally negotiate payment of debts in kind. Meanwhile, Morgan Guaranty Trust Company secretly negotiated a plan with the Mexican authorities to securitize part of that country's debt at a discount. Irritated fellow members of the Mexican Steering Committee were not informed of the plan until it was publicly announced. See Barbara Durr, "Peru Pays Banks in Fishmeal and Iron," *Financial Times*, 6 October 1987, p. 8; and Alan Murray and Peter Truell, "Loan Plan May Help Mexico, Some Banks; But It's No Panacea," *Wall Street Journal*, 30 December 1987, p. 1.

countries as Argentina (64 percent), Brazil (55 percent), Mexico (47 percent), and Venezuela (45 percent) (Table 5.12).

On the other hand, there was also a striking difference with the 1930s. Largely as a consequence of the creditors' skillful management of their balance sheets and the debtors, the region's growing payments irregularities did not threaten to destabilize the international financial system. Indeed, the banks' astute deployment of their bargaining power allowed them to profit handsomely and postpone losses for five years; moreover, those losses that gained attention in 1987 were importantly managed losses that could not detract from an impressive "growth-oriented adjustment" of the banks with respect to their problem Latin loan portfolio.[117] This contrasts sharply with the plight of the debtor countries, which have experienced losses in output and employment that would have been difficult to imagine possible back in 1982.

[117] The U.S banks' net earnings (as a percentage of assets) during 1982 to 1986 were actually higher than precrisis levels. This helped the banks double their primary capital. When coupled with cutbacks in absolute loan exposure, the result was a very marked reduction in Latin American loan/capital ratios (see Table 5.11). For data on earnings of U.S. banks see the annual editions of Salomon Brothers, *A Review of Bank Performance* (New York).

CHAPTER SIX

The Outward Transfer of Resources: What Can Be Done About It?

I HAVE TRIED to establish a convincing argument for coresponsibility in the genesis of the great Latin American debt crisis. The crisis arose out of overborrowing but also out of its necessary counterpart, overlending. At the same time the permissive instincts of bankers and borrowers received important stimulus from macroeconomic policy and banking regulation in the OECD area. Yet we saw in the previous chapter how the private banks skillfully exploited inherent objective advantages and circumstantial factors—such as their governments' heightened concern for domestic financial stability and disarray in the debtor circles—to produce a historical anomaly in which creditors have been able to pass the bulk of the costs of a systemic international payments crisis onto debtors and thereby avoid, or at least postpone, a devaluation of their assets and losses.

We also have just seen that over the last couple of years the banks have witnessed some erosion of their power to control events. Yet so far, especially in view of the magnitude of the original problem, they have done remarkably well for themselves. What started out as a crisis for the banks is now only a problem; a default by any major borrower is unlikely to create undue stress in world banking. The debtors, on the other hand, even while eventually capturing some of the monopoly rents initially garnered by the banks, have faired very poorly as they encounter a development crisis of deepening proportions. The challenge for them remains how to gain a more symmetrical distribution of burden sharing and how to channel that relief into a sustainable process of renewed growth and socioeconomic development.

A central issue in the question of burden sharing, as well as the eventual renewal of growth and development in Latin America, is the magnitude of the outward transfer of resources from debtor country to creditor country. The Latin American countries have for six straight years been transferring their domestic resources to creditor countries. This turns upside down the conventionally accepted postwar notion of North-South relations in which poorer regions are expected to receive net resources from rich nations to support global development and mutual gain in an interdependent world. This final chapter will review some of the polemics surrounding the outward transfer and then, with a view to restoring a process of growth and development in Latin America, explore ways to correct the asymmetric distribution of the costs of the debt problem.

A BRIEF OVERVIEW OF THE ISSUE OF OUTWARD TRANSFERS

It is striking that even with the relief provided by the international debt strategy, and the private bank creditors in particular, Latin America's economic performance since 1982 has been very poor. The negative social repercussions of the economic slump, as best judged by the admittedly sketchy information that is available, are even more disturbing.[1]

It is not easy to sort out and exactly weigh all the relevant factors that contributed to this dismal performance. But Latin America certainly is not an innocent victim. Persistence of inward-looking development strategies in the 1960s and 1970s made the region vulnerable to a debt crisis and not well situated to respond dynamically once the crisis broke out. Moreover, a recent examination of the adjustment process since 1982 found that with regard to the debtor countries' economic policies to confront the crisis, "in many instances the response has been sluggish, shortsighted, incoherent, or lacking continuity." On the other hand, the same study observed that domestic policies generally moved in the right direction and that important adjustments had taken place.[2] Perhaps even more importantly, however, with the outbreak of crisis a consensus rapidly emerged in Latin America concerning the need for a dramatic economic restructuring so that the region's economies can become more internationally competitive, less reliant on foreign savings, and subject to a more efficient division of labor between the state and private sector.[3] It is this new disposition that represents a window of opportunity regarding the changes needed to create more modern and dynamic economies in the region.

While Latin America has clearly contributed to its own problems, it also is obvious that even those countries most committed to adjustment

[1] World Bank, *Poverty in Latin America: The Impact of Depression* (Washington, D.C., 1986).

[2] See Andrés Bianchi, Robert Devlin, and Joseph Ramos, "Adjustment in Latin America, 1981–1986," in *Growth-Oriented Adjustment Programs*, ed. Vittorio Corbo et al. (Washington, D.C.: International Monetary Fund and World Bank, 1987), p. 197.

[3] This consensus is now readily recognized in the North. See for instance Manuel Johnson, Vice Chairman of the Board of Governors of the U.S. Federal Reserve System, "The International Debt Situation" (Washington, D.C.: U.S. Federal Reserve Board, 9 March 1988), p. 2.

TABLE 6.1. Latin America: Transfer of Financial Resources from Abroad

| Year | Transfer of Resources | | | | Memorandum Item | | |
| | Billions of Dollars | | As % of Exports of Goods and Services | | Growth Rates | | Investment ÷ GDP |
	(1)[a]	(2)[b]	(1)[a]	(2)[b]	Exports[c]	Imports[c]	
1978	14.1	16.0	23.0	26.1	9.8	16.7	23.1
1979	13.1	15.3	16.0	18.7	33.8	26.5	22.5
1980	16.7	10.9	15.5	10.1	31.3	33.3	23.7
1981	20.4	9.4	17.6	8.1	7.9	9.6	23.2
1982	− 9.7	−19.5	− 9.4	−18.9	−11.1	−18.8	19.9
1983	−29.1	−32.1	−28.5	−31.4	− 0.8	−28.0	15.2
1984	−27.5	−27.6	−24.1	−24.2	11.4	3.8	15.9
1985	−29.7	−32.0	27.2	−29.4	− 4.4	0.3	16.0
1986		−22.5		−23.8	−13.2	1.4	15.7
1987[d]		−15.7		−15.1	13.9	9.6	

SOURCE: ECLAC, Division of Statistics and Quantitative Analysis.
NOTES: The transfer is calculated as net capital inflows less factor payments (80 to 85 percent of which are interest payments). Note that there is a slight discrepancy with Table 2.1, which does not include some minor line items such as official transfer payments.
[a]Excludes the effect of the errors and omissions line of the balance of payments.
[b]Includes the effect of the errors and omissions line of the balance of payments.
[c]Goods and services.
[d]Preliminary estimates.

and transformation have had their efforts undermined by the creditors' policies. The shortcomings of the supply side have had their chief manifestation in an unprecedented involuntary transfer of domestic resources from the debtor to creditor countries[4] (Table 6.1).

To what are these large outward transfers owed? They reflect the effects of the high level of world interest rates throughout most of the 1980s, aggravated by the dramatic deterioration of the negotiated cost

---

[4] As we will see in a moment, to generate an outward transfer of resources a debtor country must adjust the current account deficit of the balance of payments. That adjustment can be voluntary, as when a country's authorities seek to reduce, or eliminate, a deficit to accommodate a lower ex ante "desired" annual level of external finance and rate of growth of indebtedness. Alternatively, the reduction of the current account balance may be an involuntary ex post response to a lower available volume of finance. (Deficits are not possible without finance.) Latin America's situation is the latter.

of credit in the first rounds of rescheduling, as well as the creditors' uniform insistence on the maintenance of commercial rates in later rounds and the massive falloff of net capital inflows beginning in mid-1982.[5] This latter phenomenon was due largely to a reluctance of banks to lend to the region, although the effects of domestic capital flight cannot be ignored.[6]

Once private creditors cease to automatically roll over interest due with new loans they exert an effective external demand for payment and an outward transfer. This in turn puts pressure on the debtor country to adjust the deficit on the current account of the balance of payments. However, within the interior of the current account the full weight of adjustment is conventionally expected to fall on the trade balance because the deficit on factor services (largely representing interest payments on the foreign debt) stems from a rigid financial contract. Unless financing is available from the country's accumulated international reserves, or from official multilateral and bilateral compensatory sources, the trade balance must register a surplus equivalent to that part of the interest payments not covered by new loans from the banks. Meanwhile, the domestic counterpart of the trade surplus is that internal sav-

---

[5] Net capital inflows peaked at $38 billion in 1981; by 1983 they had fallen to only $3 billion and since then have averaged $9 billion per annum. See United Nations Economic Commission for Latin America and the Caribbean (ECLAC), "Economic Survey of Latin America and the Caribbean, 1987: Advance Summary" (Santiago, Chile, April 1988), table 15.

[6] The subject of capital flight is much too complex to study here and could constitute a book in and of itself. Here I can point out that by using the errors and omissions line of the balance of payments as a rough and ready proxy of capital flight, Table 6.1 (columns 1 and 2) show that there were unregistered capital transactions of some $15 billion over 1982 to 1985, equivalent to nearly one-sixth of the total negative transfer recorded in the period. Moreover, we saw earlier in the study that data suggest that flight had become a serious problem several years before the crisis. Capital flight can undoubtedly be attributed mainly to domestic dynamics in the debtor country. However, it is often overlooked that external credit markets clearly complicated the problem. On the one hand, it was overlending that helped to temporarily sustain unrealistic exchange rates, fiscal and trade deficits, et cetera. On the other, the massive procyclical retreat of private creditors, and the consequent collapse of economic activity in the debtor countries, had a destabilizing effect and aggravated—indeed validated—any negative expectations of domestic private capital. Finally, the late Carlos Díaz-Alejandro pointed out that many foreign private banks and financial institutions acted as accomplices of capital flight as competitive pressures induced them to actively solicit deposits from private economic agents in the region. See Carlos Díaz-Alejandro, "Latin American Debt: I Don't Think We Are in Kansas Anymore," *Brookings Papers on Economic Activity*, no. 2 (1984), pp. 377–380. For an excellent survey of the many unresolved issues related to capital flight, see Donald Lessard and John Williamson, eds., *Capital Flight and Third World Debt* (Washington, D.C.: Institute for International Economics, 1987).

ings exceeds domestic investment or domestic absorption is less than domestic output.

Latin America's involuntary transfer of resources to its creditors since 1982 has been enormous by most any standard. The accumulated outflow has reached the sum of $150 billion (Table 6.1). To put that figure in perspective, it can be pointed out that the trade surpluses required to effect the transfer have exceeded by far those realized by France last century and Germany in the early part of this century, when each country was literally forced to effectively remit domestic resources for payment of reparations to their victors in war.[7] With regard to the internal counterpart of the trade surpluses, it is, of course, found in the drain of domestic savings. For Latin America this dimension also has been onerous: during the crisis nearly one-fifth of the region's domestic savings has been transferred abroad.[8]

The Transfers: Virtue or Vice?

Prior to the great financial collapse of mid-1982 the banks had been expanding their total loan portfolio in Latin America at a rate in excess of 25 percent per annum. With the advent of problems in Mexico the procyclical reaction was sharp: asset expansion in Latin America came to a near halt in the second half of 1982.[9] Since then new commitments have emerged only with difficulty, and in 1986 net disbursements were actually negative (see Table 2.12). The slowdown would have been even

---

[7] According to calculations made by Bianchi, Devlin, and Ramos, Latin America's trade surplus as a percentage of product was 4.3 percent between 1982 and 1985. In contrast, France's reparations to Germany, stemming from the 1871 Treaty of Frankfurt, generated trade surpluses equivalent to 2.3 percent of product between 1872 and 1875. Meanwhile, German trade surpluses after the 1919 Treaty of Versailles were positive only during 1929 to 1932, when they averaged 2.5 percent of product. See Andrés Bianchi, Robert Devlin, and Joseph Ramos, "Adjustment in Latin America, 1981–1986," p. 207.

Of course, war reparations are essentially different from debt service. Debts are voluntarily contracted, while war reparations are imposed. In theory, debts should generate a return on capital that makes them self-liquidating; there is no such dynamic in war reparations. However, if the ex post return on capital is not sufficient to service the debt—as is the case in many Latin American countries—the creditors' insistence on effective payment represents a type of lien on the economy that, in terms of its effects, may not be entirely dissimilar to a demand for war reparations. For country by country data on the transfer of resources see ECLAC, "Economic Survey of Latin America and the Caribbean, 1987: Advance Survey," table 16.

[8] United Nations Economic Commission for Latin America and the Caribbean (ECLAC), "Restrictions on Sustained Development in Latin America and the Caribbean and the Requisites for Overcoming Them" (Santiago, Chile, February 1988), p. 31.

[9] Bank for International Settlements, *International Banking Statistics, 1973–1983* (Basel, April 1984), table 5.

more dramatic had it not been for the administrative lending organized by the big banks and the IMF to save the banks' Latin American portfolio.

As mentioned in Chapter Five, in the first round of rescheduling the creditors agreed to an administrative expansion of their assets of 7 percent. However, since rates of interest at the time averaged 12 percent (including margins), the programmed negative transfer of resources from creditor to debtor was equivalent to 5 percent of the banks' outstanding commitments. This represented a dramatic turnaround because in 1981 there was a positive transfer from the banks equivalent to 5 percent of their outstanding commitments, making for a total programmed turnaround in the resource flow of 10 percent.[10] But since actual net lending between June 1982 and the end of 1983 fell short of the 7 percent formula (rising by about 5 percent), the total turnaround in flows was in fact somewhat higher, roughly 12 percent.

The negative transfer of resources from the banks has been a source of much debate. From the very outset of the crisis Latin American analysts criticized the phenomenon severely.[11] Indeed, on more than one occasion the United Nations Economic Commission for Latin America and the Caribbean termed the negative resource flow "perverse," given the crisis and the developing status of the region.[12] That criticism from Latin American circles continues unabated today and enjoys an even broader constituency.[13]

For their part many analysts in the North were initially very pleased with the management of the adjustment problem. The reduction of cur-

[10] In 1981 the average interest rate plus margin was about 17.5 percent, while the banks expanded their lending by 22.6 percent, providing for a positive transfer of 5.1 percent.

[11] United Nations Economic Commission for Latin America and the Caribbean (ECLAC), "Síntesis Preliminar de la Economía Latinoamericana durante 1983" [Preliminary Synthesis of the Latin American Economy during 1983] (Santiago, Chile, December 1983); Aldo Ferrer, "Deuda, Soberanía, y Democracia en América Latina" [Debt, Sovereignty, and Democracy in Latin America], Estudios Internacionales 17 (July–September 1984): 309–323; Raúl Prebisch, "The Latin American Periphery in the Global Crisis of Capitalism," CEPAL Review, no. 26 (August 1985), pp. 65–90; Ricardo Ffrench-Davis and Sergio Molina, "Prospects for Bank Lending to Developing Countries in the Remainder of the Eighties," Journal of Development Planning, no. 16 (1985), pp. 229–247.

[12] ECLAC, "Síntesis Preliminar de la Economía Latinoamericana durante 1983," p. 9.

[13] For more recent political statements see "Declaración y Propuesta de Personalidades sobre la Deuda Externa" [Declaration of Eminent Persons on External Debt] (Buenos Aires, 24 April 1987); and "Acapulco Commitment to Peace, Development, and Democracy, Signed on November 29, 1987, at Acapulco, Mexico" (Washington, D.C.: Organization of American States, 1 December 1987).

rent account deficits proved to be so robust that it amazed even the rosiest optimists. Indeed, some early observers approvingly termed Latin America's adjustment a spectacular "overperformance."[14] At the same time, in the early going we heard repeated expressions of confidence with respect to the success of the official strategy for dealing with the crisis.[15] Subsequent to 1985 the picture has admittedly become more complex. A growing number of important academics, U.S. Congressmen, and an occasional banker have expressed criticism of the creditors' management of the crisis; moreover, their alternative proposals usually have involved direct debt forgiveness of some type.[16] Even those who have called the shots—the big U.S. banks, the U.S. administration, and the Bretton Woods Twins—began to display more modesty regarding the achievements of the international debt management strategy; for example, by referring to the slowness of the restoration of creditworthiness in the debtor countries. Nevertheless, this latter group of officials, always cloaked in the language of the market, have tenaciously defended the official management strategy and rejected any major change of course.[17]

The official international strategy certainly has not been static; as described in Chapter Five, there have been important innovations. Yet throughout the twists and turns in the management strategy one central feature remains unaltered: the large transfer of resources from debtor to

[14] William Cline, "The Issue is Illiquidity, Not Solvency," *Challenge*, July-August 1984, p. 15; and Henry Wallich, "Professor Wallich Presents a Perspective on the External Debt Situation," *Press Review* (Bank for International Settlements), 14 January 1985, p. 1.

[15] Jacques de Larosière, "Helping to Shape a Stronger World Economy: The Tasks before the International Monetary Fund," *IMF Survey*, 24 June 1985, p. 200.

[16] Three prominent U.S. academics emerging as an alternative voice are Albert Fishlow (a very early critic), Rudiger Dornbusch, and Jeffrey Sachs. On the Hill, Senator Bill Bradley has been at the forefront of a new approach that would involve direct debt forgiveness. He has been joined by other congressmen such as La Falce, Kerry, Schumer, and Pease. More recently, in March 1988, James Robinson, Chairman of the Board of American Express Bank, argued that the official strategy was not working and proposed his own, which involved direct debt forgiveness. These alternative approaches reenter my discussion later in the chapter.

[17] For instance, see John Reed, "New Money in New Ways," *The International Economy*, October/November 1987, pp. 50–52; and David Mulford, "Recent Developments in International Debt" (Washington, D.C.: U.S. Treasury Department, 4 February 1988). Finally, the IMF has always been a steadfast defender of the management strategy. However, it must be pointed out that its new managing director, Michel Camdessus, has certainly been a relatively more candid observer of the debtors' plight and, within his obvious political limits, manifestly eager to do something about it. See "Debt Strategy Needs Strengthening, but Basic Elements Remain Valid," *IMF Survey*, 21 March 1988, pp. 89–91.

creditor nations. The proponents of the official strategy therefore of necessity defend the outward transfer as an essential ingredient for resolving the financial crisis and restoring creditworthiness to the region. William Cline, an early advocate of the outward transfer, has been more analytically explicit than most about this and therefore can help us shed light on the creditors' logic.

In his highly influential 1984 book on international debt Cline took ECLAC to task for its concern about the flow of resources from South to North. According to him, the large outward transfer of resources to the creditors was not at all perverse. Rather, he saw the outward transfer to be appropriate and in the region's best interests because it promoted the reduction of debt in relative terms and accelerated the day that the countries would restore their creditworthiness and normal access to markets. He also pointed out that the great concern about negative transfers and the compression of imports was misplaced because the orthodox adjustment programs that accompany the transfers promoted the production of tradeable goods, and especially exports. This in turn raises the capacity to import, even in the face of an outward transfer of resources to the creditors. Finally, Cline pointed out that critics of the outward transfer implicitly argue that the transfer should be zero. But a zero transfer would mean a larger accumulation of debt, which in his view would just perpetuate the excessive indebtedness of the region and inhibit restoration of creditworthiness.[18]

Cline made his influential statement in the context of his popular diagnosis that the region's debt problem was one of illiquidity and his optimism about the prospects for OECD growth rates of at least 3 percent. Hindsight is 20/20 and it is clear that the actual course of events has made it easier to spot flaws in Cline's original propositions.[19] However, even granting the world as we knew it in 1983 and 1984, the Cline argument was deficient from the start because of inadequate attention to the factor of "timing" in the adjustment process. Moreover, because northern managers of the crisis perhaps shared in this oversight, Latin America's debt problem may be more severe today than it would have been if from the outset there had been more official concern about avoiding outward transfers from the cooperative debtor countries.

---

[18] William Cline, *International Debt: Systematic Risk and Policy Response* (Washington, D.C.: Institute for International Economics, 1984), pp. 175–181.

[19] Here and elsewhere I raise some objections to Dr. Cline's work. While disagreeing on some points, I do not want to diminish the contribution of his book *International Debt.* In many aspects it is a pathbreaking effort that represents a necessary first step in any student's plan to study the debt crisis.

Finance and Adjustment in Theory   Unless a country is at a very mature stage of development it would presumably prefer to avoid an outward transfer of financial resources; that way trade deficits could be run, investment could remain higher than domestic savings, and growth could be accelerated. If obliged to undertake a premature transfer, the adjustment to this situation should be ideally as socially efficient as possible.

In simple terms, for an adjustment process to be socially efficient the trade surplus that is necessary to effect financial transfers must be mostly "produced" through a rise in savings and in the output of tradeable goods—that is, exports and import substitutes—rather than "created" through a reduction in domestic expenditure, output, and hence imports. When a trade surplus is "produced," a nation's total absorption will necessarily be less than its output, since part of what is produced must be turned over to foreign creditors, but at least economic activity and employment remain robust and standards of living can still rise. However, when a trade surplus is "created" through an economic recession, not only must total absorption be less than the domestic product but economic activity, employment, and standards of living must fall.

The problem confronting an efficient adjustment is that to produce more tradeable goods, resources must be switched, or reallocated, to these activities. Economists, to borrow from Keynes's insight,[20] often conveniently conceive of their economies as if they were purely liquid; in practice, however, they are more viscous in the short term as there are definite rigidities in the reorientation of internal expenditure and production. These rigidities exist even in the most developed economies (hence the discussion of the J-curve in the current question of the reduction of the U.S. trade deficit) and normally are considered more pronounced in more disarticulated economies such as those found in underdeveloped regions (and are further aggravated if borrowed/lent resources were deployed poorly). In other words, for an adjustment to be socially efficient and based mostly on the production of new tradeable goods it must be gradual. This requirement increases proportionately with the level of underdevelopment and structural problems of the adjusting economy. Thus, while shock treatment can be effective for an efficient price stabilization program, it can never be compatible with an efficient adjustment program.[21] Efficient adjustment simply is constrained by the factor of time.

[20] John Maynard Keynes, "The German Transfer Problem," *The Economic Journal* 39 (September 1929): 5.
[21] Bianchi, Devlin, and Ramos, "Adjustment in Latin America, 1981–1986."

Consequently, while an economy is going through the process of real-locating resources to the production of tradeable goods, it normally needs considerable amounts of compensatory financing to minimize welfare losses. In other words, financing initially must rise way above that which private markets might feel even remotely comfortable with; later, when adjustment policies and the production of tradeable goods (and a trade surplus) begin to take hold, that financing can be gradually pared back.[22] If adequate financing is not available to support the adjustment program, it cannot be efficient because it will be largely based on a compression of absorption and economic activity.

Outward transfers of resources that are squeezed from an economy via recessionary adjustment are perverse in general but are especially so for developing countries where the opportunity cost of lost income is presumably greater than that in wealthy developed countries. This type of adjustment is negative in character because it unnecessarily weakens the debtor country and its productive capacity through a deep and/or prolonged recession that indiscriminately eats into the productive muscle as well as the fat of the economy. National resources potentially available for the production of tradeable goods and a trade surplus lie idle because a scarcity of foreign exchange blocks the purchase of complementary imported inputs. Moreover, recessionary adjustment prejudices the growth of savings and investment (including investment in human capital) that is so necessary in cases like that of Latin America where economic restructuring is vital in order to produce new types of tradeable goods and to improve international competitiveness through productivity gains rather than falling real wages. The payment of debt in the midst of a situation where an economy is stagnating or contracting also exacerbates the tension between creditor and debtor that inevitably occurs when a trade account is pressured by requirements for factor payments.[23]

In sum, transfers based on recessionary adjustment are perverse because payment is made at the expense of present welfare as well as the future productive capacity of the borrower. Moreover, they are espe-

---

[22] The transitory boost in financing required for expansive adjustment receives attention in Marcelo Selowsky and Herman Van Der Tak, "The Debt Problem and Growth," *World Development* 14 (September 1986): 1107–1124.

[23] This problem always makes me recall a cartoon that appeared in a Lima magazine during the crisis. In the first panel there is pictured the president of the country and a military adviser meeting with the IMF representative. The president comments in response to the traditional IMF prescription, "Yes, we will just have to tighten our belts." In the adjacent panel of the cartoon is a peasant at the dinner table cutting up his belt and distributing it on plates to his family for supper.

cially damaging when circumstances demand an important restructuring of the debtor economy's productive structure as opposed to a mere expansion along a path that is similar to the existing pattern of production. In contrast, with appropriate time and finance, cooperative debtors can be made to efficiently produce the trade surplus needed to pay debts. In any perspective other than a short-sighted one this is clearly a more satisfactory solution for both creditor and debtor.[24]

Finance and Adjustment in Practice   I have pointed out that socially efficient adjustment demands adequate finance. In the case of Latin America the crisis itself was widely diagnosed in the North as one of illiquidity, not insolvency.[25] If so, there was an extremely compelling economic argument to provide a strong injection of cash to support the debtor economies. In the initial years of the crisis the transfer from the creditors should have been in the worst case zero, while the debt/export coefficient should have risen very sharply, albeit transitorily.

In any event, the financing provided by the international financial community fell far short of the amount required for efficient adjustment. In the abstract world of the ideal where an economy would be entirely free of distortions, efficient adjustment would require financing to cover that part of the deficit attributable to transitory shocks. The financing requirement is necessarily greater in the real world where distortions and rigidities exist. However, Ground found that during 1982 to 1985 external finance covered only 37 percent, 25 percent, 36 percent, and 16 percent of the respective annual transitory components of the deficits of the nonoil exporters.[26] Thus, what financing that became

[24] Recently there has emerged an awareness that the rapid adjustment to debt service also can be an important contributing factor to the inflationary spiral in Latin America. In effect, most of the foreign debt was contracted, or guaranteed ex post, by Latin American governments. It has proved politically and technically difficult to quickly make room for increased debt service payments in domestic fiscal budgets, giving rise to more deficits. The deficits, in turn, through a complex causal route, have pushed domestic prices upward exponentially. For more on this initially overlooked issue see Rudiger Dornbusch, "Debt, Inflation and Growth: The Case of Argentina" (Cambridge, Mass.: Massachusetts Institute of Technology, Department of Economics, February 1988); and Helmut Reisen and Axel Van Trotsenburg, *Developing Country Debt: The Budgetary and Transfer Problem* (Paris: Development Centre of the Organisation for Economic Cooperation and Development, 1988).

[25] See, for instance, Cline, *International Debt*; and Beryl Sprinkel, "Grounds for Increasing Optimism," *Economic Impact*, no. 2 (1984), pp. 35–39.

[26] Richard Lynn Ground, "Perturbaciones, Déficit, Crisis y Políticas de Ajuste: Un Enfoque Normativo" [Shocks, Deficit, Crisis, and Adjustment Policy: A Normative Focus], *El Trimestre Económico* 53 (October–December 1986): 770–771.

available could serve to avoid defaults and damage to the banks' balance sheets but not to support efficient adjustment.

The effect of the underfinancing was a massive "overadjustment." The combination of normal rigidities in the debtor economies, a less than auspicious world trading environment, and abnormally low levels of external finance caused adjustment to proceed largely on the basis of import compression, not export expansion. True, there evidently was considerable fat in the region's import bill, as suggested by the phenomenal growth rates of foreign purchases in 1979 to 1981. Nevertheless, the radical compression of imports clearly cut into productive bone, as indicated by the sharp fall in the investment coefficient and the depressed level of economic activity after 1981 (Table 6.1).

The failure to provide a critical mass of financial support for the region's adjustment efforts contributed decisively to its extraordinary high cost. Indeed, Ground has calculated the welfare losses in terms of foregone potential output during 1982 to 1985 at $800 billion, a figure that exceeds the actual value of the region's gross domestic product in 1985 and is double the size of the stock of external debt in 1987. The inefficiencies are further manifest in his calculation that for each dollar transferred abroad, eight dollars of production were lost![27] The social and political repercussions of such a negative process explain at least partly the "stop and go" adjustment policies exhibited in the debtor countries. More generally, the underfinancing has had a degenerative impact on the region, contributing to a vicious circle of uncertainty and negative expectations that increasingly raises the specter of insolvency rather than illiquidity.[28]

The central dilemma of the crisis was clear from the very beginning. In the face of the procyclical withdrawal of private banks, the IMF—whose profile in world finance had been progressively lowered—[29] was in no condition whatsoever to fill the vacuum.[30] Faced with the crisis, it

[27] Richard Lynn Ground, "Origin and Magnitude of Recessionary Adjustment in Latin America," CEPAL Review, no. 30 (December 1986), p. 71.

[28] It is interesting to note that Marxist theory predicts that in a financial crisis the capitalist system will always tend to sacrifice the value of productive capital in order to save the value of finance capital. The Marxist prediction has some striking parallels with the management of the current crisis. For a treatment of this aspect of Marxist theory see John Weeks, Capital and Exploitation (Princeton, N.J.: Princeton University Press, 1981), pp. 123–217.

[29] Until 1970 the IMF quotas were equivalent to about 10 percent of the annual value of world trade. By the outset of the crisis its participation had fallen to 4 percent. See Cline, International Debt, p. 124.

[30] Over 1982 and 1983 net flows from the banks to the nonoil-developing countries fell by $34 billion. Net lending by the Fund rose by only $9 billion. See Richard Feinberg, "LDC Debt and the Public-Sector Rescue," Challenge, July–August 1985, p. 29.

had to reposition itself. As mentioned in Chapter Five, the IMF announced two primary objectives in its management of the crisis: (a) to ensure for the banks that the countries adjusted and (b) to ensure for the countries that the banks provided finance for that adjustment. Since the Fund did not have its own resources to lend, it attempted to convert itself into a catalyst for the mobilization of private funds. Acting in conjunction with the big lenders, the Fund worked out the much discussed 7 percent formula for the expansion of bank credit. But in view of the abnormally high level of international interest rates (Table 2.14), the rigidities in resource allocation, and the depressive effects of the world recession, the 7 percent formula was wholly inadequate for socially efficient adjustment.[31] Thus the Fund achieved its first goal and failed terribly in its second. Alternatively, for the banks the IMF proved to be initially a public good, while for the debtor countries it came closer to a "public bad." Small wonder the debtor countries eventually turned their backs on it.

Even more importantly, approaching the seventh year of the crisis one does not observe a more balanced external financing environment for the Latin American countries. On the one hand, there are very poor prospects for renewed flows of private finance. For objective reasons related to rising reserves for loan losses, an involuntary loan from a commercial bank has become a rare and major event. Given those larger reserves in the banking system, even the very big debtor countries will now experience great difficulty in extracting new forced commitments from the banks.

There are, of course, the voluntary nonlending items for the banks contained in the so-called market menu of options, such as debt equity swaps and forms of securitization. But viewed from the standpoint of the immediate macroeconomic requirements for financing growth and economic restructuring in Latin America, the official market menu is very incomplete; it lists some interesting "appetizers" for the debtor countries, but the "main entrees" simply are not there. This is because

---

[31] The failure of the program also cannot be isolated from the nature of IMF conditionality. This is an old debate that I will not enter into here. Critiques can be found in United Nations, *Balance of Payments Adjustment Process in Developing Countries: Report to the Group of Twenty-Four* (New York: UNDP/UNCTAD Project INT/75/015, January 1979); Dragoslav Avramovic, "Conditionality: Facts, Theory, and Policy" (Washington, D.C.: Bank of Credit and Commerce International, May 1987); Tony Killick et al., "The IMF: Case for a Change in Emphasis," in *Adjustment Crisis in the Third World*, ed. Richard Feinberg and Valeriana Kallab (London: Transaction Books, 1984), pp. 59–82; and Richard Lynn Ground, "Orthodox Adjustment Programmes in Latin America: A Critical Look at the Policies of the International Monetary Fund," *CEPAL Review*, no. 23 (August 1984), pp. 45–82.

when left to their own devices, private markets tend to unwind from a crisis very slowly. In effect, the markets find it very difficult to isolate new debt from problematic old debt, which inhibits new lending as well as the conversion of old debt to more liquid instruments. The debt is moreover international in character, so creditors and debtors must overcome unusually complex free-rider problems and accounting, tax, and legal difficulties. Innovative financial engineering can attempt to surmount many of these obstacles, but since markets operate at the margin even in the best of times, new techniques and instruments necessarily must start small. Hence, the options in the market menu that are designed around the voluntary private portfolio adjustment of the banks will develop by themselves only gradually.[32] Unaided by comprehensive public intervention, it will take some time before those instruments in the menu, individually or in combination, can be expected to release up front the critical mass of balance of payments financing that the debtor countries need.[33] In addition, the financing that does take place will exhibit great uncertainties regarding the timing of transactions and their distribution among countries.

MEANWHILE, all the main international public lenders on which Latin America is now so dependent for new finance (the IMF, World Bank,

[32] The difficulty of the well-publicized Mexican/Morgan Guaranty Trust Company project to securitize $20 billion of Mexico's debt in early 1988 is symptomatic of the problem. Only ninety-five of Mexico's five hundred creditor banks participated, securitizing just $3.7 billion of debt at an average discount of only 30 percent. (The secondary market discount was about 50 percent.) And here the operation had some public support in the form of the U.S. government's agreement to emit a special zero-coupon U.S. Treasury bill designed to collateralize the principal of the Mexican bonds. Finally, even if the plan had fulfilled its organizers' originally buoyant expectations, the net immediate effect on the country's balance of payments financing would have been marginal: about $350 billion per annum, compared to annual interest payments of the order of $8 billion. See "Debt after Mexico," *Financial Times*, 7 March 1988, p. 14; Robert Devlin, "New Plan of U.S. Treasury for the Mexican Debt Problem" (Santiago, Chile: United Nations Economic Commission for Latin America and the Caribbean, Economic Development Division, 30 December 1987), unpublished memo; and Alexander Nicoll, "Man Who Captures Market Discount," *Financial Times*, 21 March 1988, p. 3.

[33] I have prepared a very detailed evaluation of the market menu approach for the ECLAC Secretariat. See United Nations Economic Commission for Latin America and the Caribbean, *The Evolution of the External Debt Problem in Latin America and the Caribbean*, Estudios e Informes de la CEPAL, No. 72 (Santiago, Chile, 1988). Also see Mahesh Kotecha, "Repackaging Third World Debt," *Standard and Poor's International Credit Week*, August 1987, pp. 9–10; Kenneth Telljohann, "Analytical Framework," in Salomon Brothers, "Prospects for Securitization of Less-Developed Country Loans" (New York, June 1987); and Dragoslov Avramovic, "Debt Crisis of the 1980s: The Beginning of A Wind Down?" (Washington, D.C.: Bank of Credit and Commerce International, January 1988).

TABLE 6.2. Latin America: Net Transfer from Multilateral Lenders
(billions of dollars)

	1980	1981	1982	1983	1984	1985	1986	1987
1. *Net Disbursements*	2.3	2.7	4.0	8.8	7.4	5.3	4.4	2.1
IMF	−0.1	0.1	1.2	5.7	3.3	1.5	0.2	−0.5
World Bank	1.2	1.3	1.4	1.7	2.1	1.9	2.7	1.6
IDB[a]	1.2	1.3	1.4	1.4	2.0	1.9	1.5	1.0
2. *Interest Charges*	1.0	1.2	1.3	1.7	2.2	2.7	3.6	4.0
IMF	0.1	0.1	0.1	0.3	0.6	0.9	0.9	0.8
World Bank	0.6	0.7	0.8	0.9	1.0	1.1	1.7	2.1
IDB	0.3	0.4	0.4	0.5	0.6	0.7	1.0	1.1
3. *Net Transfer (1–2)*[b]	1.1	1.5	2.8	7.2	5.2	2.6	0.7	−1.9
IMF	−0.2	. . .[c]	1.2	5.4	2.7	0.6	−0.8	−1.3
World Bank	0.5	0.6	0.6	0.8	1.1	0.8	1.0	−0.5
IDB	0.8	0.9	1.0	1.0	1.4	1.2	0.5	−0.1

SOURCE: Calculated from data provided by the Sistema Económico Latinoamericano (SELA), Caracas, Venezuela.
NOTES:
[a]Inter-American Development Bank.
[b]May not sum properly due to rounding.
[c](. . .) = zero or not large enough to quantify.

Inter-American Development Bank) have seen their financial transfer to the region slip to a point where it turned negative for all three in 1987 (Table 6.2). A $75 billion general capital increase for the World Bank may help reverse that trend. But this and other initiatives emanating from the September 1987 IMF/World Bank annual meetings (more IMF contingency financing, more flexible conditionality, et cetera), though potentially helpful, do not address in a concerted and direct way the problem of the transfer of resources to the private banks.

In sum, given the very unbalanced structure of the world financial system at the outset of the crisis, it may be that there was no way to bring forth adequate amounts of anticyclical finance for socially efficient adjustment. Perhaps the best that could have been expected was the rescue of the international financial system; indeed, in view of the historical record of repeated financial collapses following systemic international payments crises, the effective mobilization in 1982 of a decentralized world lender-of-last-resort was no small achievement. But what is unacceptable is the rose-colored glasses through which many key northern players tend to view these events. Instead of patting themselves on the back about Latin America's marvelous adjustment and viewing as troublemakers those who suggest more comprehensive solutions, it would certainly be more constructive to recognize the central failure of the international debt management strategy: its inability to evolve beyond a lender-of-last-resort function designed to protect the balance sheets of northern banks. The international financial system was saved at the expense of Latin America's development and social stability. In an interdependent world such a one-sided response is nothing to cheer about. The international community should be working intensively on institutional reforms to rectify past mistakes and to ensure that they do not reoccur in the future.

REDUCING THE TRANSFERS TO THE BANKS

One of the frailties of civilization seems to be a short memory. Keynes, referring to the burden of the allied war debt, once observed:

> It might be an exaggeration to say that it is impossible for the European Allies to pay the capital and interest due from them on these debts, but to make them do so would certainly be to impose a crushing burden. They may be expected, therefore, to make constant attempts to evade or escape payment, and these attempts will be a constant source of international friction and ill-will for many years to come. A debtor nation does not love its creditor, and it is fruitless to expect feelings of goodwill from France, Italy, and Russia towards this country [England] or towards America, if their future development is stifled for many years to come by the annual tribute which they must pay us. There will be a great incentive to them to seek their friends in other directions, and any future rupture of peaceable relations will always carry with it the enormous advantage of escaping the payment of external debts. If, on the other hand, these great debts are forgiven, a stimulus will be given to the solidarity and true friendliness of the nations lately associated.[34]

An underlying message of Keynes's work on allied debt and war reparations is that it is dangerous to permit capitalism's compulsive tendencies to enforce financial discipline during crisis to overpower the system's broader interests in growth, prosperity, and political-economic

[34] John Maynard Keynes, *The Economic Consequences of the Peace* (New York: Harcourt, Brace & Howe, 1920), pp. 278–279.

integration. The Marshall Plan, coupled with the West's economic expansion and political integration during the post-World War II period, is a great testament to the enlightened self-interest of generosity in matters of debt and reconstruction.

While Keynes made his statement in another historical context, there still are many lessons to be drawn from it for the current debt problem. Clearly any level of outward transfer from Latin America is feasible if the creditors and their governments are willing to exert sufficient political and economic pressure on the debtor countries. But as Keynes pointed out, large and protracted transfers can be politically and humanly difficult to effect. This, of course, is even more so the case if the transfer is demanded at a premature level of socioeconomic development or when a country is in a state of insolvency. Debt can be serviced efficiently—in the integrative sense of Arrow's observation cited in the preceding chapter—only when there is an environment of growth and noticeably rising living standards. Thus the financial benefits of the transfer of resources from Latin America to the creditor countries must be weighed against some important inefficiencies and costs.

For the debtor the economic cost of an outward transfer is that it siphons off domestic savings that could be used for investment; it puts restraints on import growth and consumption and limits the expansion and socioeconomic transformation of the economy. These costs almost always rub political sensibilities but can become especially destabilizing when magnified by stagnation or decline of the living standards of the debtor country's population. Moreover, transfers based on depressed debtor economies also can be technically counterproductive. Physical and human factors of production lay idle and deteriorate. Needed structural reforms are held back by low levels of investment in human and physical capital as well as the political resistance that can arise when the costs of those reforms are not diluted in growth. The heightened uncertainty and risk of depressed economies also adversely affect the confidence and initiative of the private sector, as well as the prospects for its repatriation of flight capital.

For the creditor country the debtor's outward transfer allows the banks to prosper even while they slow down, or eliminate, the expansion of their loans to the affected borrowers. However, should the outward transfer be won at the expense of reasonable economic growth in the debtor countries, there are important costs for the creditor nation as well. These include the loss of export markets (hence jobs) due to slow growth and import barriers in countries starved for foreign exchange; pressure on domestic markets from distress selling of the problem debtors' exportables; and loss of investment income from home enterprises with direct investments in those countries' depressed economies. The political price can be high, too, as a technical question of debt service degenerates into a political problem where in the last instance even countries with the strongest commitment to the international capitalist system will eventually be obliged to protect the aspirations of their own people for a better life.[35] Moreover, as internal resentment builds up in the debtor country, politicians and technicians committed to socioeconomic restructuring and international integration can have their authority undermined, giving rise to political forces more inclined toward political and economic delinking from creditor countries. Either way the consequences can include full or partial default on debts. And, of course, with sporadic defaults banks face unpredictable losses, exporters in creditor countries lose more markets, and the goal of promoting efficient socioeconomic restructuring in the debtor country can suffer if economies are forced by circumstances into a more siegelike mentality and a relatively more inward orientation.

We have already seen general indicators suggesting that the costs for the debtor countries have been enormous, while progress in restoring creditworthiness has been modest at best. While not remotely comparable, the costs of the current crisis have been building up for the creditor countries too. Export markets and hundreds of thousands of jobs have been lost in the creditor nations due to the dismal growth performance in Latin America.[36] Domestic markets increasingly lobby for protection from "cheap LDC exports," and there is great public concern over the increased supply of illegal drugs from Latin America.[37] Rates of return on direct foreign investment in the region have been cut in half, severely restricting the activity of affected firms.[38] We saw earlier that an increasing number of countries in Latin America have found it necessary to stop, or limit, debt payments unilaterally. These payments problems

[35] Industrial countries have reacted in this way. For example, during the 1930s the English and French governments failed to service their debts owed to the United States, arguing that their own people were more important than payments to foreign creditors. See Chandra Hardy, *Rescheduling Developing Country Debts, 1956–1980: Lessons & Recommendations* (Washington, D.C.: Overseas Development Council, 1981), p. 40.

[36] U.S. Congress, Democratic Committee of the Joint Economic Committee, "Trade, Deficits, Foreign Debt, and Sagging Growth" (Washington, D.C., September 1986); and U.S. Congress, Joint Economic Committee, "The Impact of the Latin American Debt Crisis on the U.S. Economy" (Washington, D.C., 10 May 1986).

[37] See William Orme, "Gephardt Losses Cheer Mexico," *Journal of Commerce*, 10 March 1988, p. 7.

[38] The data are for U.S. direct foreign investments over the period 1980 to 1985 and appear in United Nations Centre on Transnational Corporations, *Transnational Corporations in World Development* (New York, 1988), p. 82.

and arrears have undermined the credibility of financial orthodoxy, depressed bank stocks,[39] and recently imposed some unanticipated losses on the banks. A major foreign policy problem also may be brewing for the 1990s, as there are signs that the burden of debt has begun to undermine the pragmatic political coalitions that originally arose out of the crisis and that offered some promise for efficient economic restructuring and integration into the world's democratic political system.[40]

In a First Best World

What Could Be Done?   There is little disagreement now that resolution of the region's crisis will require structural economic reforms in the debtor countries and that they must be undertaken in a context of economic growth. Most Latin American countries have seriously pursued adjustments, some more successfully than others, but all at great social cost. As the creditors themselves admit, the political disposition is still there in most debtor countries to push ahead with reforms to achieve more internationally competitive economies and a state that is more functional to investment and private initiative.[41] Meanwhile, in 1985 creditor countries became converts to the growth-oriented adjustment advocated by the debtors. The most general and conspicuous missing link in the management of the crisis has been, and continues to be, a stable external economic environment, which includes predictable and sustained flows of credit to the debtor countries.

From the standpoint of world macroeconomic efficiency the first best policies to resolve the crisis are obvious. On the one hand, debtors would persist with reforms and economic restructuring. But more symmetry is needed in the adjustment process; that is, the creditor countries must simultaneously correct the severe macroeconomic disequilibria in the North. Coordinated adjustment in the North would establish a basis for: (a) higher rates of growth in the OECD area; (b) more normal international rates of interest; and (c) higher commodity prices. The stimulus of a more dynamic performance of the OECD economies would in turn naturally relieve debt burdens in Latin America and indirectly contribute to financing recovery and restructuring in the region.

---

[39] Steven Kyle and Jeffrey Sachs, "Developing Country Debt and the Market Value of Large Commercial Banks," Working Paper No. 1470 (Cambridge, Mass., National Bureau of Economic Research, September 1984).

[40] For instance, recent electoral developments in Argentina, Brazil, and Mexico are indicative of growing support for proponents of economic populism, which in the past has not been conducive to international economic integration or sustained democracy.

[41] See Mulford, "Recent Developments in International Debt"; and Johnson, "The International Debt Situation."

Indeed, a sufficiently favorable external environment could help to pull some of the debtor countries out of crisis and give them the opportunity to pursue reforms more or less autonomously through normal channels of trade and finance. The number of debtor countries in the region paralyzed by crisis would be correspondingly less. This in turn would open the prospect of the international community responding more adequately to their problems through existing multilateral financial channels.

In the absence of quick and comprehensive reforms and renewal of very dynamic and sustained growth in the OECD economies, or some type of exogenous shock that dramatically improves the debtors' terms of trade, the debt burden of most of the region's economies will be unbearable and represent an obstacle to growth and economic restructuring. In these circumstances policies must act directly on the outward transfer so that it "adjusts" to the payment capacity of the debtor, with that capacity defined in terms of minimum acceptable rates of investment and economic growth. In other words, investment and economic growth can be no longer the residuals of the debt management strategy. Rather they must become explicit targets that other parameters—in particular the transfer of resources and financing—must accommodate.

In these circumstances, and given the paralysis of private financial markets, some form of direct or indirect debt forgiveness becomes inevitable. The private market estimates that the mountain of debt contracted in the 1970s generally was overbuilt and therefore bears a real value that is considerably less than the value carried on the books of the banks. While it is true that the secondary market is small and may not be an entirely accurate measure of real values, any country loan registering a discount of 40 percent or more is a reasonably conservative sign of a bad debt.[42] To insist on an unrealistic valuation of the debt is to stifle the borrower's development and threaten an even bigger erosion of that debt's value in the future.

So many debt relief formulas have been proposed since the outset of the crisis that it would require an excessively long detour to summarize them here.[43] They span from ad hoc instruments such as partial interest

[42] Informal estimates placed secondary trading at $10 to $12 billion in 1987, although considerable double counting is involved. See Eugenio Lahera, "La Conversión de la Deuda Externa: Antecedentes, Evaluación, y Perspectivas" [Conversion of the External Debt: Antecedents, Evaluation, and Perspectives] (Santiago, Chile: United Nations Economic Commission for Latin America and the Caribbean, September 1987), p. 12.

[43] For an excellent overview of many of the proposals see Martine Guerguil, "The International Financial Crisis: Diagnoses and Prescriptions," CEPAL Review, no. 24 (December 1984), pp. 147–169. Also see Stephany Griffith-Jones, "Proposals to Manage the

rate capitalization and special public guarantees on private loans to global comprehensive schemes involving debt forgiveness. However, one proposal has repeatedly emerged in the debate about debt relief. It also is a proposal on which a growing number of observers converge. I refer to a multilateral debt facility that would convert bank debt into long-term bonds with a fixed interest rate.[44]

The precise mechanics of the debt conversion facility differ according to whose proposal one examines. However, generically, the idea proposes that a new or existing multilateral agency purchase outstanding Latin American debt from the private banks. The purchase could be effected at a discount for cash; alternatively, the debt could be exchanged for bonds emitted by the multilateral agency. In some proposals the bond captures the discount from the banks directly, while in others it is realized indirectly by exchanging loans for bonds at par but with the latter bearing below market interest rates. The banks, of course, would register a corresponding loss on their books but would receive compensation in the form of a solid off-balance sheet security

---

Debt Problem" (Brighton, Eng.: Sussex University, Institute of Development Studies, 1985); C. Fred Bergsten et al., *Bank Lending to Developing Countries: The Policy Alternatives* (Washington, D.C.: Institute for International Economics, 1985); and Patricia Wertman, "The International Debt Problem: Options for Solution" (Washington, D.C.: Library of Congress, Congressional Research Service, October 1986).

[44] To my knowledge the first proposal of this type appeared in 1978 from Albert Fishlow, "A New International Economic Order: What Kind?" in *Rich and Poor Nations in the World Economy*, ed. Albert Fishlow et al. (New York: McGraw-Hill Book Company, 1978), pp. 67–68. In the contemporary debate early proposals were made by Peter Kenen and Richard Weinert. Kenen proposed the conversion at a discount, while Weinert proposed a conversion at par but with below market interest rates, on the ground that this would spread the banks' losses over time. See Peter Kenen, "A Bailout for the Banks," *New York Times*, 6 March 1983, p. D1; and Richard Weinert, "Banks and Bankruptcy," *Foreign Policy*, no. 50 (Second Quarter, 1983), pp. 138–149. Kenen has recently updated and expanded his proposal. See Peter Kenen, "A Proposal for Reducing the Debt Burden of Developing Countries" (Princeton, N.J.: Princeton University, Department of Economics, March 1987). Another pioneer was Felix Rohatyn, "A Plan for Stretching Out Global Debt," *Business Week*, 28 February 1983, pp. 15–18. Subsequently, proposals for a multilateral facility have come from Congressman John La Falce, "Third World Debt Crisis: The Urgent Need to Confront Reality," *Congressional Record* 133, no. 34 (Washington, D.C., 5 March 1987); Congressman Don Pease, as reported in Keith Rockwell, "Bill Offers Debt Relief for 17 Nations," *Journal of Commerce*, 11 March 1988, p. 6; Arjun Sengupta, as reported in "IMF Director's Plan Would Lift Debt Weight," *Financial Times*, 25 March 1988, p. 5; James Robinson, "A Comprehensive Agenda for LDC Debt and World Trade Growth," The Amex Bank Review Special Papers, No. 13 (London, March 1988); and Percy Mistry in "Third World Debt: Beyond the Baker Plan," *The Banker*, 26 September 1987, pp. i–iv.

that has no downside risk and probably would be very marketable. Moreover, most proposals for a debt conversion facility suggest that the home country banking regulatory authorities change existing accounting and tax rules in such a way as to make sales of debt attractive to the banks.

With regard to the debtor countries the new multilateral facility would, in exchange for a coherent, bilaterally organized program of economic restructuring, agree to pass on the bulk of the discount realized on the purchase of debt. The cooperating countries' debt service would be correspondingly reduced to more manageable levels.

Various proposals exist to finance the new facility. Some suggest that its capital base be subscribed to by the creditor governments in proportion to their current participation in the World Bank and IMF. Others suggest that the major surplus countries contribute the capital, most of which would be callable, as opposed to paid-in. One of the more recent proposals out of the United States Congress suggests that the IMF's $40 billion of idle gold reserves be mobilized to establish a capital base for the new leveraged debt conversion facility.[45]

The multilateral debt conversion facility has many advantages over the ad hoc voluntary private conversions promoted in the market menu approach. On the one hand, it could systematically securitize a larger block of debt more rapidly and at lower cost for the debtor than one could possibly expect through autonomous private market channels. This would be because of rock solid public guarantees on the bonds; a global administrative perspective that could work to minimize free-rider and tax and accounting problems among banks and creditor countries; and even the political potential to make the conversion (or, alternatively, debt refinancing) obligatory for all banks, as social efficiency would probably dictate. In contrast to piecemeal private market operations the multilateral facility therefore could bring a critical mass of conversions that would immediately release balance of payments financing in amounts that are macroeconomically significant. It also would accelerate the turtlelike pace of portfolio adjustment in financial markets, thereby bringing forward the day that the debtor countries can reinitiate borrowing.

On the other hand, a multilateral facility also can better ensure that debt relief is directly functional to economic restructuring, because for a country to become eligible for relief it presumably would have to commit itself ex ante to a bilaterally organized structural adjustment program. In addition, a multilateral scheme could overcome a major bias in

---

[45] La Falce, "Third World Debt Crisis."

the current ad hoc debt management strategy: the marked tendency to favor big debtor countries over smaller ones.[46]

A less ambitious public policy would be simply the awarding on a case-by-case basis of public guarantees on market debt reduction instruments, coupled with supportive modification of tax and accounting rules for the banks. This could provide the credit enhancement needed to raise the volume of conversions to levels sufficient to generate significant balance of payments financing, now, for the debtor countries. However, ad hoc guarantees, while more effective than the hands-off policy of the official market menu approach, are not without their drawbacks. On the one hand, the distribution of relief among countries can be arbitrarily based on political factors, while the timing of that relief remains relatively uncertain. On the other hand, since ad hoc arrangements tackle free-rider and other negative externalities only in a piecemeal fashion, their cumulative cost over the medium-term could be actually more than that of a full-fledged multilateral debt reduction facility.

In any event, the establishment of a multilateral debt conversion facility in and of itself would not be enough to turn around all the debtors' economies. Many countries would still need sustained inflows of new capital to support investment, growth, and economic restructuring. This would initially have to come mostly from traditional multilateral lenders such as the IMF, World Bank, and Inter-American Development Bank in the form of direct loans and/or guarantees on private financial transactions. Moreover, to reverse negative transfers, at least for the latter two institutions, which still preserve good public images in Latin America, general capital increases will be necessary. Such increases would make much more sense, however, if they are accompanied by the multilateral debt conversion facility for problem Latin American debtors. Otherwise new capital authorizations risk pushing the multilateral lenders into a dangerous adverse portfolio selection and eventual balance sheet problems.

Why They Don't Do It   The myriad of proposals for reducing the debt overhang have repeatedly been frowned upon by the key players in the North, and even deridingly termed "radical." Objections have arisen from several angles:[47]

---

[46] This is most evident in the distribution of the new money packages.

[47] I draw from Cline, *International Debt*, pp. 133–135, but the same general arguments have regularly reappeared in the statements of bankers and U.S. government officials. See for instance, Mulford, "Recent Developments in International Debt"; and James Baker, "Statement" to the Joint Annual Meetings of the Board of Governors of the World Bank and International Monetary Fund (Washington, D.C., 30 September 1987).

—Diagnosis. Initial rejection of "radical" reform proposals stemmed from an explicit diagnosis that the debtor economies were essentially sound and only suffered from illiquidity, not insolvency. More recently the word illiquidity has disappeared from the lexicon of the debt managers. Now it is "the inherent strength of the debtor economies" that is summoned to rebuke the need for debt forgiveness.[48]

—Adverse Impact. Radical relief proposals will turn good debt into bad and choke off new lending and future access to private capital markets.

—Impact on Bank Capital. Required write-downs from radical proposals would have a destabilizing effect on the banks.

—Requirements of Public Capital. Radical plans would bail out the banks and pass the problem on to private taxpayers.

—Moral Hazard. Radical relief would adversely affect the debtors' willingness to adjust "at the expense of the creditor and the taxpayer."

Most of these objectives can be simply addressed. They generally suffer from excessively narrow reasoning.

Illiquidity was never a cogent argument to reject comprehensive or "radical" solutions, especially in view of the market's failure and the consequent chronic shortage of new financing. Even liquidity problems can be protracted, making a passive tight-fisted financing strategy, such as that employed by the creditors, socially inefficient and costly. The conventional analysis also overlooked the heavy negative externalities that customarily engulf a systemic financial crisis and that require a mass of critical public action to be broken. As observed earlier, if the negative expectations are not turned around rapidly through comprehensive public policy, an initial problem of illiquidity can tend to degenerate into insolvency.

Whether most Latin American debtor economies are inherently strong or not is ultimately a complicated empirical issue. But the creditors now tacitly admit that the general problem goes beyond a liquidity crisis. Indeed, the official buzzword since 1985 has been "structural reform" in the debtor economies. This is an admission that the status quo in the debtor countries cannot support the nominal value of debt. It also implies that relatively radical change is needed in the debtor economies. Structural change is not instantaneous; it needs considerable time. And that time factor necessarily erodes the present value of the debt. A failure to recognize the lower value of the debt now can further slow required structural change and lower the real value of that debt even

48 See for instance, Baker, "Statement."

more. If the need for a radical public solution was at least plausible in the early years of the crisis, it is compelling now, even employing the creditors' own diagnosis.

This leads to the question of adverse impact. The opportunity cost of a debt conversion facility is in fact relatively low. Without some profound change in the external environment Latin America faces prospects of a protracted period of exclusion from private capital markets. Banks perceive themselves as absolutely overexposed in the region, and it will not be until well into the 1990s that loan/capital ratios approach desired levels.[49] As for unexposed lenders such as bondholders, they were unenthusiastic about Latin America in the best of times; hence they are unlikely to risk their capital there now, at least in large amounts, as long as discounts on old debt telegraph a long and embattled cue for the region's available foreign exchange.[50] Furthermore, the trend of deregulation of domestic capital markets is expected to turn the private lenders' attention even further away from Latin America.[51]

Nor will efforts to improve creditworthiness necessarily bring a ringing response from private creditors. It was noted earlier that credit markets have not responded well to adjustments of the debtor countries' economies. However, this is entirely consistent with the historical experience of private financial markets. In effect, when a systemic payments problem arises, markets tend to experience "revulsion." Thus, credit volume becomes paralyzed generally by a "neighborhood problem"; that is, "good and bad" debtors in the vicinity of the crisis are lumped together.[52] For example, Colombia has not had a debt problem as such in the 1980s, but it has had a severe problem in securing truly voluntary syndicated loans. It also is important to point out that historically defaults have often been followed by a twenty- to thirty-year drought in access to private credit.[53] Latin America, although not in de jure default, has been in de facto default since 1982.

[49] Morgan Guaranty Trust Company, *World Financial Markets* (New York, June/July 1987), p. 3. Also see Alfred Watkins, "To Lend or Not to Lend," paper presented at a conference on Latin America and Foreign Debt, Stanford, California, Hoover Institute, September 1987.

[50] Kotecha, "Repackaging Third World Debt."

[51] Alfred Watkins, "The Impact of Recent Financial Market Developments on Latin America's Access to External Financial Resources" (Washington, D.C., February 1988).

[52] Barry Eichengreen, "Till Debt Do Us Part: The U.S. Capital Market and Foreign Lending, 1920–1955," in *Developing Country Debt* (summary volume), ed. Jeffrey Sachs (Cambridge Mass.: National Bureau of Economic Research, 1987), pp. 249–253.

[53] Charles Kindleberger, "The 1929 World Depression in Latin America—From the Outside," in *Latin America in the 1930s*, ed. Rosemary Thorp (New York: St. Martin's Press, 1984), p. 323.

The best Latin America can probably hope for as long as its debt remains a problem are sporadic private financial transactions secured by reserves, other tangible assets, or external guarantors. A multilateral debt conversion facility will not prejudice this type of access. Indeed, to the extent that the conversion helps to eliminate discounts on debt, the facility will aid, not hinder, Latin America's reentry into private capital markets.

As for the impact of comprehensive reform on bank capital, this depends very much on how any relief program is designed. Imaginative rescue programs and flexible accounting could spread losses out into the future in such a way as not to destabilize the banking system. Indeed, there are already many precedents in the domestic economies of the creditors that allow banks to amortize losses over very long periods.[54]

Regarding public capital, if the debt problem in Latin America were one of illiquidity, as originally diagnosed by the creditors, most of the liabilities from a publicly sponsored relief program never would have been more than contingent. This would have been a small price to pay to avoid the materialization of big liabilities in the future if the liquidity problem degenerated into a solvency problem. Now, however, the risks and potential costs of introducing the "radical" proposals have evidently risen sharply, and any comprehensive solution will be expensive. Nevertheless, the latest proposals for a debt conversion facility and new multilateral financing have sought to minimize paid-in capital and to exploit idle surplus resources in the North. Moreover, we saw earlier that inaction by the creditors also has public costs that are growing and are dysfunctional to world economic expansion. The costs of the conversion facility at least would be functional to resolving the problem and to promoting world economic growth.

Finally, moral hazard. Some feel that a bailout of the banks would just reward them for their recklessness in the 1970s.[55] Others fear that a bailout of the borrowers would reward them for imprudence. Excessive concern for morality can sometimes blind reality. In the middle of a crisis a bailout can indeed be good economics.

[54] Losses on securitized debts of U.S. savings and loan institutions have been allowed to be amortized over forty years. Meanwhile, problem banks regularly receive flexible treatment regarding the capital required to stay in business. See Richard Evans, "New Debts For Old—and the Swapper Is King," *Euromoney*, September 1987, p. 81; and Jerry Knight, "Bank Crisis Deepening in Texas," *Washington Post*, 27 March 1987, p. H1.

[55] The official management strategy has been so one-sided that it is hard to see how the status quo does not raise serious moral hazard problems in the banking system. At least most radical debt relief proposals make the banks pay a more visible price for their excesses of the 1970s.

I mentioned earlier that financial crises usually arise in the context of negative externalities that induce market failure. In a crisis new negative externalities develop that tend to deepen the crisis and make it protracted.[56] It is here where traditionally public intervention is desirable to reestablish order and provide a critical mass of assistance to the market that will be able to reverse expectations. With this the affected parties can recover more quickly and pay the costs of past mistakes out of future growth.

The problem of moral hazard in such bailouts can be mitigated by mentally separating old liabilities from new ones. The bailing out of old liabilities speeds recovery and can be viewed as a public good. Of course, public intervention in the market means that some of the costs will be borne by society. But this is inevitable because the negative externalities of a big crisis make it difficult to pinpoint all of the blame and to allocate the punishment correctly.[57] Simultaneously, care must be taken to ensure that new liabilities are built up in a healthier environment by avoiding a return to "business as usual." Bailouts must therefore be accompanied by systemwide reforms that discipline creditor-debtor behavior in the future. Assistance for debtors must be tied to economic and institutional reforms, while assistance for the

[56] In a boom a euphoria or mania can develop, in which independent rational evaluation is overtaken by interdependent psychology, or herd instincts. Excessive optimism builds up until the bubble is broken by an event (e.g., Mexico's technical default in mid-1982). In a crisis the market reverts to excessive pessimism. Kindleberger employs this hypothesis to analyze financial crashes throughout history. See Charles Kindleberger, *Manias, Panics, and Crashes* (New York: Basic Books, 1978).

[57] One can use the current crisis as an example of the complex interdependencies. Syndication was accepted as a part of good banking, even though in practice it created a two-tiered structure where smaller banks relied on the big banks to decide where to allocate credit. The big banks, locked into an oligopolistic structure, also suffered from interdependence of decision making. The picture is further complicated by the influence of governments that implicitly and explicitly encouraged banks to lend to LDCs by (a) funding excess liquidity, (b) permitting the discrepancy between tight home regulation and near absolute freedom abroad, (c) exhorting that banks recycle petrodollars, and (d) failing to comprehensively support official lenders as an alternative recycling mechanism. Finally, even if one could pinpoint the "bad" banks, the interdependencies in the market would mean that a failure of a big "bad" lender could damage the prospects of "good" institutions. As for borrowers, while they contracted loans on the basis of their own needs, they were also encouraged to do so by the permissive signals of the market and fashionable arguments in important international circles to the effect that bank credits were cheap and foreign indebtedness good business. And it also is true that evident contagion effects in the market due to the Mexican crisis prejudiced countries that otherwise might have avoided a debt problem. Finally, as long as a huge (perhaps "bad") debtor is in trouble, negative externalities will prejudice the efforts of neighboring "good" debtors to return to the market.

banks should be tied to write-downs and institutional and regulatory reforms. To the extent that the world monetary system contributed to the crisis, it too should be reformed.[58]

The message is simple. As we have witnessed in part by the pragmatic response of the antigovernment Reagan administration to the financial difficulties of U.S. banks arising out of problems in Latin America in 1982,[59] a systemic crisis is a public problem that demands a public solution. Unfortunately, in systems based on private markets, public solutions (public goods) are often underproduced and do not appear until the cost of a collective problem threatens to be internalized by the principal agents in the system. The Reagan administration, despite its suspicion of government, responded to the crisis with public action for fear of its repercussions on U.S. banks.[60] The scope of this intervention has been so limited because the banks (with the aid of their governments and international agencies) have been able to externalize most of the political and economic costs by passing them on to the debtors. Moreover, we have seen that the concessions to the debtors that have evolved out of the rescheduling exercises have been in practice side payments designed at the margin to prevent a bigger share of those costs entering the home market. Until there is an imminent threat of a much larger part of the costs of the crisis falling on the banks and politically sensitive segments of U.S. society, the U.S. administration has little incentive to broaden the production of international public goods. In sum, proposals for major reform remain just that, not so much because of a lack of political will but because of a lack of political necessity.

In a Second Best World

Cooperating with the creditors and their governments clearly has not had a large direct payoff for the Latin American debtors. The public goods that have appeared during the crisis are basically protective of the banks' balance sheet. Moreover, the relatively cooperative mode of most debtors ironically has probably contributed to the slow and limited production of international public goods during the crisis.

---

[58] Obviously specific proposals along this line are subject matter for a separate study.

[59] Feinberg shows how an antigovernment Reagan administration rapidly deployed the public sector to avoid a collapse of the international financial system. See Feinberg, "LDC Debt and the Public-Sector Rescue," pp. 27–34.

[60] Prior to the Mexican crisis the Europeans and others had been pressing for increased quotas in the IMF. The Reagan administration vigorously opposed any increase on the grounds that resources are better allocated by the private sector. When the crisis broke out in Mexico, where U.S. banks are heavily exposed, the administration shifted gears and quickly engineered a roughly 50 percent increase in Fund quotas.

The prospects for a major improvement in the situation are severely clouded. On the one hand, a dramatic favorable change in the debtor countries' external economic environment faces obstacles in the severe macroeconomic disequilibria in the North, which will necessarily require time to correct.[61] On the other, that same macroeconomic problem also attracts attention away from the Latin American debt problem, as the value of the dollar, Japanese, German, and U.S. trade balances, stock market fluctuations, et cetera all position themselves on the top of the North's economic agenda.

These same economic disequilibria also harden the political environment regarding the possibility for grand international initiatives on the debt. In the industrialized countries important political leadership regarding the production of international public goods has customarily come from the United States. However, that country has been economically weakened by large fiscal and balance of payments deficits that have converted it into the world's largest debtor nation. It is now being forced to retrench into greater austerity. This will tend to naturally raise resistance to international initiatives such as a new multilateral debt conversion facility and generalized increases in multilateral funding.

Meanwhile, the stronger surplus economies of the center are not accustomed to leading bold international initiatives, and especially ones that so directly affect a U.S. sphere of influence. It will take time for them to sort out their potential new international roles. Japan has made an interesting commitment to recycle $30 billion of its surplus to developing countries over the next three years (Figure 6.1), but it is not clear how much of those resources will be channeled to Latin America and what the distribution among the countries will be. Nor is it clear how quickly the money will be disbursed, especially since an important part of the resources is being channeled indirectly to developing countries through relatively slow-moving international development banks and the IMF. Finally, Japanese banks, which are major participants in the recycling project, have publicly displayed ambivalence to a program that will force them to raise exposure in problem debtor countries.[62]

The above suggests that the birth of an effective multilateral program to tackle the debt overhang in Latin America will be difficult. For sure, as long as the world economy suffers from sporadic performance and uncertainties, the pressure for "radical" debt relief programs—or at

[61] See International Monetary Fund, *World Economic Outlook* (Washington, D.C., October 1987); and Organization for Economic Cooperation and Development, *Economic Outlook*, no. 42 (Paris, December 1987).

[62] "Japanese Banks Wary of Miyazawa Debt Proposal," *Morning Press* (Washington, D.C.: International Monetary Fund, 22 September 1987).

FIGURE 6.1. Estimated Distribution of the $30 Billion Japanese Recycling Program.

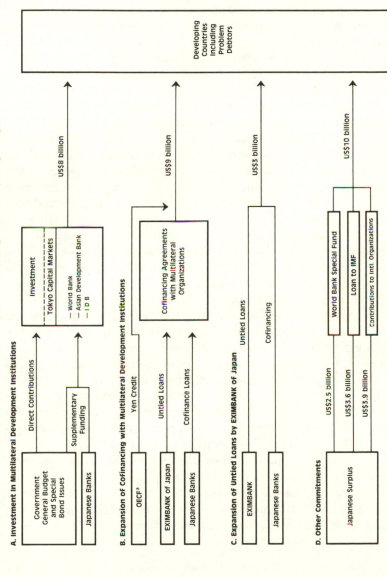

A. Investment in Multilateral Development Institutions

Government General Budget and Special Bond Issues → Direct Contributions → Investment

Japanese Banks → Supplementary Funding → Investment

Investment
Tokyo Capital Markets
— World Bank
— Asian Development Bank
— I D B

US$8 billion →

B. Expansion of Cofinancing with Multilateral Development Institutions

OECF[a] → Yen Credit

EXIMBANK of Japan → Untied Loans

Japanese Banks → Cofinance Loans

Cofinancing Agreements with Multilateral Organizations

US$9 billion →

C. Expansion of Untied Loans by EXIMBANK of Japan

EXIMBANK → Untied Loans

Japanese Banks → Cofinancing

US$3 billion →

D. Other Commitments

Japanese Surplus → US$2.5 billion → World Bank Special Fund

Japanese Surplus → US$3.6 billion → Loan to IMF

Japanese Surplus → US$3.9 billion → Contributions to Intl. Organizations

US$10 billion →

Developing Countries Including Problem Debtors

SOURCE: Based on data of the Ministry of Finance of Japan.
[a] Overseas Economic Cooperation Fund.

least additional ad hoc production of public goods—will certainly persist and grow. This is because (a) it appears that under a scenario of OECD growth rates of 2 to 3 percent the "average" Latin American country cannot normally service the debt and grow satisfactorily;[63] and (b) the market menu approach, at least as originally conceived, cannot release the balance of payments financing needed to resolve that conflict. However, given the noncommittal attitude of the Reagan administration, and the relatively low level of the Latin American debt problem on the United States' political agenda, when more public goods are produced and at what speed and comprehensiveness is anyone's guess. The possibility of a very protracted 1930s-style wind down of the debt overhang cannot be dismissed.

Be that as it may, some Latin American countries undoubtedly will, for different motives, choose to operate entirely within the creditors' current official management framework and a few of them may even prosper despite it. But given the depressive effects of the official debt strategy, many will want to explore new ways to unilaterally reduce the outward transfer. The incentives are certainly there. As indicated in Chapter Five, the breakdown of private financial markets vis-à-vis Latin America gives illiquid and insolvent borrowers alike the incentive to seek debt forgiveness. Likewise, very big debtors, which find it increasingly more difficult to squeeze an adequate volume of involuntary refinancing loans from better reserved banks, have more cause to ponder the alternative route of unilateral action. It also is clear that the significant discounts on traded Latin debt magnify the monopoly rents won by the banks when a country passively agrees to service the bulk of its obligations on commercial terms. The shortcomings of the market menu approach also encourage unilateral action because of the limited number of satisfying negotiated options it affords a debtor country. Finally, the growing cracks in the creditor cartel make nonnegotiated solutions to the transfer problem objectively more feasible.

As indicated by the large number of countries with an irregular payments status in 1987, these incentives have already taken hold in Latin America. Indeed, emerging from the crisis is an alternative "debtors' menu of options" that contains a number of unilateral strategies for reducing the transfer of resources to the creditors.

[63] "Satisfactory," of course, is normative. I will suggest a 5 percent rate of GDP growth as an acceptable minimum. Recent projections prepared by the Economic Commission for Latin America and the Caribbean suggest that without a loosening of the restriction of foreign debt, even a 3 percent rate of growth in the region will prove optimistic for the medium term. See ECLAC, "Restrictions," pp. 15–26.

Repudiation   Repudiation of the debt can be practically ruled out as an option. No country has ever given any indication of interest in this route.[64] Moreover, since the repudiation of foreign obligations is the equivalent of a "mortal sin" in the ethics of capitalism, a swift and staggering response from the creditors and their governments might be expected. Cuba in 1961 and North Korea in 1974 are modern testaments to the reprisals that can come forth as a consequence of belligerent repudiation.

The threat of sanctions is conventionally assumed to be the factor that motivates good behavior on the part of the debtor. In other words, the debtor country is little more than a *homo economicus* that will cooperate as long as the cost of noncooperation (sanctions) exceeds the benefits (nonpayment of the debt). The task of the creditor is thus to make this threat as real as possible, while restricting debt accumulation to levels below that for which sanctions would become an ineffective deterrent.[65] In practical terms the realism of this threat is presumably enhanced by the frequency with which it is raised in the commentaries on the debt crisis. For example, we can observe how William Cline highlights the consequences for an errant debtor:

> Beyond difficulties with access to long-term and short-term credit, defaulting countries could face reprisals. Foreign creditors could attach any of the foreign assets of a defaulting country, as well as its exports abroad (commercial airlines, ships, bank accounts, shipments of commodities, and so forth). For example, in 1972 Kennecott Copper Corporation successfully obtained legal seizure of Chilean copper shipments at a French port, as well as the freezing of

[64] Cuba has come the closest, suggesting that the Latin American countries immediately suspend payments. But leaders of countries indebted to the banks uniformly rejected the proposal. See "Castro's Proposal Gets Thumbs-Down," *Latin American Weekly Report*, 9 August 1985, p. 6.

[65] The conventional argumentation can be perused in the orthodox literature cited in the first part of Chapter Three. For an analysis that focuses specifically on LDCs see Jonathan Eaton and Mark Gersovitz, "Debt with Potential Repudiation: Theoretical and Empirical Analysis," *Review of Economic Studies* 48 (April 1981): 289–309; Jonathan Eaton and Mark Gersovitz, *Poor Country Borrowing in Private Financial Markets and the Repudiation Issue*, Princeton Studies in International Finance, No. 47 (Princeton, N.J.: Princeton University, Department of Economics, 1981); and Jeffrey Sachs, "Theoretical Issues in International Borrowing," Working Paper No. 1189 (Cambridge, Mass.: National Bureau of Economic Research, August 1983), pp. 19–35. For an excellent survey of the conventional literature on the dynamics of nonpayment in lender-borrower relations see Vincent Crawford, "International Lending, Long-Term Credit Relationships, and Dynamic Contract Theory" (University of California at San Diego, Department of Economics, August 1984), mimeographed.

Chilean bank accounts in New York, because Kennecott maintained that Salvador Allende had paid inadequate compensation for its expropriated copper mine. Parallel actions could certainly be expected against countries defaulting on external debt.[66]

Meanwhile, early on in the crisis Enders and Mattione performed one of the more detailed studies on the costs and benefits of repudiation with sanctions for Latin American debtors. They concluded at that time that only one country—Argentina—might view it as a rational alternative.[67]

The conventional view, however, again suffers from excessively narrow reasoning. Between the two extremes of repudiation/flagrant default and full payment that underpin the calculus of the errant borrower in the literature is a gray area of policy options that, while not free of costs, are unlikely to provoke the retaliation that has often been conventionally waved at the debtors. As Kaletsky has observed in his study of the costs of default:

> The conventional wisdom is seriously misleading. None of the reprisals listed by Cline are likely to take effect, at least in the way which he suggests. A defaulter might not get off scot-free—a flagrant repudiation of debt could quite conceivably lead to immensely damaging sanctions, but these would be of a different character and would raise quite different issues from the ones which either debtors or bankers now appear to envisage.[68]

I will now briefly explore some of the alternatives in the middle ground between repudiation/flagrant default and full payment.

Accumulation of Arrears   A conciliatory informal default in the form of a quiet accumulation of arrears is the least confrontational way to unilaterally reduce payments to the creditors. The banks could threaten to call a formal default, but there are many reasons why they probably would not take such action.

Declarations of default are legally onerous for the banks, demanding a considerable amount of their time and resources, with low probabilities for tangible returns. Again referring to Kaletsky's study:

> The law is a creditor's most obvious recourse in the event of a default. Various forms of legal redress, such as attachment of assets and sei-

---

[66] Cline, *International Debt*, p. 90.

[67] Thomas Enders and Richard Mattione, *Latin America: The Crisis of Debt and Growth* (Washington D.C.: Brookings Institution, 1983), pp. 47–50.

[68] Anatole Kaletsky, *The Costs of Default* (New York: Priority Press, 1985), p. 11.

zure of exports, are generally regarded as the ultimate deterrents against default. But bankers' hopes—and borrowers' fears—that crippling costs could be imposed on recalcitrant debtor countries through court action appear to be greatly exaggerated. Western legal systems would give private creditors only modest opportunities to disrupt a defaulting country's trade or to restrain others from doing business with it. There would be little hope of seizing its foreign currency reserves and other assets of its central bank. Even though bankers could hope to create considerable nuisance for a defaulting borrower through private lawsuits, the costs of coping with all that legal trouble would scarcely be commensurable.[69]

Why is this so? On the one hand, governments are sovereigns, and while they can be exposed to foreign law, getting courts to pass judgment against them is still in practice somewhat problematic. Moreover, even if a court rules against the country, the next stage, enforcement, also is problematic: a judgment is nothing more than a piece of paper. Finally, there are tactical considerations. A declaration of default against a conciliatory debtor could create a "martyr" that would adversely affect the behavior of other debtors. An open declaration of default also would have the disadvantage of fully exposing the unrecoverable nature of assets, perhaps provoking bigger write downs of the portfolio than if all parties remained discreetly silent. A bank also could suffer if an open confrontation provoked the country into attaching the local assets of the lender, or of its major clients, that reside within the debtor's home market.

In sum, active retaliation is likely to come only if there is a confrontational repudiation, which generates bad demonstration effects that cannot possibly be overlooked. Indeed, the key dimension may be politics since most modern default declarations and attachments have been tied up in political confrontations between the debtor and the creditor nation, in which the executive branch of the creditor's government has been a driving force in the implementation of sanctions.[70] Thus a country accumulating arrears needs to be quiet, conciliatory, and must carefully avoid direct political confrontation with its creditors' government. Other steps that probably should be taken are the following.

As part of the strategy the debtor must service normally short-term

[69] Kaletsky, *Costs of Default*, p. 21. Bernal's analysis draws a similar conclusion. See Richard Bernal, "Default as a Negotiating Tactic in Debt Rescheduling Strategies of Developing Countries: A Preliminary Note" (Kingston, Jamaica: University of West Indies, Department of Economics, September 1984), p. 7.

[70] Kaletsky, *Costs of Default*, pp. 30–31.

lines of credit in order to minimize the incentives for the banks to cut them. Some lines will inevitably be lost due to the retaliatory actions of annoyed bankers, but essential lending will be secured from institutions that perceive the profits to be made in the nearly risk-free business of trade finance.[71] Selective depositing with the banks of the debtor country's international reserves is another way to give certain lenders an incentive to keep open their lines of credit.

The borrower must additionally be prepared to make token payments to the banks at critical moments in order to demonstrate good faith. These, however, could be maintained as low as 1 to 2 percent of outstanding commitments.[72] At a rate of interest of 10 percent there would be a savings of foreign exchange on a cash flow basis of eight to nine points.[73] The savings would not be a bonanza, especially for those countries for which the debt with the banks is much less than 50 percent of the total. But other things being equal, a country would be able to lower its trade surplus (or widen a trade deficit) in support of more imports, investment, and economic growth.

Other protective action would be appropriate. Debt to foreign public and multilateral lenders should be serviced normally since in the absence of formal sanctions they may be able to provide positive transfers. Even if an institution's contribution should turn negative in a given year, a medium-term perspective should prevail in determining whether to slip into arrears with it or not. This is because the supply of public money in principle is elastic even in crisis; thus a negative transfer could quickly convert itself into a positive one given a favorable twist in negotiations with the public lender. Special patience is required with multilateral lenders since arrears with them are severely damaging to a country's image of competence and fair play.

[71] Even open trade sanctions have usually been neutralized by this neoclassical rationale. South Africa and Rhodesia were able to obtain finance, as was Allende when he was boycotted by U.S. institutions. Notwithstanding U.S. sanctions, Cuba accumulated more than a billion dollars of debt with non-U.S. private banks during the 1970s. See Bernal, "Default as a Negotiating Tactic," p. 6, and Jonathan Eaton and Lance Taylor, "Developing Country Finance and Debt," paper prepared for a conference on New Directions in Development Theory, Cambridge, Mass., Massachusetts Institute of Technology, Department of Economics, 17–19 January 1985, p. 37.

[72] Fernández has modeled the tolerance of the banks. According to him, an interest rate as low as 2 percent on outstanding debts could be preferable to the alternative of confrontation. See Javier Fernández, "Moratoria de la Deuda" [Debt Moratorium], paper prepared for the seminar on External Debt in Latin America: Actual Situation and Perspectives, organized by Centro de Estudios Monetarios de América Latina in Quito, Ecuador, 22–26 July 1985, pp. 40–41.

[73] The net savings will be less if the cost of short-term lines of credit rises, which is possible.

A country should also protect itself against potential retaliation. International reserves should be hidden (if possible) from public view and stored in safe locations, for example, outside the frontiers of the country (or countries) where the main creditor banks reside. Law firms in New York or London could be overtly contracted as part of a contingency plan to respond to potential harassment by the creditors. Also, the links between the main creditor banks and local foreign investments in the debtors' economy should be investigated to locate "pressure points" that could be subtly touched in the event that a battle of nerves begins to break out with the lenders.[74] Incentives to retaliate are also reduced if the "stick" of arrears is partially compensated by the awarding of carrots in other areas of interest to the creditors. For example, a carrot for the banks might be domestic liberalization of rules guiding participation of foreign banks in the local finance sector and expansion of debt-equity swap programs. For the governments of the banks the carrot could be in the form of the debtor country's public attitude and policies concerning issues of great political importance in the North such as drug trade, migration, voting in international fora, trade and foreign investment policy, et cetera.

Economic policy also is an often overlooked key component in the building of effective defenses. Even in the extreme case of a paralysis of payments on all old debt a country would have to continue to carefully control domestic demand so as not to erode the negotiating cushion provided by any available foreign exchange reserves. If no new fresh credit of any type were forthcoming, at least a small trade surplus would have to be maintained to service trade lines, foreign direct investments, et cetera. It also is important for the economic authorities to demonstrate an ability to use the time bought by an accumulation of arrears to correct disequilibria and move the economy in a direction consistent with eventual creditworthiness; seeing potential for some repayment, creditors have less incentive to be cantankerous.

In any event, a strategy involving informal arrears need not provoke the creditors; indeed, more than half of the debtor countries of the region have accumulated arrears for protracted periods without retaliation. The main repercussion of arrears has been more difficult access to short-term trade credit. However, the debtor should be able to manage adequately by more aggressive shopping for those lines and by rationalizing the economy's use of trade credit.

The ultimate goal of arrears' accumulation is increased foreign ex-

---

[74] The links can be direct (local branches and subsidiaries of the banks) or through corporations that are large clients of the banks or linked to them through directorates.

change availability (if only marginal in some instances) and leverage to negotiate eventual settlements that are more favorable to the country. Indeed, protracted arrears will tend to drive down the price of the banks' loan paper in secondary markets, giving the country greater opportunities to benefit from negotiations involving debt-equity swaps, buybacks, and securitization. If necessary, the debtor should be prepared to sign a less than optimal rescheduling agreement to avoid a direct confrontation; it can always fall back into noncompliance thereafter.

There are disadvantages to this strategy. First, if all of the debtors were to employ it simultaneously, losses for the banks could destabilize the international banking system. This may be a blessing in disguise, however, because it would signal to the North that the costs of the crisis were becoming more fully internalized, which would give more stimulus to a comprehensive public solution. Second, the strategy requires a strong dose of cynicism on the part of the borrower, as it would be constantly testing the tolerance of its creditors. Third, by accumulating arrears the country would be in a state of tension with international private capital. While the financial cost of that tension may be technically manageable, the internal secondary economic (or political) cost may be proportionately higher if there is not a reasonable national consensus that the debt cannot or should not be serviced on commercial terms. Finally, the tolerance of the banking system could be accidentally breached, bringing unexpected systematic sanctions.

A Unilateral Repayment Formula   The informal accumulation of arrears is admittedly a messy solution. A formal noncommercial repayment plan that establishes an explicit cue for creditors would certainly be preferable. The problem with the unilateral imposition of a precise formula is that it raises the visibility of the problem and threatens to ripple the system with a bad demonstration effect that the banks might feel obliged to respond to. Thus ventures along this line are more risky and face greater threats of retaliation. Nevertheless, such a strategy is feasible, as suggested by the mild response so far to Peru's introduction in July 1985 of the well-known "10 percent formula."[75] The proba-

---

[75] President García first established a debt service limit of 10 percent of export earnings on public medium- and long-term debt contracted before July 1985. A year later he expanded the formula to include medium-term private debt, which had been exempt. Payment of debt in kind continued to be excluded from the program. The formal limit, always flexibly applied, did help to reduce debt service. Even though export earnings fell by 13 percent, debt service actually paid declined from the equivalent of 32 percent of export earnings in 1984 to 22 percent in 1986 (the first full year of the program). Since amortiza-

bility of retaliation is reduced if several considerations are taken into account.

Since debtor-bank relations involve personal contacts and the interface of egos, a conciliatory approach is always useful; it does less damage to pride and is more hopeful.[76] Moreover, reflecting this spirit, the plan should be presented as temporary—forced on the government by the crushing weight of the recession and the legitimate popular aspirations of the nation to grow. Thus the scheme should explicitly open the possibility of a commercial repayment formula as soon as conditions permit. By formally linking payments *pari passu* with repayment capacity—as opposed to establishing, for example, a fixed twenty-year noncommercial schedule—one is forcing the bankers to take a quasi-equity position in the country. Hence, expectations about the recovery of the loan portfolio are enhanced, and immediate write-downs are potentially less.

The formula would essentially have to incorporate something akin to a bisque clause that explicitly established the conditions under which terms could be progressively raised to commercial levels.[77] To avoid the creditors' fears of cheating, performance criteria would have to include exogenously determined indicators, for example, the linking of payments to the level of the terms of trade and world export volume in the products that the debtor sells abroad.

A unilateral formula also should have a cutoff date for the debt that will be affected by the plan. That way the country at least does not preclude the possibility of finding new lenders.

The most popular formula discussed in Latin America has been the

---

tion was often refinanced, a more telling indicator is actual interest payments as a percentage of exports; over the same period that coefficient fell from 16 percent to 8 percent. As for the net transfer of resources, it declined from $538 million in 1984 to $132 million in 1986. See United Nations Economic Commission for Latin America and the Caribbean (ECLAC), *Estudio Económico de América Latina y el Caribe 1986* [Economic Survey of Latin America and the Caribbean 1986] (Santiago, Chile, 1988), table 21.

[76] President García, in contrast, has been rather confrontational, at least in public. While this has probably hurt him abroad, it initially contributed to popularity at home. In some circumstances a confrontational mode can be effective with the banks, for example, Nicaragua in 1980. But it would seem that confrontation can be best exploited by highly cohesive regimes, which is not a characteristic of most of the governments of Latin America.

[77] Bisque clauses were employed by the government of the United States for some postwar loans. For example, in 1945 the U.S. government made a loan for $4 billion to the United Kingdom. It was to be amortized in fifty years, but the bisque clause permitted the calendar to be adjusted to the economic conditions of the debtor. See George Abbott, "The Case for Cancellation," *Inter-Economics*, July 1975, pp. 217–221.

limiting of payments to some percentage of exports.[78] In mid-1984 Bolivia attempted to formally limit payments to 25 percent of exports, but events overtook the country and little commercial bank debt service has been effected since then. And as just mentioned, Peru declared and implemented the 10 percent limit on payments. The formula has several attractions. First, it is simple to monitor. Second, it is easy to comprehend at the political level and has already enjoyed considerable support in debt relief circles.[79] Third, it has some of the *pari passu* characteristics mentioned above: payments fluctuate with export earnings.

A drawback to the García formula, as I see it, is that at the macrolevel of economic policy it could act as a tax on exports. Thus a country can earn, or keep, more foreign exchange by substituting imports than it can from exporting. This obviously cannot be attractive to the creditors. Moreover, it cannot be too helpful for Peru either; as shown in Chapter Four, the country's lack of export initiative has been one of the major sources of vulnerability in the Peruvian economy.

The short-coming of the formula is correctable, however. The country could tie the 10 percent rule to the maintenance (or improvement) of the country's position in world trade. The plan also would become more attractive if the government were to introduce incentives that seriously promoted exports, particularly nontraditional ones, which have a proven record of success. Unfortunately, during the first two years of the García government export expansion was very low on the government's list of economic priorities. Indeed this deficiency has been a factor in that country's deteriorating export performance.[80]

There is an alternative formula that is somewhat more complicated but perhaps more satisfying. That is to condition debt service payments to growth. In other words, a country could program an acceptable rate of economic growth, for example, 5 percent, and allocate a high per-

---

[78] This had its expression in an early regional meeting on the debt issue. In one of the few concrete proposals to come out of the Latin American Economic Conference in Quito in January 1984 the "Plan for Action" stated: "In renegotiating the external debt, export earnings should not be committed beyond reasonable percentages consistent with the maintenance of adequate levels of internal productive activity, taking into account the characteristics proper to the individual countries' economies." "Latin American Economic Conference," *CEPAL Review*, no. 22 (April 1984), p. 43.

[79] Proposals along this line have also come forth in the North. For example, see Norman Bailey, David Luft, and Roger Robinson, "Exchange Participation Notes: An Approach to the International Fiscal Crisis," CSIS Significant Issues Series, vol. 5, no. 1 (Washington, D.C.: Georgetown University, Center for Strategic and International Studies, 1983).

[80] See note on Peru in ECLAC, *Estudio Económico de América Latina y el Caribe 1986*.

centage of the excess of foreign exchange to debt service.[81] The advantage of this type of proposal is that growth of production and income is explicitly integrated into the plan. Moreover, if the Fund and the World Bank were to fully delink themselves from the protection of the banks' balance sheets and tacitly accepted such formulas as a legitimate transitory solution, it would be easier to persuade debtor countries to participate in a formally structured adjustment program. The danger of go-it-alone formulations such as President García's is that the country, suspecting a hostile external environment, withdraws inward and delinks from the capitalist system. This has unfortunately already happened to some degree in Peru.[82]

Other unilateral formulations that debtors could consider are:

—Conversion of debt into bonds. From a position of full or partial moratorium, the debtor country could make a formal standing offer to settle arrears with individual banks by trading debts for long-term bonds. The bonds could be emitted at par, carry a long grace period (say seven years) and a twenty-five- to thirty-five-year amortization period. Banks could be given the option to accept a series A or series B bond. The series A bond would have below market interest rate (say 1 to 2 percent) but contain a bisque clause that would permit re-

[81] Costa Rica presented a proposal to its banks in June 1987 that had some of these characteristics. Essentially, interest payments would be determined on an annual basis according to the country's "capacity to pay." The capacity to pay would be determined ostensibly on the basis of the evolution of the external accounts. However, since the external accounts were broadly defined to include import levels, the country indirectly incorporated a provision for a rate of economic growth. See "Guidelines for the Rescheduling of Current & Past Due Obligations of the Government of Costa Rica" (San José, 4 June 1987).

[82] Peru had been involved in standby programs throughout the early 1980s. However, there followed a buildup of political resistance to the Fund's adjustment programs; in 1984 the country ceased to renew its standby agreement and began to accumulate arrears with the banks. In mid-1985 García's new government formalized the rejection of the Fund and the arrears' accumulation. With no new standby program a negative transfer eventually developed with the IMF. The situation provoked an accumulation of arrears with the Fund, which induced that institution in 1987 to declare Peru "ineligible" for lending. In 1987 arrears became a problem at the World Bank as well. Meanwhile, the country's initially interesting heterodox economic program has degenerated into a growing quagmire of administrative controls, while inflation and deteriorating external accounts suggest that the spurt of very strong economic growth enjoyed in 1986 and 1987 (8 percent per annum) cannot be sustained. With the potential for intensifying the moratorium exhausted the economic outlook for that country is extremely difficult. For a review of the theory underlying the Peruvian heterodox economic program see Daniel Carbonetto et al., *El Perú Heterodoxo: Un Modelo Económico* [Heterodox Peru: An Economic Model] (Lima: Instituto Nacional de Planificación, 1987).

negotiation of that rate after the fifth year, with potential enhancement up to even a full commercial rate if mutually agreed non-manipulative indicators of capacity to pay so justify. Series B bonds would incorporate a rate of interest of LIBOR plus a small margin (say, 0.5 percent). For the first five years the difference between the market rate on series B bonds and the rate paid on series A bonds would be covered by interest capitalization or new loans, whichever the bank preferred. To encourage participation in series A bonds, they would have seniority over B bonds in terms of available foreign exchange. Series A bonds also would be given preferential treatment in debt-equity swap programs.

—Interest bonds. A variant of the same plan could be applied just to future interest payments.

—Forced capitalization. For a specified period of time a debtor country could unilaterally capitalize interest payments on the debt that exceed some rate, say 2 percent nominal, or alternatively the historical real rate, which many consider to be 2 percent. A shadow commercial, or below market, interest rate could be applied to the capitalized payment for accounting purposes. The debtor country could add credibility to accumulated capitalized interest by paying the local currency equivalent into an interest-bearing escrow fund that the banks could draw upon for the purpose of making local loans or equity investment.

—Buybacks. A country could enter into moratorium and place all or part of the interest it would have otherwise paid into a special fund designed to finance the buyback of debt in the secondary market. The buybacks, however, should not be undertaken before the price dips to its anticipated floor. During the 1930s the floor price for many developing countries was 10 to 15 cents.[83]

—Payment in kind. The country offers to pay debts off to the banks by providing locally produced goods.[84]

---

[83] Kotecha, "Repackaging Third World Debt." Bolivia recently bought back nearly one-half of its commercial debt at eleven cents on the dollar. However, the resources for the buyback came from an anonymous OECD donor fund. See "Bolivia To Buy Back Debt at 11% of Face Value," *Financial Times*, 17 March 1988, p.3.

[84] In 1987 Peru successfully attracted Midland Bank and First Interstate Bank to this type of scheme. Under the plan the banks are required to purchase in foreign exchange additional Peruvian products for each dollar repaid in kind; the ratio for Midland was 2.5 and that applied to First Interstate was 3. The additional purchase compensated Peru for the imported content of the goods it exchanged for debt. See United Nations Economic Commission for Latin America and the Caribbean, "Preliminary Overview of the Latin American Economy 1987" (Santiago, Chile, December 1987), p. 9.

Finally, unless and until a unilateral formula is fully accepted by creditors, it would be wise to pursue the same protective measures outlined earlier regarding the strategy for accumulating arrears. In addition, the country would not want to formally bypass the steering committee when presenting programs to the banks; it should however, be willing and indeed encourage banks to bilaterally strike a deal with it. The country also might not want to set itself out as an example for others to follow unless there were a reasonable expectation that they would: the elimination of a bad example is one of the few important motives that the banks have for introducing sanctions. And it cannot be emphasized enough that one of the most effective protective measures is to ensure that the moratorium is an integral part of a credible economic program that promises to correct fundamental disequilibria and move the economy in a direction consistent with a viable external sector.

Cooperation among the Debtor Countries   O'Donnell has clearly stated one of the dilemmas facing a developing country wishing to unilaterally force an alternative payments plan on the banks and thereby gain a more equitable distribution of the costs of the debt crisis. On the one hand, the debtor's maximum threat if the banks do not cooperate with it—repudiation—lacks credibility. Such action could bring an overwhelming response that only a suicidal or revolutionary government could risk—neither of which characterizes the bulk of the Latin American countries. On the other, the credibility of the banks' threat for noncooperation is greater because should they let one country succeed in such an action they encounter a greater probability that others will follow.[85]

The debtor's weakness theoretically could be overcome if it joined into a club, or cartel, because, as Kaletsky points out, "it would eliminate one of the few rational arguments in favor of retaliation by creditor governments and banks, namely, the hope that retaliation against the first defaulter would have a deterrent effect on others."[86] Indeed, the framework of bilateral monopoly, which I presented in Chapter Five, begs for cooperation among the debtors. The banks have astutely perceived the advantages of cooperation by joining together in a cartel (the Bank Advisory Committee). Except for maybe Brazil and Mexico, no debtor clearly has sufficient countervailing power to confront the creditor club alone should it decide to retaliate. A socially equitable solution

[85] See O'Donnell, "External Debt: Why Don't Our Governments do the Obvious?" *CEPAL Review*, no. 27 (December 1985), pp. 27–33.
[86] Kaletsky, *Costs of Default*, p. 64.

to the crisis would perhaps have been more feasible if the monopoly power of the creditors were neutralized by the formation of a responsible look-alike debtors' cartel.

The debtors' cartel also appears desirable when we recall the earlier analysis concerning international public goods. The capitalist system tends to underproduce these items. Moreover, the Reagan administration, with its antipublic sector ideology, may be aggravating the natural constraint. While the cost of "doing nothing" is less than the benefits, the administration will likely support the status quo. As I mentioned earlier, this passive strategy is less likely to be broken until and unless the debt crisis begins to threaten the center with additional economic or political costs. Direct cooperation among the debtors is thus a way to make more transparent the potential costs of preserving the status quo, which arbitrarily sacrifices economic development for the requisites of financial discipline.

But while cooperation among the debtors is theoretically desirable, it is in practice very difficult to realize. As O'Donnell has pointedly shown, there is an equally powerful logic encouraging disunity. This countervailing logic stems from the creditors' imperative to dissuade debtor cooperation, coupled with the debtors' difficulty in overcoming a type of prisoners' dilemma, which encircles the game of cartel formation.[87]

The creditor has a strong incentive to dissuade cartel formation because when the debtors are grouped together their maximum threat—repudiation, or at least joint moratoria—immediately gains the credibility that it lacked when the countries confronted the banks individually. The banks realize this and will seek to neutralize the debtors. This is done by attempting to maintain unity among themselves—thereby preserving some of the realism of their threat of sanctions—and sacrificing some of the monopoly rents that they earned when the cartel could fully exploit the division among the debtors.

This latter consideration leads to the "side payments" that I mentioned in Chapter Five. The banks are willing to forego maximization of rents in the short term in order to protect themselves from the elimination of the greater part of those rents should the debtors form a cartel. They therefore make selective concessions to one or more of the debtors in hopes of dissuading participation in a club. The debtor in turn has a strong incentive to accept the payment because it will weigh the certain benefits of the concession against the highly uncertain benefits of the cartel. It knows that the banks might be offering side payments to other

[87] See O'Donnell, "External Debt: Why Can't Our Governments Do the Obvious?"

potential members of the cartel, making the debtors' club a highly uncertain venture. Likewise, any country contemplating a leadership role
in the formation of a cartel fears, on the one hand, the prospects of becoming isolated on the issue due to the suspected side payments to its
neighbors and, on the other, the possibility that it will be singled out for
retaliatory measures.

According to O'Donnell, it is the inability to establish clear lines of
communication and firm commitments that puts the debtors in the prisoner's dilemma. O'Donnell correctly points out that there is no easy
way to overcome this problem. But he also argues that it is not an impossible dilemma. Exploring the different ways to establish communication and firm commitments, he suggests that simultaneous national referenda on the debt issue, coupled with the countries'
submission to a supranational bargaining agent, could be a way to overcome the powerful logic of disunity. And, of course, the mere recognition of this logic is a good first step in overcoming it.

O'Donnell's review of the problems in organizing the debtors highlights the "external" threat of a side payment. As shown in Chapter
Five, these payments certainly appear to have helped to sidetrack efforts
to cooperate within Latin America. But the decisive threat to full exploitation of the possibilities inherent in the game of bilateral monopoly
may have been in fact "internal."

It must be recognized that it is inherently difficult for a debtor country
to neutralize the bargaining power of the banks. Throughout most of
the crisis the banks have had the luxury of focusing on mainly one variable in which they easily converged: service of the loan portfolio. The
governments of banks presumably had to share their concern about
payment of debt with at least foreign policy considerations, although
this latter dimension clearly has been so far largely a prisoner of financial variables.[88] In contrast, the developing countries have had to share
their negotiations on the debt with a broad range of internal national
objectives, some of which, at any given moment, superseded the debt
negotiations in importance and could indeed be prejudiced by a confrontation of any type. For instance, the newly democratic countries are
emerging from many turbulent and bloody years of military dictator-
ship. Some of these new governments give highest priority to objectives
related to the consolidation of civil society such as the promotion of better institutional control of the military; demonstration that a civil re-

---

[88] Symptomatic of this is the leading role of the U.S. Treasury and Federal Reserve in
the management of the problem. Indeed when one wants to learn about the latest event in
the debt crisis, the last place to visit in Washington, D.C., is the State Department.

gime is not inconsistent with social order; establishment of stable incentives and rules to encourage the emergence of a modern democratic entrepreneur; more, not less, political and economic integration with the center; and even the mere time to enjoy the fresh air of democracy for a while without social turmoil. These objectives moreover must be won in a context of emerging and fragile political coalitions and delicate economic conditions. While the debt may be impinging on the country's economic performance, a confrontation now with the creditors, even if successful, could prove to be a Pyrrhic victory if it destabilized other key variables of a political project.

The broad constellation of domestic conditioning factors in a debt negotiation have made it difficult for the countries to organize coherent bilateral negotiations with the creditors. This fact, coupled with considerable difference in characteristics of the region's economies, make a joint bargaining position a Herculean task. On relatively weak domestic footing, it is perhaps understandable that the Latin American governments have been very susceptible to side payments, exploiting the occasional hardening of the bargaining position of a neighbor for individual advantage.

It is probably less than a coincidence that Peru has been the only country so far able to impose a unilateral payments plan on the banks and to aggressively promote a coordinated debtor approach. In 1985 it enjoyed an elected government with a broad popular mandate built on a national consensus that Peru could not service its debt on the terms and conditions of the banks and the IMF. However, it is instructive to note that Peru had been in almost unabated conflict with the banks and the IMF since 1975, meaning it took roughly ten years of crisis for debt to mature to a degree sufficient to give it a place of paramount importance on the national political agenda.[89] Since Latin America's development crisis is now approaching its seventh year, it is reasonable to expect that a national consensus on the debt problem will begin to emerge from more countries of the region in the future.

CONCLUSIONS

We have seen that the outward transfer of resources from Latin America is an obstacle to growth and economic restructuring because of its aggravation of either the foreign exchange constraint, the savings/fiscal constraint, or both. In the absence of systematic payment guarantees from the creditor governments the voluntary market options in the so-called menu approach promise to reduce that transfer burden only

[89] For a historical overview of Peru's relations with its creditors see Oscar Ugarteche, *El Estado Deudor* [The Debtor State] (Lima: Instituto de Estudios Peruanos, 1987).

gradually over a long haul and with a high degree of uncertainty regarding the amount and timing of relief, as well as its distribution among the debtors. In the meantime, the volume of external financing needed now to support programs of economic growth and restructuring remains unsatisfied. It is thus little surprise that the countries in Latin America which have been able to sustain a process of adequate growth with price stability remain the "special case."

A strategy of growth and reconstruction in which only a few problem debtors can successfully maneuver is clearly a halfhearted international public policy. At a time when private credit markets have collapsed around Latin America, the reliance on voluntary microresponses of lenders to resolve a systemic macroeconomic financial problem is an abdication of the lessons of modern economics. Indeed, in some ways the official menu approach has thrust us back to the 1930s, when debtor and creditor were left on their own to grope inefficiently for twenty years to find ways to reduce the debt overhang of that period.

Latin American countries must confront this exceedingly difficult situation imaginatively and with a mind to redoubling efforts to bring internal and external disequilibria under control. But in view of the unrelenting weight of the transfer problem and the existence of corresponsibility in the crisis, countries are finding it necessary to force creditors to share the costs of economic restructuring and growth through the imposition of various types of informal or formal moratoria on debt payments. As the costs of the development crisis in the region escalate, this alternative in the "debtors' menu of options" could become even more widely deployed.

Regarding that alternative, so far most debtor countries have opted for the least risky tactic: informal arrears. This is understandable since virtually any formal unilateral payments plan that lowered the outward transfer sufficiently to seriously contribute to the macroeconomic financing requirements of the debtor country is sure to get a cold reception from the creditors. Yet a formal unilateral scheme has advantages in terms of establishing an orderly cue for the banks (and other creditors), while visibly demonstrating a willingness to pay. The introduction of a bisque clause enhances such plans because it could make participation by a bank more attractive than the alternative of no payment at all and an eventual cash sale of the problem loan in the secondary market (which offers no direct benefit to the debtor country). Moreover, the feasibility of such plans is rising as widening cracks in the creditor cartel indicate that more banks will be breaking out on their own to cut a deal, even at the risk of violating legal detail in loan contracts that encourage equal treatment among the creditors.

Although unilateral options can reduce the transfer, experience has shown that in and of themselves they are no guarantee for sustained growth in the debtor countries. Indeed, most de facto moratoria have so far emerged out of economic chaos and the force of events rather then as part of a planned economic strategy to gain access to foreign exchange to support reforms, investment, and growth. Even in Peru, where moratorium arose out of an initially serious economic plan, a failure to adequately manage domestic demand and promote exports has seriously undermined the medium-term growth potential of reduced transfers to the creditors. Clearly, if a lower transfer is to stimulate growth, it must emerge out of a coherent macroeconomic policy that husbands resources and channels them directly into sectors that will expand output and employment, preferably with net gains in foreign exchange earnings and certainly not with losses.

In closing, it can be said that history and common sense suggest that the question is not if, but exactly when and how, the outward net transfer of resources from Latin America will fall. The transfer could be reduced in an orderly and socially efficient way through a more ambitious international public policy initiative that recognized the collective nature of Latin America's debt problem and the efficacy of collective solutions. Barring that, it will fall only through increasingly combative negotiations between creditor and debtor, often preceded by a stoppage of payments of varying durations. The former solution is clearly preferable for the collective good of debtor and creditor countries. How realistic an option it is will depend to a large degree on the public spirit of our new political leadership in the creditor countries.

The Methodology of the Case Studies
on Bolivia and Peru

THE CASE STUDIES were developed with an institutionalist pattern model in mind. Unlike formal models that begin with a comprehensive set of relationships based on a priori deductive reasoning, pattern models start off with very simple frameworks that link "themes" initially perceived in case study fieldwork. In other words, pattern models are conceived more directly from events and are gradually made more comprehensive and general as further case study work allows the development, modification, or even rejection of existing themes, as well as the integration of new ones. The nature and explanation of pattern models does not facilitate the degree of abstraction or specification found in more traditional formalism. These models are also designed to be linked to a specific historical context and therefore have explicit limitations on the scope of their applicability.[1]

The first step to the development of pattern models is case study work. In this particular instance I was interested in patterning bank lending to developing countries during the 1970s. I thus began my study of debt accumulation in Latin America by first investigating the bank as an institution and lender to developing countries. The issue was tackled at two levels. First, I used available secondary information to study the modern international bank and developments in the eurocurrency market, with special concern for the articulation with LDCs. Second, I paralleled this first effort with very detailed case studies that generated unusually comprehensive primary data on bank lending to Peru and Bolivia and with less detailed, but nevertheless systematic, observation of lending patterns to other Latin American countries.

The two aforementioned case studies were based on a very unique data base: by tapping data in the central filing systems of the two countries, loan contracts were scrutinized on an individual basis for *every*

---

[1] There are, of course, many roads to understanding. Therefore, the use of a pattern model is not meant to cast bad light on more formal techniques. For a detailed analysis of pattern models see Paul Diesing, *Patterns of Discovery in the Social Sciences* (New York: Aldine Press, 1971); and Charles Wilber with Richard Harrison, "The Methodological Basis of Institutional Economics: Pattern Model, Storytelling and Holism," *Journal of Economic Issues* 12 (March 1978): 61–89.

recorded nondefense-related medium- and long-term commercial bank loan to the public sector (or guaranteed by it) during contemporary credit cycles. Using standardized data collection sheets, quantitative and qualitative information was gleaned from individual contracts.[2] Data were then processed to varying degrees of aggregation in order to analyze the lending behavior of individual banks as well as more general trends. These data were complemented by more aggregate data on other loans as well as on more general aspects of the economy and economic policy. The opportunity to work from a microbase, with virtually infinite possibilities for selected reaggregation of data, provided a unique view of bank lending to a developing country.

In the case of Peru the study covered two well-defined credit cycles with the banks: a relatively minor, albeit very interesting, cycle in 1965 to 1968 under the civilian Belaúnde administration, followed by a period of massive indebtedness with the banks during 1972 to 1976 under the leadership of a military government headed by General Juan Velasco (succeeded in 1975 by General Francisco Morales Bermúdez). In 1977 and 1978 Peru fell out of grace with the banks, and it was not until 1980 that a new credit cycle with them was initiated. After consolidating loans by the subsidiaries of the banks into the parent corporations, Peru had more than 170 private bank lenders and over 740 individual loan transactions for a total gross value of $2.6 billion, 86 percent of which corresponded to the period 1972 to 1976.

Bolivia's public sector did not have any significant medium- to long-term borrowing experience with commercial banks prior to 1970, and 96 percent of the value of all its borrowing during the seventies occurred in 1974 to 1979, with all but the last year being part of the economic and political program of a military regime under the leadership of General Hugo Banzer. After 1979 the access to credit was virtually cut off by the commercial lenders, and the country remained in difficulty with its creditors, despite a major rescheduling agreement in 1981 and a partial buyback of commercial debt in early 1988. During the period 1970

[2] The data were collected from the Ministry of Economy and Finance of Peru and the Central Bank of Bolivia using a common methodology designed to capture themes on the bank-borrower relationship. The methodology and data sheets are published in Robert Devlin, "Project Manual and Methodological Guidelines for the Study of the Role of Transnational Banks in the External Finance of Peru, 1965–1976" (Santiago, Chile: United Nations Joint Unit CEPAL/CET, Working Paper No. 10, E/CEPAL/R.220, 1978). The Peru study has been published in English in Robert Devlin, *Transnational Banks and the External Finance of Latin America: The Experience of Peru* (Santiago, Chile: United Nations, 1985). The Bolivia study is in Robert Devlin and Michael Mortimore, *Los Bancos Transnacionales, el Estado, y el Endeudamiento Externo en Bolivia* [Transnational Banks, the State, and External Debt in Bolivia] (Santiago, Chile: United Nations, 1983).

to 1979 Bolivia had 118 commercial creditors (after consolidation of subsidiaries) and 401 individual transactions totaling the gross amount of $1.2 billion.

Importantly, throughout the case study work my approach was largely empirical and I made no attempt to prove or reject a theory; nor did I couch the investigation in any particular theoretical framework. To the degree that I was consistently influenced by any conceptual underpinning, it was a skepticism about the blanket application of any body of established theory, especially as it applies to development.

In sum, the observation of bank behavior allowed me to discover themes on the dynamics of bank-borrower relationships, which I have linked into a somewhat abstract context in Chapter Four to explain the expansionary phase of the credit cycle. The resulting pattern model is clearly at an early stage of development and undoubtedly will benefit from more case study work and the opportunities which that provides for refinement.

Abbott, George. "The Case for Cancellation." *Inter-Economics*, July 1975, pp. 217–221.

"Acapulco Commitment to Peace, Development and Democracy, Signed on November 29, 1987, at Acapulco, Mexico." Washington, D.C.: Organization of American States, 1 December 1987.

Aggarwal, Vinod. "Cooperation in the Debt Crisis." Berkeley, Calif., University of California, September 1985.

Alexander, Charles. "Jumbo Loan, Jumbo Risks." *Time*, 3 December 1984, p. 33.

Aliber, Robert. "Towards a Theory of International Banking." *Federal Reserve Bank of San Francisco Economic Review*, Spring 1976, pp. 5–8.

American Express Bank. *Amex Bank Review* 10 (28 March 1983).

Anderson, Roger. "Bankers Assess Country Risks: Limits of Prudence." *Asian Finance*, 15 September 1977, pp. 46–47.

Angelini, Anthony; Eng, Maximo; and Lees, Francis. *International Lending, Risk, and the Euromarkets*. New York: John Wiley & Sons, 1979.

"APRA's Government Priorities." *Latin American Weekly Report*, 28 June 1985, p. 6.

"Argentina Cries All the Way to Its Bankers." *Economist*, 31 March 1984, pp. 77–78.

Aronson, Jonathan David. "The Changing Nature of the International Monetary Crisis, 1971–1974: The Role of the Banks." Paper presented at the Seventeenth Annual Meeting of the International Studies Association, Washington, D.C., February 1975.

———. *Money and Power*. Beverly Hills, Calif.: Sage Publications, Inc., 1977.

Arrow, Kenneth. "The Economics of Moral Hazard: Further Comment." *American Economic Review* 58 (June 1968): 537–539.

Arze Cuadros, Eduardo. *La Economía de Bolivia: Ordenamiento Territorial y Dominación Externa, 1492–1979* [The Economy of Bolivia: Territorial Order and External Domination, 1492–1979]. La Paz: Editorial Los Amigos del Libro, 1979.

Avramovic, Dragoslav. "Conditionality: Facts, Theory, and Policy." Washington, D.C.: Bank of Credit and Commerce International, May 1987.

———. "Debt Crisis of the 1980s: The Beginning of a Wind Down?" Washington, D.C.: Bank of Credit and Commerce International, January 1988.

———; Gulhati, Ravi; Hayes, J. Philip; Husain, S. S.; Rao, Badri; de Weille, Jan; Froland, Johan; and Wyss, Hans. *Economic Growth and External Debt*. Baltimore: The Johns Hopkins University Press, 1965.

Bailey, Norman; Luft, David; and Robinson, Roger. "Exchange Participation

Notes: An Approach to the International Financial Crisis." CSIS Significant Issues Series, vol. 5, no. 1. Washington, D.C.: Georgetown University,
Center for Strategic and International Studies, 1983.

Baker, James. "Statement" to the Joint Annual Meetings of the Board of Governors of the World Bank and International Monetary Fund. Washington,
D.C., 30 September 1987.

"Baker to See Brazil Aide." *New York Times*, 26 November 1985, p. A32.

Banco Central de Reserva del Perú. *Memoria 1976*. Lima, 1977.

———. *Memoria 1983*. Lima, 1984.

Bank for International Settlements. *Fifty-Seventh Annual Report*. Basel, 15
June 1987.

———. *Forty-Eighth Annual Report*. Basel, 1978.

———. *International Banking Developments: Fourth Quarter 1983*. Basel,
April 1984.

———. *International Banking Statistics, 1973–1983*. Basel, April 1984.

———. *The International Interbank Market*. Basel, 1983.

———. *The Maturity Distribution of International Bank Lending*. Basel, December 1983.

———. *The Maturity Distribution of International Bank Lending*. Basel, July
1985.

Banner, R. "Banks Gain from Fees by Altering Latin Debt." *New York Times*,
10 January 1983, p. D3.

Barnet, Richard, and Müller, Ronald. *Global Reach*. New York: Simon &
Schuster, 1974.

Basagni, Fabio. "Recent Developments in International Lending Practices." In
Banks and the Balance of Payments, Benjamin Cohen in collaboration
with Fabio Basagni (Montclair, N.J.: Allanheld, Osmun, 1981), pp. 78–
116.

Baumol, William. *Business Behavior, Value and Growth*. New York: Macmillan, 1959.

Bee, Robert. "Syndication." In *Offshore Lending by U.S. Commercial Banks*,
edited by F. John Mathis, pp. 151–165. Philadelphia: Robert Morris Associates, 1975.

Beek, David. "Commercial Bank Lending to Developing Countries." *Federal
Reserve Bank of New York Quarterly Review*, 2 (Summer 1977): 1–8.

Bennett, Robert. "The Intricacies of Bank Accounting." *New York Times*, 2
July 1984, p. D3.

Benston, George. "Economies of Scale of Financial Institutions." *Journal of
Money, Credit, and Banking* 4 (May 1972): 312–341.

Bergsten, C. Fred; Cline, William; and Williamson, John. *Bank Lending to Developing Countries: The Policy Alternatives*. Washington, D.C.: Institute
for International Economics, 1985.

Bernal, Richard. "Default as a Negotiating Tactic in Debt Rescheduling Strategies of Developing Countries: A Preliminary Note." Kingston, Jamaica:
University of West Indies, Department of Economics, September 1984.

Bianchi, Andrés; Devlin, Robert; and Ramos, Joseph. "Adjustment in Latin

America, 1981–1986." In *Growth-Oriented Adjustment Programs*, edited by Vittorio Corbo, Morris Goldstein, and Mohsin Khan, pp. 179–225. Washington, D.C.: International Monetary Fund and World Bank, 1987.

Biem, David. "Rescuing the LDCs." *Foreign Affairs* 55 (July 1977): 717–731.

Bishoff, Henry. "British Investment in Costa Rica." *Inter-American Economic Affairs* 7 (Summer 1973): 37–47.

Blask, Jerome. "A Survey of Country Evaluation Systems in Use." In *Financing and Risk in Developing Countries*, edited by Stephen Goodman, pp. 77–82. Proceedings of a Symposium on Developing Countries' Debt sponsored by the U.S. Export-Import Bank, Washington, D.C., August 1977.

Bloomfield, Arthur. *Patterns of Fluctuation in International Investment before 1914*. Princeton Studies in International Finance, No. 21. Princeton, N.J.: Princeton University, Department of Economics, 1968.

"BOA Methodology." *Asian Finance*, 15 September 1977, pp. 46–47.

Bogdanowicz-Bindert, Christine, and Sacks, Paul. "The Role of Information: Closing the Barn Door?" In *Uncertain Future: Commercial Banks and the Third World*, edited by Richard Feinberg and Valeriana Kallab, pp. 69–78. London: Transaction Books, 1984.

"Bolivia to Buy Back Debt at 11% of Face Value." *Financial Times*, 17 March 1988, p. 3.

Born, Karl. *International Banking in the 19th and 20th Centuries*. Translated by Volker Berghahn. New York: St. Martin's Press, 1983.

Brackenridge, Bruce. "Techniques of Credit Rating." *Asian Finance*, 15 September 1977, pp. 46–53.

Brainard, Lawrence. "More Lending to the Third World?: A Banker's View." In *Uncertain Future: Commercial Banks and the Third World*, edited by Richard Feinberg and Valeriana Kallab, pp. 31–44. London: Transaction Books, 1984.

Brandt Commission. *North-South: A Program for Survival*. Cambridge, Mass.: MIT Press, 1980.

Brau, Eduard; Abrams, Richard; Donovan, Donal; El-Erian, Mohammed; Keller, Peter; Lipsky, John; Nowak, Michael; MacIejewski, Edouard; Puckahtikon, Champen; Rennhack, Robert; Saint-Etienne, Christian; Watson, Maxwell; Williams, Richard. *Recent Multilateral Debt Restructurings with Official and Bank Creditors*. Occasional Paper No. 25. Washington, D.C.: International Monetary Fund, 1983.

Brett, E. A. *International Money and Capitalist Crisis*. Boulder, Colo.: Westview Press, 1983.

Brewer, Anthony. *Marxist Theories of Imperialism*. London: Routledge & Kegan Paul, 1980.

Brittain, W. H. Bruce. "Developing Countries' External Debts and Private Banks." *Banca Nazionale del Lavoro Quarterly Review*, December 1977, pp. 365–380.

Broad, Robin. "How about a Real Solution to Third World Debt?" *New York Times*, 28 September 1987, p. A25.

"Buddy, Can You Borrow a Dollar?" *Euromoney*, May 1978, pp. 10–15.

Cabieses, Hugo, and Otero, Carlos. *Economía Peruana* [The Peruvian Economy]. Lima: Centro de Estudios y Promoción del Desarrollo, 1977.

"Camdessus Calls for Doubling of IMF Quotas." *Morning Press*, Washington, D.C.: International Monetary Fund, 10 March 1988.

Camdessus, Michel. "Debt Strategy Needs Strengthening, but Basic Elements Remain Valid." *IMF Survey*, 21 March 1988, pp. 89–91.

———. "Statement" to the Board of Governors of the International Monetary Fund and the World Bank. Washington, D.C., 29 September 1987.

Carbonetto, Daniel; de Cabellos, M. Inés; Dancourt, Oscar; Ferrari, Cesar; Martínez, Daniel; Mezzera, Jaime; Saberbein, Gustavo; Tantalelan, Javier; and Vigier, Pierre. *El Perú Heterodoxo: Un Modelo Económico* [Heterodox Peru: An Economic Model]. Lima: Instituto Nacional de Planificación, 1987.

"Cartagena Conference of 11 Latin Nations Rejects Debtors' Cartel, Proposes Reforms." *IMF Survey*, 2 July 1984, pp. 201–202.

"Castro Escalates Debt Diplomacy." *Latin American Weekly Report*, 26 July 1985, p. 10.

Castro, Fidel. *How Latin America's and the Third World's Unpayable Foreign Debt Can and Should be Cancelled and the Pressing Need for the New International Economic Order: Interview Granted to the Mexican Daily Excelsior*. Havana: Editora Política, 1985.

"Castro's Proposal Gets Thumbs-Down." *Latin American Weekly Report*, 9 August 1985, p. 6.

Caves, Richard. "Uncertainty, Market Structure, and Performance: Galbraith as Conventional Wisdom." In *Industrial Organization and Economic Development*, edited by Jesse Markham and Gustav Papanek, pp. 283–302. Boston: Houghton Mifflin, 1970.

Chalmers, Douglas. "The Politicized State in Latin America." In *Authoritarianism and Corporatism in Latin America*, edited by James Malloy, pp. 23–45. Pittsburgh: University of Pittsburgh Press, 1977.

Chenery, Hollis, and Strout, Alan. "Foreign Assistance and Economic Development." *American Economic Review* 56 (September 1966): 679–733.

Citicorp. *1975 Annual Report*. New York, 1976.

"Citicorp Comes Clean on Third World Debt." *Economist*, 23 May 1987, p. 83.

"Citicorp Sharply Lifts Loss Reserves, Putting Its Rivals on the Spot." *Wall Street Journal*, 20 May 1987, p. 1.

Clarke, Pamela, and Field, Peter. "Boycott? No, They Just Won't Go Below ³/₄%." *Euromoney*, February 1978, p. 21.

Cline, William. *International Debt: Systematic Risk and Policy Response*. Washington, D.C.: Institute for International Economics, 1984.

———. "The Issue Is Illiquidity, Not Solvency." *Challenge*, July–August 1984, pp. 12–20.

Cohen, Benjamin in collaboration with Fabio Basagni. *Banks and the Balance of Payments*. Montclair, N.J.: Allanheld, Osmun, 1981.

Constanzo, G. A. "Statement" before the Subcommittee on Financial Institutions Supervision, Regulation, and Insurance in the U.S. House Banking, Finance, and Urban Affairs Committee, 6 April 1977.

Corea, Gamani. "The Debt Problems of Developing Countries." *Journal of Development Planning*, no. 9 (1976), pp. 53–78.

Crawford, Vincent. "International Lending, Long-Term Credit Relationships, and Dynamic Contract Theory." University of California at San Diego, Department of Economics, August 1984. Mimeographed.

Crosse, Howard, and Hempel, George. *Management Policies for Commercial Banks*. 2d ed. Englewood Cliffs, N.J.: Prentice-Hall, 1973.

Cummings, Richard. "International Credits: Milestones or Millstones?" *Journal of Commercial Bank Lending*, January 1975, pp. 40–52.

Dale, Richard, and Mattione, Richard. *Managing Global Debt*. Washington, D.C.: Brookings Institution, 1983.

D'Arista, Jane. "Private Overseas Lending: Too Far, Too Fast?" In *Debt and Less Developed Countries*, edited by Jonathan David Aronson, pp. 57–101. Boulder, Colo.: Westview Press, 1979.

Darity, William, Jr. "Loan Pushing: Doctrine and Theory." International Finance Discussion Papers, No. 253. Washington, D.C.: U.S. Federal Reserve Board, February 1985.

Davis, Steven. *The Eurobank: Its Origins, Management, and Outlook*. London: Macmillan, 1976.

"Debate Rages over Renegotiation." *Latin American Weekly Report*, 13 August 1982, pp. 2–4.

"Debt after Mexico." *Financial Times*, 7 March 1988, p. 14.

de Carmoy, Herve. "Debt and Growth in Latin America: A European Banker's Proposal." Working Paper No. 9, Institute of European-Latin American Relations, Madrid, 1987.

"Declaración y Propuesta de Personalidades sobre la Deuda Externa" [Declaration of Eminent Persons on External Debt]. Buenos Aires, 24 April 1987.

Delamaide, Darrell. *Debt Shock*. Garden City, N.Y.: Doubleday, 1984.

de Larosière, Jacques. "Fund Policy on Adjustment and Finance Clarified in Address by Managing Director." *IMF Survey*, 9 January 1984, pp. 2–6.

————. "Helping to Shape a Stronger World Economy: The Tasks before the International Monetary Fund." *IMF Survey*, 24 June 1985, pp. 200–202.

Devlin, Robert. "Banca Privada, Deuda, y Capacidad Negociadora de la Periferia: Teoría y Práctica" [Private Banks, Debt, and Negotiating Capacity of the Periphery: Theory and Practice]. *El Trimestre Económico* 51 (July–September 1984): 559–589.

————. "Deuda, Crisis, y Renegociación: El Dilema Latinoamericano" [Debt, Crisis, and Renegotiation: The Latin American Dilemma]. In *América Latina: Deuda, Crisis, y Perspectivas* [Latin America: Debt, Crisis, and Perspectives], edited by the Instituto de Cooperación Iberoamericana, pp. 67–101. Madrid: Ediciones Cultura Hispánica, 1984.

————. "External Finance and Commercial Banks: Their Role in Latin America's Capacity to Import between 1951 and 1975." *CEPAL Review*, no. 5 (first half of 1978), pp. 63–98.

———. "New Plan of U.S. Treasury for the Mexican Debt Problem." Santiago, Chile: United Nations Economic Commission for Latin America and the Caribbean, Economic Development Division, 30 December 1987. Unpublished memo.

———. "Project Manual and Methodological Guidelines for the Study of the Role of Transnational Banks in the External Finance of Peru, 1965–1976." Santiago, Chile: United Nations Joint Unit CEPAL/CET, Working Paper No. 10, E/CEPAL/R.220, 1978.

———. "Renegotiation of Latin America's Debt: An Analysis of the Monopoly Power of Private Banks." *CEPAL Review*, no. 20 (August 1983), pp. 101–112.

———. *Transnational Banks and the External Finance of Latin America: The Experience of Peru.* Santiago, Chile: United Nations, 1985.

———, and de la Piedra, Enrique. "Peru and Its Private Bankers: Scenes from an Unhappy Marriage." In *Politics and Economics of External Debt Crisis*, edited by Miguel Wionczek in collaboration with Luciano Tomassini, pp. 383–426. Boulder, Colo.: Westview Press, 1985.

———, and Mortimore, Michael. *Los Bancos Transnacionales, el Estado, y el Endeudamiento Externo en Bolivia* [Transnational Banks, the State, and External Debt in Bolivia]. Santiago, Chile: United Nations, 1983.

Díaz-Alejandro, Carlos. "The Early 1980s in Latin America: 1930s One More Time?" Paper presented at the Expert Meeting on Crisis and Development in Latin America and the Caribbean, United Nations Economic Commission for Latin America and the Caribbean, Santiago, Chile, 29 April–3 May 1985.

———. "Latin American Debt: I Don't Think We Are in Kansas Anymore." *Brookings Papers on Economic Activity*, no. 2 (1984), pp. 335–403.

———. "The Post-1971 International Financial System and Less Developed Countries." In *A World Divided*, edited by G.K. Helleiner, pp. 177–206. New York: Cambridge University Press, 1976.

Diesing, Paul. *Patterns of Discovery in the Social Sciences.* New York: Aldine Press, 1971.

Dod, David. "Restricción del Crédito de la Banca Comercial en Situaciones de Crisis de la Deuda Internacional" [Restriction of Bank Credit in Situations of International Debt Crisis]. *Monetaria* 6 (April–June 1983): 155–180.

Donaldson, T. H. *Lending in International Commercial Banking.* London: Macmillan Publishers, Ltd., 1983.

Dornbusch, Rudiger. "Debt, Inflation, and Growth: The Case of Argentina." Cambridge, Mass.: Massachusetts Institute of Technology, Department of Economics, February 1988.

———. "The International Debt Problem." Cambridge, Mass., Massachusetts Institute of Technology, Department of Economics, 1984.

———, and Fischer, Stanley. "The World Debt Problem: Origins and Prospects." *Journal of Economic Planning*, no. 16 (1985), pp. 75–78.

"Do the Bankers Take the Risks?" *Latin American Weekly Report*, 25 September 1981, pp. 10–11.

Dufey, Gunter, and Giddy, Ian. *The International Money Market*. Englewood Cliffs, N.J.: Prentice-Hall, 1978.

Dunkerley, James. *Rebellion in the Veins: Political Struggle in Bolivia, 1952–1982*. London: New Left Books (Verso edition), 1984.

Durr, Barbara. "Peru Pays Banks in Fishmeal and Iron." *Financial Times*, 6 October, 1987, p. 8.

"Earthquake Comes at Worst Time for Cash-Strapped Mexico." *Latin American Weekly Report*, 27 September 1985, p. 1.

Eaton, Jonathan, and Gersovitz, Mark. "Debt with Potential Repudiation: Theoretical and Empirical Analysis." *Review of Economic Studies* 48 (April 1981): 289–309.

———. *Poor Country Borrowing in Private Financial Markets and the Repudiation Issue*. Princeton Studies in International Finance, No. 47. Princeton, N.J.: Princeton University, Department of Economics, 1981.

Eaton, Jonathan, and Taylor, Lance. "Developing Country Finance and Debt." Paper prepared for a conference on New Directions in Development Theory, Cambridge, Mass., Massachusetts Institute of Technology, Department of Economics, 17–19 January 1985.

Edwards, Sebastián. "LDC Foreign Borrowing and Default Risk: An Empirical Investigation." *American Economic Review* 74 (September 1984): 726–734.

Eichengreen, Barry. "Till Debt Do Us Part: The U.S. Capital Market and Foreign Lending, 1920–1955." In *Developing Country Debt* (summary volume), edited by Jeffrey Sachs, pp. 249–253. Cambridge, Mass.: National Bureau of Economic Research, 1987.

Emmanuel, Arghiri. "Myths of Development vs. Myths of Underdevelopment." *New Left Review* 85 (1974): 61–82.

Encinas del Pando, José. "The Role of Military Expenditure in the Development Process: Peru, a Case Study, 1950–1980." *Ibero-Americana, Nordic Journal of Latin American Studies* 12 (1983): 51–114.

Enders, Thomas, and Mattione, Richard. *Latin America: The Crisis of Debt and Growth*. Washington, D.C.: Brookings Institution, 1983.

Ensor, Richard. "Latin America's Prickliest Borrower." *Euromoney*, June 1978, pp. 98–101.

Evans, Richard. "New Debts for Old—and the Swapper Is King." *Euromoney*, September 1987, pp. 72–81.

Feder, Gershon, and Just, Richard. "An Analysis of Credit Terms in the Eurodollar Market." *European Economic Review* 9 (1977): 221–243.

Fei, J.C.H., and Ranis, Gustav. *Development of the Labor Surplus Economy: Theory and Policy*. Homewood, Ill.: Richard D. Irwin, 1964.

Feinberg, Richard. "LDC Debt and the Public-Sector Rescue." *Challenge*, July–August 1985, pp. 27–34.

———, and Bacha, Edmar. "When Supply and Demand Don't Intersect: Latin America and the Bretton Woods Institutions in the 1980s." Paper presented at a conference on Latin America and the World Economy, sponsored by Sistema Ecónomica Latinoamericano, Caracas, May 1987.

Feis, Herbert. *Europe the World's Banker, 1870–1914.* New York: W. W. Norton, 1965.

Fernández, Javier. "Crédito Bancario Involuntario a Países" [Involuntary Bank Credit to Countries]. *Coyuntura Económica,* December 1983, pp. 198–210.

———. "Moratoria de la Deuda" [Debt Moratorium]. Paper prepared for the seminar on External Debt in Latin America: Actual Situation and Perspectives, organized by Centro de Estudios Monetarios de América Latina in Quito, Ecuador, 22–26 July 1985.

Ferrer, Aldo. "Deuda, Soberanía, y Democracia en América Latina" [Debt, Sovereignty, and Democracy in Latin America]. *Estudios Internacionales* 17 (July–September 1984): 309–323.

———. *Vivir con Lo Nuestro* [Living on Our Own]. Buenos Aires: El Cid Editor, 1983.

Ffrench-Davis, Ricardo. "Deuda Externa y Balanza de Pagos de América Latina" [External Debt and the Balance of Payments of Latin America]. In *Progreso Económico y Social en América Latina, Informe 1982* [Economic and Social Progress in Latin America, 1982 Report], pp. 177–198. Washington, D.C.: Inter-American Development Bank, 1982.

———. "External Debt, Renegotiation Frameworks and Development in Latin America." Paper presented at a seminar on Latin American External Debt, Stockholm, May 1985.

———. "International Private Lending and Borrowing Strategies of Developing Countries." *Journal of Development Planning,* no. 14 (1984), pp. 119–164.

———, and De Gregorio, José. "La Renegociación de la Deuda Externa en Chile en 1985: Antecedentes y Comentarios" [The Renegotiation of Chile's External Debt: Antecedents and Commentary]. *Colección Estudios CIEPLAN,* no. 17 (September 1985), pp. 9–32.

———, and Molina, Sergio. "Prospects for Bank Lending to Developing Countries in the Remainder of the Eighties." *Journal of Development Planning,* no. 16 (1985), pp. 229–247.

Fishlow, Albert. "Coping with the Creeping Crisis of Debt." In *Politics and Economics of External Debt Crisis,* edited by Miguel Wionczek in collaboration with Luciano Tomassini, pp. 97–144. Boulder, Colo.: Westview Press, 1985.

———. "Lessons from the Past: Capital Markets during the 19th Century and the Interwar Period." *International Organization* 39 (Summer 1985): 383–440.

———. "A New International Economic Order: What Kind?" In *Rich and Poor Nations in the World Economy,* edited by Albert Fishlow, Carlos F. Díaz-Alejandro, Richard R. Fagen, and Roger D. Hansen, pp. 11–83. New York: McGraw-Hill Book Company, 1978.

Folkerts-Landau, David. "The Changing Role of International Bank Lending in

Development Finance." Washington, D.C.: International Monetary Fund, December 1984.

Friedman, Irving. *The Emerging Role of Private Banks in the Developing World*. New York: Citicorp, 1977.

———. "The New Climate for Evaluating Country Risk." Paper presented at the International Bankers Annual Roundtable, Cannes, France, 12–14 June 1980.

———. *The World Debt Dilemma: Managing Country Risk*. Philadelphia: Robert Morris Associates, 1983.

Friedman, Milton, and Schwartz, Anna. *A Monetary History of the United States, 1867–1960*. Princeton, N.J.: Princeton University Press, 1963.

"Funaro Selects a New Team." *Latin American Weekly Report*, 13 September 1985, p. 4.

"Funaro Vows Fight against Inflation." *Latin American Weekly Report*, 6 September 1985, p. 4.

Furtado, Celso. *Não à Recessão e ao Desemprego* [No to Recession and Unemployment]. Río de Janeiro: Editorial Paz e Terra, 1983.

Galbis, Vincent. "Inflation and Interest Rate Policies in Latin America, 1967–1976." *Staff Papers* 26 (June 1979): 334–366.

Galbraith, John Kenneth. *Money*. Boston: Houghton Mifflin, 1975.

———. *The New Industrial State*. New York: New American Library, 1968.

García Zamora, Jean-Claude, and Sutin, Stewart, eds. *Financing Development in Latin America*. New York: Praeger, 1980.

Gasser, William, and Roberts, David. "Bank Lending to Developing Countries: Problems and Prospects." *Federal Reserve Bank of New York Quarterly Review* 7 (Fall 1982): 18–29.

Gilder, George. *Wealth and Poverty*. New York: Basic Books (Bantam paperback edition), 1981.

Gisselquist, David. *The Politics and Economics of International Bank Lending*. New York: Praeger, 1981.

Goodman, Laurie. "The Pricing of Syndicated Eurocurrency Credits." *Federal Reserve Bank of New York Quarterly Review* 5 (Summer 1980): 39–49.

Goodman, Stephen. "How the Big U.S. Banks Really Evaluate Sovereign Risks." *Euromoney*, February 1977, pp. 105–110.

Green, Rosario. *Estado y Banca Transnacional en México* [The State and Transnational Banks in Mexico]. Mexico City: Editorial Nueva Imagen, 1981.

Griffith-Jones, Stephany. "Proposals to Manage the Debt Problem." Brighton, Eng.: Sussex University, Institute of Development Studies, 1985.

Ground, Richard Lynn. "Origin and Magnitude of Recessionary Adjustment in Latin America." *CEPAL Review*, no. 30 (December 1986), pp. 67–85.

———. "Orthodox Adjustment Programmes in Latin America: A Critical Look at the Policies of the International Monetary Fund." *CEPAL Review*, no. 23 (August 1984), pp. 45–82.

———. "Perturbaciones, Déficit, Crisis, y Políticas de Ajuste: Un Enfoque Normativo" [Shocks, Deficit, Crisis, and Adjustment Policy: A Normative

Focus]. *El Trimestre Económico* 53 (October–December 1986): 725–792.

Group of Thirty. *Risks in International Lending.* New York, 1982.

Grubel, Herbert. "The New International Banking." *Banca Nazionale del Lavoro Quarterly Review*, September 1983, pp. 263–284.

———. "A Theory of Multinational Banking." *Banca Nazionale del Lavoro Quarterly Review*, December 1977, pp. 349–363.

Guerguil, Martine. "The International Financial Crisis: Diagnoses and Prescriptions." *CEPAL Review*, no. 24 (December 1984), pp. 147–169.

"Guidelines for the Rescheduling of Current & Past Due Obligations of the Government of Costa Rica." San José, 4 June 1987.

Guttentag, Jack, and Herring, Richard. "Commercial Bank Lending to Developing Countries: From Overlending to Underlending to Structural Reform." In *International Debt and the Developing Countries*, edited by Gordon Smith and John Cuddington, pp. 129–150. Washington, D.C.: World Bank, 1985.

———. "Credit Rationing and Financial Disorder." *Journal of Finance* 39 (December 1984): 1359–1382.

———. *The Current Crisis in International Lending.* Washington, D.C.: Brookings Institution, 1985.

———. "Provisioning, Charge-Offs and Willingness to Lend." Washington, D.C.: International Monetary Fund, June 1986.

———. "Uncertainty and Insolvency Exposure by International Banks." University of Pennsylvania, Wharton School of Business, n.d.

Gwynne, S. C. "Adventures in the Loan Trade." *Harper's*, September 1983, pp. 22–26.

Haegele, Monroe. "The Market Still Knows Best." *Euromoney*, May 1980, pp. 121–128.

Haley, John, and Seligman, Barnard. "The Development of International Banking by the United States." In *The International Banking Handbook*, edited by William Baughn and Donald Mandich, pp. 35–46. Homewood, Ill.: Dow Jones-Irwin, 1983.

Harberger, Arnold. "Comentarios del Profesor Arnold Harberger" [Comments of Professor Arnold Harberger]. In *Estudios Monetarios VII* [Monetary Studies VII], pp. 185–188. Santiago, Chile: Central Bank of Chile, 1981.

Hardy, Chandra. *Rescheduling Developing Country Debts, 1956–1980: Lessons & Recommendations.* Washington, D.C.: Overseas Development Council, 1981.

Harfield, Henry. "Legal Aspects of International Lending." In *Offshore Lending by U.S. Commercial Banks*, edited by F. John Mathis, pp. 81–89. Philadelphia: Robert Morris Associates, 1975.

Hayes, Douglas. *Bank Lending Policies.* Ann Arbor, Mich.: University of Michigan, School of Business Administration, 1977.

Hayter, Teresa. *Aid as Imperialism.* Baltimore: Penguin Books, 1971.

Hector, Gary. "Third World Debt: The Bomb Is Defused." *Fortune*, 18 February 1985, pp. 36–50.

"Hernan Somerville: La Negociación por Dentro" [Hernan Somerville: Inside the Negotiation]. *El Mercurio*, 1 March 1987, p. B1.

Hughes, Helen. "Debt and Development: The Role of Foreign Capital in Economic Growth." *World Development* 7 (February 1979): 95–112.

Hymer, Stephen. *The International Operations of National Firms*. Cambridge, Mass.: MIT Press, 1976.

"IMF Director's Plan Would Lift Debt Weight." *Financial Times*, 25 March 1988, p. 5.

Immenga, Ulrich. *Participation by Banks in Other Branches of the Economy*. Brussels: Commission of European Communities, 1975.

Institute of International Finance, Inc. "Restoring Market Access." Washington, D.C., June 1987.

Inter-American Development Bank. *Economic and Social Progress in Latin America*. Washington, D.C., 1985.

————. *External Financing of the Latin American Countries*. Washington, D.C., December 1978; December 1981; December 1982.

————. *External Public Debt of the Latin American Countries*. Washington, D.C., July 1984.

"International Banking Survey." *Economist*, 26 March 1988.

International Financing Review. London.

International Monetary Fund. *International Financial Statistics*. Washington, D.C., February 1985; May 1985.

————. *International Financial Statistics Yearbook 1985*. Washington, D.C., 1986.

————. *World Economic Outlook*. Washington, D.C., October 1987.

Ipsen, Erik. "After Mexico, the Regionals Are in Retreat." *Euromoney*, January 1983, pp. 58–65.

Jaffee, Dwight. *Credit Rationing and the Commercial Loan Market*. New York: John Wiley & Sons, 1971.

————, and Modigliani, Franco. "A Theory and Test of Credit Rationing." *American Economic Review* 59 (December 1969): 850–872.

————, and Russell, Thomas. "Imperfect Information, Uncertainty, and Credit Rationing." *Quarterly Journal of Economics* 90 (November 1976): 651–666.

"Japanese Banks Wary of Miyazawa Debt Proposal." *Morning Press*. Washington, D.C.: International Monetary Fund, 22 September 1987.

Johnson, Manuel, Vice Chairman of the Board of Governors of the U.S. Federal Reserve System. "The International Debt Situation." Washington, D.C.: U.S. Federal Reserve Board, 9 March 1988.

Kalderén, Lars, and Siddiqi, Qamar, eds., in cooperation with Francis Chronnell and Patricia Watson, *Sovereign Borrowers: Guidelines on Legal Negotiations with Commercial Lenders*. London: Dag Hammarskjöld Foundation and Butterworths, 1984.

Kaletsky, Anatole. *The Costs of Default*. New York: Priority Press, 1985.

Kane, Daniel. *The Eurodollar Market and the Years of Crisis*. New York: St. Martin's Press, 1983.

Kane, Edward, and Malkiel, Burton. "Bank Portfolio Allocation, Deposit Variability and the Availability Doctrine." *Quarterly Journal of Economics* 74 (February 1965): 113–134.

Kenen, Peter. "A Bailout for the Banks." *New York Times*, 6 March 1983, p. D1.

———. "A Proposal for Reducing the Debt Burden of Developing Countries." Princeton, N.J.: Princeton University, Department of Economics, March 1987.

Keynes, John Maynard. *The Economic Consequences of the Peace.* New York: Harcourt, Brace & Howe, 1920.

———. *The General Theory of Employment, Interest, and Money.* London: Harvest/HBJ, 1964.

———. "The German Transfer Problem." *The Economic Journal* 39 (September 1929): 1–7.

Killick, Tony; Bird, Graham; Sharpley, Jennifer; and Sutton, Mary. "The IMF: Case for a Change in Emphasis." In *Adjustment Crisis in the Third World*, edited by Richard Feinberg and Valeriana Kallab, pp. 59–82. London: Transaction Books, 1984.

Kindleberger, Charles. "Less-Developed Countries and the International Capital Market." In *Industrial Organization and Economic Development*, edited by Jesse Markham and Gustav Papanek, pp. 337–349. Boston: Houghton Mifflin, 1970.

———. *Manias, Panics, and Crashes.* New York: Basic Books, 1978.

———. "The 1929 World Depression in Latin America—From the Outside." In *Latin America in the 1930s*, edited by Rosemary Thorp, pp. 315–329. New York: St. Martin's Press, 1984.

Knight, Jerry. "Bank Crisis Deepening in Texas." *Washington Post*, 27 March 1987, p. H1.

Korth, Christopher. "The Eurocurrency Markets." In *The International Banking Handbook*, edited by William Baughn and Donald Mandich, pp. 16–35. Homewood, Ill.: Dow Jones-Irwin, 1983.

Kotecha, Mahesh. "Repackaging Third World Debt." *Standard and Poor's International Credit Week*, August 1987, pp. 9–10.

Kraft, Joseph. *The Mexican Rescue.* New York: Group of Thirty, 1984.

Kuczynski, Pedro-Pablo. "Latin American Debt." *Foreign Affairs* 61 (Winter 1982/1983): 344–364.

Kyle, Steven, and Sachs, Jeffrey. "Developing Country Debt and the Market Value of Large Commercial Banks." Working Paper No. 1470. Cambridge, Mass.: National Bureau of Economic Research, September 1984.

La Falce, John. "Third World Debt Crisis: The Urgent Need to Confront Reality." *Congressional Record* 133, no. 34. Washington, D.C., 5 March 1987.

Lahera, Eugenio. "La Conversión de la Deuda Externa: Antecedentes, Evaluación, y Perspectivas" [Conversion of the External Debt: Antecedents, Evaluation, and Perspectives]. Santiago, Chile: United Nations Economic Commission for Latin America and the Caribbean, September 1987.

———. "The Conversion of Foreign Debt Viewed from Latin America." *CEPAL Review*, no. 32 (August 1987), pp, 103–122.

Lambert, R. "New York Banks Show Strong Gains." *Financial Times*, 19 January 1983, p. 32.

Lamfalussy, A. "Monetary Reform." *Economist*, 26 October 1985, p. 6.

Langoni, Carlos. "The Way Out of the Country Debt Crisis." *Euromoney*, October 1983, pp. 20–26.

"Latin American Economic Conference." *CEPAL Review*, no. 22 (April 1984), pp. 39–52.

Lees, Frances, and Eng, Maximo. "Developing Country Access to the International Capital Markets." *Columbia Journal of World Business*, Fall 1979, pp. 80–81.

———. *International Financial Markets*. New York: Praeger, 1975.

Lessard, Donald, and Williamson, John. *Financial Intermediation beyond the Debt Crisis*. Washington, D.C.: Institute for International Economics, 1985.

———, eds. *Capital Flight and Third World Debt*. Washington, D.C.: Institute for International Economics, 1987.

Lewis, W. Arthur. "The Slowing Down of the Engine of Growth." *American Economic Review* 70 (September 1980): 555–564.

Lissakers, Karin. "Bank Regulation and International Debt." In *Uncertain Future: Commercial Banks and the Third World*, edited by Richard Feinberg and Valeriana Kallab, pp. 45–68. London: Transaction Books, 1984.

———. *International Debt, the Banks, and U.S. Foreign Policy*. Washington, D.C.: U.S. Government Printing Office, 1977.

McClelland, Peter. *Causal Explanation and Model Building in History, Economics, and the New Economic History*. Ithaca, N.Y.: Cornell University Press, 1975.

MacEwan, Arthur. "The Current Crisis in Latin America and the International Economy." *Monthly Review* 36 (February 1985): 1–18.

McKinnon, Ronald. *The Eurocurrency Market*. Princeton Essays in International Finance, No. 125. Princeton, N.J.: Princeton University, Department of Economics, 1977.

———. "The International Capital Market and Economic Liberalization in LDCs." *The Developing Economies* 22 (December 1984): 476–481.

Mandel, Ernest. *Late Capitalism*. Translated by Joris de Bres. London: New Left Books (Verso edition), 1980.

———. *The Second Slump*. Translated by Jon Rothschild. London: New Left Books (Verso edition), 1980.

Marshall, Alfred. *Principles of Economics*. London: Macmillan, 1961.

Martin, Everett. "Peru's Economic Woes Are Worrying Bankers Who Aid Third World." *Wall Street Journal*, 1 September 1977, p. 1.

Marx, Karl. *Capital*. 3 vols. 9th ed. New York: International Publishers, 1967.

Mastrapasqua, Frank. "U.S. Bank Expansion Via Foreign Branching." *Bulletin* 87–88 (January 1973): 7–71.

Mentré, Paul. *The Fund, Commercial Banks, and Member Countries*. Occasional Paper No. 26. Washington, D.C.: International Monetary Fund, 1984.

"Mexico: Hush-Hush Meeting." *Latin American Weekly Report*, 19 July 1985, p. 7.

Mills, Rodney, Jr. "U.S. Banks Are Losing Their Share of the Market." *Euromoney*, February 1980, pp. 50–62.

Minsky, Hyman. *Can "It" Happen Again?* Armonk, N.Y.: M. E. Sharp, Inc., 1982.

Mistry, Percy. "Third World Debt: Beyond the Baker Plan." *The Banker*, 26 September 1987, pp. i–iv.

Moffit, Michael. *The World's Money*. New York: Simon & Schuster (Touchstone paperback), 1983.

Montagnon, Peter. "What to Do About Countries Which Cannot Settle Their Debts." *Financial Times*, 9 March 1985, p. 16.

"The Mood Is Gloomy." *Latin American Weekly Report*, 7 October 1983, pp. 8–9.

Morgan Guaranty Trust Company. *World Financial Markets*. New York, May 1976; March 1978; September 1980; July 1981; February 1983; August 1984; January 1985; May 1985; May 1986; June/July 1987.

Mortimore, Michael. "The State and Transnational Banks: Lessons from the Bolivian Crisis of External Public Indebtedness." *CEPAL Review*, no. 14 (August 1981), pp. 127–151.

Mulford, David. "Recent Developments in International Debt." Washington, D.C.: U.S. Treasury Department, 4 February 1988.

Murray, Alan, and Truell, Peter. "Loan Plan May Help Mexico, Some Banks; But It's No Panacea." *Wall Street Journal*, 30 December 1987, p. 1.

Nash, Nathaniel. "Adjusting to 100 Failed Banks." *New York Times*, 17 November 1985, first page of business section.

Nicoll, Alexander. "Man Who Captures Market Discount." *Financial Times*, 21 March 1988, p. 3.

Noble, Kenneth. "Volcker Sees Eased Debt Terms." *New York Times*, 9 August 1985, p. D3.

North, Douglass. "International Capital Movements in Historical Perspective." In *U.S. Private and Government Investment Abroad*, edited by Raymond Mikesell, pp. 10–43. Eugene, Ore.: University of Oregon Books, 1962.

Nowzad, Bahram; Williams, Richard C.; Baumgartner, Ulrich; Dillon, K. Burke; Johnson, G. G.; Keller, Peter M.; Kincaid, G. Russell; Reichman, Thomas M.; and Tyler, Maria. *External Indebtedness of Developing Countries*. Occasional Paper No. 3. Washington, D.C.: International Monetary Fund, 1981.

Nurske, Ragnar. *Problems of Capital Formation in Underdeveloped Countries*. New York: Oxford University Press (Galaxy Books), 1967.

O'Brien, Lord. "The Prospects for the Euromarkets." *Euromoney*, September 1975, pp. 66–69.

Odle, Maurice. *Multinational Banks and Underdevelopment*. London: Pergamon Press, 1981.

O'Donnell, Guillermo. "External Debt: Why Don't Our Governments Do the Obvious?" *CEPAL Review*, no. 27 (December 1985), pp. 27–33.

Okun, Arthur. *Prices and Quantities*. Washington, D.C.: Brookings Institution, 1981.

Organization for Economic Cooperation and Development. *Economic Outlook*. No. 42. Paris, December 1987.

———. *Financial Market Trends*. Paris, October 1984.

———. *1976 Review of Development Cooperation*. Paris, 1977.

Organization of American States. *Despachos de Agencias Noticiosas* [News Agency Dispatches]. Washington, D.C., October 1987.

———. "Extract of Public Law 98–181 of the Congress of the United States Entitled: Law of National Housing and International Recovery and Financial Stability." Washington, D.C.: OAS/SERH/XIV/CEFYC/4 January 1984.

Orme, William. "Gephardt Losses Cheer Mexico." *Journal of Commerce*, 10 March 1988, p. 7.

O'Shaughnessy, Hugh. "Debtors' Conference Divided on Strategy for Service Payments." *Financial Times*, 21 June 1984, p. 4.

Page, Diane, and Rodgers, Walter. "Trends in Eurocurrency Credit Participation, 1972–1980." In *Risks in International Lending*, pp. 57–70. New York: Group of Thirty, 1982.

Parboni, Ricardo. *The Dollar and Its Rivals*. Translated by Jon Rothschild. London: New Left Books (Verso edition), 1981.

Payer, Cheryl. *The Debt Trap*. New York: Monthly Review Press, 1974.

Pearson Commission. *Partners in Development*. New York: Praeger, 1969.

Pecchioli, R. M. *The Internationalization of Banking*. Paris: Organization for Economic Cooperation and Development, 1983.

Peck Lim, Quek. "The Borrower's Trump Card Is His Weakness." *Euromoney*, October 1982, pp. 35–37.

———. "The Year of the Samurai." *Euromoney*, February 1978, pp. 10–18.

"Plazos Más Largos para Pagar Deudas Externas" [Longer Periods for Payment of External Debts]. *El Mercurio*, 31 August 1984, p. B1.

Plender, J. "Of Profits and Imprudence." *Financial Times*, 18 February 1983, p. 5.

Pöhl, Karl Otto. "Herr Pöhl Elucidates the Deutsche Bundesbank's View on the International Debt Situation." *Press Review* (Bank for International Settlements), 4 February 1985, pp. 1–6.

Polanyi, Karl. *The Great Transformation*. Boston: Beacon Press, 1957.

Prebisch, Raúl. "The Latin American Periphery in the Global Crisis of Capitalism." *CEPAL Review*, no. 26 (August 1985), pp. 65–90.

"Presidents Publicly Toughen Regional Stance on Debt Issue." *Latin American Weekly Report*, 25 May 1984, p. 1.

"Provided the Banks Stand." *Economist*, 8 September 1984, p. 82.

Reed, John. "New Money in New Ways." *The International Economy*, October/November 1987, pp. 50–52.

———. "The Role of External Private Capital Flows." In *Growth-Oriented Adjustment Programs*, edited by Vittorio Corbo, Morris Goldstein, and Mohsin Khan, pp. 417–435. Washington, D.C.: International Monetary Fund and World Bank, 1987.

Reisen, Helmut, and Van Trotsenburg, Axel. *Developing Country Debt: The Budgetary and Transfer Problem*. Paris: Development Centre of the Organisation for Economic Cooperation and Development, 1988.

"Rescheduling." *Economist*, 18 February 1984, p. 71.

Riding, Alan. "Downcast Peru is Given Lift by the New Leader." *New York Times*, 3 September 1985, p. A1.

Riner, Deborah. "Borrowers and Bankers: The Euromarket and Political Economy in Peru and Chile." Ph.D. dissertation, Princeton University, 1982.

Robichek, Walter. "Some Reflections about External Public Debt Management." In *Estudios Monetarios VII* [Monetary Studies VII], pp. 170–183. Santiago, Chile: Central Bank of Chile, December 1981.

Robinson, James. "A Comprehensive Agenda for LDC Debt and World Trade Growth," The Amex Bank Review Special Papers, No. 13. London, March 1988.

Robinson, Stuart. *Multinational Banking*. Leyden, Netherlands: A. W. Sythoff Leiden, 1974.

Rockwell, Keith. "Bill Offers Debt Relief for 17 Nations." *Journal of Commerce*, 11 March 1988, p. 6.

Roett, Riordan. "Democracy and Debt in South America: A Continent's Dilemma." *Foreign Affairs* 62 (1984): 695–720.

Rohatyn, Felix. "A Plan for Stretching Out Global Debt." *Business Week*, 28 February 1983, pp. 15–18.

Rothschild, Michael, and Stiglitz, Joseph. "Increasing Risk: 1. A Definition." *Journal of Economic Theory* 2 (1970): 225–243.

Rowen, Hobart. "IMF's Camdessus Endorses Voluntary Debt Relief Plans." *Washington Post*, 1 March 1988, p. D1.

———. "IMF Seeks to Improve Image in Third World." *Washington Post*, 26 June 1987, p. D1.

Rutledge, Graeme, and Bell, Geoffrey. "Facing Reality on Sovereign Debt." *Euromoney*, November 1984, pp. 103–105.

Sachs, Jeffrey. "External Debt and Macroeconomic Performance in Latin America and East Asia." *Brookings Papers on Economic Activity*, no. 2 (1985), pp. 523–564.

———. "LDC Debt in the 80s: Risks and Reforms." In *Crises in the Economic and Financial Structure*, edited by Paul Wachtel, pp. 197–243. Lexington, Mass.: Lexington Books, 1982.

———. "Theoretical Issues in International Borrowing." Working Paper No. 1189. Cambridge, Mass.: National Bureau of Economic Research, August 1983.

Salomon Brothers. *A Review of Bank Performance: 1983 Edition*. New York, 1983.

———. *A Review of Bank Performance: 1984 Edition*. New York, 1984.

Sampson, Anthony. *The Money Lenders*. New York: Penguin Books, 1983.

Sánchez Aguilar, E. "The International Activities of U.S. Commercial Banks: A Case Study of Mexico." Ph.D. dissertation, Harvard University, 1973.

Sargen, Nicholas. "Commercial Bank Lending to Developing Countries."

Federal Reserve Bank of San Francisco Economic Review, Spring 1976, pp. 20–31.

Sarmiento, Eduardo. *El Endeudamiento en Economías Fluctuantes y Segmentadas* [Debt in Fluctuating and Segmented Economies]. Bogotá: Fondo Editorial CEREC, 1985.

"Sarney Turns to His Neighbors." *Latin American Weekly Report*, 23 August 1985, p. 8.

Saunders, Anthony. "An Examination of the Contagion Effect in the International Loan Market." Washington, D.C.: International Monetary Fund, December 1983.

Scherer, F. M. *Industrial Market Structure and Economic Performance*. Boston: Houghton Mifflin, 1980.

Schumpeter, Joseph. *The Theory of Economic Development*. Translated by Redvers Opie. 1961. Reprint. New York: Oxford University Press, 1980.

Seiber, Marilyn. *International Borrowing by Developing Countries*. London: Pergamon Press, 1982.

Selowsky, Marcelo, and Van Der Tak, Herman. "The Debt Problem and Growth." *World Development* 14 (September 1986): 1107–1124.

Servan-Schreiber, Jean-Jacques. *El Desafío Americano* [The American Challenge]. Barcelona: Plaza y Janes, S.A., 1968.

Silk, Leonard. "Acting to Avert Debtor Cartel." *New York Times*, 20 June 1984, p. D2.

Sjaastad, Larry. "International Debt Quagmire: To Whom Do We Owe It?" *The World Economy* 6 (September 1983): 305–324.

Smith, Adam. *The Wealth of Nations*. 1937. Reprint. New York: The Modern Library, 1965.

Smith, Gordon. *The External Debt Prospects of the Non-Oil-exporting Developing Countries*. Washington, D.C.: Overseas Development Council, 1977.

Solomon, Robert. "The Perspective on the Debt of Developing Countries." *Brookings Papers on Economic Activity*. no. 2 (1977), pp. 479–510.

Spellman, Lewis. *The Depository Firm and Industry*. New York: Academic Press, 1982.

Spero, Joan. *The Failure of the Franklin National Bank*. New York: Columbia University Press, 1980.

Spindler, J. Andrew. *The Politics of International Credit*. Washington, D.C.: Brookings Institution, 1984.

Sprinkel, Beryl. "Grounds for Increasing Optimism." *Economic Impact*, no. 2 (1984), pp. 35–39.

Stallings, Barbara. *Banker to the Third World*. Berkeley: University of California Press, 1987.

Stiglitz, Joseph, and Weiss, Andrew. "Credit Rationing in Markets with Imperfect Information." *American Economic Review* 71 (June 1981): 393–410.

"Survey on International Banking." *Economist*, 26 March 1988, pp. 10–16.

Swardson, Anne. "Citicorp Move Brings New Era." *Washington Post*, 21 May 1987, p. D1.

Swoboda, Alexander. "Debt and the Efficiency and Stability of the International Financial System." In *International Debt and the Developing Countries*, edited by Gordon Smith and John Cuddington, pp. 151–175. Washington, D.C.: World Bank, 1985.

"Syndicated Loans" (Special Supplement: World Banking Survey). *Financial Times*, 21 May 1979.

Tavares, María de Conceicão, and Belluzzo, Luiz G. de Mello. "Capital Financiero y Empresa Multinacional" [Finance Capital and the Multinational Enterprise]. In *Nueva Fase del Capital Financiero* [New Phase of Finance Capital], edited by Jaime Estévez and Samuel Lichtensztejn, pp. 35–48. Mexico City: Editorial Nueva Imagen, 1981.

Taylor, Lance. "The Theory and Practice of Developing Country Debt: An Informal Guide for the Perplexed." Cambridge, Mass., Massachusetts Institute of Technology, Department of Economics, 1985. Mimeographed.

Telljohann, Kenneth. "Analytical Framework." In Salomon Brothers, "Prospects for Securitization of Less-Developed Country Loans." New York, June 1987.

"Till Debt Us Do Part." *Economist*, 28 February 1987, p. 85.

Tobin, James. "On the Efficiency of the Financial System." *Lloyds Bank Review* 153 (July 1984): 1–15.

"The Top 300." *The Banker*, June 1971, pp. 663–684.

"The Top 300." *The Banker*, June 1976, pp. 653–695.

"The Top 500." *The Banker*, June 1981, pp. 153–181.

"Tracking the Lead Bank: Who's Competing Hardest." *Euromoney*, August 1979, pp. 14–30.

Trifani, Sheila, and Villamil, Antonio. "Country Risk Analysis: Economic Considerations." In *The International Banking Handbook*, edited by William Baughn and Donald Mandich, pp. 109–112. Homewood Ill.: Dow Jones-Irwin, 1983.

Truell, Peter. "Chile and Banks Reach a Pact on Global Debt." *Wall Street Journal*, 27 February 1987, p. 6.

Ugarteche, Oscar. *El Estado Deudor* [The Debtor State]. Lima: Instituto de Estudios Peruanos, 1987.

———. "Mecanismos Institucionales del Financiamiento Externo del Perú: 1968–1978" [Institutional Mechanisms of External Finance in Peru: 1968–1978]. Santiago, Chile: United Nations Economic Commission for Latin America and the Caribbean, Joint Unit CEPAL/CET, E/CEPAL/L.205, September 1979.

United Nations. *Balance of Payments Adjustment Process in Developing Countries: Report to the Group of Twenty-Four*. New York, UNDP/UNCTAD Project INT/75/015, January 1979.

United Nations Centre on Transnational Corporations. *Transnational Corporations in World Development*. New York, 1988.

———. "Trends in Foreign Direct Investment." New York, 17 December 1987.

United Nations Conference on Trade and Development. *Handbook of International Trade and Development Statistics 1980 Supplement*. Geneva, 1981.

————. *Handbook of International Trade and Development Statistics 1981 Supplement*. Geneva, 1982.

United Nations Economic Commission for Latin America and the Caribbean. *América Latina en el Umbral de los Años 80* [Latin America on the Threshold of the 1980s]. Santiago, Chile, 1979.

————. *América Latina y el Caribe: Balance de Pagos, 1950–1984*. [Latin America and the Caribbean: Balance of Payments, 1950–1984]. Santiago, Chile, 1986.

————. *Economic Survey of Latin America 1978*. Santiago, Chile, 1979.

————. *Economic Survey of Latin America and the Caribbean 1982*. 2 vols. Santiago, Chile, 1984.

————. *Economic Survey of Latin America and the Caribbean 1983*. 2 vols. Santiago, Chile, 1985.

————. *Economic Survey of Latin America and the Caribbean 1984*. 2 vols. Santiago, Chile, 1986.

————. *Economic Survey of Latin America and the Caribbean 1985*. 1 vol. Santiago, Chile, 1987.

————. "Economic Survey of Latin America and the Caribbean, 1987. Advance Summary." Santiago, Chile, April 1988.

————. *Estudio Económico de América Latina y el Caribe 1986* [Economic Survey of Latin America and the Caribbean 1986]. 1 vol. Santiago, Chile, 1988.

————. *The Evolution of the External Debt Problem in Latin America and the Caribbean*. Estudios e Informes de la CEPAL, No. 72. Santiago, Chile, 1988.

————. *External Debt in Latin America: Adjustment Policies and Renegotiation*. Boulder, Colo.: Lynne Rienner, 1985.

————. *External Financing in Latin America*. New York, 1965.

————. *1983 Statistical Yearbook for Latin America*. Santiago, Chile, 1984.

————. "Preliminary Balance of the Latin American Economy in 1982." *Notas sobre la Economía y el Desarrollo de América Latina* 373 (January 1983).

————. "Preliminary Overview of the Latin American Economy 1986." Santiago, Chile, December 1986.

————. "Preliminary Overview of the Latin American Economy 1987." Santiago, Chile, December 1987.

————. "Restrictions on Sustained Development in Latin America and the Caribbean and the Requisites for Overcoming Them." Santiago, Chile, February 1988.

————. "Síntesis Preliminar de la Economía Latinoamericana durante 1983" [Preliminary Synthesis of the Latin American Economy during 1983]. Santiago, Chile, December 1983.

Uriarte, Manuel. "Transnational Banks and the Dynamics of Peruvian Foreign Debt and Inflation." Ph.D. dissertation, The American University, 1984.

U.S. Congress, Democratic Committee of the Joint Economic Committee. "Trade, Deficits, Foreign Debt, and Sagging Growth." Washington, D.C., September 1986.

U.S. Congress, House, Committee on Banking, Currency, and Housing. *International Banking: A Supplement to a Compendium of Papers Prepared for the FINE Study*. 94th Cong., 2d sess. Washington, D.C.: U.S. Government Printing Office, 1976.

————, Joint Economic Committee. "The Impact of the Latin American Debt Crisis on the U.S. Economy." Washington, D.C., 10 May 1986.

————, Senate, Committee on Government Affairs. *Interlocking Directorates among Major U.S. Corporations*. 97th Cong., 2d sess. Washington, D.C.: U.S. Government Printing Office, 1978.

————, Senate, Committee on Government Operations. *Disclosure of Corporate Ownership*. 93d Cong., 2d sess. Washington, D.C.: U.S. Government Printing Office, 1974.

U.S. Federal Financial Institutions Examination Council. "Statistical Release." Washington, D.C., 6 December 1982.

"U.S. Regional Banks Cut Lending to Latin America." *Press Review* (Bank for International Settlements), 27 February 1984, p. 6.

van B. Cleveland, Harold, and Brittain, W. H. Bruce. "Are the LDCs in over Their Heads?" *Foreign Affairs* 55 (July 1977): 732–750.

Vandell, Kerry. "Imperfect Information, Uncertainty, and Credit Rationing: Comment and Extension." *Quarterly Journal of Economics* 99 (November 1984):842–872.

Veblen, Thorstein. *The Theories of Business Enterprise*. New York: Charles Scribner's Sons, 1904.

Vernon, Raymond. *Sovereignty at Bay*. New York: Basic Books, 1971.

Villarroel, Juan, and Villarroel, Tanya. "Control Institucional de la Deuda Externa en Bolivia" [Institutional Control of the Bolivian External Debt]. La Paz, Bolivia, May 1981.

Wachtel, Howard. *The New Gnomes: Multinational Banks in the Third World*. TNI Pamphlet No. 4. Washington, D.C.: Transnational Institute, 1977.

Wallich, Henry. "Professor Wallich Presents a Perspective on the External Debt Situation." *Press Review* (Bank for International Settlements), 14 January 1985, pp. 1–6.

Ward, Benjamin. *What's Wrong with Economics*. New York: Basic Books, 1972.

Watkins, Alfred. "The Impact of Recent Financial Market Developments on Latin America's Access to External Financial Resources." Washington, D.C., February 1988.

————. "To Lend or Not to Lend." Paper presented at a conference on Latin America and Foreign Debt, Stanford, California, Hoover Institute, September 1987.

Watson, Paul. *Debt and Developing Countries: New Problems and New Actors*. Washington, D.C.: Overseas Development Council, 1978.

Weeks, John. *Capital and Exploitation*. Princeton, N.J.: Princeton University Press, 1981.

Weinert, Richard. "Banks and Bankruptcy." *Foreign Policy*, no. 50 (Second Quarter, 1983), pp. 138–149.

———. "Eurodollar Lending to Developing Countries." *Columbia Journal of World Business*, Winter 1973, pp. 34–38.

———. "Nicaragua's Debt Renegotiation." *Cambridge Journal of Economics* 5 (June 1981): 187–192.

Wellons, P. A. *Borrowing by Developing Countries on the Euro-Currency Market*. Paris: Organization for Economic Cooperation and Development, 1976.

———. *Passing the Buck*. Boston: Harvard Business School Press, 1987.

Wendt, Johann. "The Role of Foreign Banks in International Banking." In *The International Banking Handbook*, edited by William Baughn and Donald Mandich, pp. 47–70. Homewood, Ill.: Dow Jones-Irwin, 1983.

Wertman, Patricia. "The International Debt Problem: Options for Solution." Washington, D.C.: Library of Congress, Congressional Research Service, October 1986.

Weston, Rae. *Domestic and Multinational Banking*. New York: Columbia University Press, 1980.

Whitman, Marina. "Bridging the Gap." *Foreign Policy* 30 (Spring 1978): 148–156.

Wiesner, Eduardo. "Latin American Debt and Pending Issues." *American Economic Review* 75 (May 1985): 191–195.

Wilber, Charles, with Harrison, Richard. "The Methodological Basis of Institutional Economics: Pattern Model, Storytelling, and Holism." *Journal of Economic Issues* 12 (March 1978): 61–89.

Wilkinson, Max. "Banks Greedy over Third World." *Financial Times*, 31 March 1983, p. 10.

———. "U.S. Acted to Keep Latin America Creditworthy." *Financial Times*, 6 April 1984, p. 6.

Wionczek, Miguel. "Mexico's External Debt Revisited: Lessons of the 1985 Rescheduling Arrangement for Latin America." Paper presented at a seminar on Latin American External Debt, Stockholm, May 1985.

Wolff, Richard, and Resnick, Steven. "Classes in Marxian Theory." *Review of Radical Political Economics* 13 (Winter 1982): 1–18.

Wolfson, Martin. "Financial Crisis: Theory and Evidence in the Post-War U.S. Economy." Ph.D. dissertation, The American University, 1984.

World Bank. *Borrowing in International Capital Markets*. Washington, D.C., August 1975; August 1976; December 1978; January 1980; November 1980; November 1981.

———. *Poverty in Latin America: The Impact of Depression*. Washington, D.C., 1986.

———. *World Debt Tables*. Washington, D.C., 1981; 1982; 1983.

———. *World Development Report 1985*. Washington, D.C., 1985.